Practical Photoshop® CC 2015, Level 1©
Welcome

The authors of this book are all current or former community college instructors and Adobe Certified Instructors in Adobe Photoshop®. Together, we have taught Photoshop to thousands of students, both in traditional classrooms and online. In our 19+ years of teaching Photoshop, we have learned first hand from our students which Photoshop skills they feel are the most essential, and also which Photoshop techniques they find the most difficult to master. We have used our students' feedback to determine both the topics and the step by step tutorials in Practical Photoshop CC 2015. Marilyn Kelly, Ed.D., has carefully edited the book to make it as pedagogically-sound as possible.

The tutorials do not cover everything in Photoshop—instead we have tried to distill the important terms, skills, and techniques you will need to open, edit, create, save, and print Photoshop documents.

You will be able to download all the images used in this book from the Practical Photoshop site, http://www.practical-photoshop.com. The student files are big—most of them are high resolution so that they will print nicely. They are royalty free. We hope you will enjoy them.

We have done our best to fully edit the content for this book, but a couple of errors may have slipped in. Check the accompanying Web site: http://www.practical-photoshop.com for any corrections we might have made, and also to report any to us. Also, on the site, there will soon be videos to accompany the tutorials. Consult your instructor for specifics.

Let us leave with some thank yous:

- To the students, faculty, and staff of Santa Rosa Junior College who have been such enthusiastic Photoshop users, learners, and educators.
- To Sutter Laird for his technical support.

Barbara, Donald, Corrine, Windsor, Marilyn, & Mike

Practical Photoshop CC 2015, Level 1[©]
Table of Contents • Summary

Overview and Tutorial Guidelines 1

Tutorial 1: Photoshop Basics 9

Tutorial 2: Files for Print and Web 33

Tutorial 3: Selection 45

Tutorial 4: Layers 75

Tutorial 5: Layer Case Studies 97

Tutorial 6: Painting 117

Tutorial 7: Image Sources and Resolution 147

Tutorial 8: Design Principles & Effective Cropping 161

Tutorial 9: Adobe® Bridge® + Automations 173

Tutorial 10: Correcting Image Tonality 201

Tutorial 11: Adjusting Image Colors 217

Tutorial 12: Painting with Special Tools 235

Tutorial 13: Restoration Case Studies 255

Tutorial 14: Fun with Filters 265

Tutorial 15: Putting It All Together 283

Index 299

Practical Photoshop CC 2015, Level 1
Table of Contents

Welcome III

Table of Contents C

Overview and Tutorial Guidelines 1
Tutorial Guidelines 2
Using These Tutorials with Photoshop 2
The Photoshop Application 3
    Hardware and Software Requirements 3
    Setting up your Monitor for Photoshop 4
Adobe Photoshop CC 2015 Installation 5
    A Few Tips Before You Begin 5
    Activation & Deactivation 5
    Checking for Free Updates 6
    Adobe ID 6
    Uninstalling Adobe Photoshop CC 2015 6
The Adobe Photoshop Settings File 6
    To Restore the Default Adobe Photoshop Settings File 7
Download Tutorial Files 7

Tutorial 1: Photoshop Basics 9
Objectives 9
The Photoshop Workspace 9
    Guided Exercise 1.1: Navigate the Photoshop Workspace 9
Panel Manipulation & Customization 14
    Dock Manipulation 15
    Panel Controls 16
        Panel Menus 16
    Panel Manipulation 16
        Free-float a Panel 16

   Relocate a Panel Group 17
   Relocate an Individual Panel 17
 Document Navigation 17
  Guided Exercise 1.2: Navigate a File with View Menu Commands 17
  Guided Exercise 1.3: Use the Zoom Tool with Options 18
  Guided Exercise 1.4: Use the Navigator Panel 19
 Keyboard Shortcuts 21
  Navigation Shortcuts 21
   Context Menus 21
   Restore Tool Defaults 21
   Zoom with Context Menu 22
 Your First Photoshop Project 22
  Guided Exercise 1.5: Begin to "Carve" a Pumpkin, Photoshop Style 22
 The History Panel 24
  Guided Exercise 1.6: Use the History Panel to Undo Image Changes 24
 History Panel Keyboard Shortcuts 27
 The Layered Photoshop Document 27
  Guided Exercise 1.7: Use Layers to Finish "Carving" the Pumpkin 27
 Adobe Photoshop Help 30
  Guided Exercise 1.8: Use Photoshop Help 30
 On Your Own 31
  Navigation Shortcuts 31
 Resources and Videos 31

TUTORIAL 2: FILES FOR PRINT AND WEB 33
Objectives 33
Resolution 33
 Monitor Resolution 33
 Document Resolution 34
 Printer Resolution 34
Setting up Documents for Print 34
Printing Photoshop Documents 36
Ink Jet Paper Quality and Image Longevity 36
  Guided Exercise 2.1: Print Your Pumpkin 37

Table of Contents   Page D

  Beware of Scale to Fit Media 38
Saving Files for Fast Online Transmission.. 38
  Guided Exercise 2.2: Save a Duplicate File for the Web Using Save for Web 39
  Guided Exercise 2.3: Save a File for the Web Using Export As 42
JPEG Quality 43
How Big is Your File? 44
On Your Own 44
  Avoid the Most Common Save for Web Mistake 44
Resources and Videos 44

TUTORIAL 3: SELECTION 45

Objectives 45
Selection Principles.. 45
  How Do You Select? 46
  How Do You Deselect? 46
The Marquee Tools.. 47
  The Rectangular Marquee **Tool**... **47**
  The Elliptical Marquee **Tool** **47**
  Guided Exercise 3.1: Use the Rectangular & Elliptical Marquee **Tools** with the Move Tool 47
Modifying a Selection 49
The Magic Wand Tool 50
  Tolerance 50
  Anti-aliasing... 51
  Contiguous 51
  Sample All Layers 51
Transforming Pixels and Selections 51
  Guided Exercise 3.2 : Transform a Selection 52
The Lasso Tools 53
  The Lasso Tool Cursors 53
  The (Standard) Lasso Tool 53
  The Polygonal Lasso Tool 54
  The Magnetic Lasso Tool 54
  Guided Exercise 3.3: Use the Lasso Tool 54
The Quick Selection Tool 56

    Guided Exercise 3.4: Use The Quick Selection Tool 56
Refining Selection Edges 58
    Guided Exercise 3.5A: Use the Refine Edge Command on the Edges of the Sunflower Selection (for Photoshop CC 2015.2 and Earlier) 58
    Guided Exercise 3.5B: Use Select and Mask on the Edges of the Sunflower Selection (for Photoshop CC 2015.5) 62
Working with Selections 66
    Hiding Selection Edges 66
    The Precise or Crosshair Cursor 67
    Shrinking Selections for Cleaner Edges 67
    Refining Edge Suggestions 67
Experiment with More Selection Tools 67
    Guided Exercise 3.6: Compare the Polygonal Lasso Tool with the Quick Selection Tool 68
    Guided Exercise 3.7: Use the Magnetic Lasso Tool 70
    Guided Exercise 3.8: Combining Selection Tools 71
    Partly-Guided Exercise 3.9: Finishing the Critter 72
Copying and Pasting Selections 72
    Partly-Guided Exercise 3.10: Enhancing the Critter 73
On Your Own 74
Resources and Videos 74

TUTORIAL 4: LAYERS 75

Objectives 75
Layer Organization 75
    The Background Layer 75
    Pixel Layers 76
The Layers Panel 76
    Stacking Order 76
    Layer Components 77
    The Active Layer 77
    Layer Visibility 77
    Layer Groups 77
    Layers Panel Buttons 78
    The Layers Panel Menu 78

- Layer Filter Controls 78
- Guided Exercise 4.1: Organizing Layers 78
- Adding, Linking, & Removing Layers & Groups 80
  - Creating New Layers 80
  - Creating a Selection from a Layer 80
  - Creating a Layer from a Selection 80
  - Naming Layers 80
  - Linking Layers 81
    - To link two or more layers: 81
  - Grouping Layers 81
    - To make an empty group do one of the following: 82
    - To make a group that contains existing layers: 82
    - To remove layers from a group: 82
  - Deleting Unnecessary Layers and Groups 82
    - To delete the active layer: 82
    - To delete the active Layer Group: 83
  - Merging Layers 83
  - Guided Exercise 4.2: Layers Panel Manipulation 84
- Layer Options 85
  - Layer Blend Modes 85
  - Guided Exercise 4.3: Layer Experimentation 1 86
  - Shortcut to Preview Blend Modes 88
  - The Pass Through Blend Mode 88
  - Layer Locking 88
  - Guided Exercise 4.4: Locking Layers 89
- Layer Styles 90
  - The Styles Panel 92
    - To apply a style to a layer, or to every layer in a group: 92
  - Expanding and Contracting the Effects List 92
  - Turning Styles and Effects On and Off 92
  - Editing Styles 93
  - Opacity and Fill 93
- On Your Own 93
  - Partially Guided Exercise 4.5: Working with Layer Styles 93

    More Layers Practice 95
  Resources and Videos 95

Tutorial 5: Layer Case Studies 97

Objectives 97
Case Study 1: Type Tools and Type Layers 98
    Guided Exercise 5.1: Make Type Layers 98
    Editing Type Layers 100
    Formatting Type Layers 100
    Type Layer Options and Use 101
    Partially Guided Exercise 5.2: Edit and Format Type Layers 101
Case Study 2: Build a Composite Image 103
    Guided Exercise 5.3: Combine Three Images 103
The History Panel Revisited 107
    Guided Exercise 5.4: Layer Stacking & Blending Experimentation 107
    Guided Exercise 5.5: Use the History Panel to Select and Save States 108
    Experiment On Your Own 108
Case Study 3: Redo the Tool Critter with Layers 109
    Guided Exercise 5.6: Make a New Photoshop Document and Give It Critter Parts 109
    Guided Exercise 5.7: Layers Panel Organization 112
    Guided Exercise 5.8: Set Up a Template 112
    Guided Exercise 5.9: Use the Template to Make the Critter's Body 113
    On Your Own 116
Resources and Videos 116

Tutorial 6: Painting 117

Objectives 117
Choosing Colors 118
  Foreground Color or Background Color? 118
  The Color Picker 118
  Color Models 119
  Web-Safe and Non Web-Safe Colors 119
  The Swatches Panel 120
    To sample a swatch color: 120

- To add a swatch: 120
- To delete a swatch: 120
- To reset swatches: 120
- Color Panel 121
- Background Color Specifics 121
- The Eyedropper Tool 121
  - Eyedropper Tool Options 122
- Guided Exercise 6.1: Sample Colors 122

Brush Tool 123
- The Tool Preset Picker (1) 123
- The Brush Preset Picker (2) 123
  - Short Cuts to Remember 124
- The Brush Panel (3) 124
- Painting Modes (4) 125
- Guided Exercise 6.2: Apply Painting Modes 125
- Opacity (5) 126
- Flow (6) 126
- Guided Exercise 6.3: Compare Opacity and Flow 126
- Airbrush (7) 126
- Guided Exercise 6.4: Use the Airbrush Setting 127

Additional Painting Tools 127
- Differentiating Between the Brush Tool and the Pencil Tool 127
- The Eraser Tool 127

Fills and Strokes 128

Fill Tools 128
- The Gradient Tool 128
- Guided Exercise 6.5: Use The Gradient Tool 129
- The Paint Bucket Tool 132
- Guided Exercise 6.6: Use the Paint Bucket Tool 133

More Fill Techniques 133
- The Fill Command 133
- Filling with Layer Styles 134

Fill Layers 134
- Make a Fill layer 134

Modifying Fill Layers 135
    Guided Exercise 6.7: Fill with Layer Styles and a Fill layer 135
Stroking Techniques 138
    The Stroke Command 138
    Guided Exercise 6.8: Use the Edit > Stroke Command 138
    Stroking with a Layer Style 140
    Guided Exercise 6.9: Apply a Stroke Layer Style 140
Painting with a Variety of Tools, Options, and Commands 141
    Guided Exercise 6.10: Painting a Cartoon 141
On Your Own 145
    Design and Color Your Own Cartoon 145
Resources and Videos 145

TUTORIAL 7: IMAGE SOURCES AND RESOLUTION 147

Objectives 147
Copyright and Image Use Ethics 147
Watermarking 148
    The Digimarc Filter 148
Image Sources 149
    Public Image Sources 150
    Free Images 150
    Free Stock Photos 150
    FreeFoto 150
    Public Domain Photos 150
    Google Image Search 150
Resolution Revisited 151
    The Image Size Dialog Box 151
    Resampling 152
    Interpolation 153
Digital Cameras 153
    Digital Camera Resolution 154
    Guided Exercise 7.1: Resize a Digital Camera Image without Resampling 155
    Guided Exercise 7.2: Resize a Digital Camera Image with Resample Checked 156
    Guided Exercise 7.3: Resize Another Digital Camera Image with Resampling Checked 157

Table of Contents   Page J

Scanning Photographs & Other Printed Materials 158
    Troubleshooting Your Scanner Setup 158
    To Scan Directly into Photoshop 158
On Your Own 159
Resources and Videos 159

TUTORIAL 8: DESIGN PRINCIPLES & EFFECTIVE CROPPING.....161

Objectives 161
PARC: The Four Basic Design Principles 162
    Alignment 162
        Center Alignment 162
    Proximity 163
        No Proximity of Elements 163
        Proximity and Alignment Improve the Layout 163
    Contrast 163
    Repetition 164
Photographic Design Principles 165
    Framing 165
    Emphasis 165
    Angle of View 165
    Rule of Thirds 165
    Close Ups 166
    Balance 167
    Contrast 167
    Line and Shape 168
    Tone and Sharpness 168
    Arrangement 168
The Crop Tool 168
    Aspect Ratio Presets Menu (1) 168
    Ratio (2) 168
    Straighten Button (3) 169
    Overlay Options (4) 169
    Crop Tool Options (5) 169
    Delete Cropped Pixels (6) 169

  Content-Aware (7) 170

  Guided Exercise 8.1: Use the Crop Tool 170

  Guided Exercise 8.2:
  Use the Crop Tool to Straighten and Crop an Image 171

On Your Own 172

  Straightening Challenge 172

  Crop Evaluation 172

Resources and Videos 172

TUTORIAL 9: ADOBE® BRIDGE® + AUTOMATIONS 173

Objectives 173

Adobe® Bridge® Overview 174

  Browsing in Bridge 174

  The Tools Bar 175

    Navigation Buttons 175

    Get Photos from Camera 175

    Refine 175

  Camera Raw 176

    Open in Camera Raw 176

  Thumbnail Rotation 176

  The Workspace Switcher 177

  Quick Search 177

  The Path Bar 177

    Preview Quality 178

  Rating Images 178

    To Rate an Image from its Thumbnail: 178

    To Rate a Group of Images with the Label Menu: 179

    To Change the Rating of an Individual Image: 179

    To Change the Rating of Multiple Images: 179

    To Rate Selected Images with Keystrokes: 179

    The Filter Items by Rating Menu 179

  The Filter Panel 180

  The Sort By Menu 180

  Organization Buttons 180

Putting Bridge to Work 180
    Guided Exercise 9.1: Getting Started with Bridge 181
Additional Bridge Panels 186
    The Keywords Panel 186
        To Make a Sub Keyword: 187
        To Make a New Keyword Set: 187
        To Delete a Keyword or Set: 187
        To Assign a Keyword to One or More Files: 188
        To Remove a Keyword from One or More Files: 188
    The Filter Panel 188
    The Metadata Panel 188
        Collections Panel 189
Bridge Workspaces 189
Automations 190
Cropping & Straightening Photographs 190
    Guided Exercise 9.2: Use the Crop and Straighten Photos Command 190
Contact Sheets 191
    Guided Exercise 9.3: Make a Contact Sheet with Contact Sheet II 191
PDF Presentation 193
    Viewing PDF Slideshows 194
    Guided Exercise 9.4: Make a PDF Slideshow 195
Photomerge 197
    Guided Exercise 9.5: Use Photomerge to Make a Panorama 197
On Your Own 199
Resources and Videos 199

TUTORIAL 10: CORRECTING IMAGE TONALITY 201

Objectives 202
Tonal Range 202
    Guided Exercise 10.1: Use the Histogram Panel to Assess Image Tonality .. 203
The Image > Adjustments Menu 205
Brightness/Contrast 206
    Guided Exercise 10.2: Use Brightness/Contrast to improve a Black and White Photograph .. 206
    Avoid the Legacy Check box 207

Adjustment Layers and the Adjustments Panel 208
    Using the Adjustments Panel 208
    Guided Exercise 10.3: Make a Brightness/Contrast Adjustments Layer 209
Levels 210
    Guided Exercise 10.4: Use Levels with the Auto Setting 211
Adjusting the Tonality of Color Images 212
Auto Color Correction Options 212
    Guided Exercise 10.5: Use the Auto Color Correction Options 213
    On Your Own 215
Resources and Videos 215

TUTORIAL 11: ADJUSTING IMAGE COLORS 217

Objectives 217
Color Science 217
Color Casts 218
Color Casts and the Info Panel 218
    The Info Panel 218
    Guided Exercise 11.1: Identify and Correct a Color Cast 219
Balancing Colors with their Opposites 221
    The Color Balance Adjustment 222
    Guided Exercise 11.2: Use Color Balance to Further Correct a Color Cast 222
    Guided Exercise 11.3: Apply a Color Balance Adjustment to a Multi-layered Document 223
    Creating an Adjustment Layer with a Selection 225
Hue, Saturation, and Lightness 226
    The Hue/Saturation Adjustment 226
        Colorize 227
    Guided Exercise 11.4: Hue/Saturation Experimentation 227
    Guided Exercise 11.5: Use the Hue/Saturation Adjustment to Change the Color of a Door ... 228
Color Range 229
    Guided Exercise 11.6: Color Range + Color Balance 230
Replace Color 231
    Guided Exercise 11.7: Use Replace Color 231
On Your Own 233
Resources and Videos 233

Tutorial 12: Painting with Special Tools 235

Objectives 235
The Clone Stamp Tool 235
    Guided Exercise 12.1: Use the Clone Stamp Tool 236
    Guided Exercise 12.2: Refine Clone Stamp Tool Usage 237
Content-Aware Technology 239
    The Edit > Fill Command 239
    Guided Exercise 12.3: Use Edit > Fill with Content-Aware 239
    The Content-Aware Move Tool 240
    Guided Exercise 12.4: Use the Content-Aware Move Tool 241
The Spot Healing Brush Tool 242
    Guided Exercise 12.5: Use the Spot Healing Brush Tool 243
    Guided Exercise 12.6: Use Content-Aware Heal and Fill to Remove Unwanted Image Elements 244
The Red Eye Tool 246
    Guided Exercise 12.7: Use the Red Eye Tool 246
The History Brush Tool 247
    Guided Exercise 12.8: Use the History Brush Tool 247
    History Brush Tool Uses and Limitations 250
    Guided Exercise 12.9: More History Brush Tool Experimentation 250
The Art History Brush Tool 251
    Guided Exercise 12.10: Experiment with the Art History Brush Tool 251
On Your Own 252
Resources and Videos 253

Tutorial 13: Restoration Case Studies 255

Objectives 255
Scanning Photographs for Restoration 255
Case Study 1: Repair an Aged & Damaged Color Photograph 256
Case Study 2: Repair An Aged Color Snapshot 258
Case Study 3: Restore and Colorize An Aged
Black and White Photo 259
Sharpening Images 261
    The High Pass Filter 262
Case Study 4: Sharpen an Image with the High Pass Filter 262

On Your Own 264

Resources and Videos 264

TUTORIAL 14: FUN WITH FILTERS 265

Objectives 265

Filter Guidelines 265

The Filter Menu 266

The Clouds Filter 267

    Guided Exercise 14.1: Use the Clouds Filter to Make a Replacement Sky 267

    Guided Exercise 14.2:
    Use the Clouds Filter to Change the Color and Tone of an Image 269

Difference Clouds 269

    Guided Exercise 14.3: Use the Difference Clouds Filter 270

Motion Blur 270

    Guided Exercise 14.4: Use the Motion Blur Filter 270

    Guided Exercise 14.5: Use the Motion Blur Filter to Soften a Distracting Background 272

The Lens Flare Filter 272

    Guided Exercise 14.6: Use the Lens Flare Filter 273

The Liquify Filter 273

    The Liquify Filter Dialog Box 274

    The Liquify Tools 275

    Other Liquify Settings 276

    The Liquify Mesh 277

    Guided Exercise 14.7A: Use the Liquify Filter to Modify a Boy's Portrait (for Photoshop CC 2015.2 and Earlier) 278

    Guided Exercise 14.7B: Use the Liquify Filter to Modify a Boy's Portrait (for Photoshop CC 2015.5) 279

On Your Own 281

Resources and Videos 281

TUTORIAL 15: PUTTING IT ALL TOGETHER 283

Objectives 283

The Eraser Tools Revisited 283

    The Eraser Tool 283

    The Magic Eraser Tool 284

- The Background Eraser Tool 284
- Eraser Cautions 284
- Guided Exercise 15.1: Use the Eraser Tools to Clean Up a Selection 285
- Semi-Guided Exercise 15.2: Make a Custom Postcard 287
- Guided Exercise 15.3: Use the Magic Eraser Tool 288
- Guided Exercise 15.4: Use the Background Eraser Tool 289
- On Your Own: Make a Sunflower Postcard 291

Patterns 291
- To Define a Pattern by Selection: 291
- Guided Exercise 15.5: Making Patterns 292

Presets, Libraries, & the Preset Manager 293
- Guided Exercise 15.6: Making and Loading Libraries 293
- Semi-Guided Exercise 15.7: Use Presets to Make a Postcard 294

Resources and Videos 297
Where Do You Go From Here? 297

INDEX 299

Practical Photoshop CC 2015, Level 1[©]
Overview and Tutorial Guidelines

Adobe Photoshop® is the industry standard software for image editing. It is both very powerful and very complex. As you learn to master its complexity, you will discover that Photoshop is a magical program that should come with a warning label:

Photoshop is too much fun. It will swallow your time.

We tutorial authors have been teaching Photoshop both in-person and online since 1996. Originally, our Photoshop students were predominantly graphics professionals who needed retraining in digital imaging both for printed publications and for the newly emerging World Wide Web. Now, with digital cameras and camera phones everywhere, Photoshop has become one of the most popular computer classes we teach. In addition to graphics professionals, our students range from high-school enrichment students, to Web site developers, and to hobbyists of all ages.

Our students use Photoshop to:

- Adjust scanned or digital camera images for better screen display or printing. Photoshop lets you easily change the file format of images to use as email attachments, on Web pages, or in printed documents such as brochures and newsletters.

- Edit photographs, especially those taken with a digital camera or digitized with a scanner. Photoshop becomes an electronic darkroom.

    On the left, you can see the original digital photograph of the Golden Gate Bridge, taken by Lorene Romero. The right side shows the same photograph with a quick Photoshop edit.

Overview and Tutorial Guidelines

- Restore old and/or damaged photographs.

    The original 1921 photo, on the left, was scanned into Photoshop, restored, and colorized. You will learn to do this before the course is over.

- Modify images or start from scratch to create original artwork. Photoshop becomes an electronic playroom both for painting with pixels as well as for working with scalable objects like lines, shapes, and text. This cat face artwork was done by Nicholas Ogg.

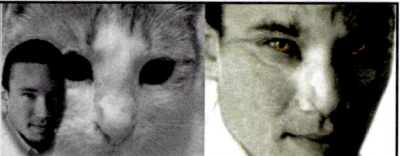

Because Photoshop is so complex, there are often several ways to accomplish the same task. To avoid overwhelming you with these variations, we typically guide you through a single method and introduce additional methods and shortcuts later in the book.

Tutorial Guidelines

At the beginning of each tutorial you will find an **Objectives** section so you know what you will accomplish by completing the tutorial. There will also be a list of practice files for you to download to follow along with the guided exercises.

At the end of each tutorial you will find an **On Your Own** section where you can continue your study of Photoshop, or further develop skills or concepts introduced in the tutorial itself. There are also additional resources as appropriate.

Graphics or computer terminology known as **KEY TERMS** are set off in bolded all caps when they are defined.

Computer menu commands and keystrokes are set off in **boldface** as are panels, bars, buttons, and other workspace elements.

Using These Tutorials with Photoshop

Photoshop menu commands often involve drilling down from a main menu to one or more submenus. We have used a greater-than sign (>) to show you the sequence to follow.

For example, **Image > Adjustments > Black & White** directs you to first click the **Image** menu, then the **Adjustments** submenu, and finally the **Black & White** command to turn a color photo into a black and white (grayscale) photo.

All Windows computers and modern Macintosh computers (except older laptops) use computer mice or trackpads with (at least) two mouse buttons. If your mouse has two or more buttons:

- **Click** means to press and release the left mouse button.

- **Right-click** means to press and release the right mouse button. If your computer only has a one button mouse or a single trackpad button, you will need to **CONTROL-CLICK** – press and hold the **control key** and then click the single button to simulate a right-click.

- **Drag** means to press the (left) mouse button and keep it down as you move the mouse.
- **Press** means to press one of the keys on the keyboard.

Photoshop often uses **MODIFIER KEYS** on the computer keyboard along with mouse clicks to extend the capabilities of those keys.

Windows typically uses the **ctrl**, **alt**, and/or **shift** keys.

Macintosh typically uses the **command** (or ⌘), **option**, **control**, and/or **shift** keys.

The **plus sign** (+) indicates when a modifier key is required. For example, you might **alt + click** (**Win**) or **option + click** (**Mac**) to perform a particular function.

When you use modifier keys, you are supposed to press the key(s) and click the mouse at the same time. Timing can be tricky. You may find it easier to first press the modifier key(s), then click or drag the mouse, and finally to release the mouse button before releasing the modifier key(s).

The Photoshop Application

Adobe produces two image-editing applications: **ADOBE PHOTOSHOP ELEMENTS** and the full **ADOBE PHOTOSHOP**. **Photoshop Elements** is a less expensive, consumer-level graphics editing application. Elements is terrific for simple image editing, but does not have the range of capabilities as the full Photoshop application. Elements offers a good training ground for moving into the professional application, as both applications use similar working environments and approaches to image production and editing.

Adobe first acquired Photoshop in 1990. Since that time, there have been several improvements, or **UPGRADES**. The most current version of Photoshop, released in June 2016, is **Photoshop CC 2015.5**.

These tutorials are designed for **Photoshop CC 2015**—not for earlier versions of Photoshop nor for **Photoshop Elements**.

Hardware and Software Requirements

Photoshop works equally well with either Macintosh or Windows computer systems. Image editing requires lots of processing power, and Photoshop works much more swiftly on newer, faster computers. Before purchasing Photoshop, make sure that your computer hardware and software are adequate. To use Photoshop effectively, you will need a fast computer, a modern operating system, and enough RAM and hard disk space to manipulate your images as you edit and save them. And, of course, you will need the Photoshop application itself. Let's look at each of these requirements in more detail.

1. A fast, powerful computer with a current operating system:

   Macintosh

   - Multicore Intel processor

- Mac OS X v10.9, v10.10, or v10.11
- 4 GB of available hard-disk space for installation; additional free space required during installation (cannot install on a volume that uses a case-sensitive file system or on removable flash storage devices)

Windows

- Intel® Core 2 or AMD Athlon® 64 processor (2GHz or faster)
- 2.6 GB of available hard-disk space for installation; additional free space required during installation (cannot install on removable flash storage devices)
- Microsoft® Windows® 7 with Service Pack 1, Windows® 8.1, or Windows® 10

2. Enough RAM (random access memory) and hard disk space to manipulate your images as you edit and save them.

   2 GB of RAM is what Adobe says. In our experience, 4 GB of RAM should be the minimum, and more is better.

3. Additional requirements:
   - 1024x768 display (1280x800 recommended) with 16-bit color and 512MB (2 GB recommended) of VRAM (video random access memory)
   - OpenGL 2.0–capable system
   - This software will not operate without activation. Broadband Internet connection and registration are required for software activation, membership validation, and access to online services. *Phone activation is not available.*

SETTING UP YOUR MONITOR FOR PHOTOSHOP

Computer monitors display patterns of colored square dots called **PIXELS**. Because those pixels are very small, we don't see them individually, but instead see the bigger "picture."

MONITOR RESOLUTION measures how many pixels fill the screen horizontally and vertically. **640 x 480** means that the monitor shows a grid of **640 pixels** across and **480 pixels** down. When you increase the monitor resolution, everything on the screen becomes smaller so you can fit more things on it. Photoshop uses many items to help you edit images, and you will need to set your monitor resolution to at least **1024 x 768** pixels to see and use all those items.

COLOR DEPTH sets how many different colors your monitor can display. For most Photoshop images, your monitor should be set to **millions of colors** (also known as **24-bit color**) so that color images look like true photographs on your screen. Here is how to check your monitor resolution and change it if needed:

Windows

1. Close or minimize any open applications so that you can see your computer desktop.
2. **Right-click** a blank area on the desktop to reveal its context menu.

3. Choose **Screen Resolution** from that context menu to view the **Screen Resolution** dialog box.

4. **Screen resolution** should be **1024 x 768 pixels** or higher.

5. Click **OK** if settings were changed, otherwise click **Close**.

Macintosh

1. Choose **Apple** ( ) > **System Preferences**.

2. Click **Displays**.

3. Click on the **Scaled** option to reveal display resolution options.

4. Choose an option which provides at least **1024 x 768 pixels** (1280x800 recommended).

5. Choose **System Preferences** > **Quit System Preferences**.

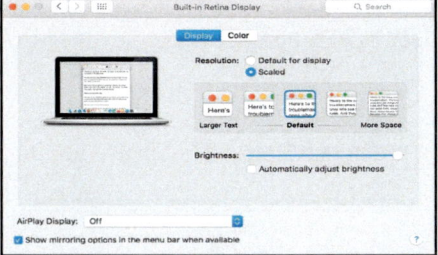

Adobe Photoshop CC 2015 Installation

Whether you install just **Photoshop CC 2015**, or the entire **Creative Cloud** collection, you will need to download the software from the Adobe Web site and follow the on-screen prompts to install the software.

A Few Tips Before You Begin

- If you are upgrading from a previous version of Photoshop, keep your serial number handy—you may need it to complete the software installation.

- If desired, uninstall and remove earlier versions of Photoshop and Bridge before you install CC 2015.

    You can run Photoshop CC 2015 on the same computer as earlier versions of Photoshop, Bridge, or Elements. However, those older versions take up valuable hard drive space, and you can get confused about which version of the software you have open. Unless you will need the older versions, remove them before you install CC 2015.

    Windows: Use the **Adobe Photoshop Uninstaller** in the **Add or Remove Programs** utility in Windows to remove Photoshop from the computer.

    Macintosh: Use the uninstaller in the **Applications > Utilities > Adobe Installers** folder to uninstall older versions of Photoshop.

Activation & Deactivation

Single-user licenses of Photoshop CC 2015 require that you activate the software online before using it for more than 30 days after its first use. According to Adobe, http://helpx.adobe.com/x-productkb/policy-pricing/activation-deactivation-products.html, this is a "simple, anonymous process." A single-user license allows you to

---

Overview and Tutorial Guidelines

place Photoshop CC 2015 onto two computers —such as work and home, or a desktop and a laptop—with the assumption that you will use Photoshop on only one machine at a time. If you want to install the software on an additional computer, you must first deactivate it on one of the original computers.

Within the Photoshop application, choose **Help** > **Deactivate**.

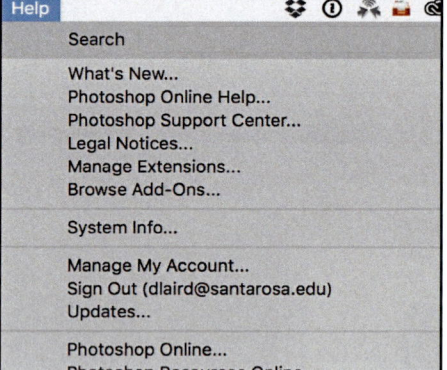

Checking for Free Updates

Photoshop CC 2015 is quite complicated, and although Adobe works hard to make it perfect, problems sometimes arise. When Adobe fixes these problems, or adds features that were not included in the shipped software, **UPDATES** become available for download and installation.

1. Open Photoshop CC 2015.

2. Choose **Help** > **Updates** to go online to the **Adobe Application Manager** to check your computer and see if any updates are available.

3. If any updates are available, you will be instructed to download and install them.
   You probably will not be able to do this if you are working in a computer lab or network.

Adobe ID

An **Adobe ID**, plus your password, gives you access to special membership benefits on Adobe.com. It is required to complete your software installation and essential for viewing special training and help features for Creative Cloud applications. For more information see:

http://helpx.adobe.com/x-productkb/policy-pricing/account-password-sign-faq.html.

Uninstalling Adobe Photoshop CC 2015

When you install your software, an uninstaller is placed in your system. In Windows, the **Add or Remove Programs** control panel should allow you to uninstall Photoshop. On the Mac, by default, the uninstaller is placed inside the **Adobe Photoshop CC 2015** folder.

The Adobe Photoshop Settings File

Application **PREFERENCES** are settings for window and panel locations, tools, dialog boxes, and color settings. Each time a tool, panel, or command setting is changed, Photoshop saves the new configurations in the **Adobe Photoshop Settings File** on the computer's hard disk.

Application **DEFAULTS** are the original settings created when the program was first installed. As you learn Photoshop, you may want to restore these defaults each time you launch the program so that your working environment is consistent, and it matches the environment described in these notes.

Occasionally, the **Adobe Photoshop Settings File** becomes corrupted, and Photoshop works very slowly or otherwise misbehaves. Restoring the **Adobe Photoshop Settings File** can often solve these problems.

To Restore the Default Adobe Photoshop Settings File

1. Check to be sure that Photoshop is not already open; exit or quit the application if necessary.

    If Photoshop is open, you will see its name on the Windows Taskbar, or its icon in the Mac OS X Dock with a triangle underneath it.

2. Locate the Photoshop application icon in the Start menu (Windows) or the Applications folder (Mac) on your hard drive.

3. Position your fingers just over the modifier keys, but do not press the keys. Capitalization matches the keyboards.

    Windows : **Ctrl+ Alt + Shift**

    Macintosh : **command + option + shift**
    The **Command** key, lower right here, is the one with the Apple logo and the cloverleaf. The **fn** key shown here is only found on laptops and some Mac keyboards.

4. Start Photoshop and then immediately press the modifier keys and keep them pressed until you see this confirmation dialog box. If you don't see it, your keystroke timing was off. **Quit** or **Exit** Photoshop and try again.

5. Click **Yes** to delete the (old) **Adobe Photoshop Settings File** and replace it with the default settings file.

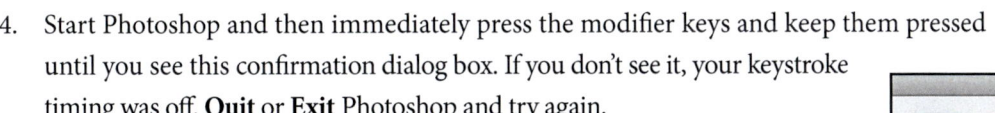

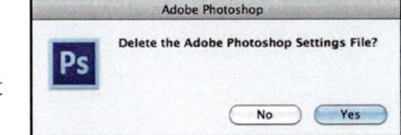

6. If you see a dialog box asking to configure your color settings, click **No** to retain the current color settings. You will not see the additional dialog box unless your color settings have been specified.

Download Tutorial Files

All the example and tutorial files used in this book can be downloaded at:
http://www.practical-photoshop.com/pages/CC-2015-level1.html

Practical Photoshop CC 2015, Level 1
Tutorial 1: Photoshop Basics

In this tutorial you will explore the Photoshop CC 2015 workspace, customize it to serve your needs, and use Photoshop to modify a photograph taken with a digital camera. The tutorial is broken up into step-by-step Guided Exercises interspersed with explanatory sections. As you work through this introductory tutorial, remember that Photoshop is a very complicated application that is best learned through repetition. The concepts and skills you learn here will be reinforced and expanded as you proceed through the tutorial series. ***Don't expect to master everything the first time through!!!***

Objectives

- Identify the major regions of the Photoshop workspace and explain the function of each: **Menu** bar and **context menus**, **Options** bar, **Tools** panel, other panels, and document window(s).

- Use the **Workspace Switcher** menu to use and change built-in workspaces.

- Manipulate and customize panels.

- Open and navigate a Photoshop document with menu commands, the **Zoom Tool**, the **Hand Tool,** and the **Navigator** panel.

- Create a layered Photoshop document from a provided starting image.

- Use the **Undo** commands and the **History** panel to reverse document changes.

- Explore **Adobe Photoshop Help**, and use it to find out more about the tools in the **Tools** panel.

The Photoshop Workspace

A **WORKSPACE** consists of the panels, menus, and keyboard shortcuts that you use with Photoshop.

Guided Exercise 1.1: Navigate the Photoshop Workspace

In this guided exercise you will use Photoshop to open and work with **01-pumpkin.jpg** that you downloaded at the end of the Overview and Tutorial Guidelines chapter.

1. Open the **Adobe Photoshop CC 2015** application.

   Windows 7

   To launch Photoshop, choose **Start** > **All Programs** > **Adobe Photoshop CC 2015**.

Macintosh

   a. Locate the **Adobe Photoshop CC 2015 application icon**. By default it is inside the **Adobe Photoshop CC 2015 folder** inside the **Applications** folder on your startup hard drive.

   b. Double-click the **Photoshop CC 2015 application icon** to open Photoshop.

   c. Press the **Photoshop icon** in the **Dock** to reveal the **Dock Menu** and choose **Keep in Dock**. Now, even when you quit Photoshop, its icon will remain in the **Dock**. You simply click its **Dock** icon to open Photoshop.

   d. If desired, follow the same procedure to open **Adobe Bridge CC** and keep it in the **Dock** as well.

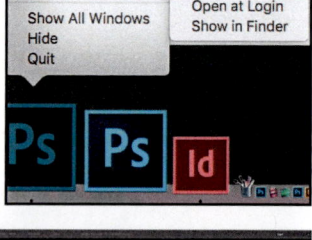

2. Once you open Photoshop, you will be shown the **Start** workspace. This Gives you quick access to any recently-opened files, as well as quick ways to create new documents.

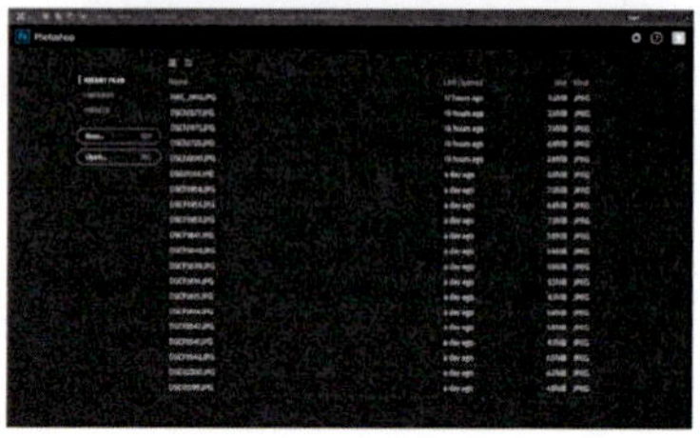

3. Open **01-pumpkin.jpg** in Photoshop:

   a. Click the **Open** button in the Start workspace or choose **File > Open** to see the **Open** dialog box.

   b. Navigate to **01-pumpkin.jpg** and click its name to select it.

   This large file, taken with a digital camera, has enough pixels for a high-quality printout on an ink jet or color laser printer. The **JPEG** format shrinks down files when saved to disk to minimize the time it takes to download those files. The image is compressed to save disk space. It takes up less than 1 MB of disk space. When opened up in Photoshop, the image is uncompressed and takes up over 12 MB of memory.

   c. Click **Open** to open **01-pumpkin.jpg** inside its document window in Photoshop.

4. Locate the major landmarks of the Photoshop workspace:

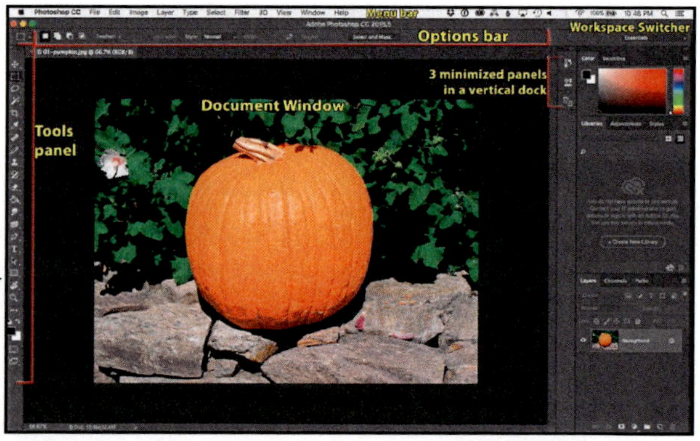

   - The **Application Frame**, always present in Windows as part of the operating system, surrounds all application components with a dark gray frame so that the entire workspace can be treated as a single unit. On the Mac you can view or hide the **Application Frame** from the bottom of the **Window** menu. By default, it is visible.

   - The **Menu** bar at the top of the workspace provides a series of menus, each of which is an organized list of Photoshop commands.

   - **Docks** are columns along the sides of the application or screen window that hold tools or panels.

Tutorial 1: Photoshop Basics   Page 10

- **Panels** are groupings that appear by default along the right edge of the workspace.
- The panel docked by default to the left edge of the workspace contains the tools that you use to create and edit Photoshop images.
- The context-sensitive **Options** bar just beneath the **Menu** bar holds settings that are specific to the chosen or **ACTIVE** tool.
- Each open Photoshop document is contained within a **document window**.
- The **Workspace Switcher** lets you choose from predefined workspaces and configure your own custom workspaces, as you will do later in this tutorial.

5. Reset the **Essentials** workspace, all tools, and the default **Foreground** and **Background** colors.

    NOTE: We are giving you the specifics here, but will not repeat these specifics for future guided exercises.

    a. To reset the **Essentials** workspace, choose **Essentials** from the **Workspace Switcher** menu if necessary and then choose **Reset Essentials** from the **Workspace Switcher** menu.

    b. To reset all tools to their defaults, **right-click** the icon of any tool at the left side of the **Options** bar and choose **Reset All Tools** from the context menu that appears.

    c. To reset colors to black and white, click the **default colors** button in the **Tools** panel **color picker**.

6. Observe how the **Options** bar contents change when you change the active tool from the **Hand Tool** to the **Zoom Tool**:

    a. Click the **Hand Tool** in the **Tools** panel to choose or **ACTIVATE** it.

    When the entire image is too big to be visible in the document window, the **Hand Tool** moves or **PANS** the image to display hidden regions of it.

    - Identify the icon of **Hand Tool** on the left edge of the **Options** bar, indicating that the **Hand Tool** is the active tool.
    - Notice that the **Options** bar contains a check box, **Scroll All Windows**, and three buttons: **100%**, **Fit Screen**, and **Fill Screen**. You will use these buttons later in this tutorial.

    b. Click the **Zoom Tool** in the **Tools** panel.

    - The **Options** bar for the **Zoom Tool** contains similar check boxes and buttons to the **Move Tool** with a few additional buttons and check boxes.

7. Use the **Workspace Switcher** on the far right end of the **Options** bar.
   The **Workspace Switcher** remains in that location no matter what tool is chosen.

   Photoshop CC 2015 ships with several preset workspaces. The default, **Essentials**, shows the most commonly-used panels, and hides those that you are less likely to use. Task-specific workspaces such as **Motion**, **Painting**, and **Photography** display the panels you are most likely to use when performing one of those tasks.

   a. To begin, the **Workspace Switcher** should display **Essentials**.
      If it is set to a different workspace, click the **Workspace Switcher** to display the **Workspace** menu and choose **Essentials** from the top of the menu.

   b. Modify your workspace: 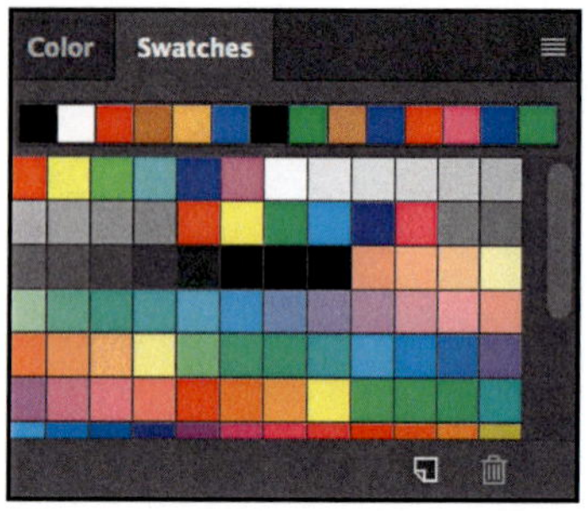
      1) On the upper right side of the screen, click the **Swatches** panel tab to bring the **Swatches** panel forward.
      2) Click other hidden panel tabs as desired to see what they contain.

   c. Choose a different workspace:
      1) Choose the **Photography** workspace.
         Notice that the panels shown on the right of the window have changed.
      2) Choose the **Photography** workspace and see the panels change again.

   d. When you are done exploring, click the **Workspace Switcher** and choose **Essentials**. Click the **Workspace Switcher a second time and** choose **Reset Essentials** near the bottom of the menu to return the panes to their locations before you changed workspaces.

      It was necessary to use the **Workspace Switcher** menu twice because the **Reset** _____ command only resets the currently chosen workspace.

      TIP: *Unless otherwise specified, periodically reset the **Essentials** workspace to keep your workspace consistent with the book.*

8. Explore the **Menu** bar and identify the **Minimize**, **Close**, and **Maximize/Restore** buttons for your operating system.

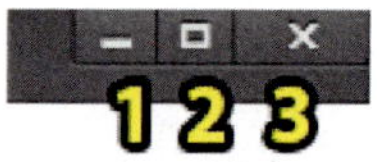

   WINDOWS:, the **Minimize** button (**1**) reduces the entire Photoshop application to the Taskbar button shown here, the **Maximize/Restore** button (**2**) toggles between having the Photoshop application cover the entire screen and appearing in a smaller window, and the **Close** button (**3**) exits Photoshop entirely.

   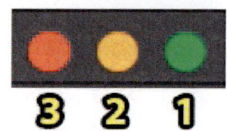

   MACINTOSH: the **Minimize** button (**2**) reduces the **Application Frame** to an icon on the **Dock**, the **Maximize/Restore** button (**1**) toggles between having the Photoshop

   Tutorial 1: Photoshop Basics   Page 12

application cover the entire screen and appearing in a smaller window, and the **Close** button (**3**) closes the active document window, but leaves the Photoshop application open.

On either system, after you minimize, simply click the minimized button on the **Taskbar** or **Dock** to reopen the **Application Frame**.

9. Manipulate the **Tools** panel:

    a. Locate the **Tools** panel, docked by default to the left edge of the **Application Frame**.

    By default, the **Tools** panel is one long skinny column.

    b. View a **TOOL TIP**, a small yellow box that contains information about the item your pointer hovers over. You will find tool tips throughout the Photoshop workspace.

      1) Without clicking, point the mouse to the tool with an eraser on it to show its yellow tool tip.

      2) The **Eraser Tool**'s tool tip is **Eraser Tool (E)**. The tool tip displays both the name of the tool and in parentheses its **KEYBOARD SHORTCUT**, the key you can type from the keyboard to choose that tool.

    c. Tools that contain a little triangle in their lower right corner hide other tools. Choose a tool hiding under the **Eraser Tool**.

      1) Click and hold the pointer down on the **Eraser Tool** to reveal the menu of tools organized under it. The **Background Eraser Tool** and the **Magic Eraser Tool** hide under the **Eraser Tool**.

      2) Drag down the list to highlight the **Background Eraser Tool** and release the pointer (mouse) button.

      Now the **Background Eraser Tool** shows in the **Tools** panel, with the other eraser tools hidden beneath it.

      3) Choose the (standard) **Eraser Tool** as you will not use the specialty erasers until the end of this course.

10. Examine the top of the document window, shown for each individual document open in Photoshop. By default, it contains an informational tab for each open document.

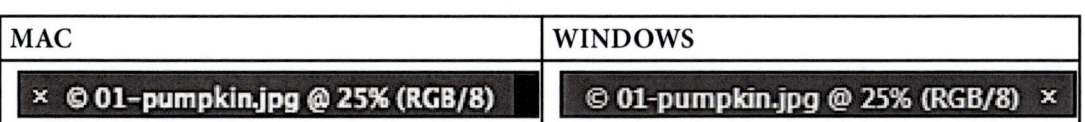

   - The **Close Box** (**x**) to close the document window.

   - The copyright symbol (©) if the image is copyrighted and the name of the file, **01_pumpkin.jpg** here.

- The zoom or magnification level @ **25%** indicates that only one quarter of the pixels are showing; the other three quarters of the pixels are hidden to view the entire document in the document window without scrolling.

- If a document has more than one layer, and a layer other than the **Background** layer is active, its name will also show at the end of the **Title** bar. Here we added **Layer 1** to the document, and **Layer 1** is active:

  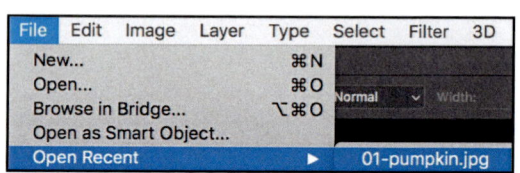

- The image mode, **RGB/8** in this document, indicates that this is an image that uses the **RGB** or red-green-blue image mode, with **8** bits to each color channel. (We won't cover 16 bit or bigger files in this course.)

11. Use the **Open Recent** command to close and reopen the pumpkin image:

    a. Click the **Close Box (x)** on the edge of the **01_pumpkin.jpg** tab. If you see a warning box asking to save the document, click **No** as you should not have made any changes.

    b. Choose **File > Open Recent** and choose **01_pumpkin.jpg**.

    By default, Photoshop keeps track of the ten most recently opened documents.
    (This feature may have been turned off if you work in a computer lab.)

12. Examine the **Status** bar at the bottom of the document window. From left to right, here is what you will see:

    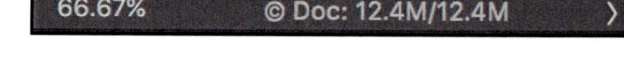

    a. **Zoom level**, **66.67%** here. To change the zoom level, highlight the number, type in a new zoom percentage like **50%**, and press **Enter** or **Return**.

    b. **Status** bar information, here Doc **12.4 M/12.4M**. This **Status** bar is set to show **Document Sizes**.

    c. Click the triangle to the right of the **Status** bar information to choose a different informational category from the **Status** bar **menu**.

    d. End up with **Document Sizes** showing (checked).

Panel Manipulation & Customization

Photoshop CC 2015 has 29 panels. Since you don't typically work with all these panels at once and since they would cover the entire screen if they were all visible and active at once, panels are either grouped in docks or accessible from the **Options** bar, depending on how a particular panel is used.

Each dock typically contains a column of **GROUPED** or clustered panels. In the **Essentials** workspace, for example, the **Color** panel, on top, is grouped with the **Swatches** panel on the right side of the **Application Frame**.

Tutorial 1: Photoshop Basics   Page 14

To view a different panel in the group, click its name tab at the top of the panel. All the panels are listed alphabetically under the **Window** menu. Check marks indicate those panels that are at the front of their panel groups, such as the **Libraries**, **Color**, and **Layers** panels in the **Essentials** workspace. The **Window** menu also lists keyboard shortcuts for the most commonly used panels, such as **F7** to open the **Layers** panel.

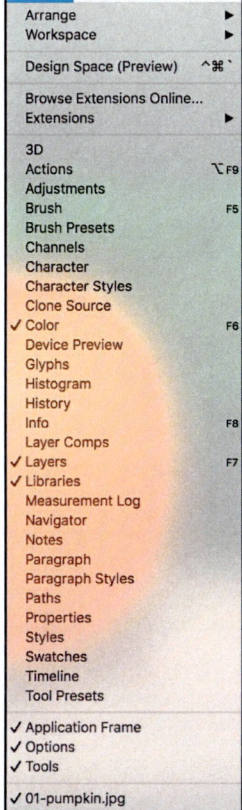

You have already seen how the **Workspace** menu lets you choose from premade workspaces. Now let's view and use the docks and individual panels.

When expanded, panels can be shrunk or expanded horizontally or vertically, but the dock itself always remains in position, either anchored to the edge of the screen or to its neighboring dock.

Dock Manipulation

The top of each dock has double arrows to collapse or expand all its panels.

- Click the right double arrows to collapse that dock. The left double arrows re-expand the dock.

- If you want, you can shrink the width of the right dock in collapsed mode to hide the labels by dragging its left edge.

The **tab** key hides the panels and bars, but with a nice twist—they are spring loaded to reappear as you mouse over them:

- Press the **tab** key. Notice that all the panels including the **Tools** panel and the **Options** bar disappear, leaving more room to work on your document.

- Without pressing the mouse button, slowly move your pointer over the left edge of the screen or application window (Windows).

    When you are in the correct spot, the **Tools** panel will appear so that you can pick a tool. Now move right, away from the **Tools** panel, and watch the **Tools** panel hide again.

- Repeat these steps, moving the pointer to the opposite (right) side of the screen to reveal the panel docks, and then move left to hide them again.

- Press the **tab** key again to reveal all the panels and bars.

Shift + tab toggles to hide and reveal only the right panel docks, but not the **Options** bar or **Tools** panel. With the narrow one-column **Tools** panel, and the **Options** bar always visible, but the panels hidden, you can see the controls you use most often, keep most of the workspace available for document editing, and quickly reveal the panels when you need them.

Tutorial 1: Photoshop Basics   Page 15

Panel Controls

Individual panels can be grouped, rearranged, reduced to icons, floated, closed, and reopened.

Shrink and Expand

- If you double-click the tab of an expanded panel, the entire group will shrink to just its top tabs, dramatically reducing its size.

- Repeat the process to expand the panel group.

Close and Reopen

In previous versions of Photoshop, people were accidentally closing panels without meaning to, so in recent versions of Photoshop it has become a bit more complicated to close panels.

1. Each panel has a panel menu, accessed from the menu button in its upper right corner. (Alternately, you can right-click the tab).

2. From the bottom of each panel menu, choose **Close** to close just that panel, or **Close Tab Group** to close all the grouped tabs, such as the **Colors** and **Styles** group.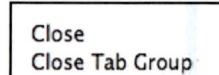

Alternately, you can choose a checked panel from the **Window** menu to close it. This will close the entire tab group and not just the single panel.

To reopen a panel and its default group, choose its name from the **Window** menu.

TIP: When we lose panels, we find it is much more efficient to use the **Workspace Switcher** to restore our workspace defaults than to start manually opening panels or groups.

Panel Menus

Each panel has a menu of commands that pertain to that particular panel.
Sometimes these commands are found elsewhere as well, and at other times they are restricted to the panel menu. Here is the **Color Panel** menu, which can modify the **Color** panel's appearance.

Panel Manipulation

There are many ways to change the appearance and location of individual panels in the docks.

Free-float a Panel

Sometimes you want to move a panel out of its dock, to float freely on top of the document window. To do this, drag a named panel such as the **Layers** panel by its tab or use the dark area at the top of the **Tools** panel to float the entire panel group.

- Position the tip of the pointer in between the **Close Box** and the **Expand** arrows (it's a small space) and drag the **Tools** panel out of its dock on top of the document window.

- Drag it back when you are done. A vertical blue line may appear as you approach the correct location.
- Release the pointer button to drop the **Tools** panel in place.

Relocate a Panel Group

Panel groups, whether collapsed or expanded, have a gray region to the right of their tabs that can be used to move the entire panel group.

- Drag the **Color/Swatches** group by the bar to the left without releasing the mouse button. You will see a blue outline showing the outline of the panel.
- Without releasing the mouse button, drag the **Color/Swatches** group above the **Layers/Channels/Paths** group. As you drag, the panels blur. When you approach the correct location, a horizontal blue line will appear at the top of the dock.
- Release the mouse button to insert the **Color/Swatches** panel into its new location.
- NOTE: if you see a blue box instead of a blue line, that is the location to merge the panels in your panel group with the underlying panel group.

Relocate an Individual Panel

If you don't like the group a panel has been placed into in one of the preset workspaces, you can drag any panel by its button (collapsed) or its tab (expanded) into a different group.

- Drag the **Styles** panel into the **Layers/Channels/Paths** group.
- If you don't like the new location, **Reset Essentials** from the **Workspace Switcher** menu to quickly put the **Styles** panel back to its original position.

Document Navigation

The viewing size of a document appears in the both the **document tab** and the **Status** bar of the active document. Changing the viewing size, or **ZOOM LEVEL**, does not change the dimensions or print size of an image—it just changes its screen display.

Guided Exercise 1.2: Navigate a File with View Menu Commands

In this guided exercise you will experiment with various menu commands to change your document view.

1. Open **01-pumpkin.jpg** if it is not already open.
2. Examine the document magnification in the **Status** bar.

    Large documents such as this one may have too many pixels to show up in your monitor, so Photoshop hides some of the pixels so that you can "see" the entire image.

Our document opened at **66.67%**. Depending on the size and setup of your monitor, your document may have a different percentage. **66.67%** means that the image is a two thirds of its actual size in both height and width, and you are viewing a low-quality version of the actual document.

3. Choose **View > Zoom In**.

   Notice that the pumpkin gets larger, but you can no longer see the entire image within the document window. Scroll bars appear on the sides of the document window to let you view the hidden parts of the document. The view magnification also changes, for us to **100%**, indicating the of the part of the image that is in the window.

4. Choose **View > 100%**. This command displays your document zoomed to **100%**.

   At **100%** magnification, you can see every pixel in the part of the document that shows in the document window; no pixels are hidden. But you cannot see the entire document because it is too large for the window.

5. Experiment with the other **View** menu commands shown here.

   Fit on Screen expands the document window to as large as can be shown on screen without being covered by panels.

   Print Size shows the image in the approximate size it will print. It is not very accurate.

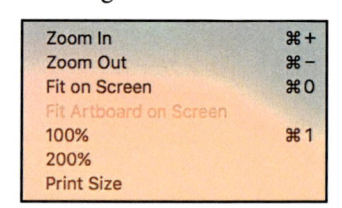

   Zoom In and **Zoom Out** let you increase and decrease magnification in set increments. If you prefer to work with keystrokes, you can zoom in and out by using the **command** key (Mac) or the **ctrl** key (Windows) along with the **plus** or **minus** keys. Each time you press the **plus** or **minus**, the zoom level increases or decreases accordingly.

Guided Exercise 1.3: Use the Zoom Tool with Options

1. Click the **Zoom Tool**, near the bottom of the **Tools** panel, to activate it. It looks like a magnifying glass.

2. Locate the **Options** bar, just below the **Menu** bar at the top of the Photoshop window.

   The far-left part of the **Options** bar always shows the **ACTIVE**, or currently-chosen, tool.

   To its right are two buttons that allow you to either **ZOOM IN** (**plus cursor**) or **ZOOM OUT** (**minus cursor**) when you use the **Zoom Tool**.

   Each time you click the **Zoom Tool** with the **plus cursor** chosen, it is the same as choosing **View > Zoom In**; the **minus cursor** is the same as **View > Zoom Out**.

3. Click the check box to the left of **Resize Windows to Fit**, and then zoom in and out several times. Notice what happens to your document window.

Tutorial 1: Photoshop Basics

- When **Resize Windows to Fit** is checked, the document window will expand or contract as you zoom in or out.
- When **Resize Window to Fit** is not checked, the document window remains a constant size.

4. In turn, click the **100%, Fit Screen,** and **Fill Screen** buttons. They function the same as the commands on the **View** menu that you have already used.

5. Use the **Scrubby Zoom** option:

    a. With the **Zoom Tool** active, make sure that the **Scrubby Zoom** option is checked.

    b. Press and drag inside the document window to the right to zoom in, focusing on the location where you are dragging.

    c. Press and drag to the left to zoom out.

    d. Uncheck the **Scrubby Zoom** option and repeat step 5 b.

    When **Scrubby Zoom** is not checked, dragging makes a **SELECTION RECTANGLE**.
    When you release the mouse, the region inside the selection rectangle zooms in dramatically.

    e. Click **Fit Screen** to view the entire image in the document window.

6. Navigate with the **Hand Tool**:

    a. Choose the **Hand Tool**.

    b. Click the **100%** button to zoom in to **100%** or actual size.

    c. Place the pointer into the center of the document and drag to one side. Notice that the document moves inside the document window, as if you were adjusting a large picture within a smaller picture frame.

    d. Click the **Fit Screen** button before continuing on to the next guided exercise.

. . . .

Guided Exercise 1.4: Use the Navigator Panel

When only a small portion of the image is visible, it is hard to tell where you are so you can make effective edits. Navigating a document with the hand tool, also called **PANNING**, can be much faster and more precise than using the document's horizontal and vertical scroll bars, especially for diagonal scrolling.

The **Navigator** panel, hidden by default in the **Essentials** workspace, provides a convenient way to navigate within a document because it always displays a thumbnail of the whole image to help you orient. In this guided exercise, you will show the **Navigator** panel and use it.

Tutorial 1: Photoshop Basics

1. Choose **Window > Navigator** to show the **Navigator** panel. It appears expanded, grouped with the **Histogram** panel. The Navigator and Histogram panel icons also appear, docked to the left edge of the original dock on the right side of the screen.

    The **Navigator** panel contains a small preview image, or **THUMBNAIL**, of the active document. In **Fit Screen** view, the entire thumbnail is surrounded by a red box, called the **PROXY**, that shows how much of the document is visible in the document window.

2. With the **Hand Tool** chosen, click the **100%** button in the **Options** bar.

    The proxy shrinks to outline only a smaller part of the pumpkin image, that which is currently visible within the document window. The **Navigator** panel shows the zoom percentage of **100%** in its lower left corner.

3. Drag the vertical scroll bar up so that you can see the top of the image. Notice that the **Navigator** panel's proxy moves as you drag.

4. Drag the horizontal scroll bar to the right so you can see the upper right corner of the image. Now the proxy should be in the upper right corner of the **Navigator** panel's preview.

5. Choose the **Hand Tool** and drag it around in the document.

    You can easily navigate diagonally with the **Hand Tool** and the **Navigator** panel's proxy updates your location in the document window.

6. Move the mouse pointer on top of the proxy in the **Navigator** panel. It changes to look like the **Hand** tool. **Drag** to change the proxy location on the Navigator thumbnail, which also changes the part of the document you see in the document window.

7. **Choose View > Zoom Out**.

    An image's view magnification is sometimes called its **ZOOM**. When you zoom out, you see a larger portion of the image in the document window, but Photoshop may need to hide some pixels

8. Click the **Zoom Out** button on the **Navigator** panel to make the zoom percentage decrease.

9. Click the **Zoom In** button on the **Navigator** panel to make the zoom percentage increase.

10. Drag the **Zoom Slider** all the way to the left. Notice that the document shrinks to **.11%** and it is virtually invisible. Zooming out this far is not very useful.

11. Slowly drag the **Zoom Slider** all the way to the right. As you drag, the zoom increases slowly. Typically, you will drag the **Zoom Slider** slowly to dynamically find the zoom percentage you need for the task at hand.

    When you reach the right end of the **Zoom Slider**, you will have magnified the document to **3200%**. Now you can see the individual pixels that make up the document, but you see such a small part of the document that you may not be able to find the proxy in the **Navigator** thumbnail. Occasionally, you may use this view to edit individual pixels in a document.

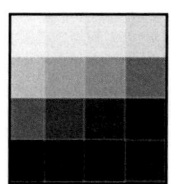

Tutorial 1: Photoshop Basics   Page 20

Keyboard Shortcuts

KEYBOARD SHORTCUTS are quick ways to execute menu commands, and to change application settings or options on the fly. Experienced Photoshop users learn keyboard shortcuts for commonly used commands to speed up their workflow.

Macintosh Laptop Users: Most modern computers use two button mice, but older Macintosh laptops still have only one button on their track pads. If you are using one of these laptops, you will need to press the **control** (or **ctrl**) key as you click to simulate the right click.

Navigation Shortcuts

Learning to navigate around an image and quickly change its view size is an important skill. You want to become familiar with zooming and scrolling around an image, and keeping track of your document viewing magnification.

Practice these navigational shortcuts:

- Double click the **Zoom Tool** to change document view to **100%**.
- Double click the **Hand Tool** to change document view to **Fit on Screen**.
- Press the **space** bar (the biggest key on the keyboard) to temporarily change from any other tool to the **Hand Tool**. Drag to pan your image. When you release the **space** bar, you will return to whatever tool you were using before you panned.
- Look at the **Zoom Tool** cursor before you click it to see if it is set to **zoom in** (plus) or **zoom out** (minus). To temporarily reverse the zoom, **alt + click** (Windows) or **option + click** (Mac).
- If a tool other than the **Zoom Tool** is active, use **Command/Ctrl + Plus** to zoom in or **Command/Ctrl + Minus** to zoom out.

Context Menus

If you **right-click** (two button mouse) or **ctrl +click** (Mac laptop trackpad) on a part of your document or workspace, its **CONTEXT MENU** of relevant commands will appear.

Restore Tool Defaults

To set an individual tool's settings back to the defaults, **right-click** the tool icon in the upper left corner of the **Options** bar and choose **Reset Tool** from the context menu that appears.

To restore all tools to their default settings, right-click the icon of the chosen tool in the **Options** bar and choose **Reset All Tools** from the context menu that appears.

Zoom with Context Menu

You can also access context-sensitive menus of commands relevant to the current tool. If you choose the **Zoom Tool** and then either **right-click** (two button mouse) or **ctrl + click** (one button mouse) on a part of your document or workspace, its **CONTEXT MENU** of relevant commands will appear. The **Hand Tool** provides only the top four options.

Your First Photoshop Project

A common problem with learning any new application is that, in the beginning, you look at a lot of "stuff" but don't get to do anything fun. Since Photoshop is so much fun, we don't want you to miss out. Here we will guide you through some exercises that let you have fun with Photoshop while you receive a very basic introduction to Photoshop painting and layer manipulation. Your goal is to experience just a little of what Photoshop can do, not to provide comprehensive coverage of each step you accomplish. As the course proceeds, we will return to each of these topics in more detail.

Guided Exercise 1.5: Begin to "Carve" a Pumpkin, Photoshop Style

1. Open **01-pumpkin.jpg** image if necessary.

2. **Locate the Color Controls** near the bottom of the **Tools** panel.
   They are the solid colored squares shown here.

   Many Photoshop tools use one or both of two user-defined colors, **Foreground** and **Background**. The big top left square shows the **FOREGROUND COLOR**; the big bottom right square shows the **BACKGROUND COLOR**.

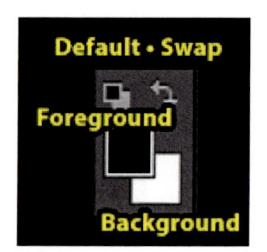

   What is the difference between the **Foreground** color and the **Background** color?

   - Painting tools such as the **Brush Tool** and the **Pencil Tool** paint using the **Foreground** color.

   - The **Eraser Tool** reveals the **Background** color when painting on the **Background** layer, the starting point for most Photoshop images

   - The **Foreground** and **Background** colors are used together to make gradient fills, and for other special effects.

   - The **swap** button which looks like a double arrow switches the **Foreground** and **Background** colors. If we clicked it with the default colors chosen, the **Foreground** color would become white and the **Background** color black.

   - By default, the **Background** color is white and the **Foreground** color is black. In a moment you will choose or **SAMPLE** a new **Foreground** color. Clicking the **default** button would then restore the black and white default colors.

3. Click the **Swatches** panel tab to bring it forward.

   By default, the **Swatches** panel hides beneath the **Color** panel. Each box is a single-color **SWATCH**.

4. Without pressing its button, move the mouse over the green swatch near the upper left corner of the **Swatches** panel.

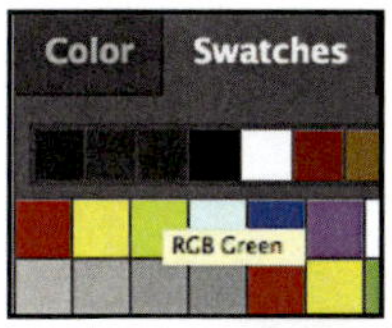

   The (mouse) pointer becomes a tiny eyedropper to signify that you can choose or sample that color, and a tool tip appears to tell you the color. Here we are sampling **RGB Green**.

5. Click that green swatch to make it the **Foreground** color. Note the change in the **Color Controls** on the **Tools** panel.

6. Restore all tools to their default settings:

   a. **Right-click** the tool icon in the upper left corner of the **Options** bar.

   b. Choose **Reset All Tools** from the context menu that appears.

   c. Click **OK** in the dialog box that appears.

7. Paint a nose on the pumpkin.

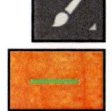

   a. Choose the **Brush Tool** and drag it in the center of the pumpkin to paint a short green line. Whoops! It's too thin.

   b. Choose **Edit > Undo Brush Tool** to remove the green line.

   NOTE: Whenever you **Undo** in Photoshop, the **Undo** command includes the name of the last tool or command you used.

   c. In the **Options** bar, click the **Brush thumbnail** to display the **Brush Preset** picker.

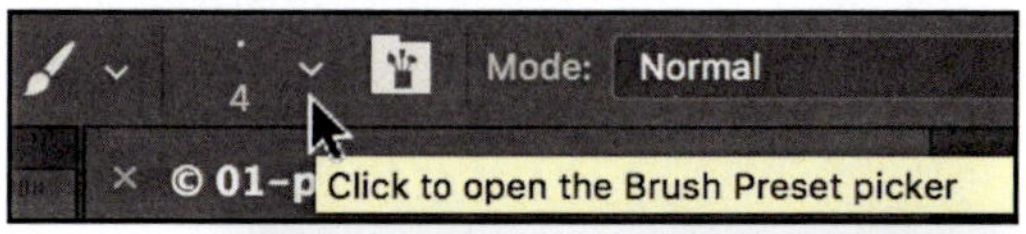

   d. Drag the **Size** slider to the right, to increase the brush size to **25 px**.

   e. Drag the **Brush Tool** to paint a short green line in the center of the pumpkin.

   That's a better thickness.

   f. Paint two more lines to make a triangle.
   It could be the nose of a jack-o'-lantern, but it is too big.

8. Attempt to erase the nose:

   a. Click the **Eraser Tool** and examine its **Options** bar.

Tutorial 1: Photoshop Basics

The **Eraser Tool**'s default settings are similar to the **Brush Tool**'s settings. An additional option, **Erase to History**, will not be covered in this course.

b. Reapply steps 7c–d to change the **Eraser Tool** brush tip size to **25 px**.

c. Drag the **Eraser Tool** across one of the green lines to erase it. Whoops, more problems:

There are still traces of green on the edges of the white. More erasing could correct that problem, but, the line will still be white, not the pumpkin image you probably expected.

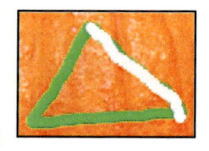

Look at the **Layers** panel and note that the pumpkin has one layer, named **Background**. When you paint directly on the Background and then use the **Eraser Tool** , you erase to the **Background** color (white by default) rather than restoring the original image.

9. Keep the pumpkin image open while you next read about the **History** panel, and then use the **History** panel to remove the green triangle to restore the original pumpkin.

The History Panel

When you need to undo just one step in Photoshop, you can choose **Edit > Undo** as we did earlier. Typically, however, if you discover a problem further down the road, like the wrong size nose on the pumpkin, **Undo** *only reverses the very last command or tool you used*.

When this happens, the Photoshop **History** panel comes to the rescue.

Every time you use a tool or command to edit your image, the **History** panel adds that particular version of the image to the bottom of the panel as a **HISTORY STATE**. The History panel lets you choose any one of these recent states to restore the image to the desired state — what the image looked like at that point in time. The **History** panel records only document-specific steps that change selections, pixels, or paths — not program-wide alterations such as a preference change or a change in document view. Program-wide alterations are not changes to the components of a particular image and so are not added to the **History** panel.

WARNING: The **History** panel is wonderful, but it has one major limitation: *History states are not saved with the image. When you close an image, its History states vanish.*

Guided Exercise 1.6: Use the History Panel to Undo Image Changes

The **History** panel is invaluable for Photoshop work because it lets you go back up to 50 steps (by default) to recover from unwanted image edits. Try it.

1. Locate the **History** panel. In the **Essentials** workspace, it is minimized to a button, to the left of the **Color/Swatches** group, just above the **Properties** button.

2. Click the **History** panel button to expand it.

   Towards the top of the **History** panel is a small thumbnail of the pumpkin image, with the **History states** listed beneath it. If the scroll bar on the right side of the panel is visible, it indicates that there are more states than you can see in the panel.

3. Drag the lower edge of the panel down to make it longer and to reveal all its **History states**, if needed.

   Here you can see seven **History states**. The default name Photoshop gives to each state is limited to the icon and the name of the tool used.

   - **Snapshot**: The appearance of the document when first opened. This state shows the document thumbnail and its file name.
   - **Open**: Opening the original document.
   - **Brush Tool**: Painting the first green line.
   - **Brush Tool**: Painting the second green line.
   - **Brush Tool**: Painting the third green line.
   - **Eraser (Tool)**: Erasing part of a white line.
   - **Eraser (Tool)**: Erasing more of the white line.
   - **Eraser (Tool)**: Erasing still more of the white line. This state is highlighted to indicate that it is the state shown in the document window.

4. Click the **Brush Tool** state immediately above the top **Eraser** state.

   When you click on a state, that activates it, and reveals the image in that state in the document window. The white eraser mark is now gone.

5. Click the **Open** state. Now the image returns to its original state before you painted on it.

6. Click the first **Eraser** state. The green triangle and white eraser line return.

7. Click the image thumbnail at the top of the **History** panel. Again the image returns to its original state before painting.

   The image thumbnail is called a **SNAPSHOT**. Each snapshot is a temporarily-stored **History state**. Right now, the **01-pumpkin.jpg** and **Open** states are identical. That's because Photoshop automatically makes that first snapshot for you in case you need to get back to the original image.

   By default the **History** panel can only record up to fifty states. When you make the fifty-first change to a document, the first state (**Open**) vanishes from the top of the list to make room for the most recent change at the bottom.

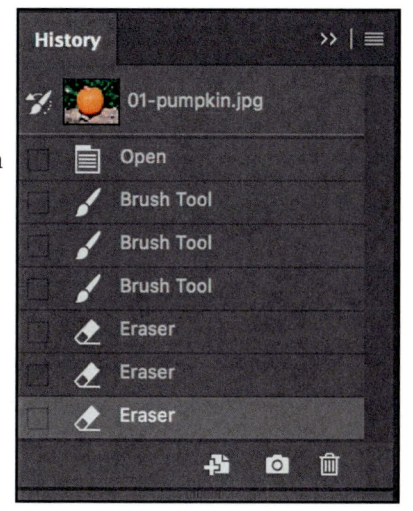

WARNING: Snapshots only remain with the document until you close the document window, or quit Photoshop. Don't expect to see them if you close your image and then reopen it.

8. Save a working copy of **01-pumpkin.jpg** in Photoshop (**PSD**) format to preserve the original and to give you more editing options. We used Mac screen shots here, but the steps are the same for Windows.

    a. **Choose File > Save As** to reveal the **Save As** dialog box.

    b. Set the location for the new version of the file. You can save it to a flash drive if working in a computer lab, or to the hard drive on your own computer.

    c. Change the format from **.jpg** to **.psd**:

    Click the arrow to the right of the **Format** box, and choose **Photoshop** from the top of the drop down list.

    The **JPEG** format was used for fast downloading. **PSD** files are optimized for Photoshop work, and permit some important features, such as saving layered documents, that **JPEGs** cannot do.

    d. Change the filename to **pumpkin1**. Do not type the period or three character extension. Photoshop will change it for you, adding the proper extension for whatever format you designated in the format box, **.psd** here.

    e. Click **Save** to save the document as **pumpkin1.psd**.

9. Choose **File > Close** to close the **pumpkin1.psd** image.

10. Choose **File > Open Recent** and choose **pumpkin1.psd** from the list of recently opened files.

    In some computer labs, you will need to choose **File > Open** and navigate to your saved file.

11. Examine the **History** panel.

    Note that the **History** panel now only displays the image snapshot and the **Open** history state. The other history states are gone—permanently. History states are stored in RAM, and not saved to disk with a document. When you close a document, if the computer freezes, or if you have a power failure, you lose your history states. For this reason, you should save your document frequently as you work on it. Each time you choose **File > Save** (**Command + S** on Mac, **Ctrl + S** on Windows), your current document state is stored on disk, and replaces the previously-saved version.

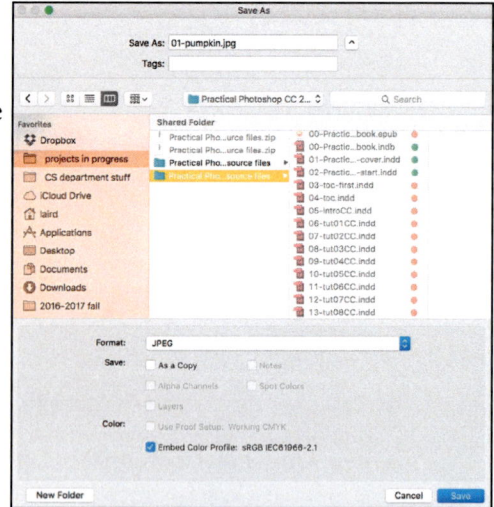

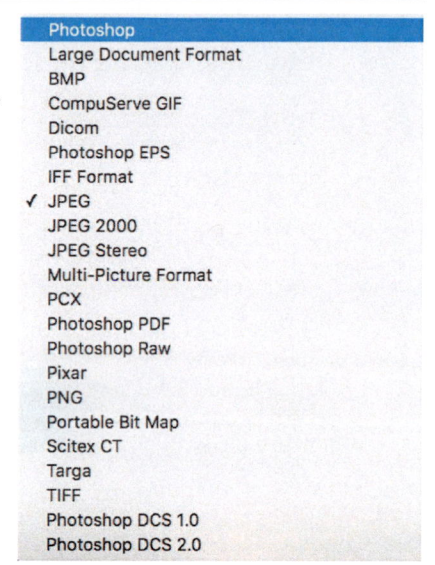

Tutorial 1: Photoshop Basics

History Panel Keyboard Shortcuts

Edit > Undo (**Ctrl + Z** or **Command + Z**) reverses the last change or history state that you made to the image. It cannot reverse more than one history state.

Edit > Redo (**Ctrl + Z** or **Command + Z**) is available just after an **Undo**. It restores the image to the way it was before the Undo.

Edit > Step Backward (**Ctrl + Alt + Z** or **Command + Option + Z**) steps you back one history state each time it is used.

Edit > Step Forward (**Ctrl + Shift + Z** or **Command + Shift + Z**) steps you forward one history state at a time. It is available if you just stepped backward.

The Layered Photoshop Document

You have already experienced the lack of editing flexibility that occurred when you tried to paint directly on top of the pumpkin pixels. Layers greatly simplify your image editing and provide some amazing special effects.

LAYERS isolate distinct parts of your image so that they can be individually viewed, positioned, or edited. Think of layers as a stack of clear plastic sheets containing image pixels and transparent areas. In the transparent areas you can see below to the layers underneath; where there is opaque imagery, you cannot.

The **Layers** panel shows the hierarchical organization of a document and lets you control the ways in which layers interact.

Guided Exercise 1.7: Use Layers to Finish "Carving" the Pumpkin

1. Open **pumpkin1.psd** image if necessary.

2. In Guided Exercise 1.6 you expanded the **History** panel on top of the **Layers** panel. Reset the **Essentials** workspace to return your panels to their default locations so that you can see the entire **Layers** panel in the bottom group of Photoshop panes. If the **Layers** panel is collapsed, click its name tab to expand it.

   This document has one layer, named **Background**. This layer shows a thumbnail of its contents. Whenever you open an image that was taken with a digital camera, it opens as the **Background** layer.

   The **Layers** panel has buttons along its bottom. Second from the right is the **New Layer** button. Click it to create a new, transparent layer named by default **Layer 1**. The new layer appears above the **Background** layer.

Tutorial 1: Photoshop Basics

Page 27

3. Notice that **Layer 1** is highlighted (lighter gray) and there is a decorative border around its thumbnail.

   The highlight and the box are the two ways that Photoshop indicates in the **Layers** panel that **Layer 1** is the **ACTIVE LAYER**, the one that you can paint on.

   Each document can have only one active layer at a time.

4. Click the **eye** symbol to the left of the **Background** thumbnail. This turns off the visibility of the **Background** so you can see **Layer 1** all by itself. When a layer is not visible, or **HIDDEN**, its eye changes to a dark square.

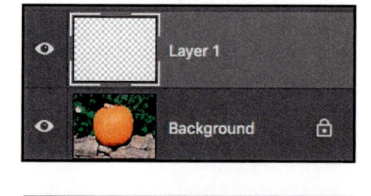

   Now all you see is a gray checkerboard. When you view a layer other than the **Background** by itself, Photoshop represents transparent regions with this checkerboard pattern. Notice that the checkerboard is also shown in **Layer 1**'s layer thumbnail.

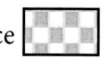

5. Click the **Background** eye again to make both layers visible.

6. Click the **Default** button in the color picker to restore the default colors—black for the **Foreground** color and white for the **Background** color.

7. Give **Layer 1** a more descriptive name:

   TIP: it is essential to give layers meaningful names because complex Photoshop documents can have more layers than you can keep track of.

   a. Double-click the name **Layer 1** in the **Layers** panel to highlight its name.

   b. Type the word "**Face**" and press the **enter** or **return** key to change the default name, **Layer 1**, to a more descriptive name.

   Notice that you did not need to delete the **Layer 1** placeholder name because the label highlighted when you double-clicked it. As soon as you typed the **F**, it replaced the text **Layer 1**.

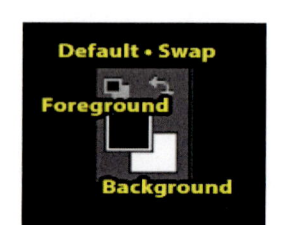

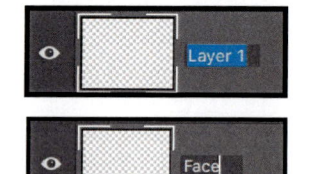

8. Paint your pumpkin's face on the **Face** layer:

   a. Check one more time to be sure the **Face** layer is active (highlighted). If it isn't, click to the right of its name to activate it.

   b. Choose the **Brush Tool**, and paint a black face on the **Face** layer.

   As you paint, make the brush tip bigger or smaller to suit your needs. Heavier, thicker lines will make your pumpkin look more carved once you finish the guided exercise.

   You might get an idea from the jack-o'-lanterns shown here. This image is from http://www.gettyimages.com.

Tutorial 1: Photoshop Basics

c. If you mess up, you can either go back in **History**, or choose the **Eraser Tool** and erase what you don't like. On any layer but the **Background** layer, the **Eraser Tool** erases to transparent, not to the **Background** color.

d. When you finish painting your face, choose **File > Save** to update the document to include the **Face** layer.

e. Now look at the **History** panel. You should see many states that say **Brush Tool** or **Eraser**, but no **Save** state. That is because the **History** panel only records document alterations, and saving does not alter the image pixels you see on screen.

9. Use the **Layers** panel settings to make your painted face look like it is carved into the pumpkin.

    Here you will just follow along step by step, but later in the course you will learn how to customize layer settings to achieve many special effects.

    a. With the Face layer active, choose **Layer > Layer Style > Bevel and Emboss** to open the **Layer Style dialog box**. This dialog box is so huge that you may need to drag it by its **Title** bar so that only the left side shows, and you can still see some of your painted face.

    b. In the **Structure** area of the **Layer Style** dialog box, change the settings to match the ones listed here.

    Style: Inner Bevel
    Technique: Smooth
    Depth: 231%
    Direction: Down
    Size: 60
    Soften: 10

10. Click **OK** to apply this layer style to the **Face** layer.

    The **Face** layer now has a section named **Effects** and a further indent listing the name of the effect that was applied. Why is it called **Effects**? Because in Adobe terminology a **Layer Style** consists of one or more individual **Effects**.

    The pumpkin looks more interesting than with the flat black paint, but it still does not look carved.

11. Use the **Fill** setting in the **Layers** panel to make the face look like it is carved into the pumpkin:

    a. Locate the **Fill** setting above the top layer of the **Layers** panel and its drop down triangle to the right of the word **Fill**.

    b. Press the triangle to reveal a slider where you can set the amount of **Fill**, from **0%** to **100%**.

Tutorial 1: Photoshop Basics   Page 29

c. Drag the slider all the way to the left, until it reaches **0%**. Notice what happens—the **Bevel & Emboss** effect stays completely visible, but the black face paint fades away making the pumpkin look carved.

d. Drag the slider a little to the right to keep just a bit of the black, if you prefer.

This pumpkin's face is faded to **16%**.

12. Choose **File > Save** to save your work. Print if desired, following the instructions in the next tutorial.

Adobe Photoshop Help

Photoshop is a tremendously complex application, and it is difficult even for Photoshop "experts" to remember all the details. Fortunately, help is only a menu away. Let's look at some of the available resources:

Guided Exercise 1.8: Use Photoshop Help

This guided exercise will give a brief introduction to using Adobe's online help system. This site is constantly changing so what you see may differ from what we demonstrate here.

By distributing Help online, Adobe can keep improving application support, and add to Help files to keep them current.

1. Choose **Help > Photoshop Online Help**.

   This launches your Web browser, if needed, and takes you to the Photoshop Help starting page.

   At the top of the page is a list of categories such as **What's New**, **Image and Color Basics**, and **Repair and Restoration**. When you click on one of the categories, the page jumps to the appropriate section.

2. Try out **Photoshop Help Online**:

   a. Click on the **Workspace** category at the top of the page.

   b. Click on the **Tool Galleries** link. This takes you to a page that includes a very useful panel overview, showing how the tools are grouped by function with the names and keyboard shortcuts for each tool.

   c. Scroll down the page to see the **Tool Galleries** with full-color examples of how each tool works.

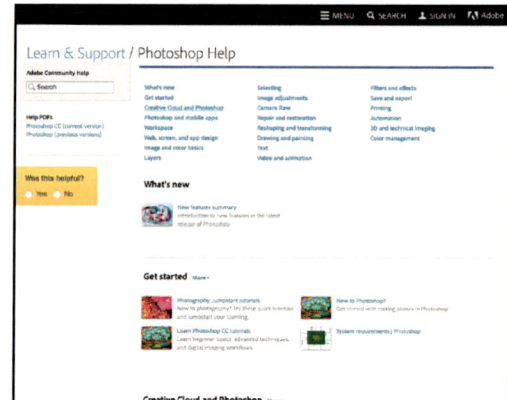

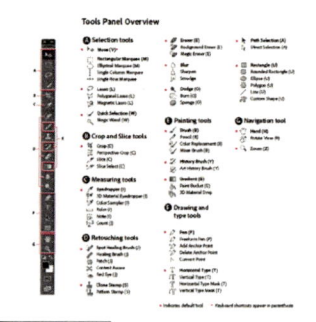

Tutorial 1: Photoshop Basics

3. Search to find more information about a specific topic:

   Sometimes you don't know where to find what you are looking for, or don't want to waste time drilling down the content topics. In either case, you can type a word or two of your question or topic into the search box at the top left side of the **Adobe Help** pages.

   a. Type **zoom** into the **Search** box and press **enter** or **return**.

      You will see articles on your topic underneath the search box. The articles may reference various versions of Photoshop, not just CC.

   b. Experiment with different search topics.

4. When you are done, you can either close the **Help** browser window or minimize it for quick reference as you continue to work.

ON YOUR OWN

Photoshop requires a lot of zooming in and out.

NAVIGATION SHORTCUTS

Practice to become an efficient navigator:

- Show the **Navigator** panel and practice using it to navigate.

- Open your completed **pumpkin1.psd** and practice these navigational shortcuts with the pointer (mouse) and the keyboard until they become second nature.

TASK	POINTER (MOUSE)	KEYBOARD
Actual Pixels or 100%	Double click the **Zoom** Tool	**Command/Ctrl + 1**
Fit on Screen	Double click the **Hand** Tool	**Command/Ctrl + 0**
Drag to pan your image	Press the **space** bar and drag	
Zoom in without the **Zoom** Tool		**Command/Ctrl + plus sign (+)**
Zoom out without the **Zoom** Tool		**Command/Ctrl + minus sign (-)**

RESOURCES AND VIDEOS

http://www.practical-photoshop.com/pages/CC2015-pp1-resources.html#01

Practical Photoshop CC 2015, Level 1
Tutorial 2: Files for Print and Web

In this tutorial you will take a first look at preparing files to be printed, emailed for screen viewing, or displayed on the World Wide Web.

Objectives

- Differentiate among monitor, document, and printer resolutions, and understand when to use each measurement.

- Distinguish between appropriate resolution for print and for Web or email images.

- Print a Photoshop document by configuring the **Print** dialog box.

- Use the **Export As** and **Save for Web (Legacy)** commands to make a copy of the print-quality document for fast online transmission.

Resolution

Resolution is a difficult concept to grasp. In nearly every class we teach, at every level, we get questions about resolution. Part of the problem is that the word **RESOLUTION** is used to measure different things. And, to make it worse, each item being measured has two kinds of measurements: a quality measurement and a quantity measurement. When measuring the **QUALITY** of an image, resolution specifies the number of pixels within a given area, (often given in pixels per inch or dots per inch), but resolution can also refer to the total **QUANTITY** of pixels in something — its absolute image dimensions.

Monitor Resolution

Let's begin with what we see on screen — **MONITOR RESOLUTION**. Monitors display patterns of colored pixels. Measured by quality, these displays are measured in **PIXELS PER INCH** or **PPI**. Monitor resolution can also refer to the physical properties of a monitor — how many total pixels it can display — its quantity. Monitor resolution determines how much of a Photoshop document can be seen when viewed at actual size (**100%**). Modern, adjustable monitors have adjustable resolution.

Some monitor numbers to keep in mind:

- The smallest computer monitor is typically **640 pixels** wide and **480 pixels high** (**640 x 480**), a quantity measurement. Handheld devices have even smaller resolution; the original iPhone had a screen resolution of **320 x 480**.

- Photoshop CC 2015 requires a screen resolution of at least **1024 x 768 pixels**.

Document Resolution

DOCUMENT RESOLUTION is the absolute measurement of a document in pixels, with width being the first number and height the second. Thus a document that is **800 x 600** is **800 pixels** wide and **600 pixels** tall. This is the "quantity" form of resolution.

Each Photoshop document also has a resolution measurement in **PIXELS PER INCH**, or **PPI** (**ppi**). This is the "quality" form of resolution. Web pages and multimedia projects typically use 72-96 ppi images both to keep file sizes down and to display properly on small or low-resolution monitors that display from 72 to 96 pixels in each inch of the computer monitor.

Printer Resolution

PRINTER RESOLUTION describes how a document is set up for printing. Printers apply dots of ink or toner onto paper or other media. Printed images are measured in **DOTS PER INCH** or **DPI** (**dpi**).

Modern desktop printers, laser or ink jet, typically print somewhere in the range from 300 to 2400 dpi.

Printed documents use resolutions of 100 ppi and up. A 4 inch by 5 inch document with an image resolution of 100 ppi will have pixel dimensions of 400 x 500 pixels, while a 4 inch by 5 inch document with an image resolution of 300 ppi will have pixel dimensions of 1200 x 1500 pixels. The small number of pixels in Web graphics make them load quickly—ideal for screen work. However, these low resolution images print poorly because they don't have enough pixels to provide the optimal number of dots for each inch of printed document.

The smaller the print dots, the higher the printer resolution setting. For instance, an image with a dpi of 150 will have smaller dots than an image set to 72 dpi. The higher the resolution, the higher quality the printout will be, up to the printer's physical capabilities. When an image is printed, each image pixel is represented with a dot of ink or toner. When an image is printed with enough dots, the human eye perceives discrete color changes as continuous, and the digital image looks like an analog photograph. Your brain blends the colors.

What can be very confusing is that an image with a low resolution can look good on the screen if not zoomed in too close. You could work away on an image believing that you have a high quality image. Then, when you print it out, you are very disappointed because the large size of the printed dots makes the image look blocky or pixilated. The bottom line is that it takes a much higher resolution for an image to look good in print than it does on screen.

Setting up Documents for Print

Before you can set up a document for printing, you need to know the resolution of the printer you are using, known as your **OUTPUT PRINTER**. The best way to do that is to read the fine print on the manual that came with your printer, but that is not always easy to do. The Internet is also a good source for finding out more information about your printer. But, just in case you lost your manual or are printing in a computer lab, here are some guidelines:

- Some printers list two resolutions, such as the HP Envy 5540 Color Printer:
  Up to 1200 x 1200 dpi or up to 4800 x 1200 optimized dpi color. You should use the lower resolution to calculate your image resolution.

- Color laser printers are usually 600 dpi printers.

- Older color ink jet printers are 720 dpi printers

- Newer photo ink jet printers are at least 1200 dpi printers.

- Graphics applications such as Photoshop measure files in **pixels per inch** (**ppi**), and the printer converts the **ppi** into **dots per inch** (**dpi**) when it prints the document.

Beginning graphics students tend to assume that if you have a 600 dpi printer, you should have at least one pixel in your image for every one of those dots. As we shall see, this is often not correct.

If you print an image that has only black and white pixels, and no shades of gray, your resolution should match that of the printer. In this case, the printer places only solid black dots onto the printout. But, if you print a photograph or graphic, either in color or in shades of gray, the **PRINTER DRIVER**, the software that tells the printer how to work, performs its own special magic called **interpolation** to fill in transitional colors between each document pixel. In addition, it generally takes an average of 3 dots of color ink to make any given printed color. For this reason, these documents only need **ONE THIRD** the ppi of the output printer for high-quality results. If your document has a higher resolution than your printer needs, the document will take longer to print; it will be a larger file that will take longer to edit, but its quality will not be any better. So, what resolution should you choose?

This simple chart, with file sizes based on a document that is 4 x 6 inches, shows the relationship between resolution and file size, and gives some recommended printer-based resolutions.

PRINTER	BLACK DOTS ONLY	COLOR AND/OR GRAYSCALE DOTS
Color laser	600 ppi	200 ppi
File size	1.03 M	2.75 M
Older color ink jet	720 ppi	240 ppi
File size	1.48 M	3.96 M
Photo ink jet	1200 ppi	300 ppi
File size	4.12 M	6.18 M

Technically, following the "rule of one-third," you should print your photo ink jet printouts at 400 dpi. However, since the human eye cannot see such small color transitions, in most cases your 400 ppi printout will not look any better than a 300 ppi printout, but your file will be much larger. For color and grayscale, think **one third**, up to around 300 ppi; for pure black and white think **one to one**.

Tutorial 2: Files for Print and Web

Printing Photoshop Documents

When you first choose **File > Print,** you will see a huge dialog box with a thumbnail of your image on the left side, and a number of controls on the right. The dialog box can be enlarged if yours does not look exactly like ours.

The left side, or **PREVIEW AREA**, shows a thumbnail of how your image will print relative to a piece of paper.

The portion of the image that will print is called the **THUMBNAIL**. Some folks question whether it really is a "thumbnail" since it is so large. Adobe calls it a thumbnail because it is smaller than the actual printed document.

The largest box with diagonal black lines represents the full page of paper as set in the **Page Setup** dialog box (usually US Letter) and the smaller white box represents the printable area for your printer.

Printers need to grab the paper to pull it through the printing mechanism. They use a small amount on the top and sides, and a larger amount on the bottom of the paper. These areas, called **MARGINS**, typically will not print. The portion of the paper that can be printed is called the **PRINTABLE AREA**.

The **Print Settings** button can be used to view and change printer-specific settings such as print quality, paper type, and number of copies. After configuring your **Print Settings**, click **Save** to save the printer settings and return to Photoshop's **Print** dialog box.

File > Print One Copy doesn't bring up any dialog box at all— it just prints a copy of your image using the settings you used last time you printed an image.

Ink Jet Paper Quality and Image Longevity

As you learn Photoshop, you will probably print your work on an ink jet printer. Ink jet paper choice has a tremendous effect both on the quality of your original output and its longevity. Ink jet prints are sharper and brighter when printed on specially-made ink jet photo paper than on junk copy paper. These specialty papers have a large amount of clay in them, and the clay keeps the print dots on top of the paper, so that those bright, crisp dots you worked so hard to create don't get absorbed into the paper and become dull and blurry. If your printouts are not as nice as you'd like, often you may not need a new printer, but simply better paper.

Unless they are printed on special, long-lasting or **ARCHIVAL PAPER**, and stored away from light, moisture, heat, and ozone, your digital printouts will not last very long. Someone we know printed some photographs of her new granddaughter using Epson Photo paper, and put them on her refrigerator, which does not receive any direct sunlight. Six weeks later, the photos were badly faded. By reading the following article on print permanence, she learned that if she had protected the photos behind glass, they would have lasted a lot longer: http://tinyurl.com/9c2rf26.

Guided Exercise 2.1: Print Your Pumpkin

In this guided exercise, you will use Photoshop's **Print** dialog box to set up your carved pumpkin document for high quality printing, and then print it. Over the years Adobe has added more and more individual settings to the **Print** dialog box, which is helpful for print professionals but can be very confusing for Photoshop beginners. In this guided exercise you will only be using the most basic print settings.

1. Open the **pumpkin1.psd** image if necessary.

2. Choose **File > Print** to open the **Print** dialog box.

   Notice that the **Print** dialog box has two panes: the left pane shows the preview of how the image will print and the right side gives a long list of settings, each of which can be expanded.

3. To simplify the **Print** dialog box, click the triangle to the left of each setting category underneath **Printer Setup** to collapse the five settings categories beneath it.

4. Configure your printer in the **Printer Setup** settings.

   a. The **Printer** drop-down menu has a list of all the printers connected to or available to your computer. Begin by choosing your desired printer from the **Printer** drop-down menu at the top of the dialog box.

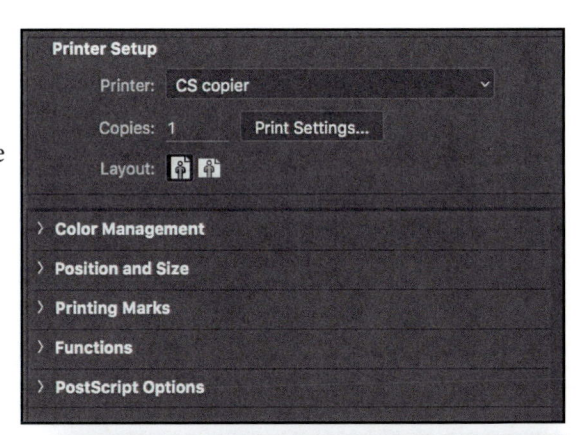

   b. Look at the thumbnail. Notice that the document is too big for the paper. You can see white space on the top and bottom, but not on the sides of the thumbnail.

5. Click the **Landscape** orientation button in the **Layout** section of **Printer Setup** to change the default **Portrait** (or tall), to **Landscape** (or wide). The document now has white space all around the thumbnail.

   Do not change any other settings in the **Print** dialog box unless you know how to use them. (These settings are for more advanced users.)

6. Click **Print** to print the document.

Beware of Scale to Fit Media

In the center of the **Print** dialog box, you will find a section called **Position and Size**. Towards the bottom of the section, the **Print Resolution** for your image is specified. For **pumpkin1.psd,** your resolution should be **300 ppi** which is optimal for most modern printers. We set it up that way when we created the tutorial. The **Height** of the printed image will be 6 inches and the **Width** almost 8 inches. Thus when printed, the image will not cover the entire 8.5 x 11 inch page or even its printable area.

If you click the **Scale to Fit Media** check box, the image enlarges proportionately to cover the printable area of your paper, approximately 8 x 10 inches. But, to enlarge the document, Photoshop lowers the print resolution from **300 ppi** to **222 ppi,** thereby slightly reducing the quality of the printout. As the preview shows you, this image will still print pretty clearly (but not quite as well as if there were **300 ppi**).

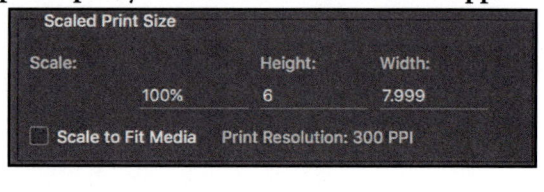

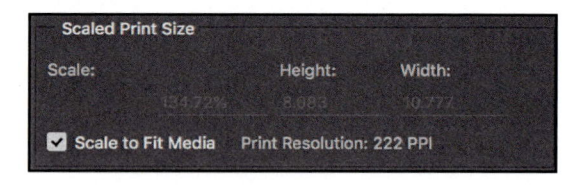

In the next section of the tutorial, you will resize a copy of the pumpkin image for fast Web transmission. Because this low-resolution copy is only **72 ppi,** it will not have enough pixels to make a high-quality printout of the same size as the original. At **300 ppi**, it will only print at about 1 1/2 by 2 inches.

Moreover, if you click **Scale to Fit Media**, although the printout will be approximately 8 x 10 inches, its print resolution will only be **56 ppi**.

The **Print** dialog box warns you by showing a very blocky or **PIXILATED** preview. That means your printout will be of very low quality.

The take home message? Use high quality images for print, and make low-quality smaller images for Web and email since smaller images transmit much more quickly online.

Saving Files for Fast Online Transmission

Assuming that you are a Photoshop beginner, we pre-configured the pumpkin image for you so that it would print properly on an ink jet or color laser printer. This image has 300 pixels per each inch of the printed image; the image is 2400 pixels wide and 1800 pixels high. Saved to disk, it started out as a JPEG file at slightly less than 1 MB. When you opened it in Photoshop and changed it to PSD format, it expanded to 12.2 MB, and once the face layer was added, it became 24.7 MB. That is a fairly big file.

When you send a file over the Internet, either attached to an email message or uploaded to a Web page, big files can cause three kinds of problems.

1. Big files take a long time for you to send (upload) and for the recipient to receive (download).

If you send someone a 24 mb file, it will take some time for the image to upload, as well as for the person on the other end to receive. The time it takes is dependent on the upload and download speeds of the Internet connections on both ends.

2. Big files can cause problems with Internet Service Providers.

Each Internet Service Provider typically gives each client a small amount of space, often 20-50 MB, to store all your downloaded files. If someone sends you a 24 MB file, or a bunch of people send you 1 MB files, you can quickly run out of room, and your provider may stop serving you. If students send their instructor large files, that instructor's email capabilities may be turned off until the inappropriately big files are deleted.

3. Big files don't display well when included in Web pages.

That's because they take so long to become visible, and because they have more pixels than the width of the monitor. Your goal is to make files that can be viewed as an email attachment or in a Web browser without scrolling. The smallest standard monitors are 640 pixels wide and 480 pixels high. Monitors, thus, are landscape (wider than they are tall). Even for folks with larger monitors, operating system and browser controls such as menus and scroll bars take some room on the screen. To allow for those controls, try to keep your Web and emailed images to 800 pixels in their largest dimension unless an assignment specifies otherwise.

Guided Exercise 2.2: Save a Duplicate File for the Web Using Save for Web

Photoshop has two commands which can be used to save a Web or email-ready copy of your image without modifying your original source image. This copy is known as an **OPTIMIZED** version of the file. In this guided exercise you will save a Web copy of your finished pumpkin image using the older **Save for Web (Legacy)** command.

1. Open **pumpkin1.psd** image if necessary.
2. Choose **File > Export > Save for Web (Legacy)**.

   Save for Web opens this huge dialog box. Be sure to click the **2-up** tab in **Views** to show both the original and optimized versions.

   The active view tab is identified by the highlighted tab in the upper left region of the dialog box.

   Original shows only the original file.

   Optimized, the default, shows only the preview of the Web file with its current optimization settings (shown on the right side of the dialog box).

   2-Up splits the image into two panes, either side by side or top and bottom depending on the pixel dimensions of the original file. The left or top preview shows the original file, and the right or bottom view shows the optimized view for easy comparison.

4-Up displays four versions of the image. The upper left image is the original. The activated pane is indicated by the colored line (Mac) or box (Win) around its preview.

You can click any other panel to activate it. When you change the optimizations settings on the right side of the dialog box, those settings only affect the activated version.

3. Choose the **2-up** view, if it is not already chosen.

4. Identify the other major regions of the **Save for Web** dialog box:

    a. The Tools are in the upper left corner of the dialog box with the **Hand Tool** chosen by default. You will only use the **Hand Tool** and the **Zoom Tool** in this course.

    When a document is too large for the whole image to fit in its preview, only its upper left corner appears in the preview panel. It is difficult to tell the quality of your Web optimization in the dark leaf corner of this image. You can use the **Hand Tool** to move about in the image to an area with more detail.

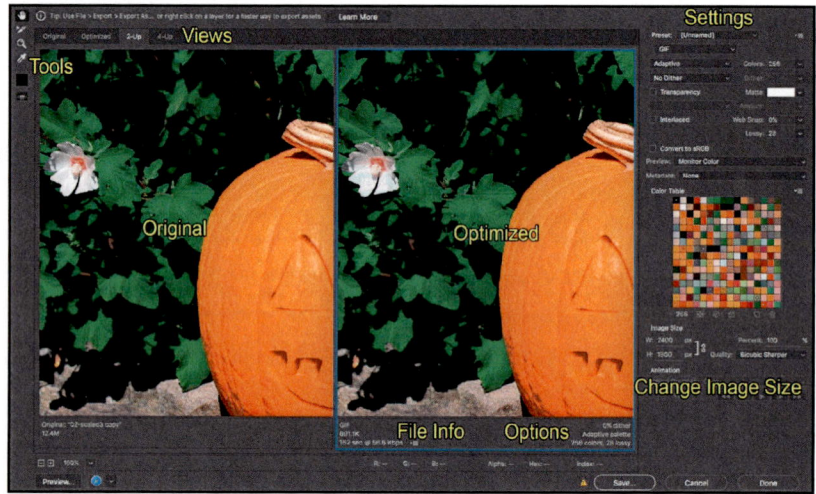

    When you drag the **Hand Tool** in one pane, all the other panes also move, so that your preview regions stay comparable.

    b. The **Settings** region is used to adjust the optimized Web file format settings to get a decent quality image with the smallest file size.

    c. The **Change Image Size** region lets you lower the total number of pixels in your Web copy so that it will load more quickly and look better on a Web page. We call this process "putting an image on a pixel diet."

    d. Underneath each preview is information about that version of the image. Here, we can see that with the default settings, this image will be in **(COMPUSERVE) GIF** format, be reduced from the original **12.4 M** (the size of the file without layers) to **1.8 M**, and that on a dialup modem (56 kb) it will take 338 seconds—or almost 6 minutes—to receive. (NOTE: your file and speed numbers may differ slightly from ours.)

5. Change the file format of the Web copy from **GIF** to **JPEG**:

The default **GIF** format works well for images with just a few colors, like logos and type, that contain up to 256 colors. The **Color Table** just above the **Change Image Size** region shows what those colors will be.

    a. Be sure the **Optimized** panel is the active one.

b. In the **Settings** region change **GIF** to **JPEG** in the drop down menu just below **Preset**.

The **Color Table** grays out because the **JPEG** file format (extension **.jpg**) supports millions of colors, not just 256, so it is better than **GIF** for preserving colors and detail in photographs and other continuous tone images.

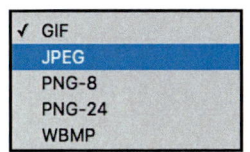

The **JPEG** format also reduces the file size of most photographs more efficiently than does the **GIF** format.

c. Check the file size at the bottom of the optimized preview.

The **JPEG** is less than half the size of the **GIF**. With the default quality of 60, the Web copy will load in 164 seconds, taking about 2.5 minutes to receive instead of almost 6 minutes.

This transmission time is better, but the image is still too big for fast Web transmission. Studies show that viewers tend to navigate off of Web pages that take more than 30 seconds to view. So, let's keep that *30 seconds* as our target download speed.

6. Reduce the number of pixels in the Web copy of the image to reduce its file size. (This image is so big that you can't even see the pumpkin in the **Save for Web** preview window.)

    a. Locate the **Image Size** section near the bottom of the right side of the dialog box.

    b. Change whichever dimension is larger, **W(idth)** here, to **800 pixels** and then press the **Tab** key to move the cursor to the next box.

    When you type in the new width and press **Tab**, the **H(eight)** recalculates to keep the image proportional, and the preview changes on screen. This image will become 25% of its original size when the new size is applied, and you will now be able to see the jack-o'-lantern.

7. Choose the **Quality** Photoshop should use to change the **Image Size**. **Bicubic Sharper**, shown here, will usually give the best results when you shrink an image.

8. Check your file size at the bottom of the optimization preview. With fewer pixels it loads much more quickly.

9. Leave the other settings in the dialog box alone, as they are for more advanced users.

10. Save the file:

    a. Click **Save** to save the Web copy of your image using your chosen settings.

    In the **Save Optimized As** dialog box that pops up next, notice that the image is already appended with **.jpg**, the three character extension for **JPEG** files.

    Name your file, making sure you are saving the file in the correct location by using the top drop down menu.

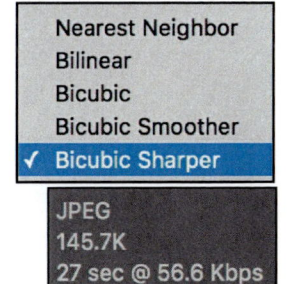

Tutorial 2: Files for Print and Web

b. Click **Save**.

When you name files for Web or email use, it is recommended that you keep the names short (under 10 characters) and do not use spaces or punctuation in the file names.

The web-sized copy, in **JPEG** format, will be saved to the place you designated with the original, and unchanged document still open. Close the original if desired.

Guided Exercise 2.3: Save a File for the Web Using Export As

The **Export As** command is new to Photoshop CC 2015.

1. Open **pumpkin1.psd** image if necessary.

2. Choose **File > Export > Export As**.

   Export As opens a huge dialog box.

3. Identify the other major regions of the **Export As** dialog box:

   a. The central pane of the dialog contains the image Thumbnail.

   b. The **File Settings** section is used to choose the file format for the exported image.

   c. The **Image Size** section lets you change the number of pixels in the exported image.

   d. The left-hand pane and Canvas Size section will not be addressed in this course.

4. Reduce the number of pixels in the exported image to reduce its file size:

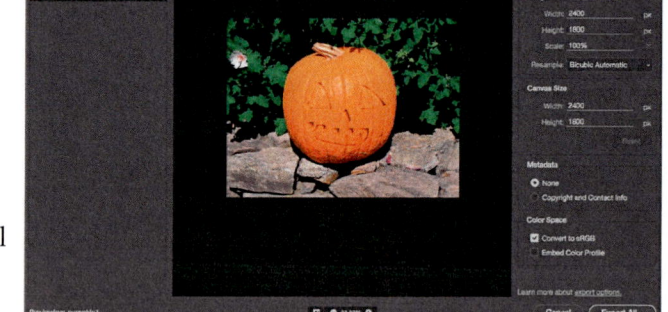

   a. Locate the **Image Size** section in the right side of the dialog box.

   b. Change whichever dimension is larger, **W(idth)** here, to **800 pixels** and then press the **Tab** key to move the cursor to the next box.

   When you type in the new width and press **Tab**, the **H(eight)** recalculates to keep the image proportional, and the preview changes on screen. Alternately, you can choose a Scale percentage from the pop-up menu in the Image Size section.

5. Set the **Resample** option Photoshop should use to change the **Image Size** to **Bicubic Sharper**.

6. Check the file size to the left of the thumbnail. With fewer pixels it is much smaller — ours is only 33.9 K.

7. Save the file:

    a. Click **Export** to save the copy of your image using your chosen settings.

    In the **Export** dialog box that pops up next, notice that the image is already appended with **.jpg**, the three character extension for **JPEG** files.

    Name your file.

    b. Click **Export**.

    The web-sized copy, in **JPEG** format, will be saved to the place you designated with the original, unchanged, document still open. Close the original if desired.

JPEG Quality

You can also change the size of an image by adjusting the **JPEG Quality** in either **Save for Web** or **Export As**. JPEG Quality is the amount that the image is compressed by approximating its color transitions mathematically rather than using the actual image pixels.

The extent to which the image distorts depends upon the color transitions of the original image, and are most noticeable with abrupt color changes. The distortion is called **JPEG ARTIFACTING**.

If you change your view in **Save for Web (Legacy)** from **2 up** to **4 up**, the additional previews will show your image with increasingly strong amounts of **JPEG artifacting**, and also decreasing file sizes (trading off file size for quality).

The **JPEG** artifacting becomes more apparent if you raise the default **100%** view to **400%** at the bottom of the dialog box.

In our experience, for images that are about 800 pixels in their larger dimension, adjusting the **Quality** until the file is between **150KB** and **250KB** will give a professional quality Web file that still loads quickly.

In most cases you should avoid **Maximum Quality**. This setting is designed to compress big, print sized files, to send to commercial print houses for publication—not for Web work.

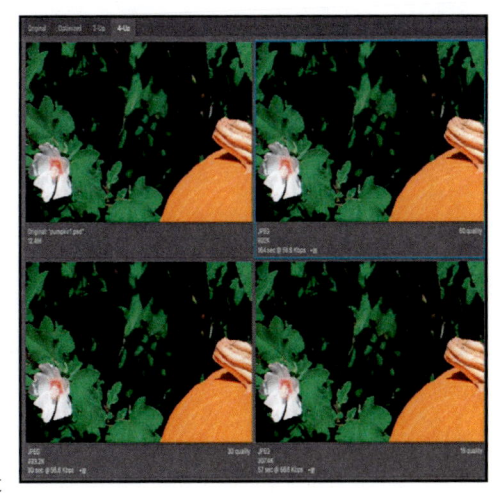

How Big is Your File?

The **SIZE** of an image can have two different values:

- **DIMENSION SIZE**: the size an image would print out (inches for the US English version of Photoshop)
- **FILE SIZE**: the space an image takes up on a hard drive or disk in bytes, kilobytes, or megabytes

    A **BIT** is the smallest unit of information on a computer. A **BYTE** is made up of 8 bits. A **KILOBYTE** (**K** or **KB**) is roughly 1,000 bytes (1,024) and a **MEGABYTE** (**M** or **MB**) is 1,024 kilobytes.

When you compress an image to send by email or put up on the Web, you need a small file that will download quickly. Usually, you will be looking at kilobytes (K or KB) unless the image is extremely small, then it will be in bytes. Images that are 1 MB or more are generally considered too large for Internet transmission. We recommend that you try to keep all course files you will send on the Web to under 200 KB unless otherwise specified.

If you want to check the size of a file after you make it, view its **Properties** (Win) or **Get Info** (Mac) from the Desktop. When you open a **JPEG** file in Photoshop, it temporarily expands for editing. Thus the **89 K JPEG** we just made opens to **791 K**.

On Your Own

We're going to cover this again because it is such a common problem for Photoshop users.

Avoid the Most Common Save for Web Mistake

Examine these settings. Although this image was placed on a pixel diet to reduce its overall pixel dimensions, its **JPEG** compression setting of **100 quality** is not strong enough and its file size of **327.4K** is too large for Web and email attachments.

Follow this strategy to avoid this common mistake:

1. Reduce the number of pixels in the **Image Size** section of the **Save for Web (Legacy)** or **Export As** dialog box.
2. Check the file size of your image.
3. Gradually reduce the quality of the image until it is small enough to meet your Web guidelines.

Another problem we often see is that folks apply the **JPEG** compression very strongly, assuming that it is best to make the smallest file possible. As you can see from the previous page, at a **Quality** of **15**, the pumpkin image artifacts badly, seriously diminishing its appearance. It's a balancing act: file size for quick transmission vs. image quality.

Resources and Videos

http://www.practical-photoshop.com/pages/CC2015-pp1-resources.html#02

Practical Photoshop CC 2015, Level 1
Tutorial 3: Selection

As you work on an image, you will make two types of changes: global adjustments that affect the entire image and localized changes that affect only certain portions of the image. To make localized changes, you need to first designate which areas to change. You do this by making **SELECTIONS**—outlining portions of an image that can be changed.

Photoshop has nine selection tools. This tutorial provides an overview of the seven most commonly used selection tools that are used to select regions of pixels:

- The **Rectangular Marquee Tool** and the **Elliptical Marquee Tool**
- The **Lasso Tool**, the **Polygonal Lasso Tool**, and the **Magnetic Lasso Tool**
- The **Magic Wand Tool**
- The **Quick Selection Tool**

Once you select a region of pixels, you can change those pixels in many ways. This tutorial focuses primarily on just three ways to use the selected region:

- Move the selected pixels to a different location on an image layer.
- Transform the selected pixels by changing their size, shape and/or rotation.
- Copy and paste selected pixels from one document to another, or from one layer to another on the same document.

Objectives

- Differentiate between selected and unselected regions of a document.
- Use the appropriate selection tool and its options to create and modify selections.
- Preview and tweak selection edges using the **Refine Edge** dialog box (Photoshop CC 2015.1 or 2015.2) or **Select and Mask** workspace (Photoshop CC 2015.5).
- Transform selections.
- Save and load selections.
- Copy and paste selections.

Selection Principles

The entire image starts out selected. The various selection tools allow you to make some image areas editable, while protecting or masking other unselected areas. For example, you may want to:

- Darken a sky without darkening the rest of an image.
- Blur or sharpen only a specific area of an image.
- Select a portion of an image and place it in another image.

The key to each of these techniques is to make careful, precise selections. In fact, many say that getting a handle on selections is the single most important Photoshop skill you can master.

Let us begin with two key selection concepts:

- **SELECTION BORDERS**, also called **MARCHING ANTS**, surround selections.
- You can select only whole pixels, not partial pixels.

    Here we have zoomed in to 1600% to show the pixel grid. The left side, **yes**, shows two selected pixels, a permitted pixel selection. The right side, **no**, shows six partially selected pixels: you cannot select parts of pixels with the pixel selection tools. We faked it here using Photoshop, of course.

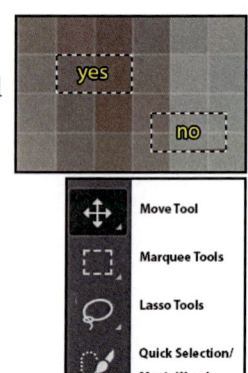

How Do You Select?

The Photoshop pixel selection tools appear just below the **Move Tool** on the **Tools** panel.

Each selection tool has specific abilities:

- All the **Marquee Tools**, as well as the **Lasso Tool** and **Polygonal Lasso Tool**, let you select by either geometric or free form areas.
- The **Magic Wand Tool**, hiding under the **Quick Selection Tool**, lets you select a consistently colored area without having to trace its outline.
- The **Quick Selection Tool** lets you select an area by painting within that area and expanding outward until the tool automatically finds and follows edges (areas of contrast) in the image.
- The **Magnetic Lasso Tool** can select by both area and color, to quickly select objects with complex edges from high-contrast backgrounds.

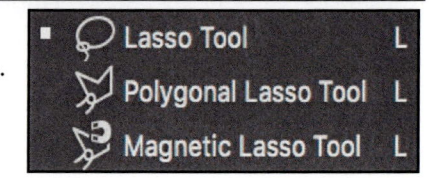

The **Move Tool**, used in conjunction with the selection tools, lets you reposition selected pixels. These tools are so important that they are clustered together at the top of the **Tools** panel.

How Do You Deselect?

When an area is selected, that area is the only one you can change. After you finish changing a selected region, you can deselect it to make the entire document editable.

- To deselect via a menu command, choose **Select > Deselect**, or use the shortcut equivalents: **Control + D** (Win) or **Command + D** (Mac).

- **Select > Reselect** activates the last selection you made in your document.

The Marquee Tools

Let's start with the simplest of the selection tools, the **Rectangular Marquee Tool** and **Elliptical Marquee Tool**.

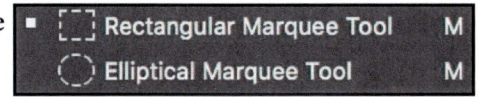

The Rectangular Marquee Tool

As you might guess, the **Rectangular Marquee Tool** is used to create rectangular-shaped selections. You can also make perfectly square selections by holding down the **Shift** key *after* starting your selection–this is known as **CONSTRAINING**.

NOTE: If you constrain a selection, be sure to release the mouse button *before* releasing the **Shift** key so that Photoshop will keep the constraint.

The Elliptical Marquee Tool

The **Elliptical Marquee Tool** is used to create elliptical, or oval, selections. When you constrain the **Elliptical Marquee Tool** with the **Shift** key, you select a round area of the document.

Guided Exercise 3.1: Use the Rectangular & Elliptical Marquee Tools with the Move Tool

In this exercise, you will use the **Marquee Tools** and the **Move Tool** to manipulate parts of an image. You'll start with an image containing photos of home workshop tools and at the end of the tutorial you will end up with a 'critter' created from these tools. When making the selections, use the **Zoom Tool** to get a closer look at what you're trying to select—zooming in will help you to make precise selections.

1. Open Photoshop.

2. Reset the **Essentials** workspace, all tools, and the default **Foreground** and **Background** colors:

   NOTE: We are giving you the specifics here, but will not repeat them for future guided exercises.

   a. Choose **Essentials** from the **Workspace Switcher** menu if necessary and then choose **Reset Essentials** from the **Workspace Switcher** menu.

   b. **Right-click** (or control-click) the current tool icon at the far left of the **Options** bar and choose **Reset All Tools** from the context menu that appears.

   c. Click the **default colors** button in the **Tools** panel **color picker**.

3. Choose **File > Open**, navigate to **03-toolcritter-start.jpg** and click **Open** to open the document within Photoshop.

The **03-toolcritter-start.jpg** document consists of workshop tools on the left and right sides, with the outline of the critter in the center.

4. Use File > Save As to save **03-toolcritter-start.jpg** as **toolcritter.psd** in the location of your choice.

    As you save, remember to choose **Photoshop** from the top of the **Format** drop-down list. Do not add **.psd** to the file name because Photoshop will automatically add the extension for you when you save the document

5. Use the **Rectangular Marquee Tool** to select the carpenter's level:

    a. Locate the carpenter's level in the upper-right portion of the document window.

    b. With the **Scrubby Zoom** option checked, use the **Zoom Tool** to click and press on the upper right corner of the document until the carpenter's level fills most of the document window.

    c. Choose the **Rectangular Marquee Tool**.

    d. Use the **Rectangular Marquee Tool** to select the level by dragging from the upper-left corner of the level to the lower-right corner.

    When you release the mouse button, you will see the **SELECTION BORDER**, or **MARCHING ANTS**, surrounding the carpenter's level.

    e. Double-click the **Hand Tool** to fit the entire document window on the screen. The level will remain selected.

6. Use the **Move Tool** to reposition the carpenter's level:

    a. Position the **Move Tool** within the selection boundary and drag the selected pixels—the carpenter's level—into the center of the critter outline, with the top of the selection near the center of the 'head' area.

    Notice that the area from where you moved the level from is now filled with white, the default **Background** color.

    b. You moved the pixels that make up the level image, replacing them with the **Background** color.

    c. Choose **Select > Deselect** to remove the marching ants. You have now made your first selection and manipulated part of an image.

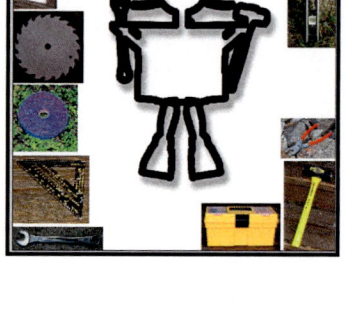

Tutorial 3: Selection

7. Select and move the roll of blue Velcro tape along the left side of the image:

    a. Locate and zoom in on the roll of blue Velcro tape along the left side of the image.

    b. Use the **Elliptical Marquee Tool** to select the blue tape.

        1) Click and hold down the mouse button on the **Rectangular Marquee Tool**, and choose the **Elliptical Marquee Tool** which is hiding beneath it.

        2) Position your cursor slightly above and to the left of the roll, and drag toward the lower-right corner of the roll.

        It can be a bit tricky to select the roll perfectly, but you can deselect and try again if it does not line up properly.

    TIP: to select from the center out rather than from edge to edge:

        1) Press and hold the **Option** key (Mac) or **Alt** key (Win) before creating the selection.

        2) Without releasing the modifier key, position your cursor in the center of the roll of tape and drag out to one of the tape edges.

        3) When you have the roll selected, release the pointer (mouse button) *before* letting go of the modifier key.

8. Double-click the **Hand Tool** to fit the entire image on the screen.

9. Use the **Move Tool** to move the roll of tape to the head of the critter.
   Notice that the roll of tape covers up the top part of the level—this is what we want.

10. Deselect the roll of tape.

11. This is a good time to choose **File > Save** to update your changes.

Modifying a Selection

It may be very difficult to make a perfect selection on the first try. If this happens, you can easily modify your starting selection by adding to, subtracting from, or intersecting with the original selection by continuing with the same or different selection tool.

When you choose any selection tool but the **Quick Selection Tool**, you will see these buttons in the **Options** bar. They allow you to easily add to, subtract from, or intersect with the current selection. You can also use keyboard shortcuts to do these modifications.

- If the default **Make new selection** button is chosen, using the chosen selection tool will deselect any previous selection so you can begin anew.

Tutorial 3: Selection Page 49

- The **Add to selection** button will allow you to outline additional areas, to make your selection larger.
  - These areas do not need to be contiguous.
  - Holding down the **Shift** key before you make an additional selection temporarily switches to the Add to selection button.
- The **Subtract from selection** button will let you outline areas to remove from your selection.
  - Holding down the **Alt** (Win) or **Option** (Mac) key as you outline temporarily switches to the **Subtract from selection** button.
- The **Intersect with selection** button restricts the selection to only in those areas that overlap with the current selection. Holding down **Alt+Shift** (Windows) or **Option+Shift** (Mac) temporarily switches to the **Intersect with selection** button.

If your selection is still not right, you can try a different approach. Since selection tools can be combined to make specific selections, you need to look at the selection job and decide how to approach it. Your best bet will be to begin your selection with the tool that will capture the majority of the area you want to select. Then, add to or subtract from the selection using any other selection tool until you have the precise selection you want.

Be patient. Careful selections can be time-consuming, but they are worth the effort in the quality of your final image. A poor selection may leave a 'halo' of pixels around the selected element, like the black edge on the left saw blade here. Select carefully to avoid pixel halos, unless they are desired.

The Magic Wand Tool

Thus far you have been using the marquee selection tools to select based on area (rectangles and ovals), but often it is more effective to select based on color.

Hiding under the **Quick Selection Tool** by default, The **Magic Wand Tool** makes selections based on similar colors.

For example, if you want to select just the clear blue sky in a photo, you can use the **Magic Wand Tool** by clicking anywhere in the sky. Any adjacent pixels of a similar color will also be selected. The **Magic Wand Tool**'s options are critical to controlling its behavior.

Tolerance

TOLERANCE determines the range of similar colors or tones that will be included in a given selection, ranging from **0** to **255**. A low value selects the few colors very similar to the pixel you click; a higher value selects a broader range of colors. The default tolerance of **32** chooses related colors, but not too many.

It is often a good place to start selecting an object with reasonably well-defined edges.

If you set the **Tolerance** to **0** and click on a pixel in a document, only those pixels the exact same color as the one you click on will be selected. If you increase the tolerance, pixels of colors similar to the one you clicked will also be selected. The higher the **Tolerance**, the wider the range of colors that will be included in the selection. With a **Tolerance** of **255**, every pixel on the active layer should theoretically be selected. In fact, the **Magic Wand Tool** sometimes leaves some pixels behind. If you want to select all the pixels, it is better to choose **Select > Select All**, or use the keyboard shortcut: **Ctrl + A** (Win) or **Command+ A** (Mac). "A" stands for all.

Anti-aliasing

ANTI-ALIASING makes soft transitions between colors by blending the color of the pixels around the edges of an object with its background. Photoshop uses anti-aliasing both for selections and for painting tools like the **Brush Tool**. Here, anti-aliasing is on for the left circle and off for the right circle.

When you make selections that are curved or diagonal — anything other than straight horizontal or vertical lines — Photoshop will typically use anti-aliasing in order to make the selection edges look smooth on screen. This is why anti-aliasing is the default setting. In most cases, you should keep anti-aliasing turned on when selecting to make the selection edge appear smoother.

Contiguous

CONTIGUOUS means touching, or next to each other. When checked (the default setting) the **Magic Wand Tool** only selects the colors of the chosen tolerance that touch each other. With **Contiguous** checked, and the default **Tolerance** of **32**, clicking in one black circle shown above would select only that black area, but not the other circle or the inside of either **O**s. With **Contiguous** unchecked, both circles and the inside of both **O**s would be selected with just one click.

Sample All Layers

If a document has more than one layer (like the pumpkin and its face in Tutorial 1) and **Sample All Layers** is unchecked (the default), the **Magic Wand Tool** uses only the tones and colors in the active layer to determine what to select. When **Sample All Layers** is checked, the **Magic Wand Tool** uses the tones and colors of all the visible layers in the document to make its selection.

Transforming Pixels and Selections

Once you've made a selection, you often will want to do more to the selected pixels than just move them. Photoshop allows you to make many changes to selected areas via the **Edit > Transform** menu.

Transform lets you scale (resize), rotate, flip, or perform other operations on the selected area.

NOTE: Once you perform the transformation, the actual pixels in the selected area will be changed. If you don't like the transformation, you may need to use the History Panel to undo the transformation.

GUIDED EXERCISE 3.2 : TRANSFORM A SELECTION

In this guided exercise, you will use the **Magic Wand Tool** to make selections based on color, and then you will transform a selected area.

1. Open the **toolcritter.psd** file, if it is not still open from the last exercise.

2. Select the saw blade with the **Magic Wand Tool**:

   a. Use the **Zoom Tool** to zoom in to the saw blade on the left side of the image.

   b. Choose the **Magic Wand Tool**.

   c. In the Options Bar, look for the **Tolerance** setting. Set it to **32** (the default setting).

   d. Click anywhere inside the gray saw blade.

   You should see one of two things, depending on exactly where you clicked: either the entire saw blade is now selected, or most of the blade is selected, but there are one or two 'islands' of non-selected pixels.

   1) In order to add these non-selected areas to your selection, choose the **Elliptical Marquee Tool**.

   2) In the **Options** bar, click the **Add to selection** button. A small plus sign (+) will appear next to your cursor.

   3) Drag over one of the non-selected areas.

   4) Repeat, as needed, to add any additional non-selected islands to the current selection. You should now have the entire saw blade selected.

   5) Click the **New selection** button in the **Options** bar to return the **Elliptical Marquee Tool** to its default setting.

3. Double-click the **Hand Tool** to see the entire image.

4. Relocate and resize the selected region:

   a. Choose the **Move Tool**.

   b. Drag the saw blade into position as one of the 'ears' of the critter. Notice that the saw blade is too big so you will need to scale it down to size.

   c. Choose **Edit > Transform > Scale**.

   d. In the **Options** bar, click the **Maintain aspect ratio** (chain link) button in between the **W** and **H** boxes so that if you change one value, the other value also changes.

e. Enter **50%** for the width (**W**) and press **tab**.
   Notice that the height (**H**) also becomes **50%**.

   f. Click the **Commit** button (check mark) at the right side of the **Options** bar.

   g. Move the saw blade into the precise location, if needed.

   HINT: use the arrow keys on the keyboard for precise placement.

5. Duplicate the saw blade to make the other ear:

   a. With the saw blade still selected, choose the **Move Tool** and move your cursor onto the saw blade.

   b. Hold down the **Option** (Mac) or **Alt** (Windows) key.

   This changes your cursor into a double arrow — one white and one black.

   c. Drag the saw blade to 'peel off' a copy and drag it into position as the other ear.

   d. Deselect.

6. Save the image by choosing **File** > **Save**.

The Lasso Tools

In addition to selecting a fixed rectangular or elliptical shape, or a color-based area, you can make a selection in any shape you want by using the **Lasso** tools.

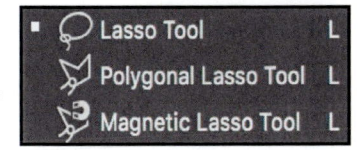

The Lasso Tool Cursors

As you move the cursor around in the document window, each of the **Lasso Cursors** shows the chosen tool with an arrowhead in its upper left. As you select with this cursor, its **HOT SPOT** or cursor point is the tip of that arrowhead. That is where Photoshop will create the selection outline as you drag the chosen **Lasso** tool to surround the item you wish to select. We colored the hot spot red here to make it apparent.

The (Standard) Lasso Tool

The **Lasso Tool** allows you to 'draw' a freehand (irregularly-shaped) selection of any shape or size. Using the **Lasso Tool**, hold the mouse button down and drag a line around the area to be selected. When you release the mouse button, Photoshop will 'close' the selection by drawing a straight line connecting the starting and ending points of your selection.

The **Lasso Tool** has two close relatives, the **Polygonal Lasso Tool** and the **Magnetic Lasso Tool**. They each have similarities to the **Lasso Tool** as well as some definite differences.

The Polygonal Lasso Tool

The **Polygonal Lasso Tool** (sometimes called the Polygon Lasso) can be used to select any shape, but by making a series of connected straight-line segments. Instead of clicking and drawing a selection, like with the **Lasso Tool**, you make a selection with the **Polygonal Lasso Tool** by creating a multi-sided polygon. In other words, clicking the mouse the first time places the starting point of the selection. When you move the mouse to a different area, you'll notice a 'rubber band effect,' a line that connects the point you clicked on with your cursor. Now, each time you click, a new vertex is added to your selected area. To complete your selection, either move the cursor close enough to the point you clicked on to start the selection (you'll see a small circle next to the cursor) and click, or double-click anywhere and the selection will be completed with a straight line connecting your starting and ending points.

The Magnetic Lasso Tool

The **Magnetic Lasso Tool** makes selections by looking for edges — areas of contrast in an image.

You use the **Magnetic Lasso Tool** by clicking on the edge of an area that you want to select, and then moving the cursor along the boundary between what you want to select and what you don't want selected. Photoshop will look for an area of contrast near the cursor and use that to determine the exact boundary of the selection. Like the **Polygonal Lasso Tool**, you can either return to your starting point and click or double-click anywhere to complete the selection.

Guided Exercise 3.3: Use the Lasso Tool

Now it is time to add the whiskers to your critter. In this guided exercise you will use the **Lasso Tool** to make selections and explore more **Edit > Transform** commands.

1. Open the **toolcritter.psd** file, if it is not still open from the last exercise.

2. Select the pliers:

    a. Use the **Zoom Tool** to zoom in on the red-handled pliers on the right edge of the image.

    b. Choose the **Lasso Tool and look at its pointer**. Remember, the hot spot for selecting is at the tip of the arrowhead, shown in red here.

    c. Starting at one end of the pliers, drag along the entire edge, ending up back where you started. Don't worry too much about making a completely precise selection — you'll clean it up next:

    - If you didn't select all of the pliers and need to add to your selection, click the **Add to selection** button in the **Options** bar and drag around the additional areas.

    - If you selected some of the rocks around the pliers by mistake, click the **Subtract from selection** button in the **Options** bar and drag around the unwanted areas.

    d. Click the **New selection** button in the **Options** bar to reset the **Lasso Tool** to its default setting.

3. Store the pliers selection so that you can access it later:

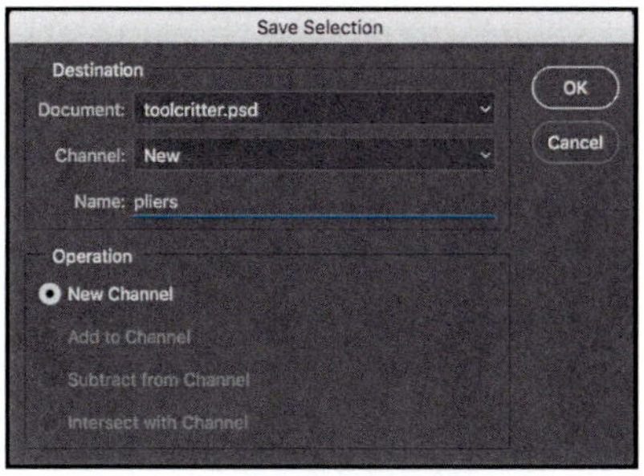

    a. Choose **Select** > **Save Selection** to display the **Save Selection** dialog box:

    b. Type **pliers** in the **Name:** box and click **OK**.

4. Double-click the **Hand Tool** to see the entire image.

5. Move the pliers into position:

    a. Choose the **Move Tool**.

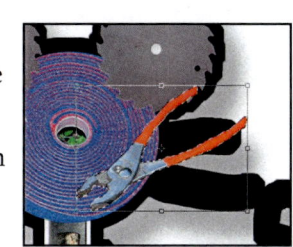

    b. Press the **Option** (Mac) or **Alt** (Windows) key and drag the selected pliers to the head of your critter, near the right edge of the roll of tape. This will "peel off" a copy of the pliers, while leaving the original ones in place, so you can use it again later.

    c. Rotate the pliers to make them appear like whiskers:

       1) Choose **Edit** > **Transform** > **Rotate**.

          You will see a box surrounding the pliers, with **HANDLES** or small squares on the edges.

       2) Move the cursor outside the rotation rectangle to make the cursor turn into a double-headed curved arrow.

       3) Drag to rotate the pliers, until they are roughly horizontal and match the outline.

    d. If the pliers are not properly lined up with the black outline, move the cursor over the pliers and drag them to the correct place.

    e. Click the **Commit Transformation button** (check mark) in the **Options** bar to confirm the rotation and move.

    f. Deselect.

6. Grab a second set of pliers for the other side of the head:

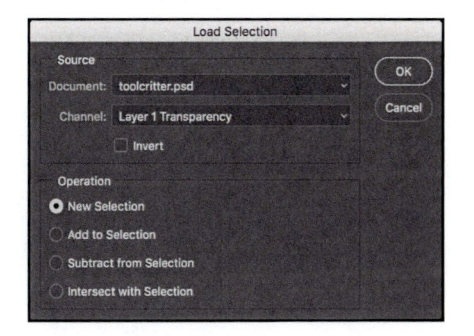

       1) Since you saved the original pliers selection, you can re-load it without having to go through the trouble of reselecting.

       2) Choose **Select** > **Load Selection**.

       3) Make sure that **Channel** is set to **pliers** and click **OK**. You should now see the original set of pliers is selected.

    a. With the **Move Tool**, drag the original set of pliers from the right edge of the image to the left side of the roll of tape.

Tutorial 3: Selection   Page 55

b. Choose **Edit > Transform > Rotate**, and rotate the pliers to be horizontal, like you did in step 6c.

Notice that the pliers do not match the outline; they are upside-down.

c. To make the pliers face the correct direction, choose **Edit > Transform > Flip Vertical**, and **Commit** the transformation.

d. Drag the pliers into position, if need be, and deselect.

7. Save **toolcritter.psd**, and close it for now. (You will finish the critter later in this tutorial.)

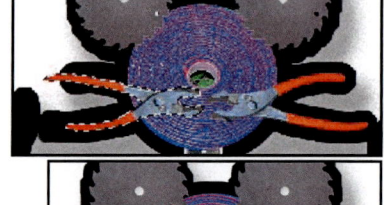

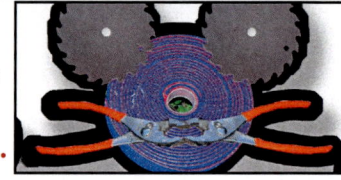

The Quick Selection Tool

The **Quick Selection Tool** works so well and is so easy to use that it is often the first selection tool you will use. Its performance is impressive in many cases, but it does not work well for selecting refined detail such as blowing hair or fine branches of a tree.

Guided Exercise 3.4: Use The Quick Selection Tool

The fastest way to understand the **Quick Selection Tool** is to try it out.

1. Reset the **Essentials** workspace, all tools, and the default **Foreground** and **Background** colors.

2. Open **03-sunflower.jpg**.

3. Choose the **Quick Selection Tool.**

4. Observe the selection controls in the **Options** bar, as they work a little differently than for the other selection tools.

   Before you make a selection, the **Make new selection** button is active. Once you make a selection, the button automatically changes to the middle **Add to selection** button so that you can enlarge your selection until your object is completely selected.

   The right **Subtract from selection** button lets you shrink your selection as needed.

   There is no Intersect with selection button.

5. Paint a short stroke across a yellow area of the sunflower.

   Notice that marching ants appear not just where you painted, but along the edge of the flower in the region you painted. Depending on the speed of your computer, it might take a little time for the selection to appear.

   Behind the scenes, Photoshop is working very hard to figure out what you want to select.

Tutorial 3: Selection

6. Slowly paint around the yellow petals of the sunflower. As you do, your selection grows until nearly all of the flower is selected.

7. Check your selection:

   a. Choose the **Zoom Tool** and make sure its **Scrubby Zoom** option is checked (the default).

   b. Press on the flower to zoom in to help make a more accurate selection; release the mouse button when the flower is adequately enlarged. Notice that some parts of the ends of the petals were not selected.

8. Choose the **Quick Selection Tool** again, and position it over the area to add to your selection (the petals here).

   Notice that the tool is too big to fix the selection; it includes foliage as well as the missing petal. Here is how the too-big brush appears on your monitor:

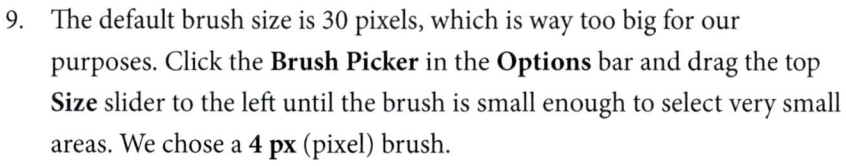

9. The default brush size is 30 pixels, which is way too big for our purposes. Click the **Brush Picker** in the **Options** bar and drag the top **Size** slider to the left until the brush is small enough to select very small areas. We chose a **4 px** (pixel) brush.

10. Click the **Auto Enhance** option in the **Options** bar to activate it.

    The **Quick Selection Tool** tends to make very sharp, almost blocky edges, which we will learn to fix later. **Auto Enhance** makes more accurate selection edges. However, it also uses a lot more of the computer's processing power, so don't keep this option checked all the time if you see it slowing down your selections.

11. Fine-tune your selection:

    a. Make sure that the brush is entirely inside the region you wish to add to the selection.

    b. With **Add to Selection** active, click—don't drag—to add individual small areas to your selection. As you do, you will probably also include areas that should not be part of the selection, like the space between the petals, as shown here.

    c. Click **Subtract from selection**, reduce the brush size further if necessary, and paint on the area you wish to remove from the selection.

12. You probably will not be able to make a perfect selection using just the **Quick Selection Tool**. Check the exactness of your selection edges and improve them using other selection tools such as the **Lasso Tool**.

13. Save your sunflower selection for later use:

    a. Choose **Select > Save Selection** to open the **Save Selection** dialog box.

       If desired, you could select and save more regions, up to a total of 20 with each image. Technically, stored selections are called **ALPHA CHANNELS**, and they reside in the **Channels** panel.

    b. Type a descriptive name in the **Name** box, and click **OK** to store the selection for future access.

    c. Choose **File > Save**.

       The **Save As** dialog box opens because your starting image is in **JPG** format and you will need to save a copy in **PSD** format to preserve the saved selection.

    d. Click the Save button to make a second version of the sunflower, **03-sunflower.psd,** with its alpha channel.

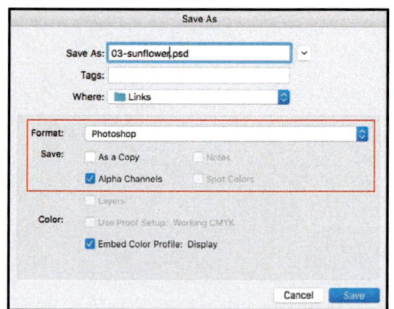

Refining Selection Edges

Look at the edges of this sunflower. What we did was to load the sunflower selection, choose **Edit > Copy**, and then paste the selected area into a new, blank document with a white background. It didn't look too bad at **100%** magnification, but when we zoomed in to **200%**, we could see how rough the edge of the selection really was. All these bad edges would look especially sloppy if we were to print the image.

Fortunately, Photoshop has tools which let you preview selections on a number of different backgrounds, and adjust the selections quite effectively.

Versions of Photoshop up through CC 2015.2 (released in November 2015) have the **Refine Edge** command. In version CC 2015.5 (released in June 2016), Refine Edge was replaced by the **Select and Mask** feature. We will show you both options.

Guided Exercise 3.5a: Use the Refine Edge Command on the Edges of the Sunflower Selection (for Photoshop CC 2015.2 and Earlier)

Let's improve our sunflower selection with the **Refine Edge** dialog box.

1. Begin with the sunflower image open and its selection loaded.

2. Either choose any of the selection tools and click on **Refine Edge** in the **Options** bar, or choose **Select > Refine Edge** to open the **Refine Edge** dialog box.

   By default, your selection is shown previewed on a white background to better see how the edge will appear.

   The **Refine Edge** dialog box contains both a **Hand Tool** and a **Zoom Tool** so that you can move the image around in its window, or zoom in or out.

Tutorial 3: Selection

Page 58

Like so many of Photoshop's dialog boxes, **Refine Edge** is full of choices, and it can be overwhelming when you first see it.

Let's examine the settings further from top to bottom.

3. Change the **View Mode** to see your selection in different ways:

- The default view is **On White**. This is an excellent view for this image because when you lift the flower off its dark background the less than perfectly selected edges show up well on white.

- **Marching Ants** shows the entire image with a dashed moving edge surrounding the selected parts of the image visible.

- **Overlay** covers the unselected areas with a transparent red color.

- **On Black** shows the selected area on a black background.

- **On White**, the default, shows the selected area on a white background.

- **Black & White** shows the selected area in white, the unselected area in black, with any partially selected or feathered areas in shades of gray.

- **On Layers** views the layer as masked by the selection.

- **Reveal Layer** views the entire layer without masking.

    a. Click the **View** thumbnail to reveal the different **View** modes, each with a tiny view of your selection.

    b. Choose the **On Black** view. Your sunflower looks particularly good on this view because it camouflages the dark edge.

    c. Choose the **Black & White** view. The sharp contrast of this view between what is selected (white) and what is not selected (black) can help pick up selection problems. You can see a black area inside two flower petals that should have been selected. This deselected area can be easily fixed by adding to the selection after leaving **Refine Edge**. (It can also be adjusted inside **Refine Edge**, but that's more advanced than this tutorial.)

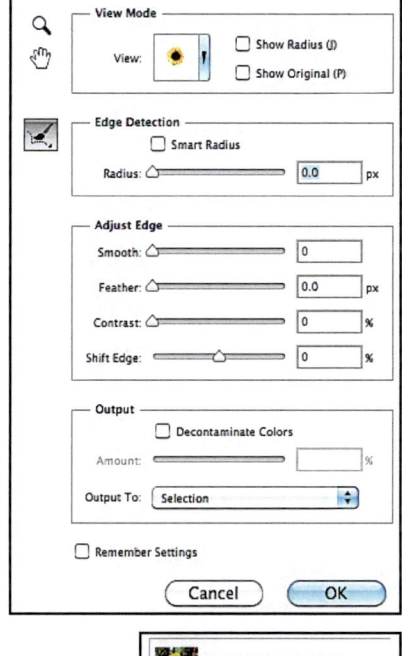

4. In **Edge Detection**, check the **Smart Radius** box and gradually increase the **Radius** setting.

    Edge Detection works by analyzing the color value of the pixels around the edge to best determine the edge pixels' opacity.

    The larger the **RADIUS**, the further out from the edge the analysis occurs.

Tutorial 3: Selection

Photoshop Help recommends that you "increase radius to create a more exact selection boundary in areas with soft transitions or fine detail, such as those in short hair or fur, or blurred boundaries."

Increasing the **Radius** can cause **ARTIFACTING** (stray pixels) but you will remove these with the **Contrast** setting. **Contrast** sharpens selection edges, and can remove artifacts and noise associated with high **Radius** settings.

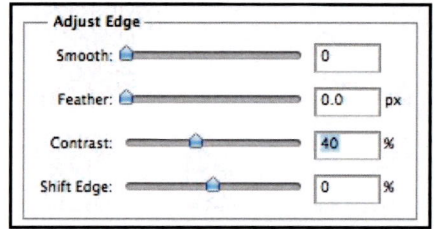

5. In the **Adjust Edge** section of the **Refine Edge** dialog box, gradually increase the **Contrast** setting until the artifacts drop away. We got good results at **40%**.

6. Explore the **Smooth** setting in **Adjust Edge**:

   Smooth evens out the irregular jagged areas of the selection border, as shown here. In most cases, you want to apply **Smooth** very gradually. Used too heavily, **Smooth** makes the edge lose definition.

	This section of green leaf was selected with the **Rectangular Marquee Tool** with no smoothing.
	Here the leaf selection is smoothed to the maximum, **100%**. While the edge is overly soft for most purposes, it might provide a nice effect for Web buttons.

The technique you will use here to set the **Smooth** value, with the **SCRUBBING CURSOR**, can be used anywhere in Photoshop where there is a settings box with a numeric value.

   a. Move the cursor to the title of the setting, **Smooth** here, until you see the double arrow scrubbing cursor. Slowly drag to the right to increase or to the left to decrease the value.

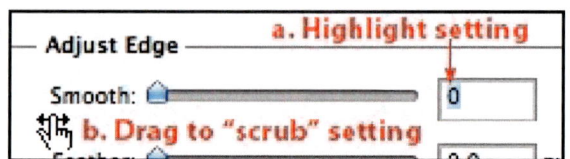

   As you drag to the right, you will see a slight softening of the edge, and the value in the **Smooth** box will go up.

   b. Without releasing the mouse, drag back and forth until you have the desired setting. *Remember, right increases and left decreases.* We found a very small increase to **3** smoothed out the edge just slightly without losing edge detail.

7. Examine your selection edge in detail using the **Zoom Tool** and the **Hand Tool** on the upper left side of the **Refine Edge** dialog box:

   a. Switch your view to **On White** and click the **Zoom Tool**.

Tutorial 3: Selection

When you choose the **Refine Edge Zoom Tool**, you concurrently choose the **Zoom Tool** in the **Tools** panel and display the **Zoom Tool** settings in the **Options** bar for your use.

  b. Use a technique you learned in Tutorial 1 to zoom in to **400%**.

  c. Click the **Hand Tool** on the upper left side of the **Refine Edge** dialog box and note that its options are displayed for your use.

  d. Press and drag on your image to pan it. By using the **Zoom Tool** and the **Hand Tool** in combination, you can gradually examine the whole selection in detail.

8. See how the **Contrast** setting affects the selection edge.

   Adding **CONTRAST** to the selection edge sharpens soft edges and removes fuzzy artifacts. Here we used the settings from before and increased **Contrast** to **40%**.

9. Contract the selection edge to diminish the dark outline around the flower petals.

   The **Shift Edge** setting contracts or expands the selection boundary from -**100%** to +**100%**.

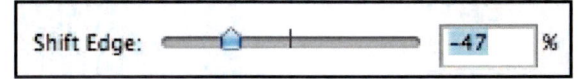

   As you contract, carefully check the results all the way around the edge. If the contraction is too strong, parts of the image you want to be visible may drop out.

   View your selection **On Black** and **Black & White** views to double-check edge problems, and tweak your settings as desired.

10. Set the selection **Output**:

    a. In the **Output To** menu, choose **New Document**. This will make of copy of just the selected pixels (the sunflower here) into its own document on a blank layer.

    b. Make sure that **Remember Settings** is checked so that **Refine Edge** keeps all the settings you worked so hard to perfect and click **OK**.

    The sunflower opens in a new **Untitled** document in its own tab in the Photoshop workspace. It is on its own layer, with the transparency of the layer shown by the checkerboard pattern.

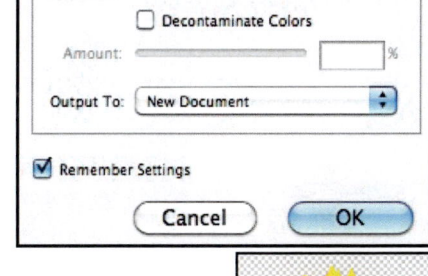

    c. Save the document as **SunflowerDone.psd** in the location of your choice.

11. Experiment with the **Feather** setting in **Refine Edge**:

    Feather creates a soft transition, or **GRADIENT**, between the selection and its surrounding pixels, moving both in and out from the selection border by the specified size of the feather, from **0** to **1000** pixels. A very small amount of feathering, like 1-4 pixels, can soften the edge just a bit so that the selection does not look like it was cut with a cookie cutter when you combine images to make a composite. Large amounts of feathering can be used for special effects.

  a. Click the tab of **03-sunflower.psd** to bring it to the front.

  b. If for some reason the sunflower is no longer selected, choose **Select > Reselect** to select the sunflower again.

  c. Choose **Select > Refine Edge**. The **Refine Edge** button is only in the **Options** bar when a selection tool is chosen. However, whenever part of an image is selected, you can chose **Select > Refine Edge** regardless of which tool is chosen.

  d. Experiment with feather settings, and view the results in different ways.

     Here we feathered the selection edge to about **20 pixels**.

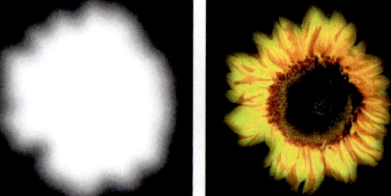

     Black & White shows just the edge transition. **On Black** and **On White** give quite different effects.

  e. Save to a new image if desired, otherwise cancel. You will use a feathered selection later in this tutorial.

12. Close **03-sunflower.jpg**.

Guided Exercise 3.5B: Use Select and Mask on the Edges of the Sunflower Selection (for Photoshop CC 2015.5)

Let's improve our sunflower selection with the new **Select and Mask** command, which replaces the **Refine Edge** command. **Select and Mask** opens a new workspace, taking over the entire screen, and gives you access to a couple of new tools.

1. Begin with the sunflower image open and its selection loaded.

2. Either choose any of the selection tools and click on **Select and Mask** in the **Options** bar, or choose **Select > Select and Mask**.

   - Along the left edge is the **Tools** panel. This contains some familiar, as well as a few new tools.

   - Along the top of the workspace is the **Options** bar, where the settings for each tool can be set.

   - The right side of the workspace contains the **Properties** panel, where the overall workspace options are located.

Tutorial 3: Selection

By default, your selection is shown previewed in an **ONION SKIN** view, where the non-selected part of the image is partially transparent to help you better see the selection edges.

3. The **Select and Mask** workspace contains the following tools:

    - The **Quick Selection Tool** works like the regular version — you drag across areas of your image to add or subtract them from the current selection.

    - The **Refine Edge Brush** is used to paint over areas where you want Photoshop to make a more precise selection, such as hair or fur.

    - The **Brush Tool** does not paint pixels, like the standard Brush tool, but instead it paints selections on or off.

    - The **Lasso**, **Hand**, and **Zoom** tools all behave the same as their standard versions.

4. The Properties panel contains a number of controls for viewing and making selections:

    - **View Mode** allows you to visualize the selection in a number of different ways. Changing the view mode changes the options available directly below the View Mode setting.

    - **Edge Detection** is used to tell Photoshop to look for fine detail along a selection edge. This is most useful when making a selection of hair or fur.

    - **Global Refinements** make overall changes to the selection edge.

    - **Output Settings** tell Photoshop what to do with the new, refined selection.

5. Change the **View Mode** to see your selection in different ways:

- The default view is **Onion Skin**. This shows the selected region at full opacity, and all non-selected regions as partially transparent.

- **Marching Ants** shows the entire image with a dashed moving edge surrounding the selected parts of the image.

- **Overlay** covers the unselected areas with a transparent red color.

- **On Black** shows the selected area on a black background.

- **On White** shows the selected area on a white background.

- **Black & White** shows the selected area in white, the unselected area in black, with any partially selected or feathered areas in shades of gray.

- **On Layers** views the layer as masked by the selection.

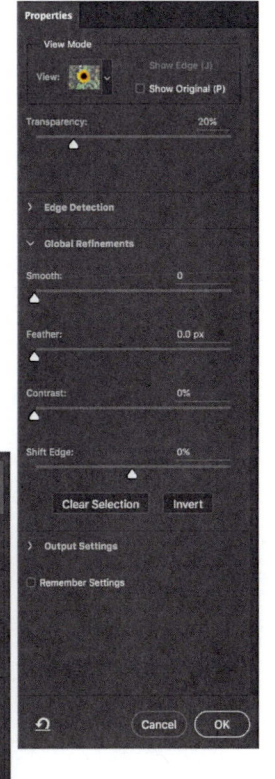

a. Click the **View** thumbnail to reveal the different **View** modes, each with a tiny view of your selection.

b. Choose the **On Black** view. Your sunflower looks particularly good on this view because it camouflages the dark edge.

c. Choose the **Black & White** view. The sharp contrast of this view between what is selected (white) and what is not selected (black) can help pick up selection problems. You can see a black area inside two flower petals that should have been selected. This deselected area can be easily fixed by adding to the selection by using the **Brush Tool** in the **Select and Mask** workspace.

6. In **Edge Detection**, check the **Smart Radius** box and gradually increase the **Radius** setting.

    Edge Detection works by analyzing the color value of the pixels around the edge to best determine the edge pixels' opacity.

    The larger the **RADIUS**, the further out from the edge the analysis occurs.

    Photoshop Help recommends that you "increase radius to create a more exact selection boundary in areas with soft transitions or fine detail, such as those in short hair or fur, or blurred boundaries."

    Increasing the **Radius** can cause **ARTIFACTING** (stray pixels) but you will remove these with the **Contrast** setting. **Contrast** sharpens selection edges, and can remove artifacts and noise associated with high **Radius** settings.

7. In the **Global Refinements** section of the **Properties** panel, gradually increase the **Contrast** setting until the artifacts drop away. We got good results at around **40%**.

8. Explore the **Smooth** setting in **Gloable Refinements**:

    Smooth evens out the irregular jagged areas of the selection border. In most cases, you want to apply **Smooth** very gradually. Used too heavily, **Smooth** makes the edge lose definition.

	This section of green leaf was selected with the **Rectangular Marquee Tool** with no smoothing.
	Here the leaf selection is smoothed to the maximum, **100%**. While the edge is overly soft for most purposes, it might provide a nice effect for Web buttons.

The technique you will use here to set the **Smooth** value, with the **SCRUBBING CURSOR**, can be used anywhere in Photoshop where there is a settings box with a numeric value.

a. Move the cursor to the title of the setting, **Smooth** here, until you see the double arrow scrubbing cursor. Slowly drag to the right to increase or to the left to decrease the value.

Tutorial 3: Selection   Page 64

As you drag to the right, you will see a slight softening of the edge, and the value in the **Smooth** box will go up.

b. Without releasing the mouse, drag back and forth until you have the desired setting. *Remember, right increases and left decreases.* We found a very small increase to **3** smoothed out the edge just slightly without losing edge detail.

9. Examine your selection edge in detail using the **Zoom Tool** and the **Hand Tool**:

    a. Switch your view to **On White** and click the **Zoom Tool**.

    When you choose the **Zoom Tool**, you concurrently choose the **Zoom Tool** in the **Tools** panel and display the **Zoom Tool** settings in the **Options** bar for your use.

    b. Use a technique you learned in Tutorial 1 to zoom in to **400%**.

    c. Click the **Hand Tool** and note that its options are displayed for your use.

    d. Press and drag on your image to pan it. By using the **Zoom Tool** and the **Hand Tool** in combination, you can gradually examine the whole selection in detail.

10. See how the **Contrast** setting affects the selection edge.

    Adding **CONTRAST** to the selection edge sharpens soft edges and removes fuzzy artifacts. Here we used the settings from before and increased **Contrast** to **40%**.

11. Contract the selection edge to diminish the dark outline around the flower petals.

    The **Shift Edge** setting contracts or expands the selection boundary from **-100%** to **+100%**.

    As you contract, carefully check the results all the way around the edge. If the contraction is too strong, parts of the image you want to be visible may drop out.

    View your selection **On Black** and **Black & White** views to double-check edge problems, and tweak your settings as desired.

12. Set the selection **Output**:

    a. In the **Output Settings** are, choose **New Document**. This will make of copy of just the selected pixels (the sunflower here) into its own document on a blank layer.

    b. Make sure that **Remember Settings** is checked so that **Refine Edge** keeps all the settings you worked so hard to perfect and click **OK**.

    The sunflower opens in a new **Untitled** document in its own tab in the Photoshop workspace. It is on its own layer, with the transparency of the layer shown by the checkerboard pattern.

c. Save the document as **SunflowerDone.psd** in the location of your choice.

13. Experiment with the **Feather** setting in the **Global Refinements** section of **Select and Mask**:

    Feather creates a soft transition, or **GRADIENT**, between the selection and its surrounding pixels, moving both in and out from the selection border by the specified size of the feather, from **0** to **1000** pixels. A very small amount of feathering, like 1-4 pixels, can soften the edge just a bit so that the selection does not look like it was cut with a cookie cutter when you combine images to make a composite. Large amounts of feathering can be used for special effects.

    a. Click the tab of **03-sunflower.psd** to bring it to the front.

    b. If for some reason the sunflower is no longer selected, choose **Select > Reselect** to select the sunflower again.

    c. Choose **Select > Select and Mask**. The **Select and Mask** button is only in the **Options** bar when a selection tool is chosen. However, whenever part of an image is selected, you can chose **Select > Select and Mask** regardless of which tool is chosen.

    d. Experiment with feather settings, and view the results in different ways.

       Here we feathered the selection edge to about **20 pixels**.

    Black & White shows just the edge transition. **On Black** and **On White** give quite different effects.

    e. Save to a new image if desired, otherwise cancel. You will use a feathered selection later in this tutorial.

14. Close **03-sunflower.psd**.

Working with Selections

Once you make a selection, Photoshop provides a number of ways in which you can improve it.

Hiding Selection Edges

Sometimes the selection's marching ants will get in the way of seeing what you are doing. You can hide the marching ants by choosing **View > Show > Selection Edges**. This command is a toggle; the second time you choose **View > Show > Selection Edges** the marching ants reappear. The toggle short-cut keys for **hiding** are **Control + H** (Windows) or **Command + H** (Mac).

Be careful! Hiding selection edges can be problematic if you forget about a hidden selection and then attempt to edit an unselected part of the document. When a document has an active selection, even if it is hidden, **Deselect** under the **Select** menu will be available (not grayed out).

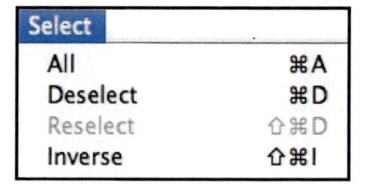

- Choose **Select > Deselect** to make the entire document or layer available for editing,
- Choose **Select > All** to place marching ants around the entire active layer in case you want to copy the contents of the layer.

The Precise or Crosshair Cursor

Cursor shapes such as pointer arrows often get in the way of making precise selections.

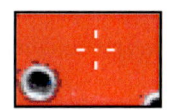

- For most tools, you can press the **Caps Lock** key to change your cursor into a crosshair, the **PRECISE CURSOR**, to make it easier to see just where you are while clicking or dragging.
- Press the **Caps Lock** key again to turn off the precise cursor and display the **STANDARD CURSOR** for the chosen tool.

Shrinking Selections for Cleaner Edges

One trick for avoiding halos is to shrink your selection slightly to remove the fringe pixels from the selection. First make a selection, and then:

1. Bring up **Select and Mask** or **Refine Edge** from the **Options** bar button or the **Select** menu.
2. Examine your selection both **On Black** and **On White**, to see which view makes the halo most apparent.
3. Move the **Shift Edge** slider to the left, and also adjust both **Contrast** and **Radius** until you achieve a pleasing edge.
4. Be sure that Output is set to Selection.

When you click **OK**, the marching ants will be in a little from the edge of the selected object because the selection is contracted.

Refining Edge Suggestions

Here are two suggestions adapted from **Photoshop Help**:

- For images where the colors of the selected object are distinct from the background, try increasing the **Radius**, applying **Contrast** to sharpen edges, then adjusting the **Shift Edge** slider.
- For grayscale images or images where the colors of the selected object and the background are very similar, try **Smooth** first, then the **Feather** option, then **Shift Edge**.

Experiment with More Selection Tools

The **Quick Selection Tool** is so effective that it is typically the first selection tool you will use. But occasionally it doesn't work very well, and one or more of the other selection tools can help you out.

Guided Exercise 3.6: Compare the Polygonal Lasso Tool with the Quick Selection Tool

When a region you are trying to select does not stand out very much from its surrounding region, the **Quick Selection Tool** can have a hard time making a decent selection. In this guided exercise you will attempt to use the **Quick Selection Tool**, and then seeing its limitations, you will use the **Polygonal Lasso Tool** for better selection success. The **Polygonal Lasso Tool** draws straight-edged segments of a selection border.

1. Open the **toolcritter.psd** file.

2. Use the **Zoom Tool** to zoom in to the triangle near the bottom-left corner of the image.

3. Use the **Quick Selection Tool** to select the triangle.

    The sheen of the metal on the triangle and the irregularity of the tones in the wood the triangle is resting on do not allow the **Quick Selection Tool** to define a clean edge to the selection.

    Here we have turned on **Overlay** view in **Refine Edge/Select and Mask** to make the selection problems more apparent.

4. Deselect.

5. Select the triangle using the **Polygonal Lasso Tool**:

    a. In the **Tools** panel, press the **Lasso Tool** and choose the **Polygonal Lasso Tool** hiding beneath it.

    b. Move the cursor to the top-right corner of the triangle (**1**) and click to 'anchor' the beginning of the selection.

    c. Move your cursor to the bottom-right edge of the triangle (**2**) and click again to place a second anchor point.

    d. Continue clicking at each corner (**3**, **4** & **5**) as you follow completely around the triangle.

    e. When you get back to your starting point at the top-right of the triangle (**1**), a small 'o' will appear next to your cursor. Click to complete the selection.

6. Remove the 'holes' — the wood visible through the two open areas of the selected triangle:

    a. Click the **Subtract from selection** button in the **Options** bar. Any selections you make now will be **SUBTRACTED** or removed from the current selection.

    b. Start with the larger triangular-shaped opening. Click in one corner to anchor the beginning of the selection.

    c. Click at each corner of the hole until you have gone completely around and completed the selection.

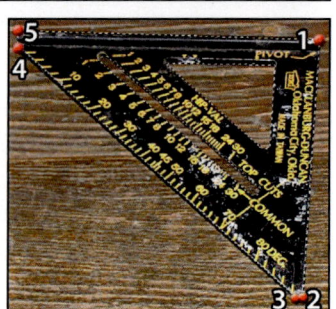

Tutorial 3: Selection

d. Repeat this procedure for the smaller, more linear hole in the triangle. You should now have just the triangle selected, and not any of the wood plank it is resting on.

7. Double-click the **Hand Tool** to see the entire image.

8. Temporarily move the triangle to a blank area of the document to make it easier to select again when you need to:

    a. Choose the **Move Tool**.

    b. Drag the triangle to the empty white space along the right edge of the image, between the original location of the level and the pliers. Make sure the triangle does not touch any other image parts. Leave the triangle here temporarily.

    c. Deselect.

9. Use the **Polygonal Lasso Tool** to select the basic outline of the black and yellow tool box, and move it into position as part of the critter's body:

    a. Zoom in to the yellow tool box along the bottom edge of the image.

    b. Choose the **Polygonal Lasso Tool**.

    c. Move your cursor to the top edge of the tool box (**1**) and click to 'anchor' the beginning of the selection.

    d. Move your cursor to the top-right edge of the tool box (**2**) and click again to place another anchor point.

    e. Continue clicking each point in sequence to go completely around the tool box. When you get back to your starting point at the top-center of the box, a small '**o**' will appear next to your cursor.

    f. Click to complete the selection.

    g. Double-click the **Hand Tool** to see the entire image.

    h. Choose the **Move Tool** and drag the tool box to the middle of the critter.

    i. Choose **Edit > Transform > Rotate 90° CCW** to turn the tool box onto its side.

    j. Use the **Move Tool** to drag the tool box into the correct position, just to the right of the level.

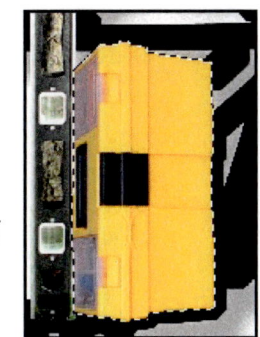

10. Duplicate the tool box for the other side of the body:

    a. Hold down the **Alt** (Windows) or **Option** (Mac) key and drag a copy to the left side of the body.

    b. Drag with the **Move Tool** into the approximate position.

    c. Choose **Edit > Transform > Flip Horizontal**.

Tutorial 3: Selection   Page 69

d. Drag with the **Move Tool** into the correct position.

e. **Deselect**.

NOTE: When you **Alt/Option drag** a selection to copy it to a new location, the duplicated pixels are temporarily on top of the active layer, so that you can use the **Move Tool** to position the duplicate pixels precisely where you want to locate them on the active layer. Once you **Deselect**, the selected pixels replace the underlying ones on the active layer, and the marching ants vanish.

11. Save the image.

For practice, select the yellow and black tool box using the **Quick Selection Tool**. Because the toolbox is so well defined against its background, the **Quick Selection Tool** works much more quickly than the **Polygonal Lasso Tool**. (We had you use the **Polygonal Lasso Tool** a second time to get more practice with that tool.) **Deselect** when you are done.

. . . .

Guided Exercise 3.7: Use the Magnetic Lasso Tool

In this guided exercise you will add the legs to your critter, starting by first selecting the red putty knife with the **Magnetic Lasso Tool**.

1. Open the **toolcritter.psd** file, if it is not still open from the last exercise.

2. Select the red putty knife:

   a. Use the **Zoom Tool** to zoom in to the red putty knife at the top-left corner of the image.

   b. Click and hold down the mouse button on the **Lasso Tool** to choose the **Magnetic Lasso Tool** which is hiding beneath it.

   c. Move the cursor to the top-left corner of the handle of the of the putty knife and click. This will set the first anchor point.

   d. Without pressing the mouse button, slowly move your cursor along the boundary between the putty knife and the wood deck it's sitting on. As you move along the edge, notice that Photoshop automatically places additional anchor points along the selection edge. These anchor points "hold" the edge in place while you complete the selection.

   If you want an anchor point in a certain location to hold the selection edge, click to place an additional point.

   If Photoshop places a point in a location you don't want, press the **delete** key to remove the most recently-placed anchor point. Then press **delete** again for each anchor point you want to delete.

   e. When you return to the starting point, click to complete the selection.

Notice that the anchor points go away. They were there temporarily to hold the selection edge in place while you worked on it.

3. Double-click the **Hand Tool** to see the entire image.

4. Use the **Move Tool** to drag the putty knife into position as the leg toward the left side of the image.

5. Duplicate the putty knife for the other leg:

    a. Hold down the **option** (Mac) or **alt** (Windows) key and drag a copy to the other side of the body.

    b. Choose **Edit > Transform > Flip Horizontal**.

    c. Drag with the **Move Tool** into the correct position.

    d. Deselect.

6. Save the image.

For experimentation, open the original **03-critter_start.jpg**, and use the **Quick Selection Tool** to select the putty knife. Which was faster for you, the **Magnetic Lasso Tool** or the **Quick Selection Tool**?

Which was more accurate? Deselect when you are done experimenting, and close the original image without saving.

· ·

GUIDED EXERCISE 3.8: COMBINING SELECTION TOOLS

Now we'll go back, get the triangle you left sitting along the right side of the image, and put it into place.

1. Open **toolcritter.psd** if it is not still open from the last exercise.

2. Double-click the **Hand Tool** to see the entire image.

3. Quickly select the triangle:

    a. Choose the **Rectangular Marquee Tool**.

    b. Drag a selection rectangle that completely encloses the triangle.

       The triangle is selected, but the selection also contains unwanted white pixels.

    c. Choose the **Magic Wand Tool**.

    d. Click the **Subtract from selection** button on the **Options** bar.

    e. Click with the **Magic Wand Tool** anywhere in the white area inside the current selection, but outside the triangle to remove the excess white pixels from the selection.

    f. Click once in each of the two holes of the triangle. Each click will remove the corresponding white pixels from the selection, to end up with just the triangle itself selected.

4. Use the **Move Tool** to drag the triangle into position on the left side of the critter.

5. Duplicate and move the triangle onto the other side of the body.

6. Choose **Edit > Transform > Flip Horizontal** to mirror the other triangle. Adjust the position as needed to match the other side.

7. Deselect, and save the image.

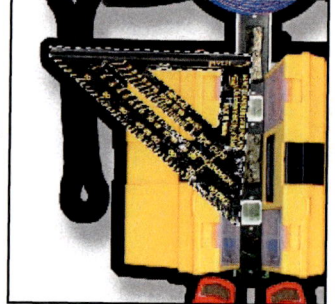

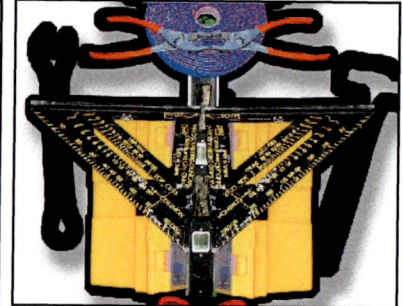

Partly-Guided Exercise 3.9: Finishing the Critter

Practice using the selection tools.

1. Using any of the tools discussed in this tutorial, select, move, and rotate the wrench and sledgehammer to place them onto the critter's 'hands'.

   Although the critter is complete, there is a lot of debris remaining.

2. Use the **Crop Tool** to remove the extra debris around the critter:

   a. Choose the **Crop Tool**.

   b. Beginning to the upper left of the critter, drag diagonally down to place a cropping rectangle around the critter, shielding the unwanted regions of the document.

   c. As needed, drag the anchor points on the rectangle edges to adjust the edges of the cropped area.

   d. Click the **Commit** button (check mark) in the **Options** bar, or press **enter** or **return** to crop out the extra debris around the critter, and to reduce the pixel dimensions of the image.

   e. Save the image. You're nearly done!

Copying and Pasting Selections

So far in this tutorial, you have worked entirely on a single layer, using the **Move Tool** to either drag or copy selected pixels from one location to another. In real life, you would rarely work this way. Instead you would move the selections onto their own layers, making them much easier to work with. Here is a preview of this more efficient technique.

Tutorial 3: Selection

Partly-Guided Exercise 3.10: Enhancing the Critter

In this Guided Exercise, you will add sunflowers to your critter.

1. Begin with **toolcritter.psd** open in Photoshop.

2. Open **SunflowerDone.psd**.

   When you open a second file, it appears in a tab in the same document window as the first image. You can then click either tab to **ACTIVATE** or bring that image forward.

3. Look at the **Layers** panel. This document contains only one layer, with the default name, **Layer 1**, containing the sunflower on a transparent background.

4. Press the **Command** key (Mac) or the **Ctrl** key (Win) and click on the layer thumbnail that contains the preview of the layer.

   TIP: Memorize this quick shortcut for selecting all the non-transparent pixels on a layer.

5. Choose **Edit > Copy** to copy the selected sunflower into the computer's clipboard.

6. Click the **toolcritter.psd** tab to activate the critter document.

7. Choose **Edit > Paste** to place the sunflower on its own layer in the very middle of the critter document.

8. Rename the new layer (**Layer 1**) **sunflowers** by double-clicking the text **Layer 1** in the **Layers** panel, typing **sunflowers**, and pressing **enter** or **return**.

9. **Command + click** (Mac) or **Ctrl + Click** (Win) on the **sunflowers** layer thumbnail to select all the non-transparent pixels on that layer.

10. Reduce the size of the sunflower (**Edit > Transform > Scale**) and move the sunflower where you want it in the image. Do not deselect it.

11. On the same layer, peel off (duplicate) at least one more sunflower to enhance your critter. You decide where to position those sunflowers.

12. Save your critter one last time, and print it if desired.

    At 300 ppi, the document will be just under 5 inches tall.

    Its file size will be fairly small because of the image's white background.

13. Close all open documents and exit Photoshop.

Tutorial 3: Selection

Page 73

ON YOUR OWN

Practice selecting elements from various images, and combining them to make new composite images. See how precise you can make the selections, and how creatively you can combine the selected elements.

RESOURCES AND VIDEOS

http://www.practical-photoshop.com/pages/CC2015-pp1-resources.html#03

Practical Photoshop CC 2015, Level 1
Tutorial 4: Layers

LAYERS isolate distinct parts of your document so that they can be individually viewed, positioned, or edited. Not only do layers help you organize the individual parts of an image, but they allow creative interactions among these layers to enhance image quality and to easily produce a variety of special effects.

Objectives

- List at least three advantages for working with layered documents.
- Identify the major landmarks of the **Layers** panel.
- Use the **Layers** panel and menu commands to create, hide, display, duplicate, group, link, lock, or delete layers.
- Understand the makeup and capabilities of two kinds of layers: the **Background** layer and standard or "pixel" layers.
- Describe the special characteristics of the **Background** layer.
- Create, name, and reorder layers and groups.
- Change layer **Opacity** and **Fill**.
- When blending layers, identify the blend color, the base color, and the result color in the document window.
- Differentiate blend modes from layer styles.
- Change the blend mode of various layers, and observe the results.
- Enhance layers with layer styles.

Layer Organization

Photoshop layers and their options are organized in the **Layers** panel.

Photoshop has several kinds of layers. In this tutorial you will work with only two — the **Background** layer and standard "pixel" layers.

The Background Layer

When you open a digital camera image, a scanned image, or most new Photoshop documents, the single layer you see is the **Background** layer. Made up of pixels, the **Background** layer has special characteristics that distinguish it from other layers that may be above it:

- The **Background** layer is always the bottom level of the document with no layers beneath it.

- The **Background** layer's position is fixed; it cannot be moved from side to side or up and down in a document.
- **OPACITY** determines the percent to which a layer hides the pixels of those beneath it. Always at the bottom of the stack, the **Background** layer is always completely (**100%**) opaque; it cannot have any transparent areas.
- When parts of the **Background** layer are erased or deleted, those areas are replaced by the **Background color** (white by default, but changeable).
- The **Background** layer cannot use any layer options such as blend modes or layer styles.
- Although most Photoshop documents have a **Background** layer, some documents consist only of other types of layers.

Pixel Layers

When layers were first introduced in Photoshop version 3, there was only one kind of layer besides the **Background** layer. Adobe simply called it a "**layer**." Each original layer contained only pixels. To differentiate these layers from others that have been introduced in later versions of Photoshop, such as the **Type** layers you will use in the next tutorial, we call these basic layers "**pixel**" layers. *This is not Adobe's terminology.*

PIXEL LAYERS are like sheets of clear film that can contain pixels of varying opacity from **0%** to **100%**. A layer of **0%** opacity is **100%** transparent; a layer of **50%** opacity is half transparent. In this **leaf** layer, the checkerboard pattern in the layer thumbnail indicates the fully transparent areas.

- When a document contains more than one layer in addition to the **Background** layer, those additional layers can be moved up and down in the stack to change the appearance of the document.
- The **Move Tool** can be used to reposition any of these layers within the document window.
- Where parts of a layer are not transparent, **BLEND MODES** determine how the visible pixels of each individual layer combine with the layers beneath it.
- Erasing part of a layer produces transparent pixels on that layer.

The Layers Panel

You can use the **Layers** panel to create, hide, display, duplicate, group, link, lock, or delete layers.

Stacking Order

The **Layers** panel displays all the layers in a document by **STACKING ORDER**, from top to bottom. If a document has a **Background** layer (some do not), the **Background** layer is always at the bottom of the stack. You can change the stacking order of any other layer by clicking on it in the **Layers** panel and dragging it up or down. In the document window, the layer at the top of the stacking order appears in front of any layers below it.

Layer Components

From left to right, each individual layer has a **Show/Hide Box**, a **THUMBNAIL** of its contents, its name, and a blank area to the right of its name that is a good spot to drag the layer when repositioning it.

In this screenshot, the **snowflake** layer is visible and the **leaf** layer is hidden. As you change the contents of a layer, its thumbnail updates.

TIP: When you drag a layer, position the pointer in the blank area to the right of the layer's name to avoid doing something unexpected to the layer.

The Active Layer

You can only paint, erase, or apply a filter to the pixels on an individual layer. This layer is called the **TARGET LAYER** or the **ACTIVE LAYER.** When you click a layer in the **Layers** panel, you activate or that layer. The **active layer** is shown by a highlight color (set by your operating system) and a special outline around its thumbnail in the **Layers** panel.

Any layer can be activated, like the **leaf** layer here. To edit a layer's pixels, the layer must be both *active* and *visible*. If the active layer is hidden, you may delete it, duplicate it, or change its name, but you cannot alter its contents.

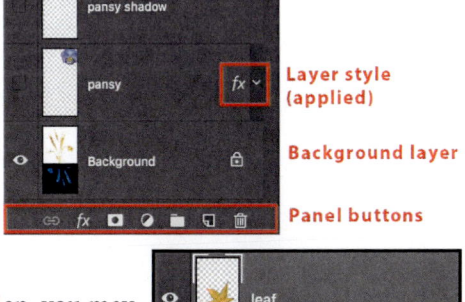

Layer Visibility

Layers can be shown or hidden. If the eye is open, then the layer is visible; if the eye is not visible (closed), then the layer is turned off or **HIDDEN**. Here the **snowflake** and **leaf** layers are visible and the **pansy shadow** layer is hidden. Hidden layers do not merge or print and they cannot be edited while hidden.

Layer Groups

LAYER GROUPS are folders that help to organize and manage layers.

The triangle to the left of the layer group name lets you click to **Expand** a group to see its contents or **Collapse** it to reduce clutter.

Layer groups function like individual layers, letting you view, select, duplicate, move, or change the stacking order of layers in a group all at once.

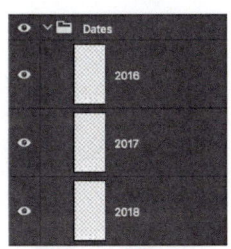

Tutorial 4: Layers

You can drag layers into and out of layer groups, or create new layers within a layer group. You can even nest groups within groups.

Layers Panel Buttons

The bottom of the **Layers** panel has seven useful buttons that you will use in this or later tutorials. These buttons are, from left to right:

1. **Link layers** lets you manipulate two or more selected layers as a unit.
2. **Add a layer style** displays a menu for applying a variety of special effects to a layer. This button says **fx** for effects.
3. **Add layer mask** lets you selectively hide parts of a layer. You will use layer masks in future courses.
4. **Create new fill or adjustment layer** provides a menu to choose the kind of fill or adjustment layer you wish to create. You will not use **Fill** or **Adjustment** layers until later in this course.
5. **Create a new group** makes an empty folder to hold a group of layers.
6. **Create a new layer** makes a new transparent pixel layer.
7. **Delete layer** deletes one or more selected layers.

The Layers Panel Menu

The upper right corner of the **Layers** panel has a button that displays the **Layers** panel menu. This menu contains many of the same commands as the **Layers** menu in the main menu bar.

Layer Filter Controls

At the top of the **Layers** panel are a series of buttons for finding layers and applying filters to them. This section of the Layers panel is most useful for animation and video, or for working with very complex documents, and will not be covered in this course.

Guided Exercise 4.1: Organizing Layers

In this guided exercise, you will work with various **Layers** panel settings to enhance a multi-layered document.

1. Open Photoshop and then open **04-layers_start.psd**.
2. Reset the **Essentials** workspace, all tools, and the default **Foreground** and **Background** colors.
3. Examine the **Status** Bar at the bottom of the application frame or document window to determine the size of the document. If you see different information than **Doc**, press the triangle on the right to display the **Status** Bar menu, and choose **Document Sizes**.

The **Status** bar shows two sizes, **4.95M** on the left and **40.1M** on the right. These document size calculation are approximate, and you might see slightly different values on your computer.

The two values mean that if the whole document was **FLATTENED** into a single layer, it would use slightly less than 5M of RAM. With its several layers, this document is 40.1M — *more than eight times as big as its flattened version* — when opened in Photoshop.

Each pixel layer requires as much RAM (memory) and disk space as the **Background** layer, except for transparent areas which do not increase the file size.

HINT: The larger your file size, the more RAM Photoshop wants. RAM is like a pie. A "slice" of the RAM pie is used to run your computer, another slice to run any open applications, another to support any files currently open in Photoshop. Photoshop requires three to five times as much RAM as the layered document size to run smoothly. Maximizing the RAM on your computer is a powerful and relatively inexpensive way to increase performance on your computer. Remember to close any open programs and files you're not using to increase your computer's power.

4. Examine the **Layers** panel.

    The **Background** layer, at the bottom of the stack, is the active layer. The **Background** layer is the only visible layer; all the other layers are hidden.

5. Position the **pansy** layers properly:

    a. Click the **Show/Hide** box for the **pansy** layer to show the flower.

    b. Click the **Show/Hide** box for the **pansy shadow** layer to show the shadow. Whoops, it is on top of the flower.

    c. Point to the blank area of the **pansy shadow** layer, just to the right of its name. Click and drag straight down until you see a dark line on the bottom of the **pansy** layer and release the mouse. Now the flower is on top of its shadow.

6. Fix the dates layers:

    a. Click the **Show/Hide** button for the **Dates** layer group near the top of the **Layers** panel. Notice that there are multiple dates jumbled together.

    b. Click the arrow to the left of the **Dates** layer group to expand its contents and notice the three date layers on top of each other.

    c. Click the **Show/Hide** button in the **2017** and **2018** layers to hide them. Now you see just **2016**.

7. Choose **File > Save As**, rename the file **layers.psd**, and save it in the location of your choice.

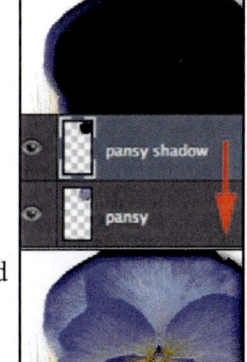

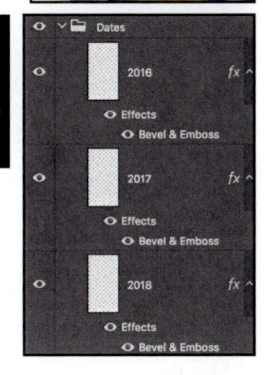

Adding, Linking, & Removing Layers & Groups

Theoretically, Photoshop allows you to create up to 8000 layers in one document. Practically speaking, it's not likely that your computer has enough RAM to support more than about 1000 layers. While layers are essential to Photoshop work, keeping track of all these layers can be challenging.

Creating New Layers

You can create new layers in a variety of ways. Whenever you make a new layer, it appears just above the currently active layer. To make a new, blank pixel layer:

- Choose **Layer > New > Layer**, or click the **New Layer** button in the **Layers** panel.

To duplicate a layer in the same document:

- Choose **Layer > Duplicate Layer**, or drag a layer thumbnail on top of the **New Layer** button.

To copy part of a layer onto its own layer:

1. Select the area.
2. Choose **Edit > Copy**.
3. Choose **Edit > Paste**.

You can copy and paste layers within the same document, or copy from one document to paste into another. You can also copy a layer from one document to another by dragging its layer thumbnail from one document to another. You will do this in Tutorial 5.

Creating a Selection from a Layer

Command/Ctrl click on a layer thumbnail to select all the non-transparent pixels on that layer in proportion to each pixel's opacity.

Creating a Layer from a Selection

Layer > New > Layer via Copy (Command/Ctrl + J) copies the selection into a new layer.

Layer > New > Layer via Cut (Command/Ctrl Shift + J) cuts the selection out of current layer and places it into a new layer.

Naming Layers

Each new pixel layer gets a default name: **Layer 1**, **Layer 2**, etc. These default names are not very useful when a document has several layers. For easier identification, you should always give your layers meaningful names as you create them.

1. In the **Layers** panel, double-click the layer name, and wait a bit until a text selection box appears around the layer name, and the name is highlighted.

2. Type a short descriptive name, and press **enter** or **return** to accept the change.

Linking Layers

Layers may be **LINKED** together to be moved, transformed, or otherwise manipulated in unison.

When layers are linked together, you can also use the **Move Tool** to drag and drop them onto another open document. Linked layers display the link symbol on the right side of their layers in the **Layers** panel.

NOTE: layers do not need to be next to each other in the **Layers** panel in order to be linked.

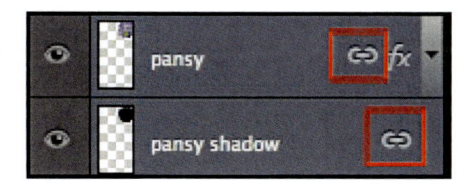

To link two or more layers:

1. Make all the layers you wish to link visible.

2. Activate the layers to be linked:

    a. Activate the first layer to be linked.

    b. Press and hold down the **Ctrl** key (Win) or the **Command** key (Mac).

    c. Click the blank spot to the right of each layer name—not the Layer name, eye, or thumbnail—for each additional layer you plan to link to the active layer. As you click, each added layer will highlight.

    d. Release the **Ctrl** or **Command** key.

3. Click the **Link Layers** button at the bottom of the **Layers** panel.

    The **link symbol** will appear at the far right of each linked layer to show that it is linked. The link symbol will only appear when one of the linked layers is active. When you activate a non-linked layer, the link symbols in the linked layers will be hidden.

    To unlink a layer, activate it and click the **Link Layers** button; it works as a toggle.

Grouping Layers

When a Photoshop document contains many layers, the ability to organize those layers is essential.

LAYER GROUPS, symbolized by folder icons, are containers for collecting, labeling, and organizing layers. There are two basic strategies for making **Layer Groups**. Either make an empty group and drag layers into that group or highlight the layers first and then make a group that contains them.

Tutorial 4: Layers

To make an empty group do one of the following:

- Use the **New Group** button at the bottom of the **Layers** panel:

    a. Click the **New Group** button at the bottom of the **Layers** panel. The group will be given a default name such as **Group 1** that you will probably want to change to a more descriptive name.

    b. Rename the group just like a layer: double-click the placeholder name **Group 1**, type in the new name, and press **enter** or **return** to accept the new name.

- Choose **New Group…** from the **Layers** panel menu or **New > Group…** from the **Layer** menu. Either of these menu choices will display the **New Group** dialog box where you can name the group, color code the group in the **Layers** panel, and choose other layer blending settings.

- Press the **Alt** (Win) or **Option** (Mac) key when you click the **New Group** button to display the New **Group** dialog box.

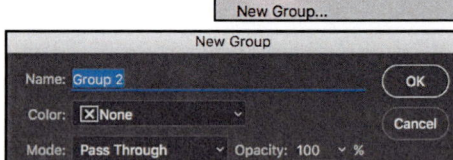

To make a group that contains existing layers:

1. Activate the layers.

2. Do one of the following:

    - Choose **Layer > New > Group from Layers…** or **New Group from Layers…** from the **Layers** panel menu. Using a menu command will display the **New Group** dialog box.

    - Type the keyboard shortcut **Command/Ctrl + G** to quickly enclose the active layers in a group, bypassing the dialog box.

    - Drag the active layers to the **New Group** button.

To remove layers from a group:

- Drag layers above or below the entire group.

Deleting Unnecessary Layers and Groups

When you delete layers and groups you no longer need, you reduce the size of your file.

To delete the active layer:

Do one of the following:

- Choose **Layer > Delete Layer**.

- Choose **Delete Layer** from the **Layers** panel menu.

- **Right-click** or **Ctrl + click** the layer name, and choose **Delete Layer** from the context menu that appears.

Tutorial 4: Layers

Page 82

- Click the **Trash** button at the bottom of the **Layers** panel.

Each of these methods displays a warning, confirming that you really want to delete the layer. Or:

- Drag the layer to the **Trash** button at the bottom of the **Layers** panel. You will not receive a warning.

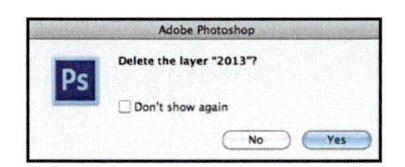

To delete the active Layer Group:

Do one of the following:

- Choose **Layer > Delete > Group**.
- Choose **Delete Group** from the **Layers** panel menu.
- **Right-click** or **Ctrl + click** the group name, and choose **Delete Group** from the context menu that appears.
- Click the **Trash** button at the bottom of the **Layers** panel.

Each of these commands will ask you if you want to delete the **Group and Contents** or the **Group Only**, which will remove the group without discarding the layers it contains.

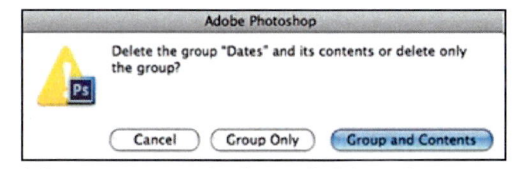

- Drag the group thumbnail to the **Trash** button at the bottom of the **Layers** panel. This will delete the group and the layers it contains without any warning (fast but potentially dangerous).

Merging Layers

MERGING LAYERS combines two or more selected layers into a single layer, taking the name of the layer lowest in the stacking order.

The advantage to merging layers is that the fewer the layers that your document contains, the smaller the file size, and the less complex the document is. The primary disadvantage to merging layers is that once merged, you can no longer manipulate those layers independently. Also, if you merge type layers they become standard pixel layers and you lose both their editability and their high-quality printing.

You may merge layers from either the **Layer** menu or the **Layers** panel menu:

- **Merge Down** combines the active layer with the layer directly below it. Both layers need to be visible to **Merge Down**.
- **Merge Visible** combines all the visible layers into a single layer without altering the hidden layers.
- **Merge Linked** combines all layers that are linked to the active layer.
- **Flatten Layers** fuses all visible document layers into a single **Background** layer and discards any hidden layers.

If one of these commands is grayed out or not present, it means that this command is not currently available. For example, you cannot merge layers if your document contains only a single layer.

· ·
Guided Exercise 4.2: Layers Panel Manipulation

Let's put some of those layers management techniques you just read about to use in the next guided exercise:

1. Open **layers.psd** if it is not already open.

2. Check the size of your layered file. It should be bigger than 25 M.

3. Choose **Essentials** from the workspace menu in the **Options** bar.

4. Delete the **Dates** group:

    a. Activate the **Dates** group.

    b. Click the **Trash** button at the bottom of the **Layers** panel.

    c. When the dialog box appears, click **Group Only** to delete the group without deleting the three date layers.

    d. Check your file size. It does not change because groups do not add or subtract document pixels.

5. Delete unnecessary layers. (Depending on the year you do this, you may have different results than us.)

    a. Activate the **2018** layer, and delete it using one of the methods described earlier in this tutorial.

    b. Check the size of your layered file. The file size has been reduced by about a half a megabyte.

    c. Delete any other hidden date layers that contain the incorrect year.

6. Group the **pansy** and **pansy shadow** layers:

    a. Activate the **pansy** layer.

    b. **Shift + click** the **pansy shadow** layer to select it as well.

    c. Choose **Layer > New > Group from Layers** to make a new group that contains the **pansy** and **pansy shadow** layers.

    d. When the **New Group from Layers** dialog box appears, type "**pansy**" into the **Name** box and click **OK**.

    e. Check the **Layers** panel. It contains a new group that contains the pansy and pansy shadow layers.

    f. With the pansy group active, use the **Move Tool** to drag the group up and right a little into the corner, so that the big black shadow in the corner is less obvious.

7. Beginning at the bottom of the **Layers** panel, click the **Show/Hide** button for each hidden layer to make all the layers visible.

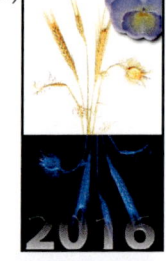

Tutorial 4: Layers

8. Hide the **gradient** layer because it obscures all the other layers.

9. Save the document.

Layer Options

The top of the **Layers** panel has controls that allow you to customize how layers can be edited, and how they interact with one another. We will just cover a few of those controls now, and some of the others as the course continues.

Layer Blend Modes

Layers can interact with those beneath them in special ways called **BLEND MODES**. Blend modes use mathematical formulas to blend the pixels on the active layer with layers underneath it to provide a variety of special effects. Because there are so many blend modes (27) and because many of the names are not very descriptive, it can be quite hard to visualize what will happen when you apply a specific blend mode. To help visualize them, blend modes are grouped on the blend mode menu by their general results. Each layer's blend mode is responsible for the way that its pixels blend with underlying pixels in the document.

> When dealing with blend modes, there are three terms to know: Base color, Blend color, and Result color.
>
> The **Blend color** is the color displayed in the active layer when you view it all by itself — the **Gradient Fill 1** layer here.

The **Base color** is the sum of all the visible colors in the layers beneath the active layer: the **beach** and **Background** layers here.

The **Result color** appears in the document window after combining the Blend and Base colors (or layers).

Guided Exercise 4.3: Layer Experimentation 1

Here you will change layer stacking order, opacity, and blend mode settings to see how they affect your image. (These screen shots use various years; yours may have a different year.)

1. Open **layers.psd** if it is not already open.

2. Experiment with layer opacity:

   a. Show the **gradient** layer at the top of the **Layers** panel. It obscures all the other layers because it is at the top of the layers stack.

   b. Click the **opacity** box to reveal its slider, and drag the slider to about **50% Opacity**. Now you partially see the obscured layers, but everything looks hazy.

3. Experiment with layer position:

   a. Return the **gradient** layer to **100% Opacity**.

   b. Position the pointer to the right of the **gradient** name on its layer.

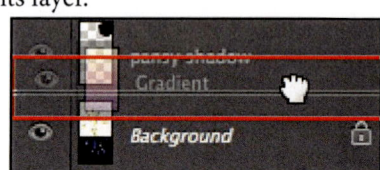

   c. Drag the **gradient** layer down onto the dividing line between the **Background** and the **pansy shadow** layers and release the pointer.

   It appears partially transparent until you release the pointer. Now all the layers except for the **Background** appear at full opacity and the gradient hides the **Background** layer.

4. Experiment with **Multiply** blend mode:

   a. Click the arrow to the right of **Normal** to reveal the **Blend Mode** menu, and choose **Multiply**. **Multiply** darkens the results along a curve, displaying the darker of the blend and base color.

   A color multiplied by white does not change, a color multiplied by black stays black.

   The left version shows the **gradient** layer at **100%** opacity, in **Multiply** blend mode, just above the **Background** layer. The right version shows the **gradient** layer, moved to the top of the stack of layers.

   b. Drag the **gradient** layer back to the top of the **Layers** panel, one layer at a time, and notice how the results change in the document window.

Tutorial 4: Layers

5. Experiment with some other blend modes:

Screen is the opposite of **Multiply**, and lightens colors along a curve. Colors screened with white become white while colors screened with black keep their color value.		**Overlay** either multiplies or screens pixels, depending on the base color. **Overlay** tends to affect midtones, leaving highlights and shadows unchanged.	
Difference gives the absolute value (mathematically) of the difference between each pixel, providing interesting, but often unpredictable colors.		**Color** treats the base as if it were a grayscale document, and applies the blend color as a wash on the image, preserving image detail.	

7. End up with **Multiply** blend mode, and drag the **gradient** layer back to just above the **Background**.

8. Activate the **leaf** layer, and change its blend mode to **Difference**. Only the leaf parts of the document change color, and the transparent regions do not change.

9. Experiment with **Dissolve** blend mode:

    a. Activate the **sun** layer, and zoom in to **100%**.

    b. Navigate so that you can see the sun in your document window.

    c. Change the blend mode of the **sun** layer to **Dissolve**. Notice that if you look very carefully, the edges of the sun become ever so slightly rough.

    d. Gradually lower the opacity of the **sun** layer, and watch how the sun changes.

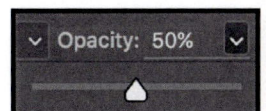

    Dissolve blend mode makes certain pixels of the layer dissolve, or disappear. As the opacity becomes lower, more of the layer dissolves. At **100% Opacity**, only the edges soften; random pixels drop out as the layer becomes more transparent. At **50% Opacity,** shown here, only 50% of the pixels on the layer are visible..

Tutorial 4: Layers   Page 87

10. Save your image, and leave it open for the next guided exercise.

Shortcut to Preview Blend Modes

You can cycle through the blend modes easily and preview them on screen by using **Shift** and the **+** (plus) or **-** (minus) keys. *To use this trick, you cannot have the blend mode menu showing, or the current mode highlighted.*

NOTE: If you have chosen a tool which has blend mode settings in the **Options** Bar, such as the **Brush Tool**, the **Shift +** shortcut will change the mode for the tool and not the layer. The shortcut will also work in some dialog boxes that use blend modes such as for layer styles or filters.

The Pass Through Blend Mode

Layer groups by default use a special blend mode called **Pass Through**. This blend mode allows all the layers within a group behave as if they were not in a group. If you assign a blend mode other than **Pass Through** to a layer group, that blend mode interacts with the settings of any individual layers in the group. You will experiment with **Pass Through** later in this tutorial.

Layer Locking

Photoshop provides five different ways to protect the contents of layers or layer groups. You can fully or partially **LOCK** layers to protect their contents.

A solid padlock to the right of the layer name indicates an entirely locked layer; a clear padlock indicates a partially locked layer. Layers must be visible in order to change their **Lock** options.

From left to right:

Lock transparent pixels (A) prevents you from changing pixel transparency. When transparency is locked, you can only paint on filled pixels, not transparent ones. You also can not delete pixels to make them transparent.

Lock image pixels (B) prevents you from changing layer pixels. When this is on, you cannot paint, erase, or apply a filter. However, you can still transform or move the entire layer.

Lock position (C) prevents you from moving a layer's contents using the **Move Tool**.

Prevent Auto-Nesting of Artboards (D) is an advanced feature which will not be discussed in this book.

Lock all (E) locks the transparency, image, position, layer styles, and blend mode of the active layer.

The **Background** layer is always locked for **Transparency** and **Position**; it cannot be **Image** locked.

GUIDED EXERCISE 4.4: LOCKING LAYERS

In this quick guided exercise you will work with the various kinds of layer locking settings.

1. Open **layers.psd** if it is not already open.

2. Activate the **leaf** layer.

3. Use transparency locking:

    a. Click the left lock option to lock the layer for transparency.

    b. Notice the clear padlock on the right side of the layer, indicating partial transparency.

    c. Sample a bright red swatch to change the **Foreground** color to red.

    d. Choose the **Brush Tool**, with a brush tip of **65 pixels**.

    e. Paint some diagonal strokes across the image.

    Notice that they only appear on the leaf itself, and because the leaf is set to **Difference** blend mode, the strokes are two tone: turquoise on the top of the leaf, and red on the bottom.

4. Display the **History** panel to step back in history to just before you used the **Brush Tool**.

5. Use **Lock image pixels**:

    a. Be sure **Transparency** locking is off. Locking is not recorded in **History** since locking does not alter image pixels.

    b. Click the **Lock image pixels** button, the one that looks like a brush.

    c. Attempt to paint on the **leaf** layer.
    You will see a null cursor as you move across the image, and a warning dialog box, if you try to paint.

    d. Click **OK**, and then click the **Lock Image** button to turn it off.

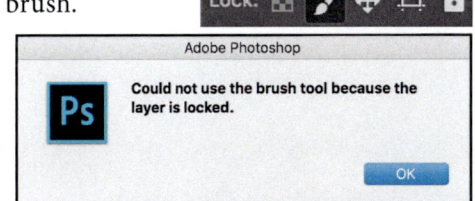

6. Use **Lock Position**:

    a. Click the **Lock Position** button.

    b. Choose the **Move Tool** and be sure **Auto-Select** is not checked in the **Options** Bar.

    c. Attempt to move the **leaf** layer. As before, you will be warned that you cannot move the layer because the layer is locked.

    d. Click **OK**, and then click the **Lock Position** button to turn it off.

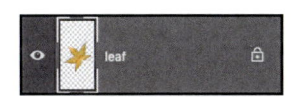

7. If you want, try the **Lock All** option. It displays the solid black lock and will not let you change the layer at all.

8. Turn off **Lock All** and leave the document open for the next guided exercise.

....

LAYER STYLES

Photoshop provides a number of special effects called **LAYER STYLES** that you can add to most layers except for the **Background** layer.

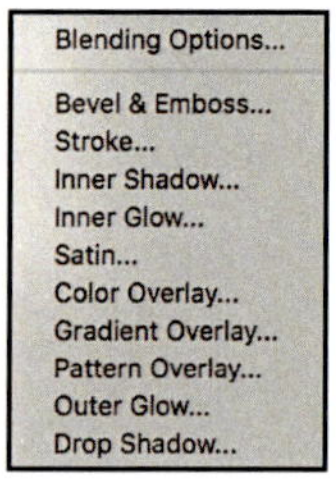

You can see the menu of these effects when you press the **Add a layer style** (**fx**) button at the bottom of the **Layers** panel. When you choose one of the styles from the menu, it opens the **Layer Styles** dialog box so that you can configure and apply one or more styles to the active layer. That style is then added to the layer in the **Layers** panel, so that you can view the style, hide it, or change its settings.

Most **Layer Styles** apply at the transition between opaque and transparent pixels, and have little if any effect on layers lacking transparent pixels such as the **gradient** layer.

The layer style samples that follow show a **sun** layer on top of a neutral gray layer and use the default settings for each layer style.

Drop Shadow adds a shadow that falls behind the contents on the layer to make the image look three dimensional. 	**Inner Shadow** adds a shadow that falls just inside the edges of the layer contents to give the layer a recessed appearance. 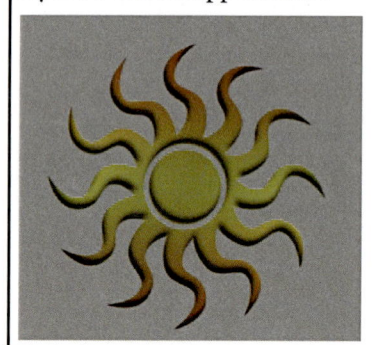	**Outer Glow** adds a glow that extends from the outside of the layer contents. 

Tutorial 4: Layers　　　　　　　　　　　　　　　　　　　　　　　　　　　　　　　　Page 90

Inner Glow adds a glow that goes from the inside edges of the layer contents.	**Bevel and Emboss** adds various combinations of highlights and shadows to a layer.	**Satin** shades the layer interior to react to the shape of the layer, typically creating a satiny finish.
Color Overlay superimposes a color (black here) on a layer.	**Gradient Overlay** superimposes a gradient on a layer.	**Pattern Overlay** superimposes a pattern on a layer.
Stroke outlines the object on the current layer using color, a gradient, or a pattern.	The real power of layer styles is the ability to configure them as you choose. Each of these suns were made by tweaking the settings for the **Bevel and Emboss** effect:	

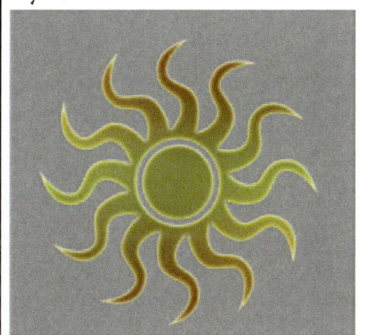

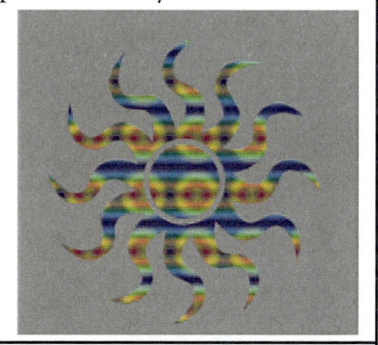

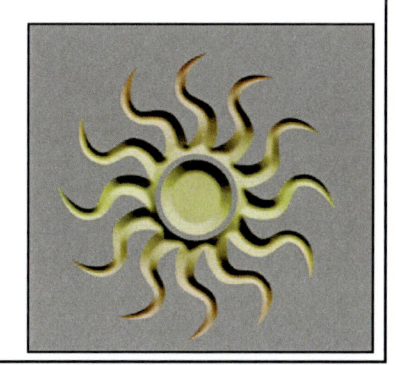

New in Photoshop CC 2015, you can add multiple instances of Stroke, Inner Shadow, Color Overlay, Gradient Overlay, or Drop Shadow to a single layer. Here is in example of the sun with the following effects applied:

- A 4-pixel green stroke along the outside of the layer.
- A 2-pixel blue stroke also along the outside of the layer.
- Two different drop shadows, each in a different direction.

THE STYLES PANEL

In addition to making your own layer style by applying one or more effects to a layer, the **Styles** panel, grouped with the Libraries and Adjustments panels, lets you apply premade styles to layers. Each of the predefined styles is made up of one or more layer effects.

TO APPLY A STYLE TO A LAYER, OR TO EVERY LAYER IN A GROUP:

1. Activate the layer or group.
2. Click a style button in the **Styles** panel. Each button applies the previewed style to the active layer.

If you activate more than one layer in the **Layers** panel, you can then click a style button to apply the style to all the active layers. Remember, you cannot apply a style to the **Background** layer.

Often you don't know exactly what the premade styles will do. That's OK. Each time you click on a different style button, you apply that style and remove the previous one.

To remove all effects from a layer or group, click the **No Style** swatch in the upper left corner of the **Styles** panel. It has a white background to distinguish it from the other styles.

EXPANDING AND CONTRACTING THE EFFECTS LIST

Within the **Layers** panel, you can click the triangle next to the **fx** symbol on the right side of an individual layer to toggle between viewing the style **Compressed** (arrow down) to save space on the **Layers** panel, or **Expanded** (arrow up) to list all the effects that make up that style. (Note that the arrows are reversed everywhere else in the Photoshop interface... Did some programmer mess up here?)

TURNING STYLES AND EFFECTS ON AND OFF

Sometimes you can't decide if you like a style or not, or if you like only some of its effects. The **Layers** panel lets you show and hide entire styles or individual effects just like entire layers by clicking the eye for an individual effect (**Bevel & Emboss** here) or for an entire style.

Tutorial 4: Layers   Page 92

Editing Styles

After you apply a style, you may decide you want to change it. Here, a ready-made style called **Chiseled Sky** has been applied to the sun layer. This layer style consists of two effects, **Bevel and Emboss** along with a **Gradient Overlay**. If you like an effect, but you want to change its options, double click the individual effect, such as **Bevel & Emboss**, to open the **Layer Style** dialog box with those settings chosen for you to modify.

Opacity and Fill

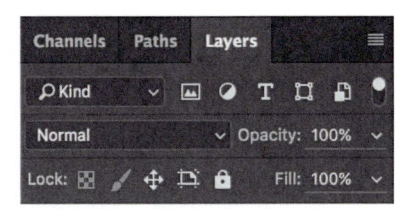

Near the top of the **Layers** panel are the **Opacity** and **Fill** settings.

Opacity controls layer transparency, from **0%** (invisible) to **100%** (solid). Adjusting **Opacity** determines the opacity of both the document pixels and any layer style applied to that layer. When you click the triangle to the right of the percentage, you show a slider that lets you drag to adjust opacity visually. Alternately, if you know the opacity value you want, you can type that percentage into the **Opacity** box. When you are done, press **return** or **enter**, or click the document window to accept the new opacity.

Fill controls the opacity of the pixels on a layer without affecting its layer style. Reducing **Fill** to **0%** is effective for creating special effects on photos. With the **Fill** set to **0%** on a text layer, the colored pixels on the layer are hidden but its layer style remains at full strength.

On Your Own

Here is your chance to play with all these fun layer style settings.

Partially Guided Exercise 4.5: Working with Layer Styles

1. Open **04-styles.psd**. This document contains two layers, a neutral gray **Background** layer, and the **sun** on its own layer.

2. Activate the **sun** layer, as you cannot apply layer styles to the **Background** layer.

3. Click the **Add a layer style** button at the bottom of the **Layers** panel and choose **Drop Shadow** from the **Layer Style** menu to open the **Layer Style** dialog box and display its **Drop Shadow** settings.

    A **DROP SHADOW** is a strategically placed shadow that makes an image look three-dimensional, as if it is being lifted off the page.

Tutorial 4: Layers   Page 93

4. Adjust the **Drop Shadow** settings:

   a. Move the huge **Layer Style** dialog box to the right side of your screen as best you can, so that you can preview your settings in the document window as you work.

   b. Drag the **Spread** and **Size** sliders to the right to increase each of them, so that the drop shadow becomes larger and softer.

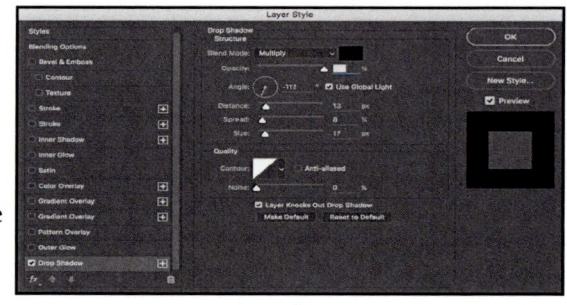

   c. Instead of working with the **Angle** and **Distance** settings, drag the shadow right inside the document window, to position it where you want it. As you drag, the **Angle** and **Distance** values update in the **Layer Style** box.

   d. Play with other settings. We also changed the shadow's color from black to purple.

   e. Click **OK** to add the drop shadow to your active layer.

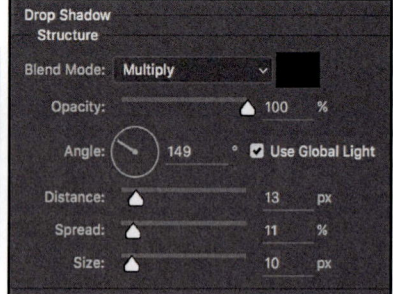

5. Observe the **Layers** panel.

   It has two components under the **sun** layer itself. The top one, **Effects**, indicates that at least one layer style has been added to the layer. The bottom one, **Drop Shadow**, shows the kind of layer style that has been added.

   Each component has a hide/show area, with the eye visible, to the left of its name. You can turn off the visibility of individual effects, or the entire group of them, by clicking to open or close the eye. You can also double click a specific style to reopen its dialog box and change its settings.

6. Add a second layer effect to the same layer:

   a. Double-click the **Effects** label in the **Layers** panel. It will open the **Layer Style** dialog box, with a bunch of advanced settings we will not cover here.

   b. Click the check box to the left of **Inner Glow**, on the left side of the dialog box.

   Notice that the inner glow of light yellow appears in the document window, but you do not see any **Inner Glow** settings within the dialog box.

   c. Now click the words **Inner Glow**, on the left side of the dialog box.

   When you click the name of a layer style, instead of just clicking its check box, the settings for that layer style appear for you to change them.

7. Experiment with the **Contour** settings, under **Quality** towards the bottom of the dialog box.

    a. Click the arrow to the right of the **Contour** thumbnail to try out different sculptural shapes with which to apply the glow.

    b. Change other settings as well, until you have a pleasing inner glow.

    c. If you dislike your settings, click **Cancel**, and try again.

8. Play around with some of the other layer styles, to get a better understanding of how they work. The possibilities are endless.

9. Click **OK** to close the **Layer Styles** dialog box.

10. Use the **Styles** panel to quickly apply ready-made layer styles:

    a. Click the **No Style** swatch in the upper left corner of the **Styles** panel to strip off any applied styles.

    b. Click on different style swatches to see how they affect your document.

    Each time you choose a swatch, it begins by removing the old style, and then adds the new one.

    c. As you change styles, examine the **Effects** list in the **Layers** panel.

    d. Turn individual styles on and off to see how they change your image. Here we began with a **Style** swatch, and then added our own inner glow and drop shadow to it.

More Layers Practice

Return to the **layers.psd** document you probably still have open in Photoshop. Choose **File > Save As** and save the document under a new name as **layers–play.psd** in the location of your choice. Now adjust blend modes and layer styles until you are happy with your results. Save and print, if desired. It is a relatively small file and will print out at about 3 x 6 inches, at 300 ppi.

Resources and Videos

http://www.practical-photoshop.com/pages/CC2015-pp1-resources.html#04

Practical Photoshop CC 2015, Level 1
Tutorial 5: Layer Case Studies

Layers are essential for building **COMPOSITE IMAGES**, collages that combine two or more images into a new image. When you build your own image, instead of one where you are guided step by step, it can be difficult to know where to start.

One approach is to find an image you like and see if it gives you any ideas for another image. Both the second image we will build in this tutorial, and the one we developed for Tutorial 4, were highly influenced by a sample file that Adobe included with an early version of Photoshop in 1995.

In Tutorial 5 you will complete three complex documents that give you an opportunity to practice and apply your growing selection and layer manipulation skills.

> **Case Study 1** shows you how to build a composite image entirely from **Type** layers.
>
> **Case Study 2** is based on the Photoshop 1995 image shown here.
>
> **Case Study 3** demonstrates a complicated layered document using the tool-critter starting file we used in Tutorial 3 . Not only does this case study emphasize the benefits of layered documents over working on a single layer, but **Case Study 3** also serves as a guide for you to develop your own critter creations.

You will then experiment with different compositions, and use the **History** panel to make decisions about which of your experiments are more effective, and to **save** your favorite document versions as distinct files.

As you build your composite images, you will add **Type** layers to your repertoire:.

Objectives

- Use the **File > New** command to set up blank Photoshop documents.
- Identify the special characteristics of a **Type** layer.
- Create, edit, and format **Type** layers.
- Build composite images by combining layers from multiple sources.
- Use the **History** panel to compare states, make snapshots, and create documents from **History** states.
- Use **Layer Groups** effectively for **Layers** panel organization.
- Experiment with layer blend modes, opacity, fill, and stacking order.
- Create a document by using a template layer.

Case Study 1: Type Tools and Type Layers

Photoshop uses the fonts installed in your operating system to create clear, crisp, and scalable type.

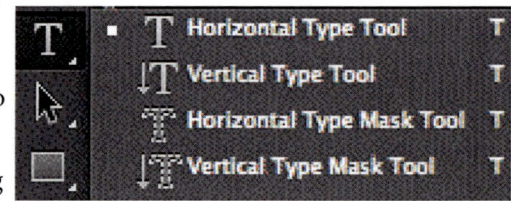

The **TYPE TOOLS** create type by placing lines or blocks of type onto **Type** layers. You can also use the **Type** tools to edit existing **Type** layers to change their fonts, type size, etc. without losing their scaling capabilities.

The **Horizontal Type Tool** is the only **Type** tool we will cover in this tutorial.

Guided Exercise 5.1: Make Type Layers

In this guided exercise you will make a new Photoshop document and add some **Type** layers to it.

1. Reset the **Essentials** workspace, all tools, and the default **Foreground** and **Background** colors.

2. Make a new blank Photoshop document with these settings:

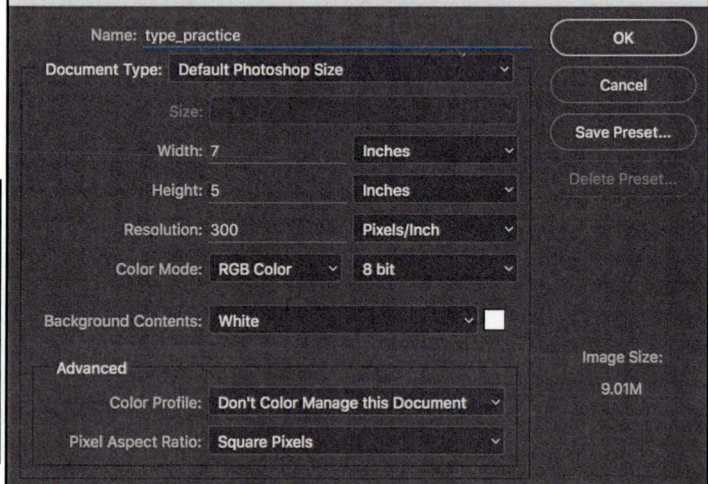

    a. Choose **File > New** to open the **New** dialog box.

    b. Choose **Default Photoshop Size** from the **Document Type** menu.

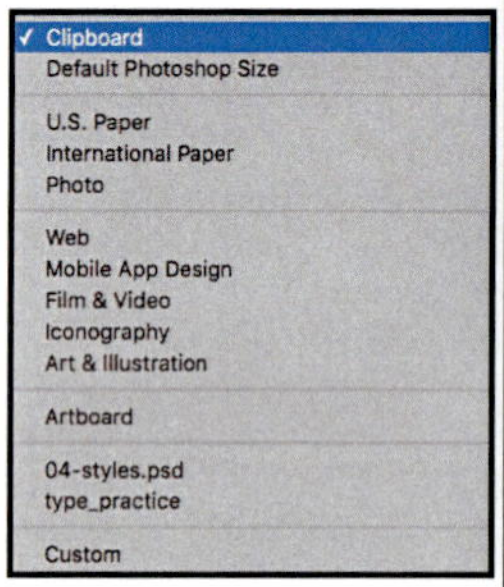

    The **Document Type** menu provides a list of commonly-used Photoshop documents. **Default Photoshop Size** makes an RGB color document, 7 x 5 inches if printed, with a resolution of 300 ppi, and a white background. These settings are perfect for our type experimentation. No matter what the resolution of the document, type layers print at the resolution the printer is capable of. You only need to worry about higher resolutions when printing photographs and other images with a lot of pixel detail.

    c. Enter **type_practice** into the **Name** box and click **OK**.

    As the tab at the top of the image shows, entering a name will label the document tab when you view the document in Photoshop even before you save it. If you don't enter a name, the tab will use a placeholder name such as **Untitled-1**.

Tutoria 5: Layer Case Studies

Page 98

3. Make a new **Type** layer:

   a. Choose the **Horizontal Type Tool**.

   b. Click on the document approximately where you want the text to start. You will see a blinking insertion point, just like in a word processing document.

   c. Type the name of a favorite pet. If you have never had a pet, then make up a name for your fantasy pet.

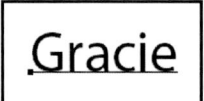

   d. As you type, notice the line under the text. It indicates that the text is active for editing.

   e. Click the **Commit** button, the check mark on the right side of the **Options** bar, to commit your text. The underlining vanishes.

   You must commit your text before Photoshop will let you do anything except for text editing or formatting. The **Cancel** button to the left of the **Commit** button allows you to stop making a **Type** layer, or to void any edits you were trying out.

   Keyboard shortcuts are faster for type creation and editing than clicking on screen buttons since your hands are on the keyboard already. The **Enter** key on the number pad commits your **Type** layer, and the **Esc** key cancels it.

4. Locate your **Type** layer in the **Layers** panel.

   When you use a type tool, you create a special layer called a **TYPE LAYER**. **Type** layers can be identified in the **Layers** panel by a large T on the layer thumbnail. Each **Type** layer will be automatically named with the first few words of the type in that layer.

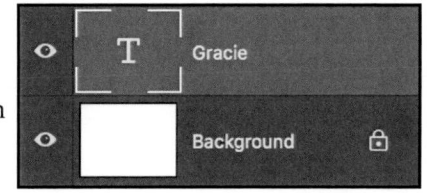

   Type layers can be formatted, moved, re-stacked, or transformed. They can also be included in layer groups and enhanced with layer styles. A **Type** layer cannot have filters applied to it or be transformed with the **Edit > Perspective** or **Edit > Distort** commands without first either **rasterizing** the layer (converting the **Type** layer to a standard or pixel layer) or turning it into a smart object (a later tutorial).

   This first **Type** layer is what is known as **POINT TYPE** because you just "point" at where you want the type to start, click, and type away. All the type stays on one line unless you press **return** or **enter** to move the cursor down to the next line. Since we are **Type** tool beginners, we are only going to work with single words and short phrases, so we won't use the other kind of type, **PARAGRAPH TYPE**.

5. Following step 2 above, make three more **Type** layers, each with individual words that describe your pet.

   In the **Layers** panel, each new type layer appears above the previous one.

6. If you don't like the location of any of your **Type** layers you can use the **Move Tool** to reposition them.

7. Remember that you must activate a layer in the **Layers** panel before you can move it.

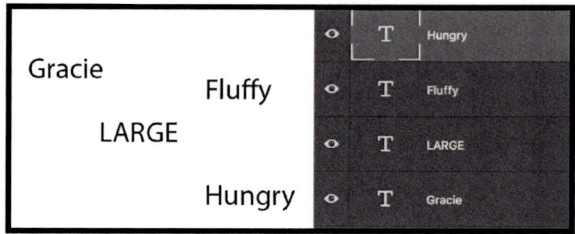

8. Save your document in the location of your choice as **type_practice.psd** and leave it open for the next guided exercise. The **PSD** (Photoshop document) format preserves the editability of the **Type** layers.

. . . .

Editing Type Layers

In principle, to edit an existing **Type** layer, you should be able to simply choose the appropriate type tool and click on the type you wish to edit. The problem is that if you don't click either directly on or very near the existing type, you will create a new blank **Type** layer instead of placing an insertion point or highlight into an existing layer. The **Layers** panel will show an extra, empty type layer when this happens.

If you have trouble clicking the correct spot, here is a workaround:

1. Double-click the **T** thumbnail in the **Layers** panel to simultaneously activate the **Type** tool and to select all the type on that layer. The **Type** layer is now active and available for editing until you **Commit** or **Cancel** it.

2. Now that you can see the type, either drag to highlight only the area you wish to retype or delete, or click to place an insertion point where you wish to add type to the layer.

3. To divide one line of text into two, place the insertion point at the division point and press **return** (Mac) or **enter** (Win).

4. **Commit** your changes.

. . . .

Formatting Type Layers

You can set basic text formatting directly from the **Options** bar, shown here with its default settings.

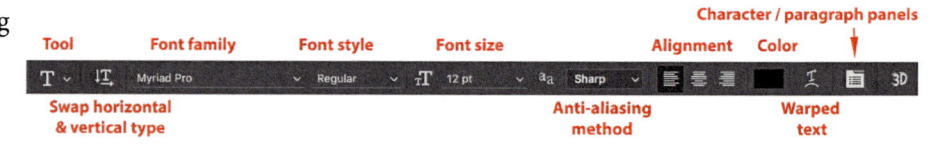

If you have a Type layer active, any changes you make will effect all the type on that layer. To change only specific text on a Type layer, highlight the desired text first. Some Options bar settings have buttons and others have drop down menus to choose from.

Font family lets you choose the font you want from the drop-down menu of the fonts that are installed and active on the computer you are using. Each font has a font sample to the right of its name to help make a font choice.

The currently chosen font is highlighted in the list. Some font families have multiple versions of that font called **FONT STYLES**. Click on the arrow to the left of the font name to see the different styles within a family. Here you can see some of the font styles for the **Myriad Pro** font family. Font style choices vary, depending on which font you have chosen.

Font size determines how big the type will be in points — with 72 points to each inch. For reference, the body type for these tutorials is 11 points in size.

Alignment determines if your lines of type will be **left aligned**, **right aligned**, or **centered**. The text in this paragraph is left-aligned.

The text **color** sample shows the current text color. To change it, click the **Color** box, and choose the color you want from the **Color Picker**. You can select (highlight) individual characters or words in a text layer and give them each of them a different color.

Type Layer Options and Use

Once created, you can work with a **Type** layer like a standard pixel layer by changing its stacking order, opacity, fill, layer style, or blend mode. If you merge a type layer with another layer, or flatten a document that contains a type layer, the type will no longer be independently editable, and the type will become fused pixels at the resolution of the overall document. ***For best printing results, avoid merging or flattening your Type layers.***

WARNING: **Type** layers need the font that created them installed on the computer that opens the file. If you move a document with a **Type** layer from one computer to another, you may not be able to view the document as created. Photoshop will warn you if this happens, and let you choose alternate fonts.

Partially Guided Exercise 5.2: Edit and Format Type Layers

In this guided exercise, you will edit and format the **Type** layers you just made. Remember, our text is just an example; you will write about your own pet.

1. After your pet's name, add a brief description:

    a. In the **Layers** panel, locate the layer that contains the name of your pet.

    b. Double-click the **T** thumbnail for that layer to simultaneously activate that layer, choose the **Horizontal Type Tool**, and highlight all the text on that layer.

c. Press the right arrow key to set the insertion point at the end of your pet's name, and then type a short phrase about your pet. Try to keep the phrase all on one line, within the boundaries of the document.

d. Commit the changes.

Notice that your **Layers panel** has updated the name of the layer with as much of your description as will fit on the Layers panel.

Also examine the **Status** bar to check your document's size. Unlike pixel layers, **Type** layers do not increase the size of the file — and sometimes strange Adobe math even shows a smaller right number, like here.

2. If desired, edit one or more of the descriptions of your pet.

3. Format your pet's name:

   a. In the **Layers** panel, locate the layer that contains the name of your pet.

   b. Double-click the **T** thumbnail for that layer to simultaneously activate that layer, choose the **Horizontal Type Tool**, and highlight all the text on that layer.

   c. Move the pointer over your pet's name. When you are in the correct position, the pointer will become an I-beam.

   d. Double click to highlight only the single word that is your pet's name.

   e. Use the **Options** bar settings to change the font family, possibly the font style, and the font size of the selected text.

   We used **Hobo Std**, **30 pt**. The type style, **Medium**, is grayed out because it is the only type style installed for this font.

   f. Select the descriptive phrase and format it differently from your pet's name.

   We formatted our type one step further by highlighting just the colon, and decreasing its size, because punctuation is less important than the name.

4. Format your other **Type** layers as desired, and use the **Move Tool** to rearrange them. Be experimental.

5. Add layer styles to each of your type layers. Remember that you can only apply a layer style to the entire layer, and not to individual words or characters.

Tutoria 5: Layer Case Studies   Page 102

6. Examine the **Status** bar. When you format your type, and add layer styles, it does increase the size of the file, but not as much as using pixel layers. Your numbers will be different than ours because you used different text and layer styles.

7. Save your document and print if desired. If you need to **Save for Web**, it will probably be smaller than 90 K because of all the white background.

Case Study 2: Build a Composite Image

Here you will learn how easy it is to combine images from different documents into a composite image. Photoshop's layer blend modes, opacity and fill settings, and layer styles easily add to the creative process.

Guided Exercise 5.3: Combine Three Images

Case Study 2 begins with a design based on the sample file, but then veers off in its own direction.

1. Open **05-beach.jpg** and save it as **layers_fun.psd** in the location of your choice.

2. Reset the **Essentials** workspace, all tools, and the default foreground and background colors.

3. Use layers and blend modes to give the image a light top and dark bottom, similar to the Adobe example:

   a. With the **Rectangular Marquee Tool**, select the bottom half of the image. The blue line you can see on your image is a non-printing **GUIDE LINE** drawn across the center of the image. It is there to help you make a precise selection.

   b. With the **Background** layer active, choose **Layer > New > Layer Via Copy** (**Command + J** for Mac or **Ctrl + J** for Windows).

   c. Name the new layer **bottom** and change its blending mode from the default **Normal** to **Multiply** to darken the bottom of the image.

   d. With the **Rectangular Marquee Tool**, select the top half of the image.

   e. With the Background layer active, choose **Layer > New > Layer Via Copy** (**Command + J** Mac or **Ctrl + J** Win) and name the new layer **top**.

   f. Change the blending mode of the **top** layer to **Screen** to lighten the top part of the document.

   g. Reduce the opacity of the **top** layer to around **40%** so it is not quite so washed out.

   h. Save your document but do not close the file.

Tutorial 5: Layer Case Studies   Page 103

4. Examine the **Status** bar to check how big your document became by adding the two extra layers. Opened in Photoshop, it has increased from **9.8 M** to over **28 M**.

5. Choose **Flatten Image** from near the bottom of the **Layers** panel menu to combine the three image layers into a single **Background** layer.

    FLATTENING an image to a single **Background** layer is a good technique for saving on RAM and storage, but only when you are *absolutely sure* you will not need to reposition any of the layers or slip another layer in between one of the layers and the **Background** layer. When the layers are flattened, you lose all these capabilities.

6. Import a sunflower from another image to become a sun in the sky with its reflection in the water:

    a. Open **SunflowerDone.psd** that you made in Tutorial 3.

    b. Select the sunflower on its layer by **Command** (Mac) or **Ctrl** (Win) clicking on the layer thumbnail.

    c. Open the **Refine Edge** dialog box or the **Select and Mask** workspace and tweak the edge settings to give a slight softening to the edge.

    Here are the settings we used:

    d. Check the edge on both the white and black preview to be sure you don't have an edge halo, set **Output** to **Selection**, and click **OK**.

    e. Choose **Edit > Copy** to copy the sunflower selection, activate the **layers_fun.psd** document window, and choose **Edit > Paste**.

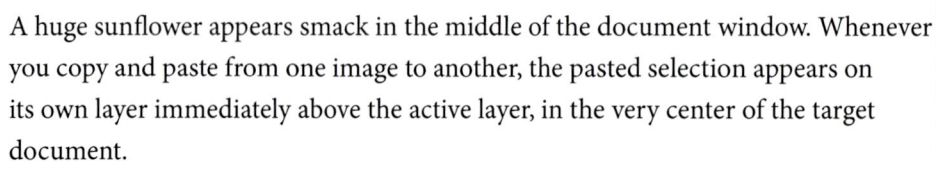

    A huge sunflower appears smack in the middle of the document window. Whenever you copy and paste from one image to another, the pasted selection appears on its own layer immediately above the active layer, in the very center of the target document.

    NOTE: the sunflower is very large because that image is higher resolution than the beach image.

    f. Close **SunflowerDone.psd**.

    Only keep the images you currently need open in Photoshop as each open image uses your computer's RAM.

    g. Rename the sunflower layer **sun**, and save **layers_fun.psd**.

    NOTE: *We won't continue to remind you, but you should save every few steps as you proceed.*

h. With the **sun** layer active, choose **Edit > Transform > Scale**, resize the sunflower to **50%** of its original size, and move it to the upper left corner of the sky, as shown here.

i. Change the blend mode of the **sun** layer to **Overlay** and lower its **Opacity** to **85%** to make it blend better with the sky.

j. Duplicate the **sun** layer, (**Layer > Duplicate Layer**), rename the layer **reflection**, and move it to the lower right quadrant of the image.

k. Lower the **Opacity** of the **reflection** layer to **50%** so that it looks like the reflection of the original sunflower.

7. Conserve your computer's RAM.

    Whenever you copy and paste, the copied item is placed in that special area of your computer's RAM called the **CLIPBOARD**. When you copy from a large document, especially if your computer does not have very much total RAM, or if you have several applications open, it is a good idea to purge the **Clipboard** to free up RAM. Try it:

    a. Choose **Edit > Purge > Clipboard**.
        Be careful not to choose **All** or you will also clear out your **History** states.

    b. Click **OK** when warned that "This cannot be undone."

8. Add a **Type** layer:

    a. Change your foreground color to white.

    b. Choose the **Horizontal Type Tool**.

    c. Click the left side of the document to set your insertion point.

    d. Type **Fun with Layers** and commit the type.

    e. Format the type layer, and position it so that it rests on the guide in the center of the document. We used **Arial Black**, a simple thick font.

9. Transform the **Type** layer to make it large enough to stretch across most of the horizon:

    a. Choose **Edit > Free Transform**.

    b. Drag the bounding box handles so that the type stretches across the full width of the document, and make the type taller if desired.

    c. Commit the transformation.

Tutorial 5: Layer Case Studies   Page 105

Notice that your **Type** layer is still a **Type** layer. You can stretch or shrink a **Type** layer without losing its editability.

10. Change layer options for the **Fun with Layers** type layer:

    a. Add a **Bevel and Emboss** layer effect of your choice to it. Here are the settings we used.

    b. Lower the **Fill** of the **Fun with Layers** layer to **20%** so that the white letters are almost transparent but the **Bevel and Emboss** layer style remains fully visible.

11. Give the **Fun with Layers** type layer a reflection:

    a. Duplicate the **Fun with Layers** layer, and choose **Edit > Transform > Flip Vertical**.

    b. Move the **Fun with Layers copy** layer beneath **Fun with Layers**, and lower its **Opacity** to **25%**, and its **Fill** to **0%** so the layer looks more like a reflection.

    c. Choose **View > Clear Guides** to remove the guide because you no longer need it.

12. Import and position an image into your document without using the Clipboard. This technique may seem a little tricker at first, but it conserves precious RAM.

    a. Open **05-branches.jpg**. It opens with its tab alongside the **layers_fun.psd** tab.

    b. Choose **Window > Arrange> 2-up Vertical** to arrange your two open documents, **layers_fun.psd** and **05-branches.jpg** next to each other.

    c. Click the **05-branches.jpg** tab to be sure it is the active document.

    d. Choose the **Move Tool**, press and hold the **Shift** key, and drag the **05-branches.jpg** **Background** layer (from the **Layers** panel) on top of the **layers_fun.psd** window.

    e. Release first the mouse button and then the **Shift** key to copy the branches into the center of the **layers-fun.psd** window.

    f. Rename the new layer **branches**, drag it to the top of the **Layers** panel, and change its blend mode to **Overlay** so that the beach image shows through.

    g. Close **05-branches.jpg**.

13. Save your work and print the document if desired.

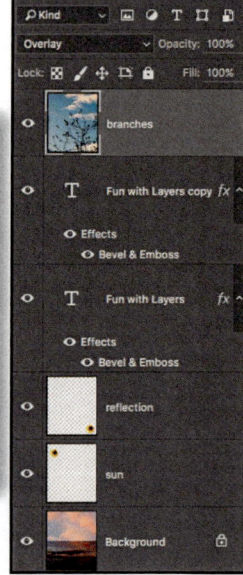

Tutoria 5: Layer Case Studies   Page 106

The History Panel Revisited

As you learned in Tutorial 1, the **History** panel records each change you make to your document as a **HISTORY STATE**. You can use these states to have better control over the various versions of your document.

At the bottom of the **History** panel are three buttons:

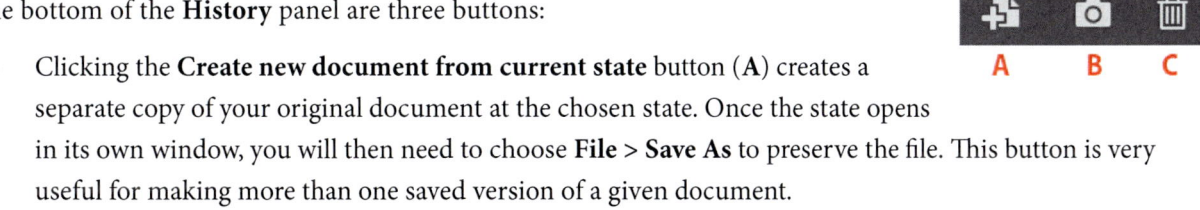

- Clicking the **Create new document from current state** button (**A**) creates a separate copy of your original document at the chosen state. Once the state opens in its own window, you will then need to choose **File > Save As** to preserve the file. This button is very useful for making more than one saved version of a given document.

- Clicking the **Create new snapshot** button (**B**) makes a named history state of the document, near the top of the **History** panel.

- Clicking the **Delete current state** button (**C**) removes either automatic states or snapshots from the **History** panel list, and from RAM.

Guided Exercise 5.4: Layer Stacking & Blending Experimentation

Here you will change layer stacking order and use the **History** panel to observe the variety of effects you can produce simply by changing the order of the layers in the **Layers** panel, or **LAYER STACKING ORDER**. Then you will use a keyboard shortcut to change layer blend modes to observe the variety of effects you can achieve.

1. With the **layers_fun.psd** document open, save it as **layers_funEX.psd** to preserve your previous project.

2. With **layers_funEX.psd** active, double-click the **Hand Tool** so that you can see the entire document in the window.

3. Use the **Dissolve** blend mode:

    a. Move the **branches** layer to the top of the **Layers** panel stacking order, if necessary, and change its blend mode to Normal.

    b. Change the **branches** layer blend mode to **Dissolve, 100% Opacity**. The document doesn't look very different because at **100% Opacity**, **Dissolve** blend mode is very, very subtle.

    c. Gradually lower the **branches** layer opacity. As you do so, parts of the layer drop out. End up at about **25% Opacity**.

4. Use keyboard shortcuts to quickly experiment with other layer blend modes:

    a. Activate the **Move Tool**, but don't move anything; the keyboard shortcut doesn't work if you have a painting tool chosen.

    b. Change the **branches** layer blend mode to **Normal**, 100% opacity.

Tutorial 5: Layer Case Studies

c. Press the **esc** key so that **Normal** blend mode is not highlighted. (Mac users will not see the highlight but you still need to begin by pressing **esc** or the next steps won't work.)

d. Press the **Shift** key, and keep it down as you press and release the **plus** key (+) and then release the **Shift** key to change the layer blend mode from **Normal** to **Dissolve**.

e. Press the **Shift** key, and keep it down as you repeatedly press and release the **plus** key (+).

Each time you press the **plus** key, the blend mode changes, to cycle through each blend mode in turn. This shortcut gives a quick way to view how the different blend modes affect your composition so you can choose the one you like the best—or take a snapshot of a few different versions for later comparison. If you like more than one version, you can save the different versions as separate files.

5. View the importance of layer stacking order:

a. Make sure the **branches** layer is at the top of the document, keeping it in the blend mode of your choice.

b. One layer at a time, drag the **branches** layer down until it is at the bottom of the stack, just above the **Background**.

c. Save your document and leave it open while you read about more uses for the **History** panel, and then finish the case study with the next guided exercise.

Guided Exercise 5.5: Use the History Panel to Select and Save States

1. Begin with **layers-fun.psd** open, and the **History** panel visible. (Choose **Window > History** if necessary.)

2. Use the **History** panel to compare layer blending for each position of the branches layer, to determine which position you like the best. Notice the subtle changes in the image colors as the layer order changes.

3. Make a snapshot of the position you like the best and name the snapshot **branches blending**.

4. Save and print as desired, and close all open documents.

Experiment On Your Own

The **05-play** folder contains other images that you can use to experiment with layer blending. Here are two examples:

Example 1: A single image with selections

1. Use the **Elliptical Marquee Tool** to select individual ovals and then copy those pixels onto layers.

2. Blend each oval layer with the **Background** using a different **Blend Mode**.

3. Experiment with layer **Opacity** (all **100%** here).

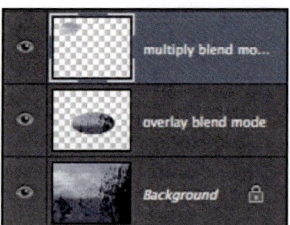

Example 2: Blending two images

1. The first image was divided into quadrants, and a copy of each quadrant was placed on its own layer and blended with the **Background** using different blend modes.

2. The leaf was brought in from another photo, placed on the top, and set to **Overlay** blend mode.

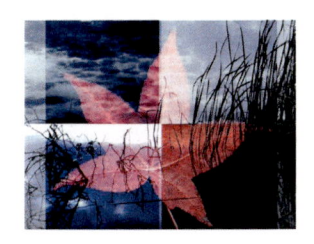

Case Study 3: Redo the Tool Critter with Layers

In the Selection Tutorial, you worked on just one layer with selection tools and the **Move Tool** to build a tool critter. Here you will build another tool critter, but this time you will use layers to compare and contrast the two approaches.

Working with layers is much more powerful, but that power comes with a cost—a much bigger, more complex document that of course uses more RAM.

Guided Exercise 5.6: Make a New Photoshop Document and Give It Critter Parts

As you recently learned, Photoshop comes pre-loaded with **New Document** templates that are perfectly set up to make high-quality printed documents. These templates are very handy if you know before you start how big you want your finished document to be. In this guided exercise you will start with an appropriately-sized blank document, and bring in layers to build your composition.

1. Reset the **Essentials** workspace, all tools, and the default **Foreground** and **Background** colors.

2. Set up the blank document:

    a. Within Photoshop, choose **File > New**.

    b. Type **my_critter** into the **Name** box.

    c. Choose **Photo** from the **Document Type** drop-down menu.

    The **Photo** preset changes the **Size** menu to list only common photographic print sizes. It also sets the **Resolution** to **300 pixels/inch**, the color mode to **RGB Color**, and the **Background Contents** to **White**.

    d. Choose **Landscape, 5 x 7** from the **Size** menu and click **OK.**

    e. Save **my_critter.psd** in the location of your choice.

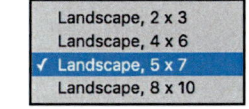

3. Individually select each of the "critter tools" you will need for this project and place each on its own layer:

    a. Open **03-toolcritter_start.jpg**. You now have 2 open documents.

b. Select the needed "critter tools" and copy each onto its own layer. Let's try a few different strategies so you can compare them. Begin with the **Copy/Paste** method:

   1) Use the **Quick Selection Tool** to select the saw blade.

   2) Examine the selection in the **Refine Edge** dialog box or **Select and Mask** workspace to be sure that the selection is nice and clean, and that you like the edge transition when previewed on both black and white backgrounds. Adjust as desired, choose **Output to Selection**, and click **OK**.

   3) Choose **Edit > Copy** or **Command/Ctrl + C** to place a copy of the selected area into the computer's Clipboard.

   4) Choose **Edit > Paste** or **Command/Ctrl + V** to add a new layer containing the selected area just above the active layer (the **Background** layer here).

   5) Rename the new layer **saw blade**.

   The **Copy/Paste** method is logical, but it takes two commands, and uses some of the computer's memory for the clipboard contents.

c. Contrast with the **Layer via Copy** method:

   1) Activate the **Background** layer because it is the one that contains the desired pixels.

   2) Select the blue Velcro tape roll, and give it a **Refine Edge** checkup.

   3) Choose **Layer > New > Layer via Copy**.

   These down-out-down menus can be hard to control. For frequently used commands, it is better to memorize and use keystrokes. Here you should use **Command + J** (Mac) or **Ctrl + J** (Win).

   4) Rename the layer **tape**.

   Layer via Copy is certainly easier than **Copy/Paste**, especially if you memorize the quick keystrokes, and it does not clog up your clipboard's memory either.

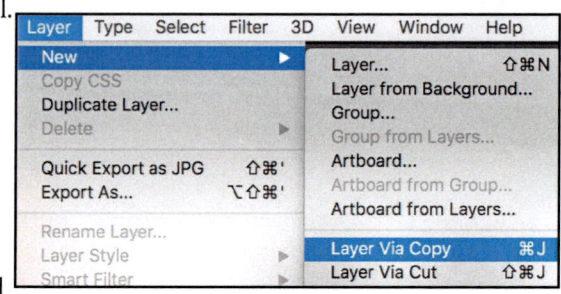

d. We will not use all the tools for this project. You will just need: **pliers, tool box, tape, putty knife, triangle, and saw blade**. As you work, remember that you will have to keep activating the **Background** layer because it is the one that has the original tool pixels.

   1) Activate the **Background** layer.

   2) Zoom in on the desired region and select with whichever selection tool will best grab as much of the desired region as possible, as quickly as possible.

In many cases, the **Quick Selection Tool** will work well, but you may need to add to or subtract from your selection until you get it to be precise. You will probably find that the **Polygonal Lasso Tool** is superior to any other tool for selecting the triangle. And, speaking of the triangle, don't forget to remove its "holes" from your selection.

3) Use **Refine Edge** or **Select and Mask** to preview and adjust each selection.

4) Copy each selection to its own layer using the technique you prefer, and name each layer descriptively. We recommend you use the same names we used to make the directions easier to follow.

5) Be sure that you have these six tool layers before continuing: **pliers**, **tool box**, **tape**, **putty knife**, **triangle**, and **saw blade**. They do not need to be in this order.

4. Combine the individual tool layers into a single group:

   a. In the **Layers** panel, click the top layer, press the **Shift** key, and click the second to the bottom layer to activate all the layers except the **Background** layer.

   b. From the **Layers** panel menu, choose **New Group from Layers**, name the group **critter parts**, and click **OK**.

5. Copy the **critter parts** group from **03-toolcritter_start.jpg** to **my_critter.psd**:

   Dragging a layer, group or selection from one document to another copies them from the source to the target document.

   Pressing the **Shift** key as you drag centers the imported item(s). This duplication technique does not use the **Clipboard**.

   a. Arrange the two document windows so that you can see both of them.

   b. Activate the **03-toolcritter_start.jpg** window by clicking in it.

   c. **Drag** the **critter parts** group from the right side of the **Layers** panel onto the **my_critter.psd** document window, pressing and holding down the **Shift** key *before* releasing the mouse to center the contents of the duplicated group within the **my_critter.psd** document window.

6. **Save my_critter.psd**.

7. Close **03-toolcritter_start.jpg** without saving.

8. Rearrange the tool layers within the document so that they are fully visible along the bottom:

   a. Choose the **Move Tool**.

   b. On the left side of the **Options** bar, check **Auto-Select** and choose **Layer**, not the default **Group** from the pop-up menu.

Tutorial 5: Layer Case Studies

c. **Drag** the individual tools to the bottom of the document window.

d. Uncheck **Auto-Select** so that you do not accidentally move the wrong layer as you proceed.

9. Save one last time and leave **my_critter.psd** open for the next guided exercise.

Guided Exercise 5.7: Layers Panel Organization

Here you will make another layer group, and move the appropriate critter part layers into it.

1. Make and name a new group:

    a. Activate the **Background** layer.

    b. **Option + click** (Mac) or **Alt + click** (Win) the **Create a new group** button at the bottom of the **Layers** panel.

    Alt or **Option** clicking automatically opens the **New Group** dialog box to type in the group's name.

    c. Type **Head** and click **OK**.

2. Enlarge the **Layers** panel and drag the **saw blade**, **triangle**, **tape**, and **putty knife** layers from the **critter parts** group into the **Head** group.

3. Rename the **critter parts** group **Body**.

4. Duplicate the **putty knife** layer and move the duplicate into the **Body** group, as this part will be used for both the head and the body:

    a. Activate the **putty knife** layer. It is in the **Head** group.

    b. Holding down the **Option** key (Mac) or the **Alt** key **(Win),** drag the **putty knife** layer into the **Body** group to place a copy of the layer into the group.

5. Collapse all the groups and activate the **Background** layer.

    In spite of all this layer organization, the document window appears unchanged because no layers obscure each other except for the **putty knife** layer which is superimposed on top of the **putty knife copy** layer.

Guided Exercise 5.8: Set Up a Template

A useful technique for building a composite image is to hand sketch the placement of the components in a composite image, and then to scan the sketch and bring it into Photoshop to use as a **TEMPLATE** or guide. We have already made a guide image for you. Here you will import and configure a template layer to help you arrange your critter's parts.

1. Begin with **my_critter.psd** open in Photoshop and both layer groups collapsed to make the **Layers** panel more compact.

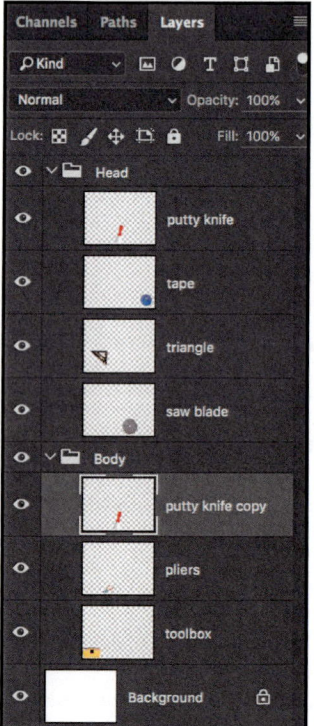

2. Activate the **Background** layer because the imported layer will appear immediately above the active layer.

3. Open **05-critter_template.jpg**.

4. Change its **Background** into a pixel layer so that it will be easier to identify when you bring it into the other document:

    a. In the **Layers** panel, double click the **Background** layer to show the **New Layer** dialog box.

    b. Type **critter template** into the **Name** box and click **OK**.

    Notice that the layer options section of the **Layers** panel is no longer grayed out.

    When you convert the **Background** to a pixel layer, you can change its opacity, fill, blend mode, and locking options—even if it is the only layer in the document.

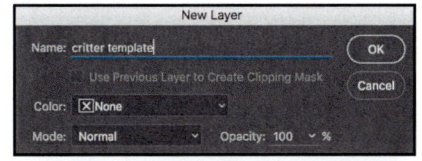

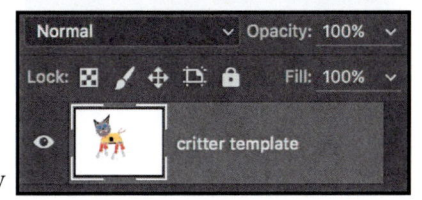

5. Move the **critter template** layer into position in the **my_critter.psd** document:

    a. Choose **Window > Arrange > 2-up Vertical** to see the two document windows side by side.

    b. Activate the **05-critter_template.jpg** document by clicking in it.

    c. **Drag** the **critter template** layer from the right side of the **Layers** panel onto the **my_critter.psd** document window, pressing and holding down the **Shift** key before releasing the mouse to center the contents of the layer within the **my_critter.psd** document window.

    d. Lower the **Opacity** of the **critter template** layer to **35%**. Your **Layers** panel should resemble the one shown here.

    Don't worry if your tools slightly overlap the template. You'll be repositioning those tools next.

6. Close **05-critter_template.jpg** without saving it.

7. **Save my_critter.psd** and leave it open to begin assembling the critter.

Guided Exercise 5.9: Use the Template to Make the Critter's Body

Here you will explore different techniques for assembling the tool box and some tools into the critter's body.

1. Show the **Body** group and expand it to see its layers and be sure the **tool box** layer is at the top of the **Body** group; rearrange them if necessary.

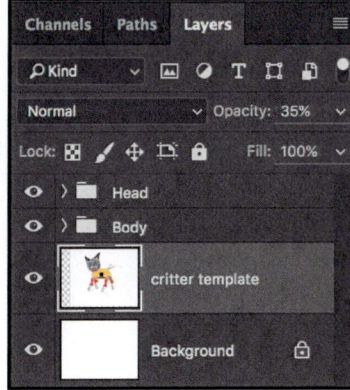

2. Use a quick shortcut to duplicate the **putty knife copy** layers, as you will need a total of four of them:

   a. Rename **putty knife copy** to **putty knife 1**.

   b. Position the mouse just to the right of the **putty knife 1** layer name.

   c. Drag the **putty knife 1** layer on top of the **Create a new layer** button at the bottom of the **Layers** panel and release the mouse to duplicate the layer.

   d. Repeat steps 2 b-c two more times so that you have four **putty knife** layers. Notice that the layers are somewhat conveniently named **putty knife1**, **putty knife1 copy**, **putty knife1 copy 2,** and **putty knife1 copy 3**.

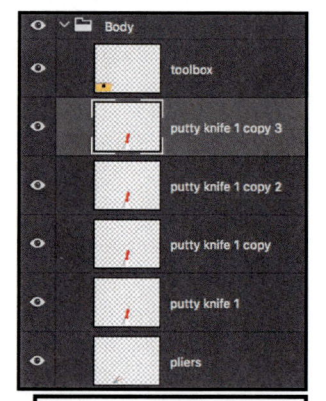

3. Put the **putty knife** legs into place:

   a. Hide the **Head** group so you don't accidentally move one of those layers.

   b. Choose the **Move Tool** with **Auto-Select Layer** checked.

   c. Drag the top **putty knife** to approximately where it belongs.

   d. Then drag the other three putty knives in line. Notice that there is one left. You will use it when you make the critter's head.

   e. Click on the far right putty knife (in the document window), choose **Edit > Free Transform**, rotate the putty knife into position, and commit your transformation.

   f. Repeat with the other putty knives as needed, until all four are just where you want them.

4. Give the critter a tail:

   a. Choose the **Move Tool** with **Auto-Select Layer** checked.

   b. Drag the **pliers** in place.

5. Turn the **tool box** into the critter's body:

   a. Choose the **Move Tool** with **Auto-Select Layer** checked.

   b. Drag the **tool box** roughly into place.

   c. Choose **Edit > Free Transform** and rotate the tool box about **180 degrees**. Press the **Ctrl** key (Win) or the **Command** key (Mac) and drag the individual corner handles to skew the toolbox to give it the correct shape. It can be approximate.

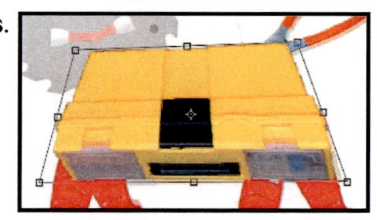

   d. **Commit** your transformation.

6. Collapse the **Body** group, and click the **Lock All** button to lock the group and all its layers so you don't accidentally move them.

7. Give the critter a head:

    a. Expand the **Head** group.

    b. Choose the **Move Tool** with **Auto-Select Layer** checked.

    c. Drag the **saw blade** in place to make the critter's head.

    d. Drag the **tape layer** on top of the **saw blade** and transform it smaller to make one of the critter's eyes.

    e. Duplicate the **tape** layer and move it to make the second eye.

8. Make the critter's ears:

    a. Be sure the **triangle** layer is beneath the **saw blade** layer. Then move the **triangle** in place and transform it to make the first ear.

    b. Duplicate the **triangle** layer, and position and transform the duplicate to make the second ear.

9. **Uncheck Auto Select Layer** so you don't accidentally activate and move the wrong layer.

10. Activate the **critter template** layer, and drag it to the side so that you can see how to make the critter's mouth.

11. Use the **putty knife** layer in the **Head** group to make one side of the mouth, transforming as needed.

12. Duplicate the **putty knife** layer and flip it horizontally to make the other side of the mouth.

13. Hide the template layer.

14. Collapse the **Head** group, but keep it active.

15. Use the **Move Tool** to readjust the **Head** position relative to the **Body**, until you are happy with its position.

16. If desired, use the **Type Tool** to add a title and name to your critter.

17. Use the **Crop** tool to remove the extra white space from the document's edges.

18. **Save** your masterpiece and print if desired.

    If you need to **Save for Web**, it may be quite a bit below 99 K because of the solid white background.

On Your Own

Using either the tool critter pieces we provided or images that you supply, build another composite critter. Be creative, and have fun.

Resources and Videos

http://www.practical-photoshop.com/pages/CC2015-pp1-resources.html#05

Practical Photoshop CC 2015, Level 1
Tutorial 6: Painting

Just like traditional artwork, when you paint in Photoshop, you begin by first choosing your paint color, and then your brush. But because this is Photoshop, you have a dizzying array of options to work with, and these options can be overwhelming. Instead of trying to master everything at once, relax and approach this chapter as an assigned play time with a new paint box. The more you play, the better you will learn how to use and customize these three basic painting tools: the **Brush Tool**, the **Pencil Tool**, and the **Eraser Tool**.

Two more Photoshop painting tools, the **Paint Bucket Tool** and the **Gradient Tool**, let you fill layers and selections with solid colors, patterns and gradients. In addition, you create special layers, called FILL LAYERS, for more flexibility with solid colors, patterns, and gradients. Finally, you will use the **Overlay** and **Stroke** layer styles to non-destructively add solid colors, gradients, and patterns to all the non-transparent regions of layers, or to just their edges.

Objectives

- Use the **Color Picker**, the **Color** panel, the **Swatches** panel, and the **Eyedropper Tool** to sample (choose) and manipulate **Foreground** and **Background** colors.

- Configure the **Brush Tool** using the **Brush Preset** picker and the **Options** bar settings and experiment with those settings.

  - Paint with a variety of blending modes and observe their effects.

  - Explore **Opacity**, **Flow**, and **Airbrush** settings.

  - Adjust the **Size** and **Hardness** settings of tools that use brushes for effective painting.

- Differentiate between the **Brush Tool** and the **Pencil Tool**.

- Compare the use of the **Eraser Tool** on the **Background** layer and on standard pixel layers.

- Use the **Paint Bucket Tool** and the **Gradient Tool** to fill selected areas with patterns, gradients, and solid colors, and to set options to control the results.

- Create and use **Fill** layers filled with solid colors, gradients, and patterns.

- Use the **Overlay** and **Stroke** layer styles, and compare their uses with those of **Fill** tools and **Fill** layers.

Choosing Colors

Brush and **Fill** tools often use the **Foreground** and **Background** colors. There are many ways to specify these colors. Painting tools such as the **Brush Tool** and the **Pencil Tool** paint in the **Foreground** color. The **Paint Bucket Tool** can fill a layer or selection with the **Foreground** color.

Foreground Color or Background Color?

In earlier tutorials, you changed your **Foreground** color from the **Swatches** panel, and restored the default black and white colors in the **Tools** panel.

The **Tools** panel displays square color samples of the **Foreground** and **Background** colors. If you click one of those color samples, it opens the **Color Picker** so that you can change that color or *sample a color* in Photoshop jargon.

The top of the **Color Picker** dialog box will specify either **Foreground Color** or **Background Color** as an extra check that you are changing the desired color.

The **Color** panel also lets you activate either the **Foreground Color** or the **Background Color**, with the **Foreground Color** active by default. Whichever color is active will be surrounded by an extra box or frame.

- To activate either the **Background** or the **Foreground** color, click (don't double click) inside its box in the **Color** panel.

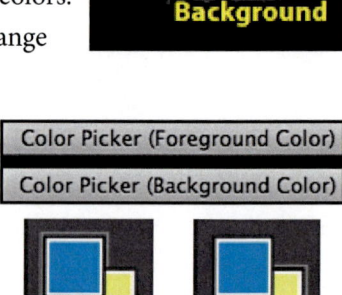

The Color Picker

Within the **Color Picker**, you can choose colors numerically or by clicking in the **Color Field**, the big box on the left side of the **Color Picker**.

To sample a color from the **Color Field**:

1. Locate the **Spectrum** in the middle of the **Color Picker**.

2. Drag its slider triangles or click the part of the spectrum in which you are interested. The **Color Field** will change to display tones of that hue.

3. Click inside the **Color Field** on the desired color.

   Here the circle shows the **Sampled Color** which you can also see in the **Changed** box. Each time you click to sample a different color, the **Changed** box will update.

Tutorial 6: Painting

Page 118

Color Models

COLOR MODELS are methods of describing, measuring, and displaying colors numerically by using specific numbers to define a certain color. Photoshop translates each pixel's numeric value into a color or shade of gray to appear on screen or to print. The **Color Picker** shows the numeric values of the sampled colors for the **HSB**, **RGB**, **Lab**, and **CMYK** color models. If you change the numbers in one or more of the boxes, it changes both the sampled color, and the numbers for the other color models.

We will only work with two color models in this course: **RGB** and **CMYK.**

> The **RGB COLOR MODEL**, named for its additive primaries **red**, **green**, and **blue,** describes transmitted light. Your computer display transmits colors based on the **RGB** color model.

> The **CMYK COLOR MODEL**, named for its subtractive primaries **cyan**, **magenta**, and **yellow** with the addition of black (**K** for **kohl**). **CMYK** color is also known as **PROCESS COLOR**. Process color is quite magical. Instead of mixing and painting many, many different colors of ink or paint, process color combines cyan, magenta, and yellow inks or dyes, along with black for ink jet and color laser printers, to print color photographs that look very close to the "real" thing.

The **gamut indicator** is a triangle with an exclamation point in the center, just to the left of the **Cancel** button. This icon appears to warn you that the color chosen is not a **PRINTABLE COLOR**. In other words, the sampled color cannot be created with **CMYK** color inks. The **gamut indicator** appears when the color that you see on screen and its CMYK printable version are not the same color.

- Click the small color box below the **gamut indicator** to sample the closest printable color.
- The sampled color will change to the one in the box, and the gamut warning will vanish.

Web-Safe and Non Web-Safe Colors

In the early days of the Internet, most color computer monitors could only display 256 different colors. And to make things more complicated, the Mac and Windows operating systems did not *totally* agree upon which 256 colors they would display. Only 216 were the same, becoming the **WEB-SAFE COLORS**. If you chose any other colors, those colors would be approximated by **DITHERING** or displaying a checkerboard pattern of the two closest Web-safe tones, so early Web designers were very careful to choose Web-safe colors for their sites to get smooth solid colors when needed.

If **Only Web Colors** is checked, you will only be able to sample one of the 216 Web-safe colors.

The **color field** will have large areas of discrete colors instead of tonal gradients.

The **Web Warning Indicator** is a cube that represents a pixel. It appears when a color is not Web-safe. Click the small color box below the cube to sample the closest Web-safe color. In practice, don't worry much about this indicator. Modern monitors can display a great many colors—even the so-called "non-safe" ones.

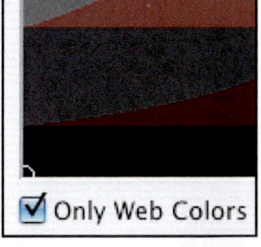

Tutorial 6: Painting

THE SWATCHES PANEL

Use the **Swatches** panel to choose common preset colors, or to store color samples that you will want to access again. Each square of color is a single color **SWATCH**. Along the top of the panel are swatches of the 16 most recently-used colors.

TO SAMPLE A SWATCH COLOR:

- With the **Foreground** color active in the **Color** panel, click a swatch in the **Swatches** panel to make it the **Foreground** color.

- **Command-click** (Mac) or **Ctrl-click** (Win) a swatch to make it the **Background** color.

TO ADD A SWATCH:

1. Point your mouse to a blank area of the **Swatches** panel. When you are in the right spot, the **Paint Bucket** icon will appear.

2. Click in that blank area of the **Swatches** panel.

3. Type a name in the **Color Swatch Name** dialog box, and click **OK**. The current **Foreground** color has now been stored as a swatch.

You can also add a swatch by clicking the **Add to Swatches** button in the **Color Picker** dialog box.

TO DELETE A SWATCH:

1. Press **Option** (Mac) or **Alt** (Win) and point the mouse over the swatch you wish to delete. When you are in the correct location, you will see a scissors icon over the swatch.

2. With **Option/Alt** still depressed, click the swatch to delete. The swatch will vanish without a warning.

   Be careful when you delete swatches, as the process is not undoable. If you accidentally delete the **Preset** swatches, you can reset the entire set. However, this process will also remove any custom swatches you have made.

TO RESET SWATCHES:

1. Click the **Swatches** panel menu button in the upper right corner of the panel to view the **Swatches** panel menu.

2. Choose **Reset Swatches**.

3. When the warning dialog box appears, here are your choices:
   - **OK** will return to the original default set of swatches.

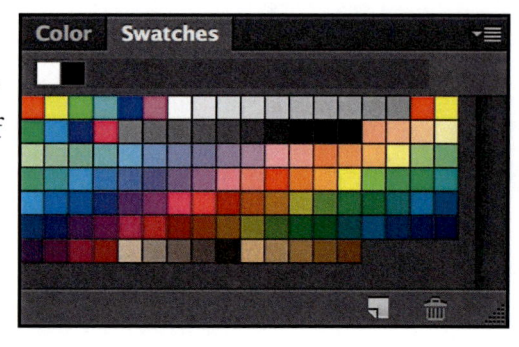

- **Append** will add the default set of swatches to the end of your currently displayed swatches. You won't lose any custom swatches, but you will have two swatches of most of the originals.
- **Cancel** will not make any changes to the current swatch set.

Color Panel

The **Color** panel, grouped with the **Swatches** panel, also lets you change the **Foreground** and **Background** colors. Each time you make a color change, the new color appears in the color selection box in both the **Tools** panel and the **Color** panel.

Here are three quick ways to change a color using the **Color** panel:

- Drag the triangle beside the spectrum at the right side of the panel.
- Click in the large color field to choose a color.
- Double-click either the **Foreground** or **Background** color sample to display the **Color Picker**.

Background Color Specifics

The **Background** color is only utilized by certain tools and commands.

- On the **Background** layer, the **Eraser Tool** reveals the **Background** color.
- The **Background** color also appears if you delete, cut, or move a selection from the **Background** layer.
- The **Gradient Tool** paints its default gradient from the **Foreground** to the **Background** color.

The Eyedropper Tool

Often you will want to sample a color from your image rather than trying to guess the color from the panels or pickers. The **Eyedropper Tool** lets you choose or **SAMPLE** a color from an open Photoshop document simply by clicking on it.

With the **Foreground** color active in the **Color** panel, when you press on the document without releasing the pointer button you will see the **Sampling Ring** to help you better choose the desired color.

- The **Sampling Ring** is surrounded by a neutral gray ring to better compare the sampled color on the top half with the original color on the bottom half of the ring.
- As you drag the pointer, the sampled color updates to whatever color is under the tip of the pointer.

- Release the pointer button to choose the currently sampled color as your new **Foreground** color.

Here are two color-sampling tricks:

- When the **Foreground** color is active, press the **Alt /Option** while sampling to choose a new **Background** color.
- When the **Background** color is active, press the **Alt /Option** while sampling to choose a new **Foreground** color.

Eyedropper Tool Options

The **Options** bar lets you change the **Sample Size** from the default **Point Sample** (the 1 pixel default) to **3 x 3 Average** or **5 x 5 Average** (measured in pixels), up to **101 x 101** for very large images. Larger samples average the color of pixels in the given area and can be more representative of the color you seek.

....

Guided Exercise 6.1: Sample Colors

Do this simple guided exercise to see a demonstration of the **Eyedropper Tool** in action.

1. Reset the **Essentials** workspace, all tools, and the default **Foreground** and **Background** colors.
2. Open **06-frog.jpg** and zoom to **600%** magnification so that you can easily see the individual pixels that make up the frog.

    Viewed at **600%** or higher, you can see the grid that separates each pixel.

3. Use **Point Sample** to sample a frog-green **Foreground** color:

    a. Reset your colors to the default black and white, and click (don't double-click) the **Foreground** color sample in the **Color** panel to be sure that the **Foreground** color is active.

    b. Choose the **Eyedropper Tool**.

    c. Using the default **Point Sample** option, click a green pixel on the frog's body to make that green color the **Foreground** color.

    d. Click on several different pixels and watch the **Foreground** color change in both the **Tools** panel and the **Color** panel.

    Observe that **Point Sample** is so small that it is easy to sample a non-green color depending on which individual pixel you sample.

4. In the **Options** bar, change the sample size to **5 x 5 average**, and click on different green pixels. Notice that there is much less variety between samples when you use a slightly larger region to do your sampling.

Tutorial 6: Painting

5. **Alt/Option + click** on a yellow part of one of the feet to make the yellow color the **Background** color.
6. Keep **06-frog.jpg** open to use in the next guided exercise.

Brush Tool

The **Brush Tool** has a variety of useful settings. The default settings are shown here. Let's look at them in order from left to right.

The Tool Preset Picker (1)

Whenever you choose a tool, its icon appears in the left end of the **Options** bar. This icon is actually a button; clicking the button reveals the **Tool Preset Picker**. We'll save that for a later course.

This is also the hot spot for resetting either an individual tool or all the tools.

The Brush Preset Picker (2)

Photoshop brushes can simulate the effect of real world paint media such as oil paint, watercolors, pastels, charcoal and crayons. Photoshop comes with many special **Preset Brushes** and provides many different settings to create a plethora of effects. Here we just want you to grasp the basics of working with preset brushes to adjust their **size**, **hardness**, or **opacity**.

There are two spots where you can pick brushes: the **Brush Preset Picker** on the left side of the **Options** bar, and the **Brushes** panel. The **Brush Preset Picker** is much easier to use, so we will cover it here and leave the **Brushes** panel for later courses.

The **Brush Preset Picker** drops down to reveal a number of settings and an assortment of **Preset** brushes to choose from.

- **Thumbnail (A)** at the top of the **Brush Preset Picker** shows the thumbnail of the currently active brush with its settings below. Here, the chosen round brush is fuzzy or soft around the edge. The number **13** means that the brush is 13 pixels in diameter, *even though its thumbnail is much smaller.*

- **Size (B)** lets you change the size of your brush. You can either move the slider or type in a size number. Photoshop remembers the brush settings for each tool independently. Thus, the brush size you choose for the **Brush Tool** will not hold when you switch to the **Pencil Tool**.

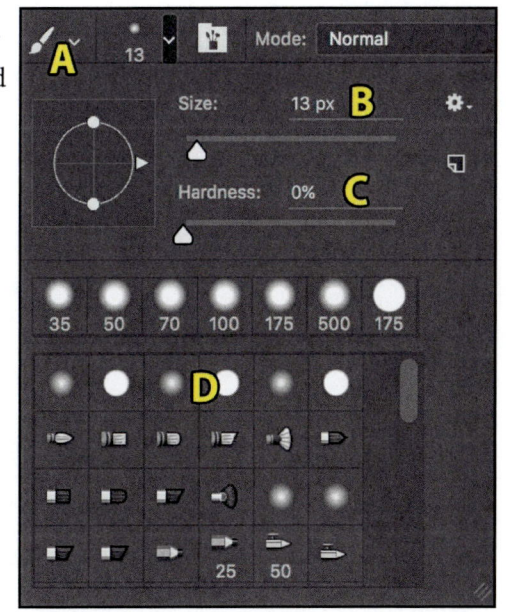

- **Hardness (C)** determines how many **ANTI-ALIASING** or transitional tones there will be on the edges of your brush strokes.

The default preset brushes are either **100%** or **0%** hardness. **100%** hardness has a minimal amount of anti-aliasing and **0%** has the maximum amount of anti-aliasing. With the **Hardness** slider you can vary hardness between **0%** and **100%**. When a brush has **0%** hardness, it is known as a **SOFT-EDGED BRUSH**.

The three brush samples shown here all have the same master diameter. The harder the brush the more color it will apply to the edges of the brush.

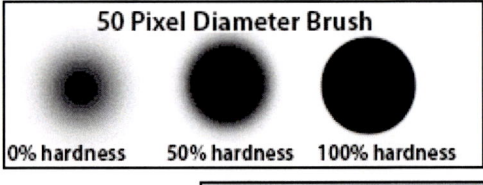

- **Built-In Brush Presets (D)**, accessed via the pop-out menu, allow you to load additional **Brush Presets** that come with Photoshop as well as custom brushes that you save. 76 brushes are loaded by default. There are more sets of **Brush Presets** ready to load from the pop-out menu, such as **Calligraphic Brushes**, **Natural Brushes**, **Faux Finish Brushes**, and **Wet Media Brushes** to name a few. These brushes are stored in the **Presets** folder inside the Photoshop folder on your hard drive. All brushes stored there will appear in this menu.

When you click on a brush set from the pop-out menu, you will be given a choice to append (add) them to the current list. You can also choose **Load Brushes** to browse to anywhere on your computer or removable media to load a saved brush set. **Replace Brushes** does the same, but replaces what you had before with the newly selected brushes. Explore loading some **Brush Presets**. Then choose **Reset Brushes** from the pop-out menu to restore the default set of preset brushes.

SHORT CUTS TO REMEMBER

- Within a document window, the **Brush Tool's** context menu will temporarily reveal the **Brush Preset Picker**. **Right-Click** (or **Control + Click** on Mac trackpad) to get to the context menu.
- Use the bracket keys [ ] to the right of the **P** key to quickly decrease [or increase] the size of your brush.
- Use the **Shift** plus the bracket keys to increase and decrease the hardness of the brush.

. . . .

THE BRUSH PANEL (3)

Clicking on this button will open the **Brushes Panel** with more advanced **Brush** options that we will not cover in this tutorial.

Painting Modes (4)

PAINTING MODES control how the colors of what you paint—the **BLEND**—interact with the color of the pixels currently on the layer you are painting on—the **BASE**—to produce the **RESULT**, the colors that actually appear on the layer in the document window.

NOTE: *Painting modes permanently alter the layer's pixels.*

Guided Exercise 6.2: Apply Painting Modes

This guided exercise demonstrates some special effects you can achieve by painting with modes other than the default **Normal**.

1. Open **06-frog.jpg**, if it is not already open.

2. Choose the **Brush Tool**.

3. In the **Brush Preset Picker**, select a medium size, soft brush: **35 pixel diameter, 0% hardness**.

4. In the **Options** bar, set the **Mode** to **Overlay**.

5. Click the **Foreground Color** box in the **Tools** panel.

6. In the **Color Picker** choose a bright red color.

7. Paint on the frog in the document window. Change brush size as needed. Remember that the [and] keys decrease or increase brush size.

8. Click the **Foreground** Color box in the **Tools** panel and choose a bright blue color in the **Color Picker**.

9. Paint on the frog's feet. Notice that the blue does not show up well. Change the **Mode** to **Color**. Try painting the feet again. The blue color comes in strong. **Undo**, reduce the **Opacity** setting to about **30%** and try again.

10. Increase the **Opacity** and paint the eyes.

    Using this technique, you can change the color of an object, while preserving its texture and tonal range. This method is often used to change the color of a subject's eyes.

    Color blending mode works very similar to **Overlay**; painting with a chosen color will yield a color very close to the chosen color. Other blending modes will lighten, intensify, or in the case of **Difference**, paint the opposite of the chosen color. For instance, the red color used on the frog set to **Difference** would turn it to a dark, saturated green.

Tutorial 6: Painting

Opacity (5)

Returning to the **Brush Tool** options, **Opacity** sets the maximum amount you can see through a brush stroke.

Opacity controls the entire brush stroke. Without releasing the mouse, no matter how many times the painted areas overlap, the opacity stays as set. A setting of 100% opacity produces very opaque paint with no transparency so that the underlying pixels will be completely covered. Reducing the opacity permits any underlying pixels to partially show.

Flow (6)

Flow determines how quickly the color paints, so that you end up with the specified opacity. Notice that the painted area darkens where it overlaps—up to the specified opacity.

Guided Exercise 6.3: Compare Opacity and Flow

This guided exercise demonstrates the difference between the **Opacity** and **Flow** settings.

1. Create a new document by choosing **File > New**.
2. In the **New** dialog box, choose the Preset: **Default Photoshop Size** and click **OK**.
3. Choose the **Brush Tool** from the **Tools** panel.
4. Configure your brush:
    a. Choose a large brush from the **Brush Preset Picker**.
    b. Click the **Foreground Color** box in the **Tools** panel and select a deep color from the **Color Picker**.
    c. Set the **Opacity** to **50%** and the **Flow** to **100%**.
5. Paint with one stroke, keeping the mouse clicked down, repeatedly painting over the same area.
6. Set the **Opacity** to **100%** and the **Flow** to **50%**.
7. Again, paint with one stroke repeatedly over the same area with the mouse held down.

    Notice the difference. With reduced opacity, the paint never accumulates over **50%**. With reduced flow, the paint will accumulate to **100%** but will take more passes than with the flow set to **100%**.

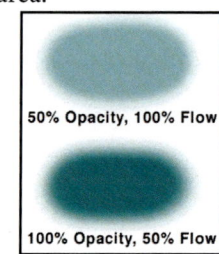

Airbrush (7)

The **Airbrush** setting simulates a real world airbrush. It allows color to build up if the mouse is held in one spot.

Guided Exercise 6.4: Use the Airbrush Setting

Compare painting with the **Airbrush** setting turned on and off.

1. Reset the **Essentials** workspace, all tools, and the default **Foreground** and **Background** colors.
2. Create a new document by choosing **File** > **New**.
3. In the **New** dialog box, choose the **Preset: Default Photoshop Size** and click **OK**.
4. Choose a fairly large brush with a deep color and set its **Opacity** to **50%** or above.
5. Click with the mouse in the document; keep the mouse depressed while you hold the brush in the same location.
6. Choose the **Airbrush** setting in the **Options** bar.
7. Click with the pointer at a different spot in the document; keep the mouse depressed while you hold the brush in the same spot.

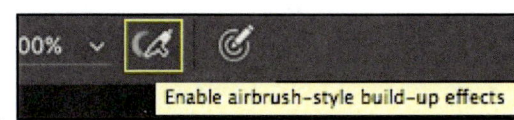

   You will see that the paint will accumulate, bleeding as if the paper were absorbing it.

Additional Painting Tools

Any tool that uses a brush is considered a **PAINTING TOOL**. Here we will examine two more painting tools: The **Pencil Tool** and the **Eraser Tool**.

Differentiating Between the Brush Tool and the Pencil Tool

Grouped with the **Brush Tool**, the **Pencil Tool** differs from the **Brush Tool** in one key way. The **Pencil Tool** always draws hard-edged lines or areas, without anti-aliasing, while the **Brush Tool** always paints with anti-aliasing. Even with **100%** hardness, there will be anti-aliasing with the **Brush Tool**.

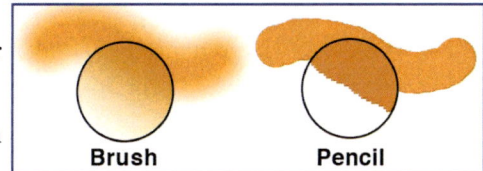

The **Pencil Tool** is best used for drawing a straight line or editing on a pixel by pixel basis. For example, in the extreme close-up view of this illustration of an eye, the **Pencil Tool** could be set to draw with a one pixel wide brush. This method makes it easy to edit the two pixels next to the arrow.

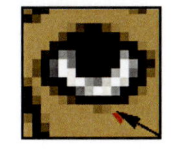

The Eraser Tool

The **Eraser Tool** is used to remove pixels from a layer or to selectively lower the transparency of areas of a layer. Using the **Eraser Tool** on the **Background** layer will erase the painted area to the current **Background** color. Used on any other pixel layer, the **Eraser Tool** will erase to transparency.

The **Eraser Tool**'s options are similar to those of the **Brush Tool**, but there are special **Eraser Tool Mode** settings to select which type of eraser to use:

- The **Brush** setting is like using the **Brush Tool**. From the **Brush Picker** you can choose from **Brush Presets**, adjust **Opacity** and **Flow**, or choose the **Airbrush** option.

- The **Pencil** setting is similar to using the **Pencil Tool**. You can choose from **Brush Presets**, but the brushes can only be non anti-aliased brushes. **Brush** and **Opacity** are the only option for **Pencil** mode.

- The **Block** setting is for removing blocks of pixels with a non anti-aliased brush. There are no **Brush Presets** and no **Opacity** or **Flow** options available. The block setting also uses a square brush shape.

Fills and Strokes

To **FILL** in Photoshop is to put something—typically a color, a pattern, or a gradient—into a selection or onto a layer. You can fill with a command, by using tools, by making special layers called **FILL LAYERS**, or by using certain layer styles.

To **STROKE** in Photoshop is to place a border around a selection or object. You can stroke with commands, with certain layer styles, or with vector paths. We will not cover the third kind of stroke in this tutorial.

Fill Tools

There are three **Fill** tools in **Photoshop**, the **Paint Bucket Tool**, the **Gradient Tool**, and the **3D Material Drop Tool** (not covered in this course).

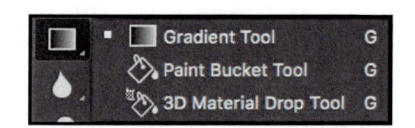

The Gradient Tool

The **Gradient Tool** paints transitions of color or tone across a layer or a selection. Its tool options affect the way it works. At **100% Opacity** in **Normal** painting mode, the gradient will replace all the pixels on the active layer or selection.

By default, the **Gradient Tool** draws gradients using the **Foreground** and **Background** colors displayed in the **Tools** panel, using the **Linear Gradient** style shown here transitioning from **black** to **white** at **100% Opacity**.

Results depend on where and for what distance you set the angle and length as you drag the tool across the document. Each arrow shows approximately the distance and direction the **Gradient Tool** was dragged.

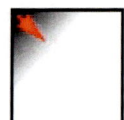

In addition to **Linear**, the **Gradient Tool** has four other style options: **Radial**, **Angle**, **Reflected**, and **Diamond**, as shown on the **Options** bar. Again, the arrows show the start and end of the dragging.

Press the down arrow to the right of the gradient thumbnail to display the **Gradient Picker**, where you can click to choose from a variety of gradients. The default gradient presets are shown here, using a red **Foreground** color and a blue **Background** color.

Here are some commonly used presets:

1. The default **Foreground to Background** gradient.

2. Next is the **Foreground to Transparent** gradient. When chosen, the gradient fades from the **Foreground** color to transparent, and completely ignores the **Background** color.

3. The other gradient presets ignore the **Foreground** and **Background** colors, and apply specified colors, beginning with **Black to White**.

4. The second to the last of the default preset gradients will paint stripes, circles, and diamonds of the **Foreground** color with areas of transparency, for special effects.

Clicking the gradient thumbnail will select the **Gradient Editor** for creating custom gradients; it will not be covered in this course.

Guided Exercise 6.5: Use The Gradient Tool

The best way to learn how to use the **Gradient Tool** is to just get in there and play with it. This exercise will guide you through some play time with the **Gradient Tool**. To really have fun with this image, we will use a separate layer, set to **Color** blending mode, so that the gradients you use will change the hues of the photo, but its tones and textures will remain.

1. Reset the **Essentials** workspace, all tools, and the default **Foreground** and **Background** colors.

2. Open **06-stained_glass.jpg** and save it as **stained_glass.psd** in the location of your choice.

3. Cover your image with a gradient:

    a. In the **Options** bar, click on the arrow to the right of the gradient thumbnail to display the **Gradient Picker** and choose the **Red to Green** gradient preset.

b. Make sure that **Linear Gradient** is the chosen shape option.

c. In the document window, click and hold near the top of the image, drag down to the middle of the image and let go of the mouse.

Notice that the whole image is affected by the gradient. When you use the **Gradient** tool without a selection, the gradient fills the entire layer. Also notice that from the point you stopped dragging in the middle of the image to the bottom is pure green.

d. **Undo** the gradient.

It is very rare to apply a gradient to a layer containing an image because the gradient completely replaces all the image detail. Instead, gradients are typically applied to blank layers or to selected regions on a layer.

4. Make a new layer on which to place your gradient experimentations:

    a. Create a new layer by clicking the **New Layer** button at the bottom of the **Layers** panel.

    b. Name the layer **gradient experimentations**.

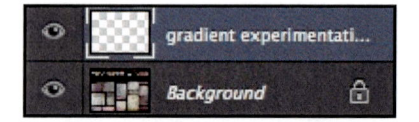

5. Make approximately the same gradient on the **gradient experimentations** layer, and configure it so that you can see the stained glass picture through it:

    a. Paint the gradient on the **gradient experimentations** layer.

    b. At the top of the **Layers** panel, change the layer blending mode from **Normal** to **Color** so that you can see the detail of the image, but all the panes of glass are either red, green, or transitions between the two colors.

    c. Experiment with some other blending modes to see how they affect this image. Try **Overlay**, **Multiply**, **Screen**, and **Difference** blending modes.

    We particularly liked **Overlay** because it made the colors glisten, bringing out the translucent qualities of the glass.

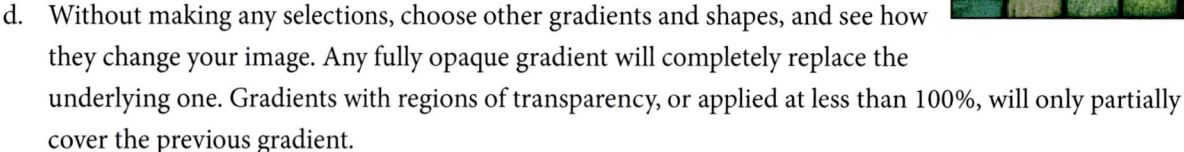

    d. Without making any selections, choose other gradients and shapes, and see how they change your image. Any fully opaque gradient will completely replace the underlying one. Gradients with regions of transparency, or applied at less than 100%, will only partially cover the previous gradient.

6. Paint gradients onto selections:

    a. Either back up in **History** to before you painted any gradients on the image or, with the gradient experimentations layer active, choose **Select > Select All** and then press the **Delete** key to remove any gradients from the gradient experimentations layer.

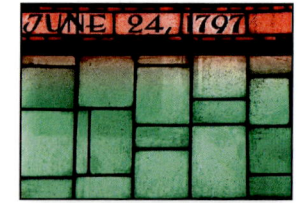

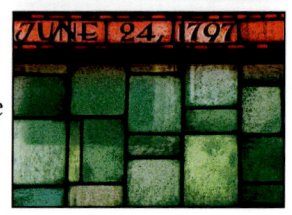

b. Set the blending mode of the **gradient experimentations** layer to **Color**.

c. Choose the **Rectangular Marquee Tool** from the **Tools** panel.

d. Draw a rectangular selection around an individual stained glass rectangle. Try to surround all the colored pixels of the rectangle. It is OK to grab some of the black around the edges.

e. Choose the **Gradient Tool**. From the **Gradient Picker**, choose one of the preset gradients. Drag with the pointer inside the selection.

f. Choose the **Rectangular Marquee Tool** and draw a marquee around another rectangle in the image.

g. Click the **Foreground Color** selection box and select a color in the **Color Picker**. Do the same for the **Background** color.

h. Choose the **Gradient Tool**. From the **Gradient Picker**, choose the upper left thumbnail, **Foreground** to **Background**.

i. Drag with the pointer inside the selection.

j. Change the layer blending mode to **Normal** to see the gradient in its normal state.

k. Change the blending mode back to **Color**. Continue on, using the **Rectangular Marquee Tool** to select different rectangles.

   Here are some suggestions for experimentation:

   - Change colors by choosing new **Foreground** and **Background** colors.
   - Experiment with drawing the gradient in different directions.
   - Try out the other shape options.
   - To make your work go faster, use the shortcut keys of **M** for the **Marquee Tool** and **G** for the **Gradient Tool**.   
   - If you forget to draw a marquee before drawing the gradient, the gradient will fill the layer. Undo and continue.

l. When you have filled all the rectangles, go to the **Layers** panel and change the blending mode back to **Normal**. Examine the gradients in their pure form.

Note that you could have set the painting mode for the **Gradient Tool** to **Color** to get the same effect as we did here with setting the layer blending mode. However, using a separate layer provides more flexibility:

- You have not applied color changes directly into your pixels.

Tutorial 6: Painting   Page 131

- You can change the layer blending mode to see the gradients in their normal state.
- You can change layer blending modes and opacity settings to better control how the gradient colors blend with the underlying image.

THE PAINT BUCKET TOOL

The **Paint Bucket Tool** fills a layer or selection with the **Foreground** color or a pattern. We will only work with the **Foreground** color here.

With its default settings, the **Paint Bucket Tool** replaces pixels with the **Foreground** color. When you click on an image with the **Paint Bucket Tool**, it fills areas similar in color to the spot where you clicked. The **Paint Bucket Tool** is useful for filling areas with solid color, such as a flat color **Background** or a logo design.

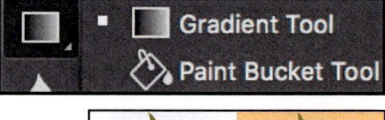

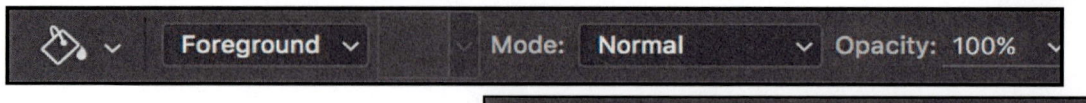

You already used **Tolerance** with the **Magic Wand Tool** in the selections tutorial. When a layer or selection contains pixels of varying colors or tones, **Tolerance** controls how the **Paint Bucket Tool** will fill the selection.

Like all other painting tools, the **Paint Bucket Tool** can only change pixels on an individual layer. When **Sample All Layers** is checked, **Tolerance** applies to all visible document layers, but still only paints on the active layer.

Even with **Tolerance** to the max (**255**) you may need to click the **Paint Bucket** more than once to completely fill an area. In such a case, you may prefer to avoid the **Paint Bucket Tool** altogether. Instead, choose **Edit > Fill** and fill **100%** to fill a selection completely in one step. (We will do that later in this tutorial.)

Let's look at some of the other **Paint Bucket** tool options:

- Set an **Opacity** amount lower than **100%** if you don't want to fill the area with completely opaque pixels.
- Like the **Magic Wand Tool**, **Tolerance** controls how close the color needs to be to the one clicked on to be filled with the **Paint Bucket Tool**. The higher the number, the wider the range of tones that will be filled with one click of the **Paint Bucket Tool**.
- Leave **Anti-aliased** checked for smooth edges.
- **Contiguous** determines whether or not the filled pixels need to touch the source click. With **Contiguous** checked, you will only affect neighboring areas. With **Contiguous** unchecked, you will affect all the pixels in the active layer that have colors that fall within the set **Tolerance**.

Tutorial 6: Painting

- When a document has more than one visible layer, the **All Layers** option becomes active. When checked, the **Paint Bucket Tool** will fill based on colors read from all the visible layers but the fill will only appear on the active layer.

When you have a selection, using the **Paint Bucket Tool** affects only the areas of the selection. Without a selection, if the active layer is either transparent or a solid color, the **Paint Bucket Tool** will fill the entire layer.

Guided Exercise 6.6: Use the Paint Bucket Tool

This short guided exercise illustrates the use of the **Tolerance** and **Contiguous** settings.

1. Reset the **Essentials** workspace, all tools, and the default **Foreground** and **Background** colors.
2. Open **06-paint_bucket.jpg**.
3. Choose the **Paint Bucket Tool**.
4. Choose a yellow-orange **Foreground** color. 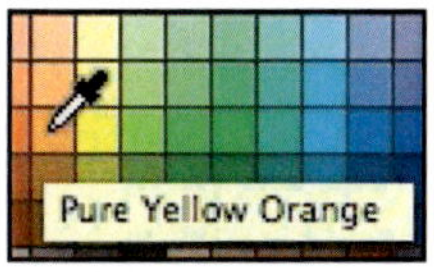
5. Begin with the default settings of **Opacity 100%**, **Tolerance 32**, and **Contiguous checked**.
6. Move your cursor into the document window, click on a light green area of the central leaf, and view the results.
7. **Undo** the results (**Command/Ctrl + Z**).
8. Change the **Tolerance** setting to **64** and click on the same spot.
9. **Undo**, turn **Contiguous** off, and click in the same spot.
10. **Undo**, set the **Tolerance** to **80**, and click again.

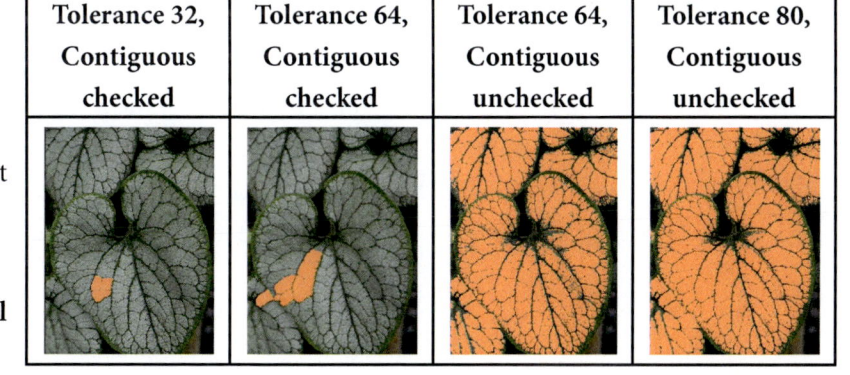

More Fill Techniques

The Fill Command

Edit > Fill displays the **Fill** dialog box for filling selections or layers with individual colors or patterns.

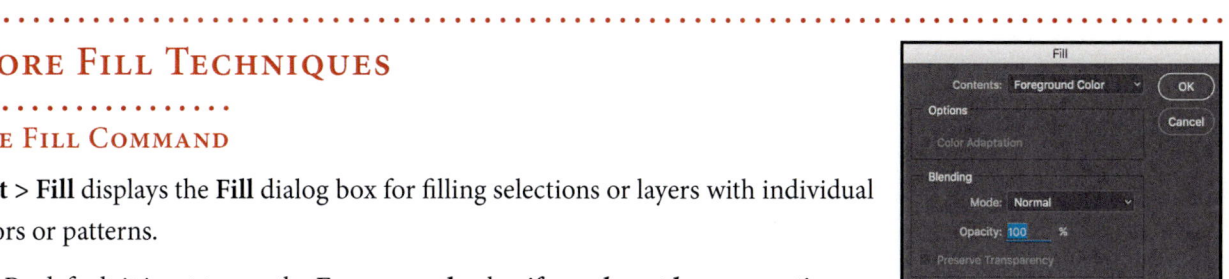

- By default it is set to use the **Foreground** color *if you do not have an active selection*. If a region on the **Background** layer is selected, it will instead default to **Content-Aware** fill. Do not use **Content-Aware** now. We will explain **Content-Aware** fill in a later tutorial.

- Click on the **Use** drop down menu to choose a pattern or other solid color.

TIP: Since the **Fill** command does not rely on **Tolerance**, it often does a better job of filling at 100% than the **Paint Bucket Tool**.

Fill shortcut commands that do not show the **Fill** dialog box or apply **Content-Aware** filling to a selection:

- **Option + delete** (Mac) or **alt + delete** (Windows) deletes to fill with the current **Foreground** color.

- **Command + delete** (Mac) or **ctrl + delete** (Windows) deletes to fill with the current **Background** color.

Filling with Layer Styles

Overlay layer styles let you apply editable color, gradient, and pattern fills to the non-transparent regions of layers. (Remember, you cannot apply layer styles to the **Background** layer.)

Fill Layers

Fill layers are, simply enough, layers filled with a solid color, gradient, or pattern. Not only are these specialty layers easy to make and to edit, but they also add very little size to your document, especially when compared to a standard pixel layer. We often use **Fill** layers to place solid color layers underneath layers with some transparency because they are speedy, easily editable, and do not add much to the size of the file.

Make a Fill layer

1. Activate the layer that the new **Fill** layer should cover.

2. Click the **New fill or adjustment layer** button at the bottom of the **Layers** panel to reveal its pop-up menu.

3. Choose one of the top three menu items to view its **Fill** layer dialog box.

    Solid Color fills the active layer with a solid color chosen from the **Color Picker**. Initially it is set to the **Foreground Color**.

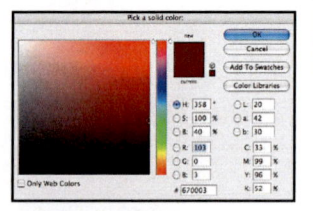

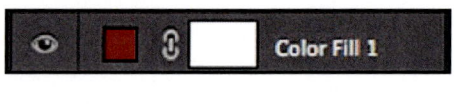

Gradient fills a layer with a gradient chosen from the **Gradient Preset Picker**.

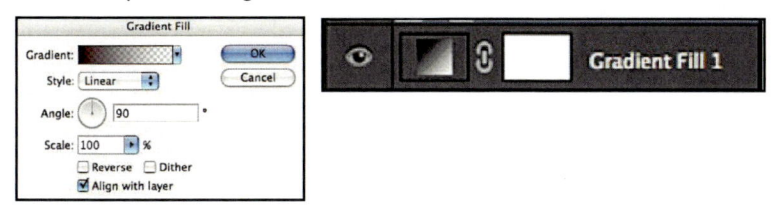

Pattern fills a layer with a pattern chosen from the **Pattern Preset Picker**.

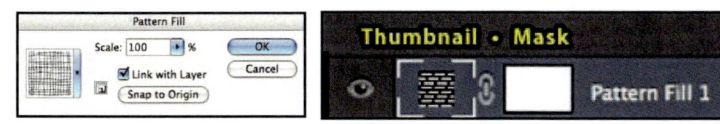

4. Change the settings in the **Fill** dialog box as desired, and click **OK** to create the new **Fill** layer.

   Each **Fill** layer is inserted just above the **active** layer in stacking order. In the **Layers** panel, the white box to the right of the **Fill** thumbnail is a **LAYER MASK**. We discuss masks in Practical Photoshop Level 2.

Modifying Fill Layers

If you don't like the way your **Fill** layer looks, here is how to modify it:

1. Double click on its layer thumbnail (not its mask) to bring up its dialog box.
2. Change the settings, and click **OK**.

This process makes it very easy to pick a different **Fill** color, gradient, or pattern — or to change other settings in the dialog box.

After you make a **Fill** layer, you can change its layer options just like for any other layer, and also change its position in the document stacking order.

Guided Exercise 6.7: Fill with Layer Styles and a Fill layer

In this guided exercise you will use layer styles to change the appearance of a dahlia flower non-destructively, and then use **Fill** layers to place the flower on a variety of different backgrounds. This technique works best for a single subject isolated onto its own layer.

1. Reset the **Essentials** workspace, all tools, and the default **Foreground** and **Background** colors.
2. Open **06-dahlia.psd**.
3. Examine the **Layers** panel to notice that the **dahlia** is on a transparent layer with a solid white **Color Fill** layer below.

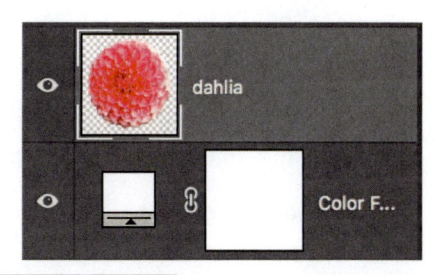

Tutorial 6: Painting
Page 135

4. With the **dahlia** layer active, apply a **Color Overlay** layer style to the **dahlia** layer:

    a. Click the **Add a layer style** button at the bottom of the **Layers** panel to reveal its pop-up menu and choose **Color Overlay**.

    By default, the non-transparent regions of the layer are covered with a purple overlay. The controls for the **Color Overlay** layer style are quite simple. You can change the overlay color, its blending mode, and its opacity.

    b. Save as **06-dahlia2.psd** in the location of your choice.

5. Change the blend mode of the overlay:

    a. Double click **Color Overlay** in the **Layers** Panel to open the **Layer Style** dialog box.

    b. Change the blend mode to **Color Burn**. Notice how you can still see the influence of the purple overlay, but some of the original color shows through, bringing additional depth to the colors of the flower.

    c. Click on various other blend modes, and observe how they change the colors of the dahlia.

    d. End with the one you like the best, lower the **Opacity** if desired, and click **OK** when you are satisfied with your results. We chose **Subtract** because it made such a major change to the flower.

6. Experiment further with the **Color Overlay** settings by changing blending modes, color, and opacity until you achieve results that you like and then click **OK**.

7. Apply a **Gradient Overlay** layer style:

    a. Double click **Color Overlay** in the **Layers** panel to open the **Layer Style** dialog box.

    b. Click the check box to the left of **Color Overlay**, to turn off that layer style, and then click the **Gradient Overlay** name to turn it on and also to reveal the **Gradient Overlay** settings in the **Layer Style** dialog box.

    c. Click the down arrow to the right of the gradient thumbnail to reveal the **Gradient Picker**. The **Gradient Picker** shows swatches of the currently loaded gradients, but Photoshop has lots more gradients hiding.

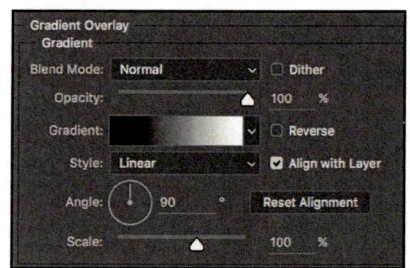

    d. Click the triangle on the right side of the **Gradient Picker** to reveal its menu. At the bottom of the menu are more gradient libraries that you can add to your picker.

    e. Choose **Metals** to load the **Pastels** gradient library, and then click **Append** when the next dialog box opens.

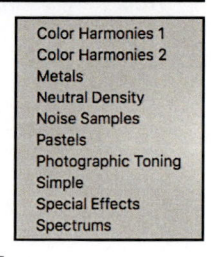

Tutorial 6: Painting

f. Change the blending mode to **Color**, and then choose one of the pastel gradients to make the dahlia resemble a colorful dyed flower.

g. Try out other gradients and options, ending up with settings of your choosing.

We used the blue, yellow, pink gradient, set to **Color** blending mode.

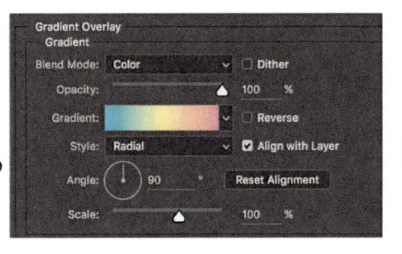

8. If desired, you could also add a **Pattern Overlay** style to the layer. Then, in the **Layers** panel, you can individually show and hide each style to determine what looks the best. You can also double click any of the styles to reopen them and change their settings.

We did not use a **Pattern Overlay** on the dahlia, but you would follow roughly the same procedure as for the **Gradient Overlay** to apply a pattern to your layer. The **Pattern Preset Picker** initially shows only a handful of patterns, but the picker menu has many additional pattern libraries to load.

9. Change the plain white **Fill** layer to a more interesting color:

    a. Double click the layer thumbnail on the left side of the **Color Fill 1** layer to open the **Color Picker**.

    b. Drag the **Color Picker** window to the side and sample different colors by clicking on the image itself until you find a background which is harmonious with the flower, and then click **OK**.

10. Add a **Gradient Fill** layer to add depth to your background:

    a. Make sure that **Color Fill 1** is the active layer.

    b. Click the **New fill or adjustment layer** button at the bottom of the **Layers** panel, and choose **Gradient** near the top of the menu.

    c. Change the gradient settings until you find one you like, and click **OK**.

    We used the **Background** to **Transparent** gradient with the **Foreground** color set to black, style set to **Linear**, and **Reversed** unchecked.

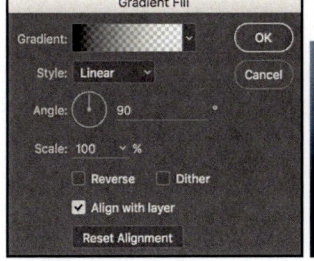

11. Add a **Pattern Fill** layer to the background, to make the background less smooth:

    a. Make sure that **Gradient Fill 1** is the active layer.

    b. Click the **New fill or adjustment layer** button at the bottom of the **Layers** panel, and choose **Patterns**.

c. Change the pattern settings until you find one you like and click **OK**.

We loaded the **Texture Fill** gradients library and chose the **Leather** gradient to fill the background with a gray leather texture.

Then we changed the blending mode of the **Pattern Fill 1** layer to **Overlay** and lowered the opacity of the layer to **50%**.

12. Save your image and keep it open for a later guided exercise.

Stroking Techniques

A **STROKE** is a border or edge that surrounds a selection, the non-transparent pixels of a layer, or other Photoshop elements.

The Stroke Command

Edit > Stroke displays the **Stroke** dialog box for stroking selections or bordering pixel edges on layers with areas of transparency. You can only stroke with individual colors, not gradients or patterns.

The **Stroke** dialog box provides a color swatch for selecting color. You can choose to stroke the inside, outside or on the center of the edge of a selection or image. You may also set a blending mode and opacity for the stroke.

The **Stroke** command is handy for putting a border around an image. The command will be grayed out in the **Edit** menu if you do not have a selection or any transparent pixels on the active layer.

Choose **Select All** before applying a stroke around the edge of the entire image, and be sure to apply the stroke to the **Inside**.

Guided Exercise 6.8: Use the Edit > Stroke Command

In the next short exercise, you will experiment with stroking an image and a selection.

1. Open **06-maple.psd**.

2. Look at the **Layers** panel. Notice that the maple leaf is on a transparent layer. Underneath is just a **Fill** layer of white.

3. Paint a stroke around the leaf:

    a. Make sure the **Maple** layer is the active layer.

    b. Choose **Edit > Stroke**.

    c. In the **Stroke** dialog box, click on the color swatch.

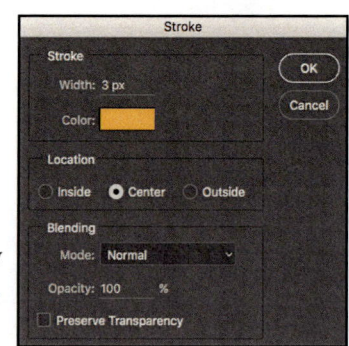

    d. In the **Color Picker**, click in the **Spectrum** column near the bottom to view red/orange colors. Move your cursor to the upper-right corner of the **Color Field** and click. Notice that the **Gamut Indicator** is visible. This means the orange color selected will not print with CMYK inks. Click on the little box under the indicator to select the closest in gamut color.

   e. Click **OK**.

   f. Back in the **Stroke** dialog box, set the **Width** to **3** pixels and **Location** to **Center** and click **OK**. Because part of the layer is transparent, the pixel information on the layer can be stroked.

4. **Undo (Command/Ctrl + Z)** to paint a different stroke.

5. Paint a stroke with partial transparency around the leaf:

   a. Choose the **Eraser Tool** from the **Tools** panel. In the **Options** bar, set the **Mode** to **Brush** and the **Opacity** to **60%**.

   a. From the **Brush Picker**, choose a large, soft brush (**65** pixels diameter with a **Hardness** of **0%**).

   b. Paint with the Eraser around the edges of the leaf so that they are nicely faded.

   c. Choose **Edit > Stroke**. Leave the settings the same as before and click **OK**.
      Notice that the stroke bleeds into the soft pixels of partial transparency.

   d. In the **Layers** panel, turn on **Lock Transparent Pixels**.

   e. Reduce your brush size to **30** pixels and keep **Hardness** at **0%**.

   f. Use the **Color Picker** to choose a dark maroon color.

   g. Paint around the edge of the leaf with the **Brush Tool**. Notice that the paint is restricted to just the leaf. No new pixels are added to the layer.

6. Sample a color from the image and use it to stroke the "edge":

   a. Choose the **Eyedropper** tool from the **Tools** Panel.

   b. Click on a deep green spot in the leaf to sample the color.

   c. To stroke the edge, we will need a selection. **Select All** using the keys **Command + A** (Mac) or **Ctrl + A** (Win).

   d. Create a new layer by clicking the **New Layer** button at the bottom of the **Layers** panel, and name that layer **border**.

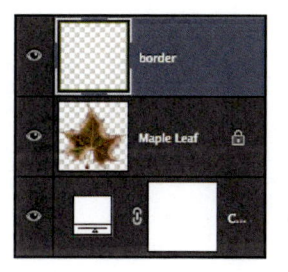

Tutorial 6: Painting   Page 139

If you begin with a selection, you can stroke the selection edge on any layer you choose. Placing the stroke onto its own layer makes it easy to change in the future.

e. Choose **Edit > Stroke**.

In the **Stroke** dialog box, notice that the color swatch reflects the **Foreground** color you sampled from the leaf.

f. Change the **Location** setting to **Inside**. Leave the **Width** set to **10** pixels and click **OK** to place a green border around the edge of the image.

7. Close the file without saving, as this exercise was just for experimentation.

Stroking with a Layer Style

The **Edit > Stroke** command has three serious drawbacks:

- It can only be applied to pixel layers, or to selections on pixel layers.
- The pixel stroke it makes is **DESTRUCTIVE**, meaning that it replaces pixels of other colors with the stroke, so that it is very difficult if not impossible to remove or alter the stroke in a later Photoshop session.
- The stroke is always hard-edged; you cannot get a soft-edged or feathered stroke with this method.

In contrast, the **Stroke** layer style is non-destructive, and has many more options for applying a stroke to a layer. But the **Stroke** layer style is also limited because it is so sensitive that it can place strokes around undesired areas.

Guided Exercise 6.9: Apply a Stroke Layer Style

Here you will place a stroke around the dahlia to finish the image.

1. Open **06-dahlia2.psd** if it is not already open.

2. Apply a **Stroke** layer style:

    a. Activate the **dahlia** layer.

    b. Click the **Add a layer style** button at the bottom of the **Layers** panel and choose **Stroke** at the bottom of the menu.

    c. Set the Size to 40 pixels.

    d. Be sure the stroke color is set to red by clicking the **Color** box and sampling a red swatch, if need be.

    e. Click **OK** to apply the **Stroke** layer style.

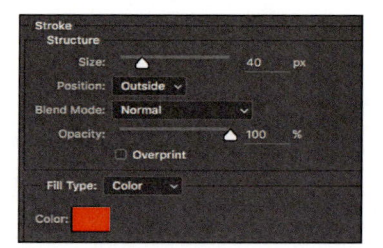

3. Change the color of the **Stroke** layer style:

    a. Double click **Stroke** in the **Layers** panel to open the **Layer Style** dialog box at the **Stroke** setting.

    b. Click the **Color** thumbnail to open the **Color Picker**, and then click on different regions of your image until you have a stroke color you like. We sampled a very light blue from the center of the flower.

    c. Since the 40-pixel stroke is so visually distracting, change the size to around 10 pixels. The thin stroke adds just a bit of definition to the flower's edge.

    Changing the **Fill Type** from the default **Color** to **Gradient** or **Pattern** provides even more ways to configure your stroke. For example, we found that stroking with a fairly big stroke (**92** pixels) set to the **Frozen Rain** pattern (included in the **Textures** library), with a blending mode of only **77%**, set to **Overlay** worked very nicely.

    This pattern stroke, instead of making a sharp outline, subtly added more grain to the part of the background that surrounds the puppet.

4. Save your completed dahlia, and print if desired.

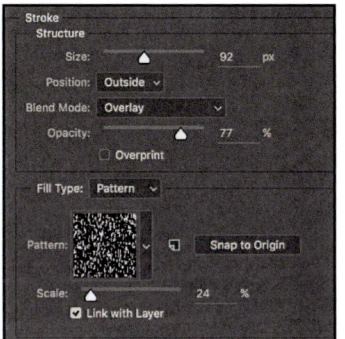

Painting with a Variety of Tools, Options, and Commands

The painting tools and commands will hopefully become more familiar as you use them to paint a cartoon image of a woman and her dog. These techniques are actually used for comic book development where the artist first hand-sketches the drawings and then either scans them into Photoshop or redraws the drawings in either Photoshop or Adobe Illustrator. Finally, Photoshop is used to colorize the drawing.

Guided Exercise 6.10: Painting a Cartoon

In this exercise, you will paint on a cartoon image using tools and commands introduced in this chapter. You will work with the **Swatches** and **Color** panels, load brush presets, and practice changing brush settings.

1. Reset the **Essentials** workspace, all tools, and the default **Foreground** and **Background** colors.

2. Open **06-cartoon.psd** and save it as **cartoon.psd**.

3. Open the **Layers** panel and examine the layers.

There are two layers. The top **Outlines** layer is mostly transparent with black cartoon lines. This layer is locked so that you don't accidentally paint on it or move it. Keep the **Outlines** layer at the top of the layer stack throughout this exercise. The bottom layer is a white **Color Fill** layer.

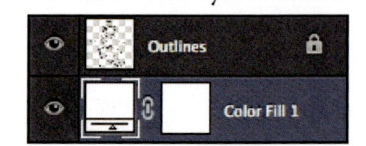

4. Paint the sky with the **Gradient Tool**:

   a. Make sure the **Color Fill 1** layer is active.

   b. Create a new layer by clicking the **New Layer** button at the bottom of the **Layers** panel. The new layer should appear as the middle layer.

   c. Rename the new layer **Sky**. You will use this layer to create a gradient to represent the sky.

   d. Use the **Quick Selection** tool with **Sample All Layers** checked to quickly select the sky region behind the woman. (Selecting the region first will limit the gradient to that region.)

   e. Click on the **Foreground Color** swatch in the **Tools** panel to display the **Color Picker**. Type in these **RGB** values: **R-52, G-138, B-218**. Notice the **Gamut Indicator** appears. This means that the color selected will not print with **CMYK** inks. Click the little box below the warning triangle to choose the closest printable blue and click **OK**.

   f. Click on the **Background Color** swatch in the **Tools** panel, then choose a light blue color and click **OK**.

   g. Choose the **Gradient Tool** from the **Tools** panel.

   h. In the **Options** bar, click the arrow to the right of the gradient thumbnail to display the **Gradient Picker**.

   i. Choose the first selection, **Foreground to Background**, with the shape option set to **Linear Gradient**, the first shape.

   j. In the document window, click at the top of the image and drag straight downward with the mouse to the bottom of the selection.

5. Color the glasses for the woman and her dog with more gradients:

   a. Create a new layer above the Sky layer and name it **Glasses**.

   b. Make a dark green **Foreground** color and a light green **Background** color by sampling your colors from the **Color Picker**.

   c. Select both sides of the woman's sunglasses.

   d. With the **Gradient Tool**, click at the bottom of the selection and drag to the top.

   e. Choose different Foreground and Background colors.

   f. Select the dog's sunglasses, and paint a gradient in them using the colors you chose.

6. Make and save a color swatch:

   It is helpful to create a swatch for each of the major colors that you use for a given project. Later, if you want to switch back to a color, you can quickly get it from the **Swatches** panel.

   a. In the **Color** Picker sample a red-brown or adobe color for the **Foreground** color.

   b. Click on the **Swatches** tab at the top of its panel group to switch to the **Swatches** panel.

   c. Move the cursor over a blank area of the **Swatches** panel to see the **paint bucket** icon.

   d. Click to create a swatch of the chosen color.

   e. In the **Color Swatch Name** dialog box name the swatch **Hills** and click **OK**.

7. Add a new layer, and name it **Hills**.

8. Paint the **Hills** layer with a brush from a brush library:

   a. Choose the **Brush Tool**.

   b. Click the **Brush Preset** picker and then its panel menu, and choose **Dry Media Brushes** near the bottom of the list to load the **Dry Media Brushes**.

   c. In the dialog box that pops up, click the **Append** button to add the **Dry Media Brushes** to the list of current brushes.

   d. Again, from the **Brush Preset** picker pop-out menu, choose the **Small List** option for viewing brushes. This option shows both a small brush thumbnail, and its text name to make it easier to find a special brush.

   e. Scroll down the brush presets to choose **Pastel on Charcoal Paper**. This brush simulates textured paper.

   f. In the **Options** bar, set **Flow** to **20%**. The more you paint with the **Pastel on Charcoal** brush, the more it will become a solid color. To preserve its texture effect, you will want the paint to flow more slowly.

   g. Paint with the brush over the hills area in the background. Go ahead and paint roughly; do not worry about staying within the lines. Be sure to not obscure the texture effect of the brush by painting the hills a solid color.

   h. Choose the **Eraser Tool**. Choose a soft, round brush, adjusting the size as needed. Paint with the **Eraser Tool** to clean up any stray paint outside of the lines.

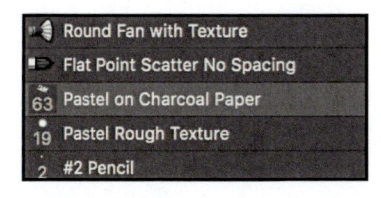

Tutorial 6: Painting   Page 143

9. Paint grassy stuff onto the lower background region:

    a. Sample a light green color with more yellow in it, and create a swatch for it in the **Swatches Panel**.

    b. Create a new layer and name it **Grass**.

    c. Choose the **Brush Tool**, and the **Oil Medium Wet Flow** brush.

    d. Leave the **Flow** set to **20%**. Begin painting in the background from the hills forward. Again, paint roughly, knowing you can clean up with the **Eraser Tool**. Adjust the size of the brush as you see fit. Try to get a painterly effect.

    e. Adjust the brush **Opacity** down to about **35%**, leaving **Flow** at **20%** or lower. Choose first a darker green, and then a lighter green and paint over the same area with both colors to get color variations.

    f. Again use the **Eraser Tool** to eliminate any stray paint.

10. Use another specialty brush to paint blades of grass onto the foreground:

    a. Choose the **Brush Tool**. In the **Brush Preset** picker, click on the pop-out menu button and choose the **Small Thumbnail** view (the default). This view will give you a thumbnail of the brush shape.

    b. Scroll down the **Brush** presets and choose a brush that looks like 3 strands of grass. If you let the cursor hover over it, you will see a tool tip that says **Grass**.

    c. The **Grass** preset is set to a large size, **134 pixels**. Adjust the size down as you see fit.

    d. The **Grass** brush works with both the **Foreground** and **Background** colors. Choose a light and a dark green, but lighter and darker than the ones you already used.

    e. Experiment with changing the **Opacity** and **Flow**. A low flow seems to work well. Paint over the foreground. Go for as subtle or as intense an effect that you want.

11. Create a new layer for the woman and one for the dog. Continue painting and experimenting with brushes and settings.

12. Make a new swatch for every color you use. Create a new layer if you think you want to erase to clean up your painting. For instance, the woman's dress might need a new layer, so your brush strokes can be cleaned off of the woman's skin. Try loading the **Special Effect** brush presets to find a brush that will paint a pattern on the dress.

13. Save your image, and print if desired.

After experimenting with different methods of selecting colors, viewing your brush presets in the **Brush Picker**, and using different brushes, you will start to develop your own favorite way of working. Make a note of the brushes that you like.

On Your Own

Design and Color Your Own Cartoon

1. Open the original **06-cartoon.psd** and save it as **mycartoon.psd**.

2. Erase everything on the **outlines** layer (activate the layer, select all, and then press the Delete key).

3. Use the **Brush Tool** with black paint to paint your own cartoon outlines onto the **outlines** layer.

4. Use the techniques you learned in Tutorial 6 to colorize your cartoon.

Resources and Videos

http://www.practical-photoshop.com/pages/CC2015-pp1-resources.html#06

Practical Photoshop CC 2015, Level 1
Tutorial 7: Image Sources and Resolution

There are basically four ways that you can acquire digital images:

- Start with a new blank document, and paint the image from scratch. This is probably the least common source.
- Take photographs with a digital camera or phone.
- Use a **SCANNER**, a machine that converts printed images or slides into digital images.
- Use images made by someone else that were posted on an Internet site or distributed on a disk.

In this tutorial, you will examine image sources and then take a closer look at image resolution, including digital camera and scanning resolutions and image resizing.

Objectives

- Define copyright, and give at least one reason why it is unethical (and probably violates copyright law) to copy images off the Internet without permission.
- Describe how to embed and read a digital watermark.
- Visit at least one online image source, read its fair use agreement, and download an image.
- Use the **Image Size** dialog box to evaluate image resolution and change image sizes.
- Explain the relationship between image interpolation and resampling.
- Relate the megapixels that digital cameras capture to image pixel dimensions, print size, and resolution.
- Change the print resolution of a digital camera image with and without resampling, and evaluate the consequences of each.
- Scan a photograph directly into Photoshop.

Copyright and Image Use Ethics

Just because you can scan an image into your computer or download it from the World Wide Web, that does not mean that you have the right to use it. A common misconception is that if your are using an image as a student, or a not-for-profit venture, you can use it freely. This is not true. If you see an image that you want to use, email the webmaster for that site or person who posted the image and ask permission.

> We expect that you will only use digital images that you have the rights to use in any projects you develop. ***Do the right thing!***

You can read more about copyright at: http://www.copyright.gov

Here are a couple of quotes to give you more copyright information:

> "Since the advent of personal computers, digital media files have become easy to copy an unlimited number of times without any degradation in the quality of subsequent copies.... The popularity of the Internet and file sharing tools have made the distribution of copyrighted digital media files simple.
>
> The unauthorized availability of multiple perfect copies of copyrighted materials is perceived by much of the media industry as a threat to its viability and profitability, particularly within the music and movie industries. Digital media publishers typically have business models that rely on their ability to collect a fee for each copy made of a digital work, and sometimes for each performance of said work."

http://en.wikipedia.org/wiki/Digital_rights_management

> "**COPYRIGHT** is the body of legal rights that protect creative works from being reproduced, performed, or disseminated by others without permission. The owner of copyright has the exclusive right to reproduce a protected work; to prepare derivative works that only slightly change the protected work; to sell or lend copies of the protected work to the public; to perform protected works in public for profit; and to display copyrighted works publicly. These basic exclusive rights of copyright owners are subject to exceptions depending on the type of work and the type of use made by others."

Microsoft Encarta 1996

WATERMARKING

Prior to digital graphics, a **WATERMARK** was a distinguishing symbol or "mark" that was impressed into paper when it was made. If you held the paper up to the light, you could see its watermark.

Digital photographers and artists add watermarks to their images to mark their creations as their own. The image shown here belongs to http://www.photospin.com; there is a clear watermark across this low-resolution image downloaded from their Web site. If you want to use a high-resolution version of this image, without the watermark, you will need to purchase the license from **Photospin** to use the image.

THE DIGIMARC FILTER

Digimarc makes a filter that embeds an invisible, or nearly invisible watermark into digital images. According to the Digimarc Web site, this software can "allow users to embed into audio, images, video and printed documents a digital code that is imperceptible during normal use but readable by computers and software." Prior to Photoshop CC 2015, the Digimarc filters were automatically installed when you installed Photoshop. Now, you first need to go to http://www.digimarc.com/products/guardian/images/adobe-photoshop-cc-2015-notice to download, then install the filters. Once installed, you can follow these directions to use the filters:

Here is how to embed and read a **Digimarc** watermark:

1. Open an image to watermark within Photoshop.

2. Choose **Image > Duplicate** to preserve your unwatermarked original.

3. Choose **Filter > Digimarc > Embed Watermark** to embed a demonstration watermark into an image.

4. Determine how effective you want your watermark to be, trading off visibility with durability (the more visible the watermark, the more durable or difficult to remove it is), and click **OK** to embed your watermark.

5. The **Verification** box will appear. Click **OK** to dismiss it.

6. Save your image to permanently embed the watermark into the image.

Filter > Digimarc > Read Watermark lets you check an image to see if it has an embedded watermark or not.

NOTE: *The Digimarc filter bundled with Photoshop is only for demonstration purposes.* To embed your personal watermark into images, you must purchase the professional version of **Digimarc**, starting at $59 for 1000 images. https://www.digimarc.com/application/photography.

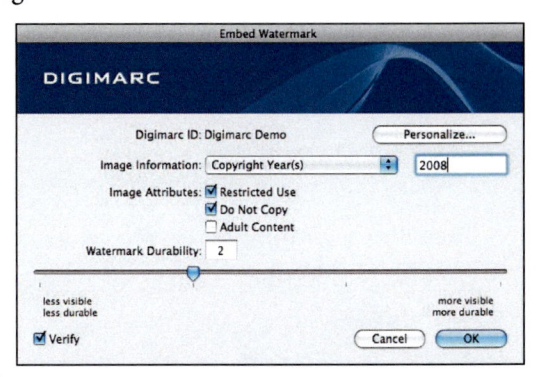

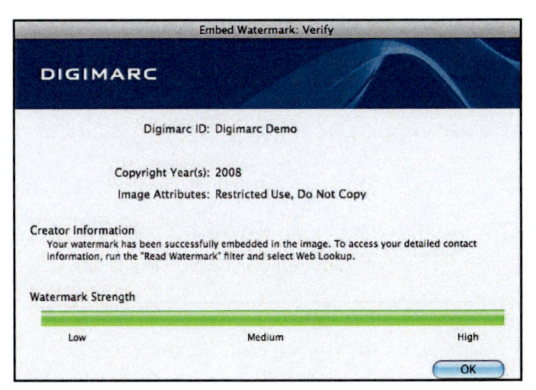

If you search the Web for digital watermarks in Photoshop, you will see tutorials for a number of ways to make your own watermarks.

Image Sources

There are many digital image sources on the Web. You can obtain some of these images for free; you will have to pay for others. Each image Web site has a use statement on it somewhere that explains how you can use the images. Many of these sites allow you free downloading and use for personal, non-commercial experimentation, but expect you to pay a royalty fee if you use the images commercially.

Be careful about the resolution of images you download. Online digital images are typically at screen resolution (72 ppi), and do not contain enough pixels for high quality printing.

Many talented photographers post photos online at specific sites for anyone to use, as long as you follow the fair use guidelines posted on the site. Below are some examples of sites where you can download "free" images. Most of these sites expect you to establish a user name and password in order to download high-resolution images.

Public Image Sources

Don't overlook government sources of images. With few exceptions, any images created by the Federal government are considered public domain. Here are a couple of public sources:

- **NASA** (http://www.nasa.gov) has a large library of space-related images. Usage information is available at http://www.nasa.gov/audience/formedia/features/MP_Photo_Guidelines.html.

- The **Library of Congress** (http://www.loc.gov) has an extremely large Prints & Photographs collection. As per their usage guidelines at http://www.loc.gov/rr/print/195_copr.html, all images are noted as to copyright status.

Free Images

According to their Web site, the **Free Images** (http://www.freeimages.com) is "the leading source of free stock photos." Their use terms are very generous. You can use any of the photos in their system "free of charge for any commercial or personal design work if you obey the specified restrictions concerning each photo you download." If you use an image, they ask that you email the artist and let the contributor know how you will use the image.

Professional photographers and hobbyists from throughout the world contribute images to the Free Images and evaluate each other's work. It is a tremendous resource.

Free Stock Photos

Free Stock Photos is a smaller but similar site to Free Images, with an additional restriction that you credit Free Stock Photos whenever you use one of their images. http://freestockphotos.com.

FreeFoto

According to their Web site, http://www.freefoto.com allows for free Internet use of their images, provided you give credit and a link back to their site. For commercial usage, their images are available for a reasonable licensing fee.

Public Domain Photos

Public Domain Photos claims to have the "largest collection of public domain photos on the Internet." Their warning: "All photos on this Web site are public domain. You may use these images for any purpose, including commercial. But if some photo contains logos and products you need to be careful. Using someone else's trademark commercially can get you sued." http://www.public-domain-photos.com/

Google Image Search

You can search for images using **Google's** very powerful searching capabilities: http://images.google.com.

WARNING: *Google takes no responsibility for keeping track of the copyright status of any of the images it locates. It is your responsibility to go to the source site(s) and check each image's usage terms.*

Resolution Revisited

In Tutorial 2, you were introduced to resolution, and you sized some images for printing and screen purposes. Now that you have had more Photoshop experience it is time to take a second look at resolution, to evaluate images with unknown resolutions, and to better understand what Photoshop is doing when it changes the resolution of an image. Let us begin with the **Image Size** dialog box.

The Image Size Dialog Box

The **Image > Image Size** command opens a dialog box where you can view and change the resolution of an image. The **Image Size** dialog box is critical for setting up documents for printing.

Let's locate the key regions of the **Image Size** dialog box, and see how they work. We have used **07-bridge.jpg**, if you want to open it and follow along:

Choose **Image > Image Size.**

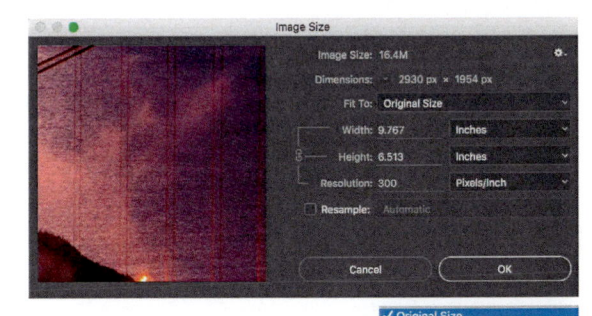

- **07-bridge.jpg** is **1.1M** compressed in **JPEG** format and saved to disk. However, Image Size show a size of **16.4M**. The bigger number is the total size of the file in **RAM** for editing in Photoshop.

- Next you see the Dimensions (number of pixels) of the document — 2930 px x 1954 px here.

- Below that is the **Fit To** menu. This allows you to choose from among a number of preset image dimensions at specific **PPI** settings. Choosing one of these presets will resample the image to get as close as possible to the chosen preset, without distorting the proportions.

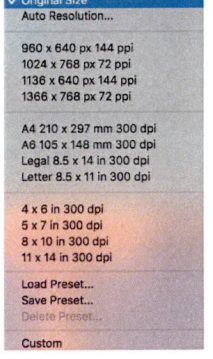

- Next are the values for **Width** and **Height**. If you change one of these values, you change the quantity of pixels in the document—as well as the total file size.

  Notice the chain or link icon to the left of the **Width** and **Height.** They are linked so that if you change one value, the other changes to keep your document in proportion. Click the link symbol to unlink the width and height values, if you want to distort the image. Typically you would leave them linked.

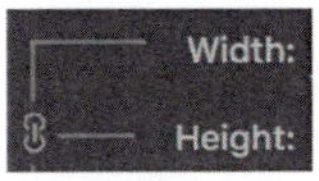

  Sometimes it is convenient to resize a document by **Percent** rather than **Pixels**. For example, this screenshot was shrunk to **75%** to make it fit better on the page. The drop-down menu to the right of **Width** or **Height** lets you change your dimensions measurement from **Pixels** to **Percent**. When you switch, it starts at **100%**; type in a new percentage to change the file size.

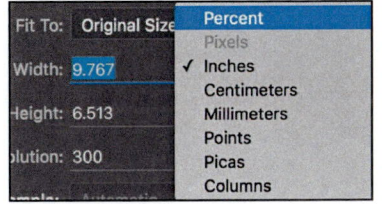

Tutorial 7: Image Sources and Resolution

Width and **Height** give the physical size of the document as it will print. Often measured in inches, Photoshop documents can also be measured in percent, pixels, centimeters, millimeters, points, picas, or columns (used to resize images to set sizes for newspaper or magazine work). **Resolution**, measured in **PIXELS PER INCH (PPI)**, relates to the **DOTS PER INCH (DPI)** the printer will output.

NOTE: *You will rarely ever set a print-ready Photoshop document to more than 300 ppi* because **300 ppi** contains enough information for modern high resolution printers to interpolate to their higher **1200+ dpi** when they print.

- If a document contains more than **300 ppi**, it will take much longer to print, but its output will not be any better than the **300 ppi** document.

- **Resample** changes image dimensions by either adding or discarding pixels. The file size will change as pixels are added or removed. Uncheck **Resample** when you do not want to change the image's pixel dimensions.

- **Scale Styles,** available in the pop-out menu in the upper-right corner of the Image Size dialog box, proportionally adjusts special layer effects such as drop shadows so that they stay in proportion when image dimensions are changed. Typically you should keep **Scale Styles** checked.

Resampling

When you **RESAMPLE** an image, you change both the its pixel dimensions and its file size.

DOWNSAMPLING permanently removes pixels. The image becomes smaller, both in quality resolution (fewer pixels such as 150 ppi to 72 ppi) and in quantity resolution or dimensions (8 x 6 inches to 4 x 3). The quality of the image will degrade a little, becoming more blurry.

UPSAMPLING means that you are asking Photoshop to add pixels to the image to enlarge its pixel dimensions. Photoshop has to mathematically generate the additional pixels, and this typically degrades the image as well.

You can sometimes get away with a small amount of upsampling, but the more you upsample the worse the image quality becomes. This cannot be compensated for with any magical Photoshop trick.

The left square shows a 10 x 10 pixel document with a resolution of 10 ppi in which each pixel was given a different color. The right square was upsampled from the original to 20 x 20 pixels at a resolution of 20 ppi.

If you look closely, you can see that pixel colors were not added uniformly when upsampled. The reddish purple and maroon colors bled into areas where you would not want them. The overall effect is to blur the image. Now imagine doing the same enlargement to a photograph. Image detail will be greatly compromised.

Tutorial 7: Image Sources and Resolution

Try it on your own with a digital photograph and see what happens to the image. Choose **Image > Image Size** and check **Resample**. Change either the **Width** or **Height** dimensions, or else change the **Resolution** to a much higher number.

Interpolation

IMAGE INTERPOLATION describes the method used when scaling, resizing, rotating, or otherwise transforming images and selections. It is the method Photoshop uses to mathematically determine how to fill in the "missing" pixels when upsampling, or precisely how to remove the excess pixels when downsampling an image. Since interpolation can degrade image quality, it is important to pick the method that will do the best job.

Of the six choices of **interpolation** provided in the **Image Size** dialog box, four of them will give you the best results:

- **Automatic** will automatically choose one of the six resampling methods, depending on whether you are upsampling or downsampling.
- **Bicubic**, gives reasonably precise resampling, resulting in fairly smooth tonal gradations.
- **Bicubic Smoother** is designed for minimizing artifacts when **UPSAMPLING** images.
- **Bicubic Sharper** is used to minimize softening of images when **DOWNSAMPLING**. This is the interpolation method used for almost all the screen images in these notes. Occasionally **Bicubic Sharper** will over-sharpen image areas. If that happens, undo and use plain **Bicubic** instead.

With **Resample Image off** (unchecked) you can no longer change the overall file size and pixel dimensions, but you can still change the (print) Width and Height or **Resolution** so that when printed, there will be more or fewer pixels per inch. This is the setting to use when you set up a document for printing. You will do this later in this tutorial.

Digital Cameras

Images captured by older or consumer-level digital cameras typically have no ppi or dpi—the only resolution they measure is the absolute width and height of images in pixels, such as 640 x 480, the resolution of the original digital cameras. While some newer cameras assign a print ppi to digital images, older cameras did not have this ability. When images from older digital camera are opened, Photoshop needs to assign a ppi and automatically gives them **72 ppi**.

To change the print resolution of an image, you typically resize it with **Resample** unchecked or "off" to increase the print resolution without adding or removing any pixels. This will decrease print size, but increase ppi.

Compare these three image size examples:

Before resizing, this relatively low-resolution image, **07-leaves.jpg**, has **Pixel Dimensions** of 1024 x 768. Its **Document Size** when printed is **14.222 x 10.667 inches**.

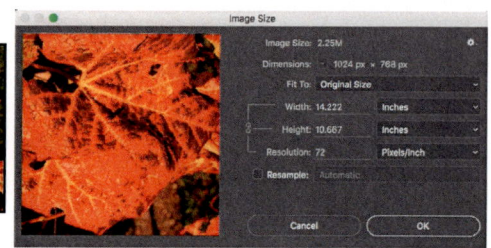

It is too big to fit on a standard piece of letter-size printing paper. Even though the paper is 8 1/2 x 11 inches, when you take **PRINTER MARGINS**, the region of the paper that most printers can't print, into account, you are left with about 8 x 10 inches of printable area.

If **Resample** is **checked** and the **Resolution** set to 300, changing the **Resolution** box value also changes the image's **Pixel Dimensions** to 4267x3200 pixels. Bigger numbers **UPSAMPLE** the image and smaller numbers **DOWNSAMPLE** it.

Next, **Resample** was **unchecked**, and the **Resolution** was changed from **72** to **300 ppi**. Notice that the document's **Pixel Dimensions** did not change. But, with the increased resolution of **300 ppi**, the (printed) **Width and Height** is much smaller, **3.1413 x 2.56 inches**.

Let's add one more size to the mix. Many ink jet printers give excellent results with the **Resolution** set to **240 ppi**, *lower* than the **300 ppi** Adobe recommends. **240 ppi** lets you print a physically larger image, without resampling. With a resolution of **240 ppi**, the (printed) **Width and Height** enlarges to **4.267 x 3.2 inches**.

In sum, when **Resample** is unchecked, if you change the image's resolution, you do not change the image's pixel dimensions, nor the size of the file. To avoid resampling your pixels, you will typically keep it unchecked.

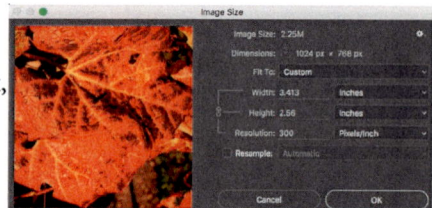

. . . .

Digital Camera Resolution

Different digital cameras capture different quantities of pixels, measured in millions of pixels, or **MEGAPIXELS**. The same camera can be set to capture different resolutions as well. **HIGH-RESOLUTION** means the image has enough pixels to print the desired size at 240-300 ppi without resampling. The number of pixels captured limits the printed size of a high-quality image.

The chart on the next page can help you to calculate the biggest image you can print based on image pixel dimension. Some of the print sizes have been rounded down.

GUIDED EXERCISE 7.1: RESIZE A DIGITAL CAMERA IMAGE WITHOUT RESAMPLING

In this guided exercise, you will open a high-resolution digital camera image and resize the image without resampling. With each resize, you should print the image, so that you can see the relationship between ppi and print quality.

If you are using an ink jet printer, be sure to print on photo paper to best assess the differences in print quality.

Megapixels	Pixel Dimensions	Print Size
0.3 megapixels	640 x 480	72 ppi: 8.9 x 6.7 inches
		240 ppi: 2.7 x 2 inches
		300 ppi: 2.1 x 1.6 inches
5 megapixels	2560 x 1920	72 ppi: 35.6 x 26.7 inches
		240 ppi: 10.7 x 8 inches
		300 ppi: 8.5 x 6.4 inches
8 megapixels	3264 x 2468	772 ppi: 45.3 x 34.3 inches
		240 ppi: 13.6 x 10.3 inches
		300 ppi: 10.9 x 8.2 inches
12 megapixels	4000 x 3000	72 ppi: 55.6 x 41.7 inches
		240 ppi: 16.7 x 12.5 inches
		300 ppi: 13.3 x 10 inches
16 megapixels	4608 x 3456	72 ppi: 64 x 48 inches
		240 ppi: 19.2 x 14.4 inches
		300 ppi: 15.4 x 11.5 inches
18 megapixels	5196 x 3464	72 ppi: 72 x 48 inches
		240 ppi: 21.7 x 14.4 inches
		300 ppi: 17.3 x 11.6 inches

1. Open **07-rugs.jpg** and save it as **rugs.psd** in the location of your choice.

2. Examine the edges of the document window.

   By default, they do not show dimensions. If that is the case, choose **View > Rulers** to display horizontal and vertical rulers on the edges of the document window.

3. From the **Status** bar pop-up menu, choose **Document Dimensions** so that you can keep track of resolution changes as we work with this image.

   Unaltered, the document will print at about **41.7 x 33.3 inches**, at **72 ppi**.

   If the document dimensions are not shown in inches:, **right-click** (two button mouse) or **ctrl + click** (one button mouse) on one of the rulers and choose **Inches** from the context menu that appears.

4. At the original **72 ppi**, print in **Landscape** (wide) to fit as much of the image as possible onto 8.5 x 11 inch paper. You will compare this output with changes in ppi you will make for two more printouts:

   a. Choose **File > Print**.

   b. Click the **Landscape** button in **Layout** near the top of the dialog box.

   c. In the **Position and Size** settings, *do not* click **Scale to Fit Media**.

   d. Since the image size is larger than the 8.5 x 11 inch paper size, only the center of the image will print, and the rest will be cut off.

   e. Click **Proceed** when you get the warning that the image is larger than the paper's printable area; some clipping will occur.

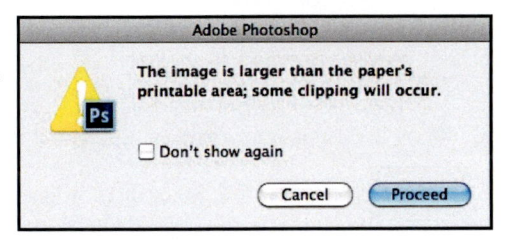

Tutorial 7: Image Sources and Resolution

f. Examine the printout. Only the center of the photograph prints, and while the details of the rugs are visible, they are not very sharp.

5. Use the **Image Size** dialog box to resize the image without resampling, and print a second version:

   a. Choose **Image > Image Size** to open the **Image Size** dialog box.

      Notice the pixel dimensions, **3000 x 2400**.

   b. Uncheck **Resample** if necessary, type **240** into the **Resolution** box, and click **OK**.

      The **Status** bar now tells you that the document will print at approximately **12.5 by 10 inches** at **240 ppi**.

      The document pixels are unchanged because you increased the print resolution *without* changing the document dimensions.

   c. Print the document a second time with **Layout** set to **Landscape** and **Scale to Fit Media** unchecked like before.

      Now your printout includes *almost* all of the photograph. The rugs are much sharper, but cover less of the overall image.

6. Repeat step 5 with your **Resolution** set to **300 ppi** with **Resample** unchecked.

   Now the entire document will print at **10 x 8 inches** as you have crunched more pixels (to become printed dots) in each inch of the document.

7. Save **rugs.psd**. This is now the **300 ppi** version.

. . . .

GUIDED EXERCISE 7.2: RESIZE A DIGITAL CAMERA IMAGE WITH RESAMPLE CHECKED

In this guided exercise, you will duplicate **rugs.psd** and resize the image with **Resample** checked to compare the printouts at **240 ppi** and **300 ppi**.

1. With **rugs.psd** open, choose **File > Save As**, and save the duplicate as **rugs240.psd** in the location of your choice.

2. Choose **Image > Image Size** to open the **Image Size** dialog box, check **Resample**, type **240** into the **Resolution** box, and click **OK**.

   With **Resample** checked, pixels are discarded and the document shrinks from **20.5M** to **13.2M** (when open in Photoshop).

3. Print the document again compare its quality with the **300 ppi** printout.

   - Most modern ink jet and color laser printers recommend **300 ppi** for best quality printouts.

- If you don't see a quality difference, **240 ppi** is probably an adequate resolution for your printer. The advantage to **240 ppi** is that the file size is considerably smaller and the lower resolution file will print more quickly.

- If you do see a significant difference or if you will be sending images to a service that requires **300 ppi**, then by all means stick with **300 ppi**.

GUIDED EXERCISE 7.3: RESIZE ANOTHER DIGITAL CAMERA IMAGE WITH RESAMPLING CHECKED

In this guided exercise, you will open a high-resolution digital camera image and reduce the file size from **300 ppi** to **72 ppi** with **Resample** checked. Then you will increase the ppi back to **300 ppi**, and examine the quality of the re-enlarged image.

1. Open **07-bodie.jpg** and save it as **bodie.psd** in the location of your choice.

   This document has the same pixel dimensions as **07-rugs.jpg**, 3000 x 2400.

2. Choose **Image > Duplicate** to make a second version of the image.

3. Downsample the duplicate to **72 ppi**:

   a. Choose **Image > Image Size** to open the **Image Size** dialog box.

   b. With **Resample** checked, type **72** into the **Resolution** box.

   Bicubic Automatic will use **Bicubic Sharper** interpolation to remove pixels and the file size will shrink from **20.6M** to **1.19M**.

   c. Click **OK**.

   If you saved this version now, without changing the image's **Width** or **Height**, you would have a much smaller version of the original image that you could save in **JPG** format and email to a friend.

4. Upsample the image back to its original size:

   a. Choose **Image > Image Size**.

   b. Set the pixel **Width** to **3000**, and click **OK** to upsample the file.

   c. **Bicubic Automatic** used **Bicubic Smoother** interpolation to "reconstruct" the missing pixels and the image enlarges back to **20.6M**.

5. Compare the quality of the two files:

   a. Double-click the **Zoom Tool** to view the copy at **100%**.

   b. In the **Navigator** panel, move the proxy over the sign on the front bumper in the thumbnail.

c. Choose **Window > Arrange > Match Zoom and Location** to view both open documents at the same zoom percentage (**100%**) and document location.

Notice how blurry the resampled image is compared to the original. You can barely read the sign on the altered image, even though the resampled image has the same pixel dimensions as the original.

This example demonstrates why it is so important to capture an image at appropriate resolution, rather than try to add image resolution with the **Resample** check box. Every time you resample, either upward or downward, you lose quality.

Scanning Photographs & Other Printed Materials

SCANNERS are machines that convert prints or slides (analog images) into digital files to be used by the computer. To decide how to scan an image, you should know how you plan to use it. Scan images to be placed on the Web at **72 ppi**. Scan color and grayscale print images at **300 dpi** (higher if you plan to enlarge them).

If you scan at too high a resolution, your file will be huge, and take a long time to edit and to print—but your printout will not be of better quality. The printer indiscriminately throws away pixel information when it prints. It is better to scan at appropriate resolution and control the image yourself.

If you scan at too low a resolution, your image quality will suffer because the computer interpolates or uses pixel mathematics to fill in missing data. Your image may appear jagged, pixilated, or blurry.

Troubleshooting Your Scanner Setup

Some scanners allow you to scan directly into Photoshop, while others require you to use their proprietary applications. See the specific instructions for your scanner to see which method you will use.

To Scan Directly into Photoshop

1. Place your photograph, drawing, or painting onto the flatbed scanner. (We do not teach slide scanning in beginning Photoshop.)

2. Choose **File > Import > Your Scanner** (the name varies from one scanner to another). This command opens the scanning software.

3. Choose the resolution you want to use for your printed file and specify that you want to scan a color photograph. Remember that if you are enlarging a small image, you will need to scan at a high enough resolution, then use the **Image > Image Size** command to change the print resolution.

4. Use the scanning software to scan your image.

5. When your scan is complete, Photoshop will display the scanned image as an unsaved Photoshop file.

6. Choose **File > Save As**, name the file, and save it in Photoshop format (**PSD**).

7. Remove your original media from the bed of the scanner.

NOTE: not all scanners have software to scan directly into Photoshop. Instead, you must open the scanning software from the desktop, and save the scanned image before opening in Photoshop. When asked what file format to use, choose **TIFF** because that format preserves the most image detail of the original scan. Open Photoshop, and then choose **File > Open** to open the **TIFF** file. Choose **File > Save As** and save the file in native Photoshop or **PSD** format before you edit it.

HINT: keep original scans untouched, and edit a copy of the scanned image so that you don't need to rescan the image if you "mess up."

On Your Own

With your own images, experiment with the various resizing techniques shown in this tutorial.

Resources and Videos

http://www.practical-photoshop.com/pages/CC2015-pp1-resources.html#07

Practical Photoshop CC 2015, Level 1
Tutorial 8: Design Principles & Effective Cropping

DESIGN PRINCIPLES are guidelines that suggest how to best arrange the various elements of a composition. In page layout or desktop publishing, design principles apply to color scheme and typography, as well as to the relationship between text and graphics on an entire document, and on each printed page. In Web design, effective use of design principles apply to the appearance of the overall site, as well as the composition of individual graphic elements and photographs. We will explore some of these design principles in this tutorial.

In Photoshop, some design principles are more relevant than others. For starters, each Photoshop document is a single page rather than a multi-page publication or Web site. Next, since most Photoshop documents are based on photographs, there are special considerations to be made for photographic composition.

Photographers have control of many elements that can make the distinction between just OK and great photographs. As a photographer, you need to develop and use your photographer's eye to see beyond the usual. There are some basic principles that will help you when you go out and shoot photos.

Then, as you work on projects where you blend together or build a **COMPOSITE** of several images, design principles can guide you to make more effective compositions.

Depending on the media you are working in, and who you consult, you will find different lists of design principles. For example, **about.com** (http://desktoppub.about.com/cs/basic/g/principles.htm) lists the following, in alphabetical order: alignment, balance, consistency, contrast, proximity, repetition, unity, and white space. We have based this tutorial on the design principles from Robin Williams' short book, *The Non-Designers Design Book* (Peachpit Press, 2008, ISBN-10: 0-321-53404-2) that we recommend you read for more examples and ideas about using design principles to improve your design work.

Thank you Robin. http://www.peachpit.com/store/non-designers-design-book-9780321534040

So why are we including a tutorial on design principles in the middle of a Photoshop text? First, because understanding and using design principles in your Photoshop work can guide you to make more pleasing compositions.

Second, because Adobe includes design principles in the **Adobe Certified Associate** (**ACA**) exam that some of you may want to take after you complete this course, and a second semester of Photoshop. You can learn more about the ACA exam, and download the learning objectives for the exam at http://www.adobe.com/education/resources/certificate-programs.edu.html.

Objectives

- Identify the four basic design principles from *The Non-Designers Design Book* called **PARC**—**proximity**, **alignment**, **repetition**, and **contrast**—and explain how to apply these principles to compositions.

- Examine the photographic principles listed in Adobe's ACA study prep guide, and apply them to photographic examples.
- Use the photographic design principles to crop photographs.

PARC: The Four Basic Design Principles

The **PARC** acronym stands for **proximity**, **alignment**, **repetition**, and **contrast**, the four basic design principles. These principles relate to one another, and you will use them together to make effective designs. We will present the principles in the following order; **alignment**, **proximity**, **contrast**, and **repetition**. Although the order does not follow the acronym, it will be simpler for you to follow. These first examples use page layout samples because it is easier to assess the design with examples based on text, not images.

As you examine these text-based examples, try to visualize how you can relate them to photographic images and compositions.

Alignment

ALIGNMENT, sometimes called **JUSTIFICATION,** is the lining up of the top, bottom, sides, or middle of text or graphic elements on a page. Using just one alignment per page, or two at the most, will help unify the page.

> The principle of alignment states that **nothing should be placed on the page arbitrarily. Every item should have a visual connection with something else on the page**.... Even when elements are physically separated from each other, if they are aligned, there is an invisible line that connects them, both in your eye and in your mind.
>
> — Robin Williams, *The Non-Designer's Design Book*

Without alignment, the elements of a page or composition look haphazard, and it is difficult to know where to look first, or next. When elements are aligned, the document or image looks unified.

CENTER ALIGNMENT

CENTER ALIGNMENT places all the lines of text, or other elements, into the middle of the page as shown here. Center aligned text can be hard to read, and boring to look at. It is best to avoid center alignment except in some formal layouts, such as wedding invitations.

Sticking elements into the corners of a layout separates rather than unifies the elements, and is also discouraged.

RIGHT ALIGNMENT or **LEFT ALIGNMENT** places all the lines of text to the right or left side. This business card is right aligned, leaving some breathing space along the right edge. This card is more professional and inviting than the others and has a much cleaner look because of its strong vertical line.

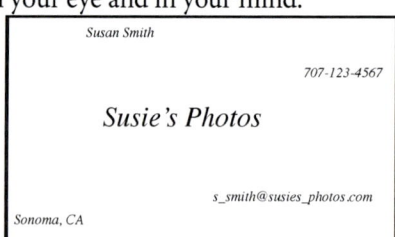

Proximity

PROXIMITY means closeness.

> The principle of proximity states that you **group related items together**—move them physically close to each other—so the related items are seen as a cohesive group, rather than a bunch of unrelated bits. Items or groups of information that are not related to each other should not be close in proximity (nearness) to the other elements which gives the reader an instant visual clue as to the organization and content of the page.
> — Robin Williams, *The Non-Designer's Design Book*

The purpose of proximity is to organize. Grouped elements are much more organized than items scattered across the page. But, be careful with proximity. Use blank areas, known as **WHITE SPACE**, to separate unrelated elements. Also take care not to include too many elements or your project will become cluttered and confusing.

No Proximity of Elements

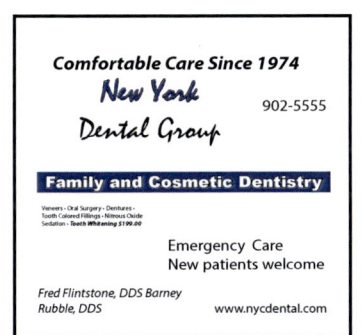

In this example, taken from a telephone book (with names changed to protect the innocent), the information is spread all around the advertisement without thought to proximity.

Elements are stuck in corners and the white space is very uniform making the advertisement boring. In addition, some elements that are not related are grouped together, such as the company name and the telephone number. The advertisement seems very disorganized, like information is just tossed in.

Proximity and Alignment Improve the Layout

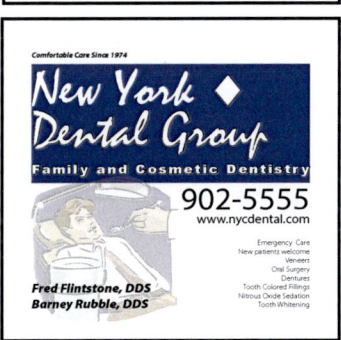

By grouping similar elements, the advertisement becomes organized, cohesive and readable. We also used the principle of alignment to unify the recreated advertisement.

Contrast

CONTRAST occurs when two design elements are different; the greater the difference, the greater the contrast.

> Contrast is one of the most effective ways to add visual interest to your page—a striking interest that makes you want to look at the page—and to create an organizational hierarchy among different elements. The important "rule" to remember is that for contrast to be effective, it must be strong. Don't be a wimp!
>
> Contrast is created when two elements are different. If the two elements are sort of different, but not really, then you don't have contrast. The principle of contrast states that **If two items are not exactly the same, then make them different. Really different.**
> — Robin Williams, *The Non-Designer's Design Book*

Contrast, whether in a photo or a résumé or a newsletter, makes the viewer want to look at the piece. Contrast also organizes the information by directing the eye from one item to another to help the viewer decide what is important to look at first, second, etc.

To create contrast, make two elements very different; slightly different does not work. It is somewhat similar to photography. In photography, we think of contrast in tonal values. A high contrast image has very light highlights and very dark shadows. It is the difference between the two that provides contrast. With print, we look to create contrast with type, color, texture, graphics, lines, etc. Compare these two business cards:

Here, with the exception of the business name, all the type is the same size with same font. The only contrast is that the business name uses a larger font, and begins with a small logo graphic that is close to the same size of the company name. ***Boring***!

Simple changes in contrast make this version much more appealing and eye-catching. The variety of fonts and sizes give contrast for much more visual interest.

The graphic is much larger, adding size contrast. We have organized the information on the card on the right by contrast. You immediately know what is the most important piece of information — the name of the company. Second in importance, the telephone number jumps out at you.

Repetition

REPETITION means that design elements appear more than once to unify the design.

> The principle of **REPETITION** states that you repeat some aspect of the design throughout the entire piece. Repetition can be thought of as consistency.
>
> — Robin Williams, *The Non-Designer's Design Book*

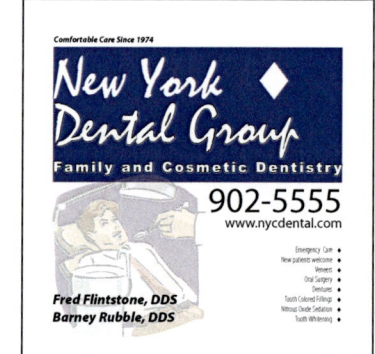

Here, we began by looking for an element to repeat, and chose the large diamond between New York and Dental Group.

To reinforce the right justification we had already used, we added diamonds to the end of each list item to subtly emphasize each of the dental services in the list.

Repetition is important in a one page piece and even more so with a longer document because repetition make the pages seem like they belong together. The repeated element may be a bullet, a shape, a color that you use consistently, or perhaps your use of white space. Even something as basic as page numbers in the same place on all the pages adds to the repetition. Whatever you decide to use to repeat, make it strong.

Photographic Design Principles

Everyone has their own idea of what makes a great photo, but there are some basic principles to look for when you are composing your photo in the viewfinder. Here are some favorites:

Framing

If you think of a framed printout of a photograph, then **FRAMING** means to decide before you shoot what to include within that frame. Your photographs will be more visually striking if you try to fill their frames with relevant and interesting elements. Often a frame included in the image helps orient the viewer.

Emphasis

EMPHASIS means drawing attention to a subject within the photograph, to tell the viewer where to look first. Photographically, this emphasis is called a **FOCAL POINT**.

There are many ways to create a focal point: size, color, texture, lines, tonal values. Which way you choose to emphasize the subject matter is up to you, but every image needs a focal point. This image of a canoe uses the red color and angle of the canoe as a focal point.

Angle of View

When you take pictures from the subject's eye level, you capture the subject realistically. Changing that angle alters the point of view.

Try altering your vantage point and perspective. Use a ladder and shoot down on the subject. Get down on the ground and shoot up. Shoot at weird angles. Unusual angles make the viewer stop and look.

Rule of Thirds

If you place your subject right smack in the middle of a photograph, it is not very visually interesting. Offsetting the subject helps to focus the viewer's eyes on the subject.

Here is a camera hint: When you use a digital camera, it is usually set up to focus in the very center of the viewfinder. Many cameras allow you to move that focus off center. Learn to change the focal point, and you will greatly improve your images. Rather than placing your subject in the center of the photo, place it off center. ***Think of a box, and divide it into thirds horizontally and vertically*** to give you nine regions.

Tutorial 8: Design Principles & Effective Cropping

If you place your subject at the intersection of these regions, your photograph will typically become much more interesting. Here the original photograph has been cropped using the rule of thirds:

Original

The girl is straight in the center, surrounded uniformly by the field, and the stone she is sitting on is almost as prominent as she is.

Cropped

In the cropped version, the girl's face is in the upper left "third," the unimportant rock is diminished, and the girl herself fills much more of the photograph.

. . . .

Close Ups

The distance from the camera to the subject often makes a big difference in good composition. Pictures that are **CLOSE UPS** rather than shot further away from the subject are more intimate and engage the viewer.

Let's take a look at another example of how cropping in closer, following the rule of thirds, improves a photograph:

Original

In spite of the dramatic setting, the original fountain picture is ordinary.
The fountain is right in the middle, and there is so much background that the eye does not know where to look.

Cropped

In the cropped version, the fountain and the water become the focal point. The water that was shot at a slow shutter speed becomes much more interesting than in the original uncropped version.

MACRO photography can create extreme close ups and dramatic images. Details of a subject make for creative and interesting photos as well. ***Get in close!*** The close up of these grapes is much more dramatic than if the cluster were take from a focal point of 3 or 4 feet away.

Compare these two flower photographs. The close-up is much more engaging.

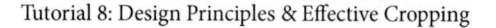

Tutorial 8: Design Principles & Effective Cropping Page 166

Balance

When items are **BALANCED**, they are evenly distributed. In a visually balanced photograph, no one section or element is heavier than another. Compare these two bell photographs:

The original shows almost the whole bell, but it is so massive that the photo seems unbalanced.

In the cropped version, there is nice balance between the bell and its holder. Applying the rule of thirds makes the composition much more dynamic. In this case, you can almost hear the bell ringing.

Balance does not have to be even. Some elements will have a large sense of weight and others will have a small sense of weight. In the grape closeup, notice the balance between the grapes in sunlight and those in shadow.

Contrast

CONTRAST is variety; it is used to hold the viewer's attention. Contrast can guide the eye through the artwork, or just provide visual interest.

Contrast can create a focal point by using tonal differences. Notice the textural contrast between the sky and the grapes in the photo on the previous page. The grapes have both color contrast and light/dark contrast. There is also contrast between the bell and its holder.

Photographically, there are many kinds of contrast.

- Light and dark contrast
- Size contrast
- Color contrast
- Texture contrast
- Movement contrast.

Patterns and textures can provide interesting studies in balance and contrast, as shown in the two photos to the right.

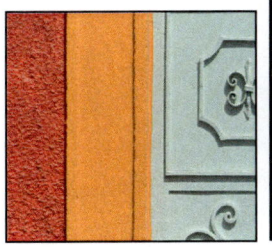

LINE AND SHAPE

Lines can be very effective in guiding the viewer's eye where you want it to go. Any lines that you see in the viewfinder should be looked at and possibly emphasized in the composition.

TONE AND SHARPNESS

Light and focus can draw attention to (or away from) your subject. Notice the repetition of the women's clothing, legs, and shoes.

ARRANGEMENT

The arrangement of elements in a photo can be very compelling. Not seeing the women's faces in the photo makes them very mysterious.

THE CROP TOOL

Objects that are not essential to the subject of a photograph can be distracting. Sometimes changing the camera's perspective or angle will remove or de-emphasize distractions. At other times, you can remove the distracting stuff in Photoshop. That's where the **Crop Tool** comes in.

The **Crop Tool** allows you to remove, or crop off, unwanted portions of your image, as well as change its overall composition. Here are the **Options** bar settings for the **Crop Tool**:

ASPECT RATIO PRESETS MENU (1)

ASPECT RATIO is the relationship between **width** and **height**. The **Aspect Ratio Presets** menu allows you to choose from preset aspect ratios to use with the **Crop Tool**.

These preset ratios are useful for cropping digital camera images to print at standard photograph sizes, such as **5" x 7"** or **8" x 10"**.

- The default setting of **Ratio** allows you to crop to any aspect ratio.

- As you crop, you can easily switch between portrait and landscape aspect ratios. You will do that shortly.

RATIO (2)

The Ratio boxes allow you to enter your own custom ratio numbers. If you commonly use the same custom proportions, you can add those custom proportions to the **Aspect Ratio Presets** menu by first entering the numbers into the Ratio boxes, and then choosing **New Crop Preset** from the **Aspect Ratio Presets** menu. The new preset will then show up on the **Aspect Ratio Presets** menu.

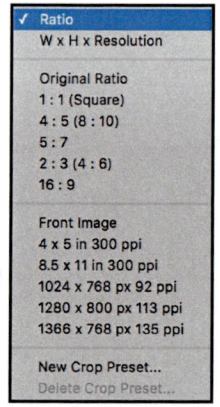

Straighten Button (3)

Before Straightening	After Straightening

This photo was taken inside the German World War II bunker at the then-occupied Stalheim Hotel in Norway that looks out onto the dramatic Voss Valley. Quarters were cramped so it was difficult to hold the camera straight.

The **Straighten** button allows you to straighten your image by drawing a line along what should be either vertical or horizontal. When you release the pointer, the image rotates so that the line you drew is either absolute horizontal or absolute vertical, depending on how you drew it. Try it yourself with **08-stalheim.jpg**.

After you straighten, the **Straighten** button is no longer active. You need to click the **Straighten** button again to change your straightening angle.

Overlay Options (4)

The **Overlay Options** menu provides a number of **Crop Tool** overlays to help you make an effective crop such as **Rule of Thirds**, **Grid**, and **Golden Spiral**. From this menu, you can also control the visibility of the **Overlay**.

Crop Tool Options (5)

The **Crop Tool Options** menu lets you customize the appearance and behavior of the **Crop Tool**. Options include **Use Classic Mode** (to make the **Crop Tool** work like it did in Photoshop CS5), and changing the visibility, **Color**, and **Opacity** of the **CROP SHIELD** which darkens to better show which parts of the image will be preserved and which will be cropped off.

Delete Cropped Pixels (6)

The **Delete Cropped Pixels** check box lets you decide whether the portion of the image that you crop off will be permanently deleted, or merely hidden.

- **Unchecked** preserves the cropped off region, *as long as the file is saved in PSD format* so that you can change the cropping at a later point in time. The file size stays the same.
- **Checked**, the portion of the image that is shielded will be permanently discarded when you **Commit** the crop. The file size gets smaller. Use this setting when you are sure you won't need to change the crop in the future.

Content-Aware (7)

The **Content Aware** check box controls whether Photoshop will attempt to fill in any empty space created when straightening an image during cropping. When checked, Photoshop will analyze the areas surrounding the empty spaces to make a guess as to what should go into the blank areas.

Guided Exercise 8.1: Use the Crop Tool

In this guided exercise you will use the **Crop Tool** with the **Rule of Thirds** to crop a wide-angle photograph of a boy standing on a large boulder.

1. **Reset** the **Crop Tool** and open **08-crop-boy.jpg**.

2. Examine the file size in the **Status** bar.

   This image starts out at **12.16 inches x 9.12 inches** at a resolution of **300 pixels/inch**. It is a large file.

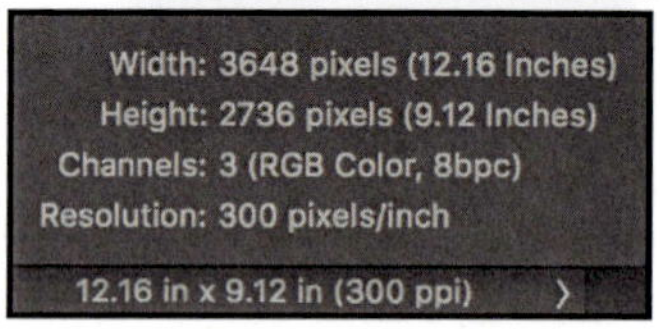

3. Choose the **Crop Tool.**

   Your image is automatically surrounded by a dashed box but you will not see the crop overlay yet.

4. Drag the handle on the upper left corner of the image diagonally down a bit.

   As you drag, notice that the crop overlay appears. Also notice the box displaying the current print size of the image in inches.

5. Drag the crop box handles until the crop box approximately surrounds the area you want to keep.

   When you release the mouse, the regions of the document outside the crop box become **SHIELDED** (darker) so that you can better evaluate how the cropped image will look.

6. To take full advantage of the **Rule of Thirds**, place one of the grid intersections directly over the boy. To fine-tune the position of the crop box, drag anywhere within the box to move the image, while leaving the crop box in place.

7. To apply the crop, do one of the following:

   - Double-click inside the cropped area.
   - Click the **Commit** button on the right side of the **Options** bar.

- Press **enter** or **return**.
- Right-click on the document and choose **Crop** from the bottom of the **Context** menu.

The unwanted edge pixels have been removed and the actual image size shrinks to focus on the image subject.

With the default **Delete Cropped Pixels** checked, the file size gets smaller. You can check this from the **Status** bar.

We didn't provide a number here because your crop size will probably be different from ours.

8. Close the image without saving. It is just for experimentation.

. . . .

Guided Exercise 8.2:
Use the Crop Tool to Straighten and Crop an Image

In this guided exercise you will straighten and crop a photo to improve its composition.

1. Open **08-crop_lake.jpg**.

2. Notice that the horizon line is not straight.

   We drew a red arrow here so you can better see the problem:

3. Straighten the image:

   a. Choose the **Crop** tool.

   b. Click the **Straighten** button in the **Options** bar.

   c. In the document window, drag a line from the distant shoreline on the left edge to the shoreline on the right. The shoreline is slightly curved, so it will not line up exactly. When you release the mouse, the image will straighten, using the line you drew as a horizontal reference.

   d. You should now see your straightened image with the shield covering the parts of the image that are cropped off.

   It is much better, but the image still has some distracting objects.

4. Drag the lower-right corner handle up and to the left until the rocks in the foreground and the people on the right are outside of the crop region.

5. Drag the corner handles until you have the crop positioned to your liking. Be careful not to drag any of the corners outside of the image, or that area will fill with background-colored pixels (white by default) when you actually crop.

Tutorial 8: Design Principles & Effective Cropping

6. Apply the crop.

7. Admire your cropping skill, then close without saving, as you will not use the image again.

ON YOUR OWN

STRAIGHTENING CHALLENGE

1. Open **08.damsel_fly.jpg**. It was taken in the Denver Botanical Garden.

   Taken quickly, while the damsel fly briefly landed on the plank, there was not time to zoom in or focus. But, surprisingly the damsel fly itself is quite clear.

2. Crop and straighten the image to your liking, using the design principles used in this tutorial. This is only one example.

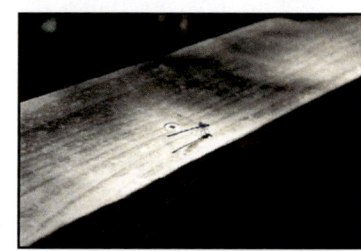

CROP EVALUATION

1. Take a series of photographs of the same subject using some of the design principles covered in this tutorial.

2. Evaluate the images, either on your own, or with colleagues or fellow students, to decide which images you prefer, and why.

3. Crop as appropriate and re-evaluate.

RESOURCES AND VIDEOS

http://www.practical-photoshop.com/pages/CC2015-pp1-resources.html#08

Practical Photoshop CC 2015, Level 1
Tutorial 9: Adobe® Bridge® + Automations

As you work with digital images, you will soon acquire many of them—and managing images can be a challenge. **Adobe® Bridge®**, the image management application that accompanies Photoshop CC 2015, will help you organize your image collection, keep track of who "owns" each image, and how each image can be legally used.

Adobe Bridge is indispensable for anyone who manages large numbers of digital images, and especially for digital camera users. When searching for a file in Bridge, you can:

- View thumbnails of every image in a folder to easily find what you are looking for without needing to open the files in Photoshop.

- View data about a file such as the date it was created, the date it was last modified, its size, etc..

- Select numerous files and open them all at once.

- Reorganize files by renaming, copying, or moving files from one location to another—all within Bridge.

Objectives

- Move back and forth between Bridge and Photoshop.

- Explain what **Camera Raw** is, and how to use Bridge as an intermediary to open **Raw** files.

- Identify the major landmarks of the Bridge application, and its preset workspaces.

- Use Bridge to:

    - View and arrange thumbnails of multiple images.

    - Assign ratings, and reorganize images by rating.

    - View and edit non-image file information called **METADATA.**

    - Preview a **Camera Raw** file, and open it in Photoshop.

    - Assign keywords to images, and use the **Filter** panel to find images by keyword.

- Understand the benefits of using automations.

- Use **File > Automate** in Photoshop to:

    - Make a contact sheet with **Contact Sheet II**.

    - Divide multiple images scanned into a single document into individual documents with **Crop and Straighten Photos**.

- Create a **PDF** slideshow with transitions and then view the slideshow in Adobe Acrobat or Adobe Reader.
- Combine images into a panorama using the **Photomerge** command.

Adobe® Bridge® Overview

Adobe Bridge is a stand-alone application that comes with any of the other Adobe CC applications. Technically, Bridge is what is known as **BROWSING SOFTWARE** because it lets you examine and manipulate media *attached* to your computer such as optical disks, flash drives, cameras, media cards, or external hard drives. However, when any of these external image sources are *detached* from the system, Bridge can not view their images.

NOTE: before continuing, so that your applications will match ours:

1. Restore the Adobe Photoshop Settings File following the instructions in Tutorial 1.
2. Close Bridge if it is open.

Browsing in Bridge

Choose **File > Browse in Bridge** or the shortcut keys **command + option + O** (Mac) or **ctrl + alt + O** (Win) to switch to Bridge.

At the top of the application window, you will see a series of bars that look almost the same in either Mac or Windows. This is the Mac version:

In either Mac or Windows the **Menu** bar is the top bar, followed by the **Tools** bar and the **Path** bar. Below the bars is a central **Content** panel that displays **THUMBNAILS** or small versions of the items in the currently browsed folder along with several more panels on either side.

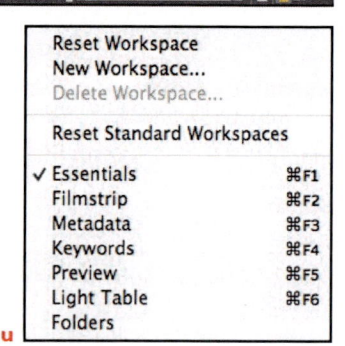

Let's begin by resetting the Bridge **Standard Workspace**:

1. Bridge has a **Workspace Switcher** just like Photoshop. In the **Tools** bar, click the arrow to the right of the list of workspaces, and choose **Reset Standard Workspaces** from the **workspaces** menu.

    Notice the thin vertical bar on the left edge of the **Workspace Switcher**. You can drag this **expand/shrink** bar left or right to expand or shrink the **workspace** buttons.

Tutorial 9: Adobe Bridge & Automations　　　　　　　　　　　　　　　　　　Page 174

When you can see the buttons, you can click on any one of them to change workspaces without the **Workspace Switcher** menu.

When the Bridge window is small, the **Workspace Switcher** is hidden. If you do not see the **Workspace Switcher**, choose **Window > Workspace** to see the **workspaces** menu.

2. If **Essentials** is not the current workspace, choose **Essentials** from the **workspaces** menu.

Now let's examine each region of Bridge individually:

. . . .

The Tools Bar

The various **Tools** bar components will show or hide, depending on the size of the Bridge window or application frame. Maximize the Bridge application window or frame so you can see all the components. Examine them, from left to right:

Navigation Buttons

- **Back** and **Forward buttons**: These buttons work like the back and forward buttons in Web browsers to move to the previous or next viewed folder.

- **Favorites**: Lists items in the **Favorites** folder, and folders in the **Parent Directory**.

- **Recent**: Reveals a recent application like Photoshop or goes to a recent folder. You can select Dreamweaver, Fireworks, Go Live, Illustrator, InDesign, or Photoshop, and choose recent files that were opened by these applications.

    Back: click the boomerang to return to Photoshop.

The next group of buttons lets you manipulate the items being browsed in a variety of useful ways.

Get Photos from Camera

Get Photos from Camera loads a small program called the **Photo Downloader** that streamlines the transfer of images from a digital camera or media card.

The **Photo Downloader** lets you choose where to save the images, rename them, save copies to another folder, and add non-image data including copyright information. **Resources** at the end of this tutorial provides an online tutorial for using the **Photo Downloader**.

Refine

The **Refine** menu provides three choices for working with images:

- **Review Mode** lets you review a folder of images on a full screen, cycling from one to the next.

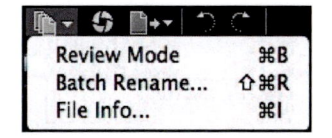

- **Batch Rename** lets you copy, move, and rename groups of images.
- **File Info** lets you view and edit the **METADATA** or non-image information associated with one or more images.

Camera Raw

Some digital cameras have the ability to save images in a special format called **CAMERA RAW** (or simply **Raw**) that stores the uncompressed information collected by the image sensor without applying any changes or formatting.

Open in Camera Raw

When you attempt to open a **Raw** file, you will first open the intermediary **Camera Raw** dialog box.

Open in Camera Raw lets you open **TIFF**, **JPEG** and **Raw** files within the **Camera Raw** dialog box so that you can edit them using **Camera Raw's** powerful non-destructive editing capabilities. For our beginning course, just accept the default settings by clicking the **Open Image** button to open the image in Photoshop. (We cover **Camera Raw** in later courses.)

NOTE: if a **TIFF** or **JPEG** file has previously been adjusted in **Camera Raw** that file will open first in **Camera Raw** as well. If that happens, just click **Open Image** to open the image in Photoshop.

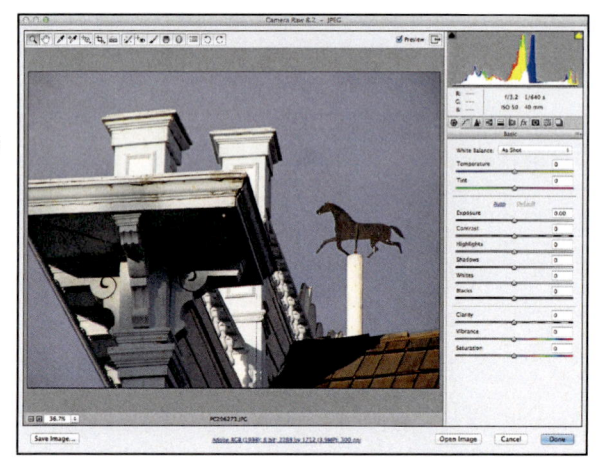

Thumbnail Rotation

Digital cameras only take landscape oriented photographs. To take a portrait image, you turn the camera on its side. Most of the time, the camera's software automatically rotates the portrait images when you **Get Photos from Camera**. If you have an older camera, or if you have turned off auto-rotate on your camera, Bridge will show only landscape thumbnails and the photos will be in landscape orientation when opened in Photoshop.

The rotation arrows let you turn an image either **Counter Clockwise** or **Clockwise** so that the image is oriented correctly both in Bridge and in Photoshop. Each click of a rotation button turns the thumbnail **90º** in the indicated direction.

- Bridge can only rotate the views of **JPEG**, **PSD**, **TIFF**, and **Camera Raw** file images.

WARNING: Rotating thumbnails does not rotate the actual image unless you actually open the file in Photoshop and save it.

Fortunately, Photoshop will prompt you that the rotated image has not been saved, and ask if you wish to save it when you close the image or quit Photoshop.

The Workspace Switcher

You already used the **Workspace Switcher** to reset the **Essentials** workspace.

Quick Search

The far right section contains the **Quick Search** box.

Quick Search lets you search using the Adobe Bridge search engine or the search engine from your operating system: Windows Desktop Search (Windows) or Spotlight (Mac OS). Each works a bit differently.

- Bridge searches filenames and image keywords, looking within the currently selected folder and all subfolders or within Computer (Windows 7/8/10 & Mac OS).

- Operating system search engines look for filenames, folder names, and image keywords, looking in the currently selected folder or in Computer (Windows 7/8/10 & Mac OS).

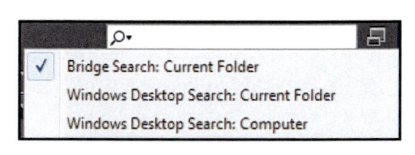

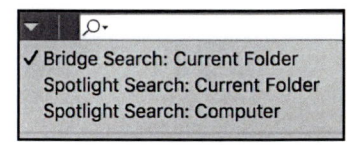

To use **Quick Search**:

1. Click the magnifying glass icon in the **Quick Search** field and choose the desired search method (Bridge or operating system).

2. In the search box, type in your search criteria.

3. Press **enter** (Windows) or **return** (Mac OS).

The Path Bar

The **Path** bar shows the location of the currently viewed folder. The **Window** menu lets you hide or show the **Path** bar. If you do not see the **Path** bar, turn it on by choosing **Window > Path** Bar.

We only are showing part of the **Path** bar here, Windows above and Mac below:

Not only does the **Path** bar show you the location of the folder you are browsing, but it also serves as a quick way to navigate to a different folder on the path. For example, on the Mac path, clicking the **2009** folder will display thumbnails of the items in the **2009** folder in the **Contents** panel.

Tutorial 9: Adobe Bridge & Automations					Page 177

Preview Quality

As you browse the images in a folder, you often have to wait while Bridge generates the thumbnail and large preview of each image.

Preview Quality options set the quality of image previews in Bridge.

- The default **Always High Quality** displays better previews at all times for better viewing but slower performance.

- **High Quality On Demand** uses embedded previews until you click on an image to view it in the **Preview** panel. Then Bridge creates a high quality, color managed **Preview**.

- **Prefer Embedded (Faster)** generates low-quality previews more quickly and take up less storage space. **Prefer Embedded (Faster)** is a good option for viewing a large number of images quickly, as long as you remember that the previews are not as accurate as the **High Quality** previews.

If you find that Bridge is taking a long time to generate previews for your chosen folder:

- Click the **Browse Quickly by Preferring Embedded Images** button to temporarily switch to **Prefer Embedded (Faster)**. When active, it changes color to be more obvious.

- Click the **Browse Quickly by Preferring Embedded Images** button again to turn it off, to return the former quality option.

Rating Images

To help manage your image collection, Bridge lets you assign ratings to your images starting with **Reject**, to **None** (the default), and from **1–5 Stars** and then to search based on those ratings.

To Rate an Image from its Thumbnail:

- Click its thumbnail in the **Content** panel to activate it.

- Click on one of the small dots below the image to rate the image from 1-5 stars.

    When you click a dot, that dot and the ones to the left of it will become stars.

If you don't see the dots, enlarge the thumbnails by dragging the **Thumbnail Size** slider at the bottom of the **Content** panel to the right.

To give several images the same rating, it can be faster to first select the images and then to rate them from the **Label** menu.

To Rate a Group of Images with the Label Menu:

1. **Click** the first thumbnail in the **Content** panel to activate it.
2. **Shift-click** the last of a consecutive group of images or individually **Command + click** (Mac) or **Ctrl + click** (Win) on each additional thumbnail to add it to the selected images.
3. Choose the desired rating from the **Label** menu (in the Bridge **Menu** bar).

As you rate images, avoid "grade inflation." If half of your images are rated five star, then your ratings will not tell you very much. Make your images really earn every star you give them, and save five stars for the one or two best photos you take for that shoot.

You always have the ability to change ratings later if you change your mind.

To Change the Rating of an Individual Image:

- In the image thumbnail, click the desired star level to give the image that rating.
- To assign **No Rating**, click the **Null** sign (ø) to the left of the star dots.

To Change the Rating of Multiple Images:

Select the images in the **Content** panel and do one of the following.

- Choose **Label > Increase Rating** or **Label > Decrease Rating**.
- Choose **Label > No Rating**.
- Choose **Label > Reject** to add a red **Reject** rating.

    We rejected this cherry blossom photo because of the busy background behind the blossoms. However, we did not simply discard the image because the flowers are nicely in focus and we may want to crop the image later for a close-up.

To Rate Selected Images with Keystrokes:

No Rating: **Command/Ctrl + 0** (zero)

Star Rating: **Command/Ctrl + rank** (1–5)

The Filter Items by Rating Menu

The **Star** button on the **Path** menu displays the **Filter by Ratings menu**, where you can show only those images that meet specific criteria.

Tutorial 9: Adobe Bridge & Automations

The Filter Panel

Once you have applied ratings to some images, you can use the **Filter** panel to display only those images that have a given star rating or higher.

You can also use the **Filter by Ratings** button in the **Path** bar.

The Sort By Menu

To the right of the **Star** menu is the **Sort by** menu. **Sort by** determine the order in which thumbnails will be displayed in the **Content** panel. The menu displays the current sorting criteria for determining image order in the **Content** panel. Its menu lets you sort by a variety of criteria, with a check mark showing the criterion currently in use (**by Filename** here). Click the caret symbol (^) to switch between **ascending** (A–Z) and **descending** (Z–A) order.

In addition to using the **Sort by** menu to order thumbnails, you can drag image thumbnails individually to change their order in the **Content** panel. When you do, the **Sort by** menu changes to **Sort Manually**.

Organization Buttons

The last three buttons let you navigate to recently viewed items, make new folders to organize your images, and delete unwanted images.

Open recent: Lists previously viewed items.

New folder: Lets you create a new folder inside the current folder.

Delete: *Permanently deletes* images of selected thumbnails from Bridge and puts the files into the **Trash** (Mac) or **Recycle Bin** (Win).

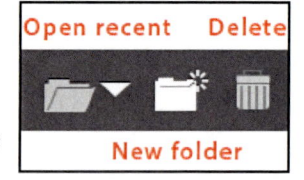

Putting Bridge to Work

In the first part of this tutorial, we have shown you a bunch of things you can do with Bridge, but you won't really understand them until you get a chance to work with Bridge yourself. Now it is your turn.

Bur first, we are going to show you how we used Bridge to prepare the files for the next Guided Exercise.

Windsor Green took the photographs in Oaxaca, Mexico, and uploaded them to Barbara Heiman for processing.

- Some of the images are in **JPEG** format and others are in **PSD** format.

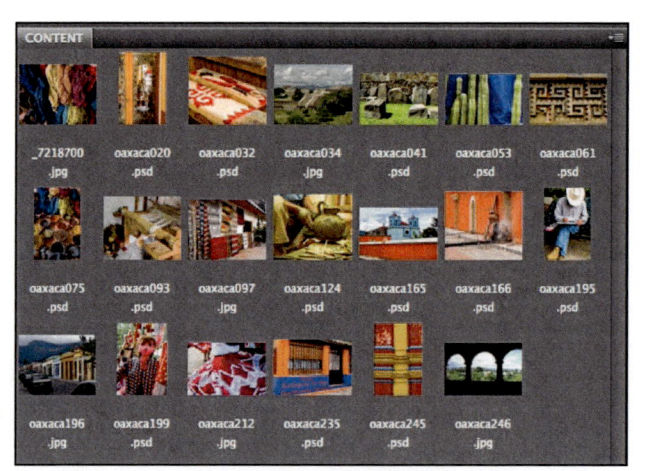

- Barbara checked out the size of the folder and discovered it was **87.3 M**—awfully big for a simple Bridge exercise. Compressed, the folder was still over **77 M**.
- The folder consisted of 20 files, 14 **PSDs** and 6 **JPEGs**.
- If the **PSDs** were converted to **JPEG** format, the folder size would get much smaller.

Here is what Barbara did:

1. Chose **By Type** from the **Sort By** menu, to put all the files of each file type together.
2. Clicked the first **.PSD** file in the **Content** panel, and then **Shift + clicked** the last file to select all of them.
3. Chose **Tools** > **Photoshop** > **Image Processor** to make a **JPEG** copy of each of the selected **PSD** files.
4. Made a new folder that contained just the **JPEG** versions of the files you are going to work with, **09-bridge**. The original files will not be changed.

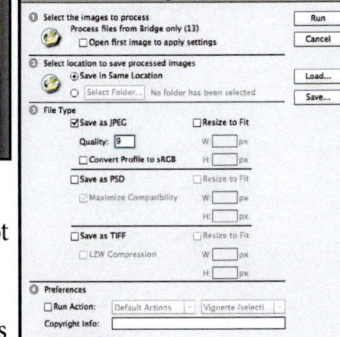

   The new folder of 20 high-quality images is now about **18.4 M**, and compressed it is **18 M**. Still big, but manageable. There is not a big change between the compressed and uncompressed folder sizes because the **JPEGs** were individually compressed when saved.

. . . .

Guided Exercise 9.1: Getting Started with Bridge

Before you do this exercise:

1. Locate the **09-bridge.zip** folder that you downloaded with the rest of the files and folders for this course.
2. Put **09-bridge.zip** onto the Desktop, and decompress it.
3. Rename the expanded folder **bridge-working**. The zip file still contains the original images.

In this guided exercise you will use the **Content** panel to rotate, rename, reorder, and rank images. As you do so, you will use the **Preview** panel to better view your images.

1. Open Photoshop, then close any open images.
2. Choose **File** > **Browse in Bridge**.
3. Click **Essentials** in the Bridge **Workspace Switcher** to be sure you are using the default **Essentials** workspace.

   If you don't see the **Essentials** button, choose **Essentials** from the **Window** > **Workspace** menu.
4. Choose **Reset Essentials** from the **Workspace** menu to be sure your workspace matches ours.

5. Identify the major regions of the **Essentials** workspace:
   - The various bars at the top of the window.
   - The three panels that fill most of the window.
   - The **Status** bar at the bottom of the Bridge window.

6. Use the **Favorites** panel to browse to the **bridge-working** folder:

   a. Locate the **Favorites** panel. It is in the left panel, grouped with the **Folders** panel.

   The **Favorites** panel displays a two part list. You may see different choices in your **Favorites** panel as the specific items are determined by what is checked in **Bridge Preferences**.

   Computer shows all the storage devices currently connected to your computer. The lower part of the **Favorites** panel shows the **Desktop**, **Documents** and **Pictures** folders, along with any custom items (none here).

   Clicking on an item in the **Favorites** panel will take you to that location.

   b. Click **Desktop** to view thumbnails of all the items on your **Desktop** in the **Content** panel.

   c. Click the **Folders** tab, grouped with **Favorites**, and then click the arrow to the right of **Desktop** to display the folders on your desktop.

   The **Folders** panel shows a navigational tree structure of the contents of your hard disk and other attached storage devices, such as camera media cards, flash drives, optical disks, or additional hard disks. Items in the **Folders** panel expand and collapse like groups in the Photoshop **Layers** panel.

   We are not going to do it here, but the **Folders** panel is a convenient place to navigate from one folder to another, and even from one storage device to another, all within Bridge. Whenever you click on an item, Bridge displays the contents of that item in the **Content** panel.

   d. In the **Folders** tab, click the **bridge-working** folder and observe the browsing results:
      - The **Path** bar shows the path from the **Desktop** to the **bridge-working** folder.
      - The **Content** panel shows the contents of the **bridge-working** folder. The panel has a vertical scroll bar because there are so many images.

7. Add the **bridge-working** folder to your **Favorites** panel:

   a. Click **Desktop** in the **Path** Bar to browse that location.

   b. Drag the **bridge-working** folder to the bottom of the **Favorites** panel, being careful not to drop it onto any of the items in **Favorites**, so that you don't accidentally move the folder.

   When you are in the correct location, a horizontal bar will appear.

   c. Release the mouse to make the **Favorite**. You may need to scroll down the **Favorites** panel to see it.

   If you don't see the new **Favorite**, you accidentally moved the folder instead of making a **Favorite**. In that case, immediately choose **Edit > Undo Move** and try again.

   Because it is so easy to accidentally move a folder rather than to make it a **Favorite**, here is an alternate technique: either **right-click** (two button mouse) or **ctrl + click** (one button trackpad) the desired folder, and choose **Add to Favorites** from the context menu that appears.

   To remove a favorite, either **right-click** (two button mouse) or **ctrl + click** (one button trackpad) the desired item, and choose **Remove from Favorites** from the context menu that appears.

8. Preview and rotate a thumbnail:

   a. Enlarge the thumbnails:

      1) Locate the **Thumbnail Size Slider** on the **Status** bar at the bottom of the Bridge window.

      2) Drag the slider to the right to increase the size of the thumbnails in the **Content** panel so that you can see them better.

   b. Choose and rotate a thumbnail:

      1) Click on thumbnail **oaxaca195.jpg** to select it.

      When you select a thumbnail, it also appears in the **Preview** panel.

      If desired, you can drag the panel edges of the neighboring panels to enlarge the **Preview** panel.

      2) Click the **Rotate 90 Degrees Counter-Clockwise** button to orient this portrait image properly.

Tutorial 9: Adobe Bridge & Automations   Page 183

The image rotates in both the **Content** and the **Preview** panels.

To rotate the actual pixels, you would double click the thumbnail in the **Content** panel, not the preview to open the image in Photoshop, save it, and then close it. If you had more than one file to rotate in the same direction, you could select each in turn and then click the rotation button to rotate them simultaneously. Each time you select an additional thumbnail, it also appears in the **Preview** panel.

9. Rename an image:

    a. Click on thumbnail **_7218700.jpg** to select it.

    b. Click the file name beneath the thumbnail to select the file name but *NOT* its file extension. That is because just changing the file's extension does not actually change its format. Bridge is warning you by highlighting only the name, but not the dot or the extension.

    Be careful not to double-click or you will open the file in Photoshop. If that happens, close the file, activate Bridge, and try again. If you find yourself having difficulty getting the Bridge thumbnails into rename mode, it may be easier to **right-click** the thumbnail to view its context menu and then choose **Rename**.

    c. Type **Yarn**, and press the **enter** or **return** key.

    Three things happened here:

    - The new name of the file, **yarn.jpg**, appears in both the **Content** and **Preview** panels.
    - The file's name changes within the filing system of your operating system, and not just within Bridge. So, only rename files if you need to.
    - The thumbnail probably moves to the last spot in the **Content** panel because of the change in alphabetical order: **y** for **yarn** is near the end of the alphabet.

10. Preview **yarn.jpg** using the **Loupe Tool**:

    a. Click on thumbnail **yarn.jpg** in the **Content** panel.

    b. Click inside the thumbnail in the **Preview** panel to see the **Loupe Tool**.

    The bottom of the **Preview** panel will now display the **Loupe Tool**'s magnification, which starts out at **100%** or **actual size**.

The **Preview** thumbnail can be so small that it is difficult to assess the quality of a high resolution image to see if it is in focus and has proper detail where you want it.

- Click the **Preview** thumbnail to reveal the **Loupe Tool** to magnify the clicked area to better assess its quality.

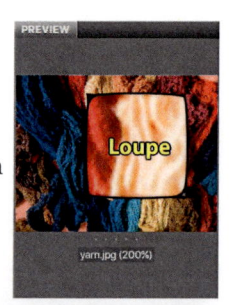

- Click in a new location, or drag the **Loupe Tool** around to examine different parts of the thumbnail.
- To dismiss the **Loupe Tool** click inside the magnified area of the tool.

c. Enlarge the **Loupe Tool**'s zoom level by pressing the plus (+) key.

d. Reduce the zoom level with the minus (-) key. If your mouse has a scroll wheel, you can also use it to zoom the **Loupe** in or out. On this image, we could zoom between **100%** and **800%**.

e. Drag the **Loupe Tool** around in the image to preview different parts.

f. Click inside the magnified area of the **Loupe Tool** to dismiss it.

When more than one thumbnail is selected, each shows up in the **Preview** panel. If you want to compare the quality of, say, two images, you can click on each to place an individual **Loupe** on each preview. This can be very helpful if you are trying to pick between two very similar images without having to open them both in Photoshop.

To better assess similar images you can synchronize multiple Loupe tools in the **Preview** panel by using **Ctrl-click** or **Ctrl-drag** (Windows) or **Command-click** or **Command-drag** (Mac OS) on one of the images.

11. Change thumbnail order:

    You can drag thumbnails from one location to another within the **Content** panel to change their viewing order. When you do this, **Sort by File Name** in the **Path** bar changes to **Sort Manually**.

    a. One at a time, drag all the images that have yarn, or weavers in them, to the top of the **Content** panel.

    b. Notice **Sort Manually** in the **Path**.

12. Use Bridge to open an image in Photoshop:

    Double click a thumbnail to open it in the application that is associated with its file type. By default, image files such as **GIFs** and **JPGs** will open in Photoshop. A **.doc** file will open in Microsoft Word, even from Adobe Bridge.

    a. Double click the **yarn.jpg** thumbnail.

    b. Wait while the image opens in Photoshop. Bridge will go into the background.

    c. Close the image in Photoshop without saving, and go back to Bridge.

13. Rename a group of images all at once using the **Batch Rename** command:

    Batch Rename is very powerful. With it you can rename a group of files in place, as we will do here. More advanced folks can use **Batch Rename** to move or copy a group of files, and give them new names in the process. But with power comes the ability to mess things up.

    WARNING: *Batch Rename permanently changes the files it affects, and there is no Undo.*

a. In the **Content** panel, select the five weaving images.

b. Choose **Tools > Batch Rename** to open yet another huge dialog box, so big that we are not showing you the whole thing here.

c. At the top of the dialog box, choose **Default** from the **Presets** menu and then look at the **Preview** name at the bottom of the dialog box.

The **Current filename**, **oaxaca032.jpg** is the name of the first selected file, and the ridiculously long **New filename** is what **Default** will generate.

d. For the **Destination Folder** choose **Rename in Same Folder**.

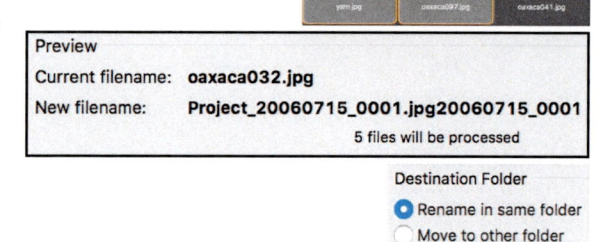

e. In the **New Filenames** section, make the following changes:

   1) For the top **Text**, highlight all the text and then change it to **weaving**.

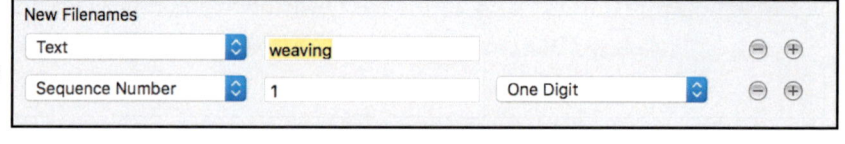

   2) Click the **Minus** (–) radio button to the right of **Date Time** to delete that entry and likewise delete the lower **Text** entry.

   3) For **Sequence Number**, start with **1** but change **Four Digits** to **One Digit** as you are only renaming six files.

   4) Under **Options**, be sure that all the available **Compatibility** items are checked, so that you can move the image freely from one operating system to another. This is the Mac version:

   5) Observe the **Preview** area, to see the new name of the first image in your series.

   6) Click **Rename** to simultaneously change the names of all the selected images and in this case to move them to the bottom of the **Content** panel.

This guided exercise has shown you just a small part of the Bridge's capabilities. But wait, there's more!

Additional Bridge Panels

Bridge has eight panels, as listed in the **Window** menu, and so far you have only used four of them. Here are some others:

The Keywords Panel

KEYWORDS are user-defined descriptive words or phrases that you can attach to individual files or groups of files to better manage your digital library. Keywords are grouped into keyword sets. Bridge starts with four sets—**Event**,

People, **Place**, and **Other Keywords**—but you can add (or remove) an unlimited number of keywords and keyword sets. When you attach a keyword to an image, that is called **TAGGING** the image. This witch image is tagged with two keyword phrases, **witch** and **Salem MA**.

When images are tagged, the keywords are summarized in the **Filter** panel.

If you click the check box on the left side of a keyword in the **Filter** panel, like **seven gables** here, only images with that keyword assigned will appear in the **Content** panel.

Three tiny buttons at the bottom of the **Keyword** panel may be used to make new keywords and keyword sets, and to deleted unwanted ones.

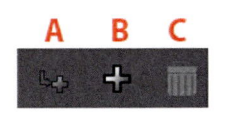

To Make a Sub Keyword:

1. Highlight the **Keyword Set** that will hold the new keyword.
2. Click the **New Sub Keyword Set** button (**A**).

   A blank box will appear below the current keyword set, for you to type in your new sub keyword.

3. After typing a name or short phrase, press **enter** or **return** to accept your set name. Bridge will automatically organize the keywords in alphabetical order.

To Make a New Keyword Set:

1. Scroll down to the space below all the keywords and click to deselect all keywords and sub keywords.
2. Click the **New Keyword** button (**B**).

   A blank keyword will appear at the top of the list, with a box for you to type in your new keyword.

3. After typing the new keyword, press **enter** or **return** to accept your keyword. Bridge will automatically organize the keyword sets in alphabetical order, and highlight the new set so that you can add keywords to it, like you did above.

To Delete a Keyword or Set:

1. Highlight the keyword or set to delete.
2. Click the **Delete** button (**C**).
3. Click **Yes** when the warning box appears.

TO ASSIGN A KEYWORD TO ONE OR MORE FILES:

1. Select one or more image thumbnails.

2. In the **Keywords** panel, click the box to the far left of the name of the keyword you want to add.

   A check mark appears in the box next to the keyword when it is added to a file, like **Spring** here.

TO REMOVE A KEYWORD FROM ONE OR MORE FILES:

1. Select one or more image thumbnails.

2. Click the box next to the name of the keyword you want to remove.

   The check mark will vanish from the box to the left of the keyword.

THE FILTER PANEL

The **Filter** panel is a real time saver because you can sort and filter files that appear in the **Content** panel based on a variety of useful criteria. It shows only filter criteria that apply to the current images displayed in the Content panel.

For example, you can click on a filter to see just the landscape-oriented images in a folder, or just those in **JPEG** format. If you assign keywords to images, those will also appear in the **Filter** panel for quick sorting.

THE METADATA PANEL

METADATA is textual information about an image. When a single image is previewed, the top of the **Metadata** panel gives its file dimensions and size, and other information.

The **Metadata** panel organizes metadata into several sections, each of which can be expanded or collapsed by clicking the triangle to the left of the category.

- At the top of the **Metadata** panel are two boxes, one that summarizes camera settings and the other that summarizes image settings.

- **File Properties** gives standard information including file name, size in pixels, creation date, modified date, color mode, print resolution, and color profile.

- **IPTC Core** (**International Press Telecommunications Council**) has editable fields where you can add descriptions, keywords, author, or copyright information. It is a very long list with only a few of the categories shown here.

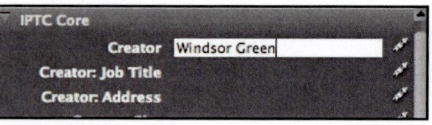

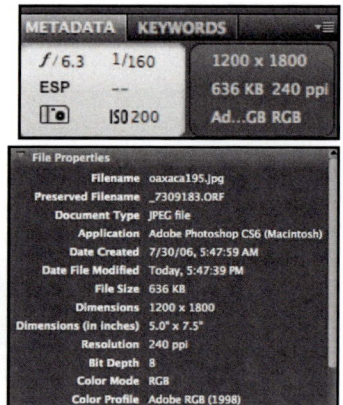

- For digital cameras, **Camera Data** (**Exif**) stores information about the camera settings used when the shot was taken. Set by each digital camera model, **Camera Data** generally contains the camera make and model, exposure time, shutter speed, f-stop, aperture, focal length, flash mode, metering mode, etc.

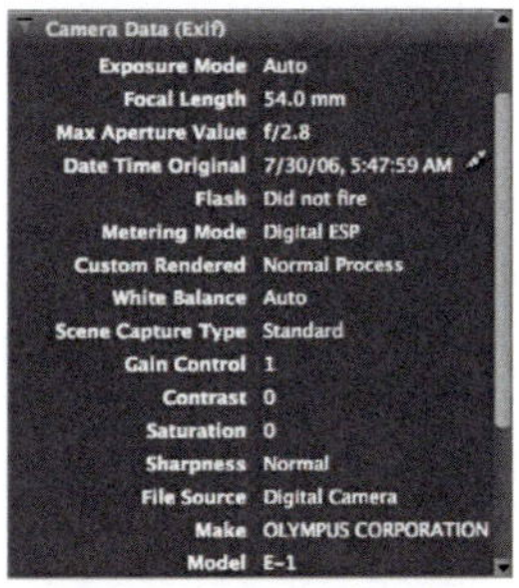

    Here is the **Camera Data** for **oaxaca195.jpg**.

If an image was shot in **Camera Raw** like the Salem witch, any adjustments made in the **Adobe Camera Raw** dialog box will also be displayed in the **Metadata** panel. Otherwise, the **Camera Raw** section will not be displayed.

Collections Panel

COLLECTIONS allow you to group photos in one place, even if they're located in different folders or on different hard drives. We will not use the **Collections** panel in this course.

Bridge Workspaces

The **Workspace switcher** begins with seven preset workspaces to make it easy to switch from one workspace to another. Here are some of our favorites:

> The **Essentials** workspace, which you have already used, displays the **Favorites**, **Folders**, **Filter**, **Collections**, **Content**, **Preview**, **Metadata**, and **Keywords** panels. The panels you haven't used yet will make more sense when we look at a few of the other workspaces.

> The **Filmstrip** workspace displays the **Content** panel as thumbnails in a scrolling horizontal row, with a large preview of the currently selected item(s) in the **Preview** panel above it. The **Filmstrip** workspace also displays the **Folders**, **Favorites**, **Filters**, and **Collections** panels. **Filmstrip** is terrific when previewing a bunch of images. The right and left arrow keys on the keyboard can be used to quickly move from image to image.

> The **Metadata** workspace displays the **Content** panel with a thumbnail of each image along with textual information about that image, such as the file date, size on disk, pixel dimensions, file format, and ratings, along with the **Favorites**, **Filters**, and **Metadata** panels. It is very long.

> The **Keywords** workspace shows the **Content** panel slightly differently, along with a larger thumbnail. It also shows the **Favorites**, **Keywords**, and **Filter** panels.

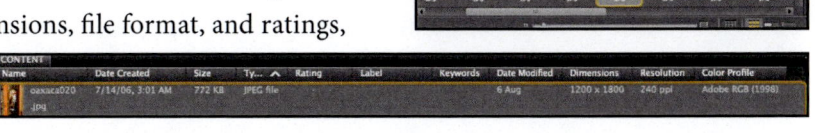

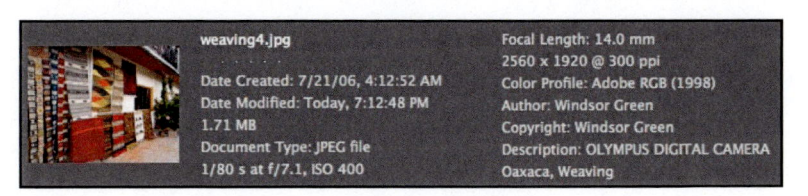

Tutorial 9: Adobe Bridge & Automations   Page 189

The **Preview** workspace displays the **Content** panel as a vertical column of image thumbnails, with a large **Preview** panel showing the selected image(s). It also shows the **Favorites**, **Folder**, **Filter**, and **Collections** panels.

The **Light Table** workspace displays only the **Content** panel.

The **Folders** workspace shows a large **Content** panel, along with the **Favorites** and **Folders** panels. It is used primarily for organizing images into folders.

Automations

AUTOMATIONS allow you to process groups of images at once, often in special ways. The automation commands in Photoshop are organized under the **File > Automate** menu. You will use just four of the Automate commands in this tutorial: **Crop and Straighten Photos, PDF Presentation, Contact Sheet II,** and **Photomerge**.

The copyrighted photographs you will use for most of the automation examples were taken by Windsor Green in Oaxaca, Mexico.

Cropping & Straightening Photographs

You have already used the **Crop Tool** with its **Straighten** button to straighten and crop individual photographs. If you scan a group of small images into a single file, or scan or photograph photo album pages, **Crop and Straighten Photos** will straighten and save each individual image into its own file.

Guided Exercise 9.2: Use the Crop and Straighten Photos Command

In this simple exercise, you will apply the **Crop and Straighten Photos** command to an individual photograph and then to a photo album page with two photographs.

1. Within Photoshop, open **09-metal.jpg**.

2. Choose **File > Automate > Crop and Straighten Photos**. Wait while Photoshop opens a duplicate of the original image, and automatically crops and straightens it.

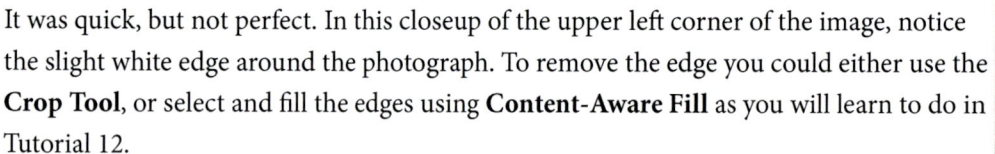

   It was quick, but not perfect. In this closeup of the upper left corner of the image, notice the slight white edge around the photograph. To remove the edge you could either use the **Crop Tool**, or select and fill the edges using **Content-Aware Fill** as you will learn to do in Tutorial 12.

3. Close both open documents. There is no need to save the cropped and straightened image because you are just experimenting.

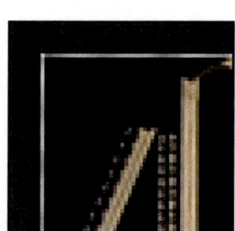

4. Open **09-crop_straighten.jpg**.

   This file showing two snapshots of London from 1952 is a scan of a page from a old family photo album.

5. Choose **File** > **Automate** > **Crop and Straighten Photos**.

   Wait while Photoshop generates two duplicate images, one for each snapshot, and automatically crops and straightens them. Notice that each image was only cropped to the edge of the entire photograph and that each image includes the once white border.

   If you were going to restore these photographs, it might be best to begin by crop off the border to better adjust the tones and colors in the actual image.

6. Close these documents as well. They are too badly aged and damaged for a beginning Photoshop learner to restore.

Contact Sheets

A **CONTACT SHEET** is a collection of image thumbnails that you can either view on screen or print. Contact sheets are useful for showing a client many images from a photo shoot, or for keeping as an image catalog for images backed up to disk.

Let's create contact sheets with Photoshop's **Contact Sheet II** automation:

Guided Exercise 9.3: Make a Contact Sheet with Contact Sheet II

In this guided exercise you will select images from the Bridge **Content** panel and then turn them into a contact sheet.

1. Begin in the **Essentials** workspace in Bridge, browsing the **bridge-working** folder.

2. Switch the workspace to **Light Table** and enlarge the thumbnails so that they are easy to see.

3. Select just the five weaving images.

4. Make a contact sheet using the default settings:

   a. In Bridge, choose **Tools** > **Photoshop** > **Contact Sheet II**.

Tutorial 9: Adobe Bridge & Automations

b. Examine the huge **Contact Sheet II** dialog box:

Begin with the default settings. The top section, **Source Images**, lets you either use selected files from Bridge, as we are, or navigate to a specific folder and use all the images within that folder.

The **Document** section is where you specify the size of the document, its resolution, and other details. By default, the contact sheet will be **8 x 10 inches**, **RGB color**, with a resolution of **100 ppi**. Change the resolution to **300ppi** for good print settings. If you wanted to email a low resolution version to someone, you could change the resolution to **72 ppi**. You could also manually reverse the **Width** and **Height** to make a contact sheet that printed landscape, not portrait.

When **Flatten All Layers** is checked, the ending contact sheet will be flattened to a single layer to limit the file size. When **Flatten All Layers** is unchecked, every thumbnail and label is on its own layer, and you can individually edit each layer. That is a good option if you want to display your contact sheet on a background other than white, or if you want text color other than black.

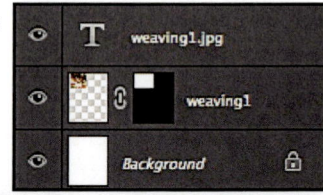

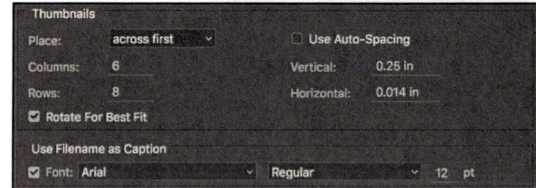

The **Thumbnails** section provides some basic size and positioning for the image thumbnails.

The most important settings here are the number of **Columns** and **Rows**. The higher the numbers, the more thumbnails that will fit on a page, but the smaller they will be. For example, **6 x 8** will lay out 48 small images on a page. If you have more than 48 images, Photoshop will keep making new pages (files) until all the thumbnails have been included.

The **Use Filenames as Captions** section lets you set the font and size for the captions, or hide captions when unchecked.

c. Without changing any settings, click **OK** to generate the contact sheet.

d. Wait while Photoshop opens, resizes, and closes each image and builds the contact sheet. It is fast for only 5 images, but can take quite a while for a lot of images.

e. This layout is not very good for only 5 images because most of the page is blank, so close the generated **ContactSheet-001** without saving it.

5. Make another contact sheet with larger thumbnails:

   a. In Bridge, make sure the six weaving images are highlighted.

   b. Choose **Tools** > **Photoshop** > **Contact Sheet** II.

   c. In the **Contact Sheet II** dialog box, change **Columns** to **2** and **Rows** to **3** to make fewer, but larger thumbnails on each page.

   d. Click **OK** and wait to see your new contact sheet.

6. Save and print the contact sheet if desired. It is a **PSD** file.

Notice that while the contact sheet has nice big thumbnails, each thumbnail is a different size because the original images did not have the same pixel dimensions. Also notice that there is no place for a header, footer, or other identification for the overall contact sheet. The **Contact Sheet II** automation is quick, but basic.

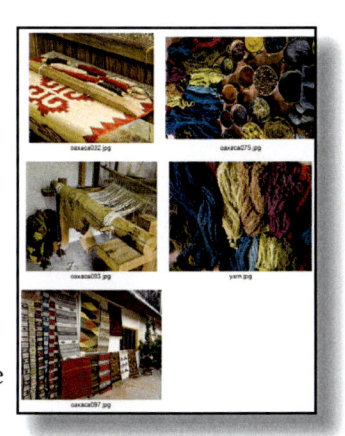

PDF Presentation

The **PDF Presentation** command in Photoshop lets you create a multiple page **PDF** document from images you choose. **PDF** stands for **Portable Document Format**. **PDF** files have some distinct advantages over **PSD** files:

- **PSD** documents are only one page long while **PDFs** can contain many pages.

- **Adobe Reader** and other programs, as well as Mac OS X, allow you to open and view **PDF** files. Adobe Reader is a free download. You typically need a specific image editing application, such as Photoshop, to view **PSD** files.

- **PDFs** can be password protected so that they can be viewed, but not printed — or not even viewed at all without the password.

The PDF files created by the **PDF Presentation** command are very simple, containing one image per page. You can opt to create the PDF file from all images you have open in Photoshop, or you can choose any images on your computer. The PDF can be viewed as a multi-page file, or as a PDF slide show.

The **File** > **Automate** > **PDF Presentation** command has a few configurable options:

- **Source Files** allows you to choose to include all open files, or browse your computer to add images.

- The **Output Options** section is where you choose what type of document you are creating, and how it appears:

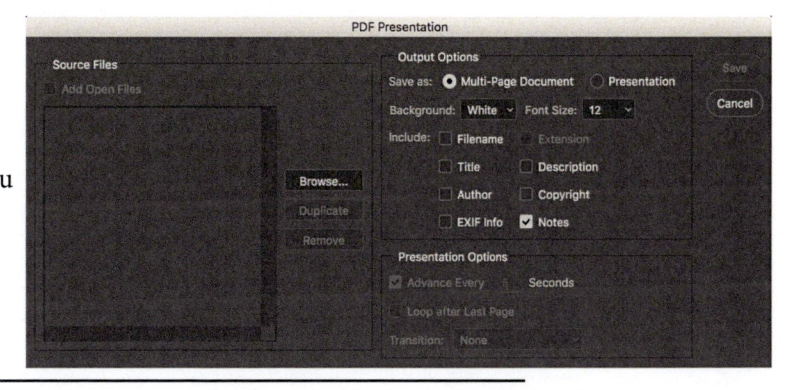

Tutorial 9: Adobe Bridge & Automations   Page 193

- **Multi-Page Document** creates a PDF file containing one page per image chosen in the Source Files section.

- **Presentation** creates a PDF with the ability to play as a slide show in your PDF reader application.

- **Background** allows you to choose the background color for your document. You can pick white, black, or gray as the background color.

- **Include** lets you decide which of seven different pieces of metadata — information stored within many images — will appear beneath each image. The choices are Filename (with or without the file extension), Title, Description, Author, Copyright, EXIF Info, and Notes.

- **Font Size** lets you choose the size of the font used for displaying this metadata.

- The **Presentation Options** section becomes available when you choose to create a Presentation. If you chose to create a Multi-Page Document, this section will be grayed out. It contains:

    - **Advance Every** allows you to set how long each slide appears on your screen before advancing to the next slide.

    - **Loop after Last Page** will set the slide show to loop until it is stopped.

    - **Transition** allows you to have no transition from one slide to another, or to choose from any one of 23 different transitions. You can also choose to have a random transition applied to each slide change.

Once you select your options in the PDF Presentation dialog box and click Save, you will be shown a standard Save dialog box. After clicking Save there, you will then be shown a Save Adobe PDF dialog. This is a very complex dialog box with many options. For now, just accept the default settings you see there. Once the PDF is saved, you can open it with your PDF reader to view the results.

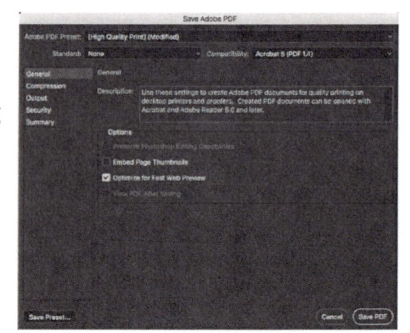

Viewing PDF Slideshows

You will need an application that can display **PDFs** and play **PDF** slide shows to complete the next tutorial. Anyone who needs to get **PDF** viewing software can download Adobe Reader for free from Adobe at: http://get.adobe.com/reader/otherversions

Windows users, you *may* need to download software to view **PDFs**:

1. Choose **All Programs** from the **Start** menu, and look for **Adobe Reader 9.x** or **Adobe Acrobat 7.x** or higher.

2. If you find one of these applications, you are fine to proceed. Otherwise, you must download and install Adobe Reader—fortunately free—in order to view **PDF** documents, including the slideshow you are going to make next.

Mac folks:

> Look for either **Adobe Acrobat** or **Adobe Reader** in the **Applications** folder. If you don't find it, you will need to download it.
>
> **Preview for Mac** does not play PDF slide shows satisfactorily. **Preview** could open our **PDF** just fine, but we needed to choose **View > Slideshow** in order to see the first slide, and then we had to click the **Play** triangle at the bottom of the slide to start the slideshow.

Guided Exercise 9.4: Make a PDF Slideshow

A **PDF** slideshow is a convenient way to automatically display a set of images one at a time, on screen. Here is how to do it using the PDF Presentation command in Photoshop:

1. Start by setting up a folder of images to include in your slide show. If necessary, open **Bridge** and navigate to the **bridge-working** folder.

2. Duplicate the folder so that you do not disturb the original file names and custom order:

    a. Use the **Path** bar to back up one organizational level, so that you browse the location that contains the **bridge-working** folder, probably the **Desktop**.

    b. Choose the **Essentials** workspace.

    c. Click once to activate—but not to open—the **bridge-working** folder.

    d. Choose **Edit > Duplicate** to copy the **bridge-working** folder.

    e. In the **Path** bar, choose **Sort by Filename** (if not already chosen) to view the duplicated folder alongside its original.

    f. Rename **bridge-working** to **bridge_slideshow**.

    g. Double-click the **bridge_slideshow** folder to view its contents in the **Content** panel.

3. Pick *any eight* of the images in the **Content** panel to use in your slideshow and give each a descriptive name:

    a. Change the names of each your chosen images to a very short description.

    Capitalize as you want your slideshow captions to appear. Spaces are OK, but *avoid punctuation* because certain punctuation marks can really confuse computer operating systems.

    b. To rename the files, **right-clicking** and choosing **Rename** from the context menu may be the fastest approach.

4. Switch back to Photoshop and choose **File > Automate > PDF Presentation**.

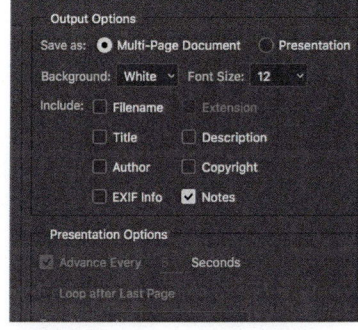

Tutorial 9: Adobe Bridge & Automations

5. Choose which images will appear in your slide show:

    a. In the **Source Files** section of the PDF Presentation dialog box, click the Browse button and navigate to the bridge_slideshow folder you created earlier.

    b. Command- or Control- click on the eight files you renamed in step 3.

    c. Change the order in which the images will appear in the slide show by dragging them up or down in the list of files.

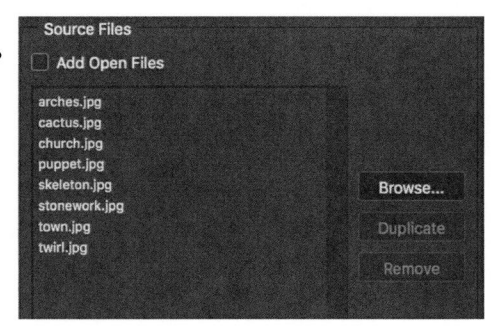

6. Configure the **Output Options** settings to create a slide show, rather than a multi-page document:

    a. Select **Presentation** in the **Output Options** section of the dialog box.

    b. If desired, change the **Background** color from the default white to another color. We chose **Black**, because we think these colorful photographs will show up nicely on a black background.

    c. Set up the text to **Include** under each slide.

        1) Check **Filename**, but not **Extension**.

        2) Set the font size for the included text. We chose **16 pt**.

7. Configure the **Presentation Options** settings so that the slideshow will play as you like. You will not be able to see the effects of these settings until you actually save the **PDF** and view it in Acrobat or Reader.

    a. **Advance Every ___ Seconds** sets the rate at which the slides will change. In our impression, the default **5 seconds** was way too long. **2 seconds** seemed about right to us.

    b. **Loop After Last Page** makes the slideshow play continuously. When unchecked, the slideshow will only play once.

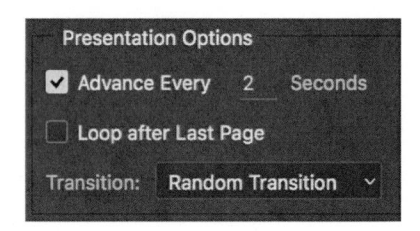

    As you play the slideshow, press the **escape** key to end the slideshow and return to the main Acrobat or Reader window.

    c. **Transition** is the effect that the slideshow will use when it changes from one slide to another. We chose **Random Transition** because we like to be surprised.

8. Click **Save** to save your slide show. Remember to accept the defaults in the Save Adobe PDF dialog box.

9. View your slideshow. First open your **PDF** viewer, then choose **File > Open** and open your slideshow **PDF**. Then choose **View > Full Screen** for Acrobat or Adobe Reader.

10. After viewing your slideshow, press the **esc** (escape) key to end the slideshow and return to the normal view of your document.

11. If you are pleased with your slideshow, **Quit** or **Exit** Acrobat or Reader, as you are done.

12. If you want to work further on your slideshow settings, close the slideshow document window as you can't change an open document created in a different application. Then switch back to Photoshop, and choose the PDF Presentation command again.

    Unless you change your file names as you preview to make different versions of your slideshow, Adobe will warn you that your new preview will replace (delete) the old version of the file.

13. It is fine to overwrite in this case, so click **Yes**.

PHOTOMERGE

Have you ever had a time where you wanted to take a photo of a panoramic view, but it was just too wide to capture in one photo? If so, you either settled for one photo which captured only part of the view, or took multiple images, each capturing only part of the scene, like these images of the Panamint Valley, near Death Valley, in California.

If you then tried to bring the images into Photoshop and manually line up the layers, you would probably end up with a mess like this. Each image looks fine on its own, but when you put them together, the individual distortions caused by the wide-angle lens make them not overlap nicely. Fortunately, Photoshop has the **Photomerge** command, which excels at stitching together individual images to form one large panoramic image.

GUIDED EXERCISE 9.5: USE PHOTOMERGE TO MAKE A PANORAMA

Let's use Photomerge to combine the four images of the Panamint Valley into one wide-angle panorama.

1. Start by closing any open images in Photoshop.

2. Open **pm1.jpg**, **pm2.jpg**, **pm3.jpg**, and **pm4.jpg** from the **09-photomerge** folder inside the **student_images** folder.

3. Choose **File > Automate > Photomerge** to bring up the Photomerge dialog box.

4. In the **Source Files** section of the dialog, be sure **Use** is set to **Files**.

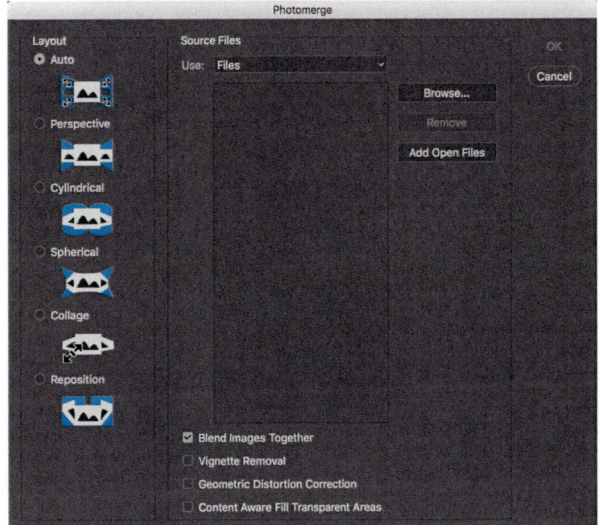

5. Click the **Add Open Files** button to add the four images to the **Source Files** list.

6. Choose a layout — how Photoshop is to stitch the images together.

    There are six different layout choices:

    - **Perspective** chooses one of the images to be the reference for the horizon, and distorts the other images to fit to the chosen reference image. This emphasizes the image vanishing point, but can radically exaggerate the edges of the panorama.

    - **Cylindrical** maps the stitched images as if they were on the outside of an unfolded cylinder.

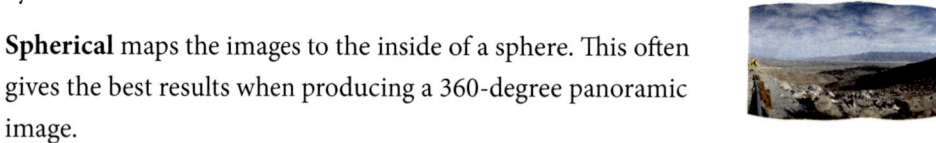

    - **Spherical** maps the images to the inside of a sphere. This often gives the best results when producing a 360-degree panoramic image.

    - **Collage** aligns the images, transforming — rotating or scaling — each image as needed.

    - **Reposition** aligns the source images, matching overlapping content, without transforming any of the source images.

    - If you want to let Photoshop decide which layout option to use, **Auto** analyzes your images and chooses either Perspective, Cylindrical, or Spherical.

7. Make sure **Blend Images Together** is the only option checked at the bottom of the **Source Files** section.

8. Click the **OK** button, then sit back while Photoshop combines copies of each image into one document, matches the overlapping sections, and blends the boundaries between the images. Depending on the size of the images, and the processor and memory in your computer, this may take a few minutes.

Depending on which layout method you chose, you may notice areas of transparency around your finished panorama. These appear because of the transformations necessary to line up the overlapping portions of the source images.

9. Close the panorama you created, then choose **File > Automate > Photomerge** again. Follow the same steps as last time, but this time check the **Content Aware Fill Transparent Areas** box. Once it creates your panorama, Photoshop will try to guess what the missing areas would look like. In general, it depends on the content of the source images and the layout method chosen as to how good of a job it does.

On Your Own

- Arrange a folder of images of your choice. Be sure to define keywords and use those keywords to tag your images. Then use the **Filter** panel to view image subsets.

- Using your own folder of images, create a **PSD** contact sheet with **Contact Sheet II**, a print quality **PDF** contact sheet, and a **PDF** slideshow.

- Use **Photomerge** to combine two or more images into a panorama image.

Resources and Videos

http://www.practical-photoshop.com/pages/CC2015-pp1-resources.html#09

Practical Photoshop CC 2015, Level 1
Tutorial 10: Correcting Image Tonality

Photoshop provides an amazing range of tools and commands for improving both scans of printed photographs and images taken with digital cameras and smart phones. In general, you should correct images beginning with **GLOBAL ADJUSTMENTS** that affect the entire image. Later in the correction process, you will make **LOCAL ADJUSTMENTS** to correct specific problems that the global adjustments did not fix. Here is why you should fix the overall problems first:

- There is no reason to spend time removing dust, scratches, mold, or other artifacts from parts of an image you will later trim off.
- When you adjust an image's overall tone and color, artifacts frequently become more (or less) obvious. If you wait until you have finalized the color and tone corrections before removing artifacts, you only have to clean up artifacts once.

Here is an overview of the image correction steps that professionals typically follow:

1. Obtain a digital image by either transferring it from your camera, phone, or tablet or scanning it from film or from a printed photograph. When scanning, be sure that you digitize the image with adequate resolution to make a high-quality print at your largest desired size.
2. Open the digital image within Photoshop, and choose **File > Save As** to save a working copy of the image with a slightly different name. Do not alter the original, known as the **ARCHIVAL VERSION**, so that it is preserved in its pristine state.
3. **CROP** the working copy to reduce unwanted pixels from its perimeter and straighten the image if appropriate.
4. Improve overall image tone and color as needed.
5. Fix localized problems.
6. Make "artistic" changes as desired.
7. Sharpen the image if needed.
8. Save and print.
9. Make a Web version if desired.

This tutorial begins a four part series on image correction:

Tutorial 10: perform basic image corrections by adjusting the lights and darks of images using non-destructive adjustment layers.

Tutorial 11: assess and improve color and tone, and sharpen images for printing.

Tutorial 12: use special tools to fix local problems or otherwise change specific parts of images.

Tutorial 13: do some case studies to further understand the restoration process.

Objectives

- Delineate the steps you should take to correct or restore a photograph.
- Evaluate image tone with the **Histogram** panel.
- Use the **Brightness/Contrast** command to improve image tone.
- Explain the benefits of using **Adjustment** layers over the **Image > Adjustments** commands.
- Identify the key landmarks of the **Adjustments** panel and the associated **Properties** panel.
- Improve image tone with the **Levels** adjustment.
- Modify adjustment layers using the **Properties** and **Layers** panels.

Tonal Range

The **TONAL RANGE** or **DYNAMIC RANGE** of an image is determined by the way its pixels are distributed throughout the image. When we speak of the tonal range of an image, we are describing:

- How many light, dark or medium level pixels are in the image.
- How much contrast is in the image.
- If the image is predominantly light or dark.
- If the image was captured with an incorrect exposure.

Pixels range in brightness from **0** (**black**) to **255** (**white**). Tonal range is divided into three areas: **HIGHLIGHTS**, **MIDTONES**, and **SHADOWS**.

HIGHLIGHTS	Lightest pixels	205 - 255
MIDTONES	Midrange pixels	65 - 204
SHADOWS	Darkest pixels	0 - 64

A properly balanced image typically has pixels in all three areas, however there is no right or wrong image tonality. Some images are meant to be predominantly light or dark, based on the lighting conditions and subject matter.

The **KEY** of an image describes the appropriately-adjusted tonal range of an image.

- Images with predominantly light subjects such as sunny days at the beach, or polar bears on the snow are called **HIGH KEY IMAGES**.
- Images of dark subjects such as roasted coffee beans or nighttime scenery are **LOW KEY IMAGES**.
- Most images are **AVERAGE KEY** with most of the image in the midtone range, plus some highlight and shadow pixels to enhance detail.

Other images have problems with tonality that diminish their quality. Here are some common problems with image tonality.

Problem	Tonal Description
Flat images that lack contrast	Image pixels concentrate in the midtone range with few or no highlights and shadows.
Images that are too light	Image pixels concentrate in the highlight to midtone range, lacking shadows.
Images that are too dark	Image pixels concentrate in the shadow to midtone range, lacking highlights.

Photoshop allows us to redistribute an image's tones to fix these common image problems. But before we attempt to fix anything, we need to analyze the tonal problems. The **Histogram** panel helps us in this analysis.

Here is one of the photographs from Oaxaca that you used in the Bridge tutorials. It is an average key image. Its **HISTOGRAM** is the graphic display of its color and tones. This graph displays the pixel values, based on their level of brightness, ranging from **0** (black) to **255** (white).

In its default **Colors** view, the graph is in color to show where on the graph the image's red, green, blue, cyan, magenta, and yellow colors appear.

The pixel values of the image are plotted along the horizontal axis; the height of the graph at any point represents the total number of pixels in the image with that brightness level.

Here we are viewing the **Histogram** panel in **Expanded** view and have changed its **Channel** from **Color** to **Luminosity** to see just the image tones. Notice that the graph has pixels all the way from the far left to the far right of the graph, with most of the image on the left side — the darker tones. The Expanded view also gives us some additional statistical information about the distribution of pixels in the image.

. . . .

GUIDED EXERCISE 10.1: USE THE HISTOGRAM PANEL TO ASSESS IMAGE TONALITY

In this guided exercise you will change your workspace to **Photography** and then examine the **Histogram** of a variety of grayscale images to better understand image tonality.

1. Reset all tools, and the default **Foreground** and **Background** colors.

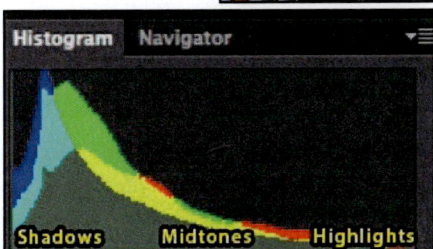

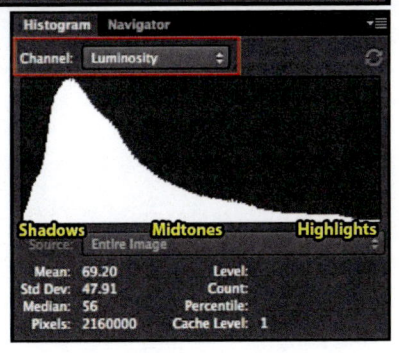

2. Close any open documents and choose **Window > Workspace > Photography**. Note that the panels in the right dock change, topped by a group that contains the **Histogram** and **Navigator** panels. The **Histogram** panel will be empty until you open an image.

3. Open **10-cobweb.jpg** to configure and examine its **Histogram**:

    a. Click the **Cached Data Warning** triangle in the upper right corner of the **Histogram** panel to update the image cache.

    The **Histogram** changes slightly as Photoshop calculates a more accurate graph. You will need to update each time you open an image or adjust it to view the most accurate **Histogram**.

    b. In the **Histogram** panel menu, change the view from **Compact View** to **Expanded View**.

    c. The (Color) **Channel** is **Gray** meaning that this is a **GRAYSCALE** image: the entire image is composed of only white, black, and gray pixels.

    d. Notice that the **Histogram** itself extends virtually all the way to the ends of the graph.

    Based on the **Histogram** alone, we can expect this image to have good contrast. Inspecting the image we can see clear detail in both the lightest areas of the image such as the cobweb and dark areas behind the lock.

4. Close **10-cobweb.jpg** and open **10-twins.jpg**.

    Notice both how light and washed out this image is, and how its **Histogram** has no shadow pixels and very few true highlights.

    This picture, taken in 1921, has faded with time, and seriously lacks contrast. We drew red boxes on either end of the **Histogram** to show where their are very few or no pixels for the lightest highlights and darkest shadows.

5. Close **10-twins.jpg** and open **10-maze_gr.jpg**.

    10-maze_gr.jpg is a modern picture that was photographed in a shadow, and lacks highlights.

    Notice that the **Histogram** does not have any highlights and very few light midtones.

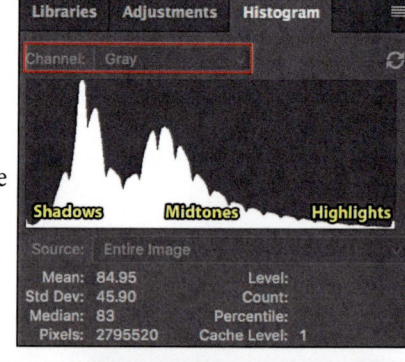

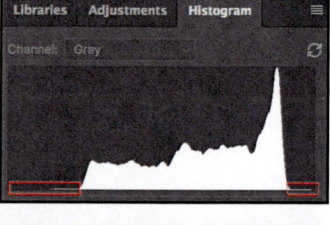

6. Close **10-maze_gr.jpg** and open **10-loraine_gr.jpg**.

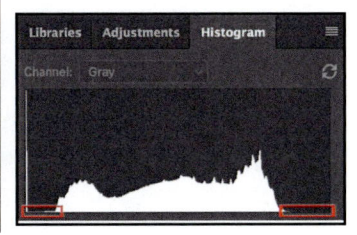

   At first glance, this **Histogram** looks reasonably good. Its tones extend across most of the tonal range except for the darkest shadows and the lightest highlights.

   However, when we look at the picture itself, it looks quite washed out.

   The scan of the photo album page includes both the photo itself and the black paper from the album page.

   The dark pixels from the black paper are part of the scanned image and are included in the **Histogram** — you can see the large spike at the left edge of the histogram.

7. Choose **File > Automate > Crop and Straighten Photos** to straighten the photo and get rid of the black background.

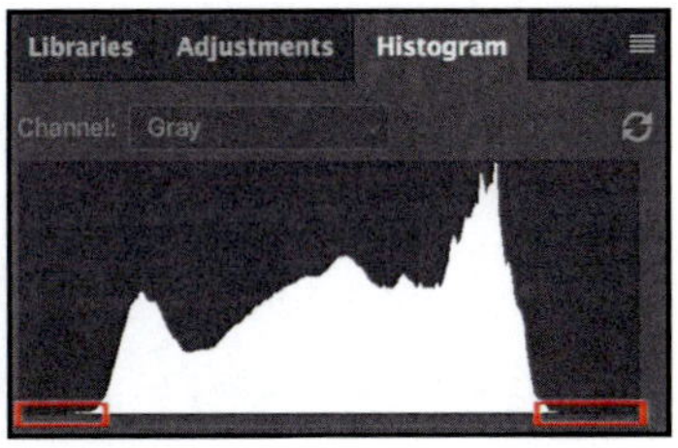

8. Use the **Crop Tool** to further trim off any mounting edges of the image, so that all that remains is the photograph itself.

   Notice that the revised **Histogram** has no highlights, and virtually no shadows. Eliminating the matting from the album gives us a much more accurate **Histogram** of the photograph itself, to better determine how to fix the image.

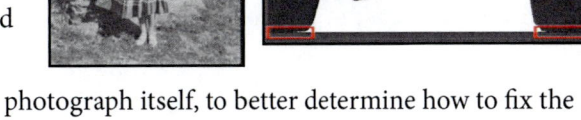

9. Save the cropped version of Loraine as **10-loraine_gr_crop.psd** to use later in this tutorial.

....

The Image > Adjustments Menu

Photoshop has many powerful ways of adjusting images. Many image adjustment commands can be found under the **Image > Adjustments** menu. When you use any of these commands, you change the actual color and/or tone of the image's pixels.

We will introduce the following commands in this tutorial:

- **Brightness/Contrast**
- **Levels**
- **Hue/Saturation**

Brightness/Contrast

The simplest tonal adjustment command is **Brightness/Contrast**. The **BRIGHTNESS** slider lightens or darkens. If you drag the **Brightness** slider to the right, you expand image highlights; if you drag the **Brightness** slider to the left, you expand image shadows.

The **CONTRAST** slider enhances or limits the differences between light and dark areas. The **Contrast** slider expands or shrinks the overall range of tonal values in the image.

Guided Exercise 10.2: Use Brightness/Contrast to improve a Black and White Photograph

In this guided exercise you will use the **Brightness/Contrast** command to improve the tonality of a grayscale image.

1. Open the **10-maze_gr.jpg** image that you viewed earlier. In assessing the **Histogram** of the image, we saw that it lacks highlights.

2. Zoom in to **100%** so that you can see all the image pixels. When image pixels are hidden, it is harder to evaluate image adjustments.

3. Choose **Image > Adjustments > Brightness/Contrast** to open the **Brightness/Contrast** dialog box. When first opened, both **Brightness** and **Contrast** have values of zero (**0**).

    - Dragging a slider to the **right increases** the adjustment.
    - Dragging a slider to the **left decreases** the adjustment.

4. Make these adjustments:

    a. If necessary, drag the **Brightness/Contrast** dialog box to the side of the document window so you can see how your adjustments affect the image.

    b. Slide the **Brightness** slider to the right, to **+60** to lighten the image, and notice how brightening the image improves its detail and lightens the image.

    c. Examine the **Histogram** without clicking the refresh triangle.

    The gray part of the graph shows the original image's tonal distribution; the white graph shows the tonal distribution moving to the right, becoming lighter with the increase in **Brightness**.

    Since the subject itself is pretty dark, it is not a problem that there are still very few highlights.

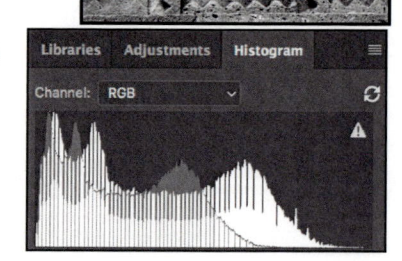

Tutorial 10: Correcting Image Tonality

The **Histogram** now contains white lines throughout; it is no longer solid black. When the adjustment redistributes the tonality of the image, it skips some of the brightness values. Adjusting the image makes the tones less continuous than in the original image. These divisions are called **COMBING** because they look like the teeth of a comb. Combing is typical of an adjusted photograph and is not a problem unless the adjustment is so extreme that the spaces between pixel tones are very wide.

   d. Slide the **Contrast** slider to **+30**, and observe the changes.

       The increased contrast enhances the maze detail particularly in the lower part of the image.

   e. Click **OK** to accept these settings.

No Adjustment	Brightness + 60	Contrast +30

5. Examine the **Layers** panel and observe that the image still has only one layer, the **Background**.

When you use the **Image > Adjustments** commands, they alter the value of the actual image pixels. If you were to save the image at this point, then close it, you could not remove or change the **Brightness/Contrast** adjustment you just made. This kind of image adjustment is known as a **DESTRUCTIVE** adjustment for this reason.

6. Go back in **History** to the original state of the image, and leave it open for the next guided exercise.

Avoid the Legacy Check box

A quick warning. Do not check the **Use Legacy** check box in the **Brightness/Contrast** dialog box, unless you need results like this:

The maze becomes washed out, and there are no longer good shadows.

Here is why the results are so different, from Photoshop Help:

Brightness/Contrast applies proportionate (nonlinear) adjustments to image pixels, as with **Levels** and **Curves** adjustments. When **Use Legacy** is selected, **Brightness/Contrast** simply shifts all pixel values higher or lower when adjusting brightness. Shifting the image pixels this way can cause **CLIPPING**: loss of image detail in highlight or shadow areas.

For this reason, using the **Brightness/Contrast** command in **Legacy** mode is not recommended for high-end output.

Adjustment Layers and the Adjustments Panel

Image adjustment is very sensitive, and sometimes what looks good on screen does not print well—or you discover a better technique for fixing your image and want to return to the original and try something different. To provide flexibility, and also to allow you to edit image tones non-destructively, Photoshop developed adjustment layers and the **Adjustments** panel.

An **ADJUSTMENT LAYER** is a special layer that can be edited or even deleted without altering the color or tone of the original image pixels.

Adjustment layers can be manipulated like any other layers. You can adjust their visibility and their blending mode. You can show or hide them by clicking the eye icon. You can move them up or down a stack of layers to determine which part of the image (beneath the adjustment layer) will be affected by the adjustment.

The **Adjustments** panel lets you easily create adjustment layers, choose among preset adjustments for some adjustments, and modify your adjustment settings, all in one spot.

NOTE: Nearly every adjustment in the **Image** > **Adjustments** menu can be accessed from the **Adjustments** panel. To obtain all of these benefits, you should choose your adjustments from the **Adjustments** panel rather than the **Image** > **Adjustments** menu whenever possible.

Using the Adjustments Panel

The top of the panel contains buttons for each of the available adjustments, sixteen in all.

If you hover over an adjustment button, such as **Brightness/Contrast** here, the button highlights and its name appears at the top of the **Adjustments** panel.

When you click an adjustment button, two things happen:

- Its adjustment layer is added to the **Layers** panel.
- The **Properties** panel with the specific adjustment settings opens.

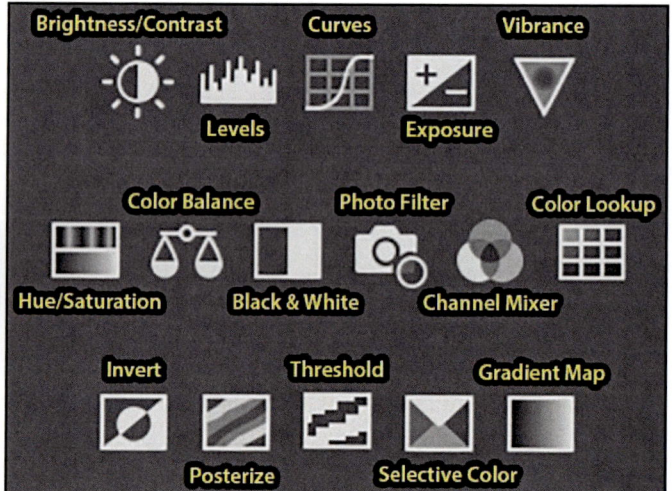

Tutorial 10: Correcting Image Tonality

Once you create an adjustment layer, a series of control buttons will appear at the bottom of the **Properties Panel**.

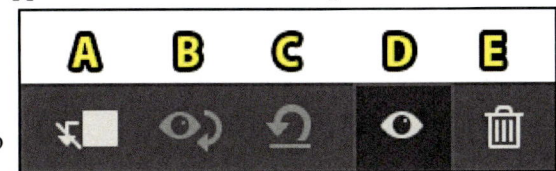

Most of the buttons will not activate until you make an adjustment layer:

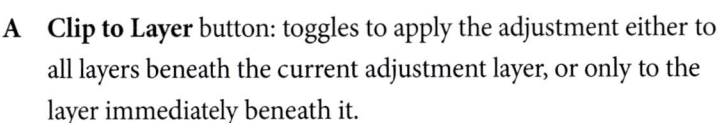

A **Clip to Layer** button: toggles to apply the adjustment either to all layers beneath the current adjustment layer, or only to the layer immediately beneath it.

B **View previous state** button: shows the image before making the latest adjustment.

C **Reset to adjustment defaults** button: restores the adjustment to an earlier state. When more than one change has been made, the first click returns to the previous state and a second click restores the adjustment to its default state.

D **Visibility** button: toggles to hide or show the current adjustment layer. When hidden, the adjustments do not apply.

E **Trash** button: discards the adjustment layer. When you click the **Trash** button, you will be warned in case you clicked it accidentally. Click **Yes** to delete the adjustment or **No** to cancel.

GUIDED EXERCISE 10.3: MAKE A BRIGHTNESS/CONTRAST ADJUSTMENTS LAYER

In this guided exercise you will use the **Adjustments** panel to add a **Brightness/Contrast** adjustment layer to the maze photo you previously adjusted from the **Image > Adjustments** menu.

1. Open **10-maze_gr.jpg** if it is not already open.

2. In the Adjustments panel, point to the **Brightness/Contrast** button.
   It is the top left adjustment.

   The button highlights and its name appears at the top of the **Adjustments** panel.

3. Click the **Brightness/Contrast** button to create a new **Brightness/Contrast** adjustment layer in the **Layers** panel.

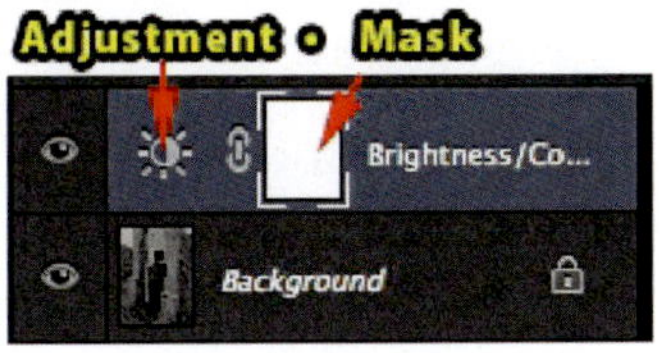

   The adjustment icon on the left is used to reveal the **Properties** panel to change the adjustments for that layer; the thumbnail on the right is a **MASK** to selectively apply the adjustment to only part of the image.

   The **Properties** panel opens automatically with the **Brightness/Contrast** settings displayed.

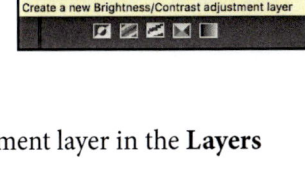

4. In the **Properties** panel, use the same settings as before to increase **Brightness** to **+60** and **Contrast** to **+30,** with **Use Legacy** unchecked, of course.

   Play around with the settings to fine tune your adjustment. There is no absolutely "correct" setting as image tonality is subjective. It depends on how much contrast you like.

5. Click the **Properties tab** or the **Collapse** arrows to shrink the **Properties** panel to a button.

6. Differentiate between the **Adjustment** icons in the **Layers** panel and in the **Adjustments** panel:

   a. In the **Brightness/Contrast** layer, double-click the **Brightness/Contrast** icon to reveal the **Properties** panel. Use this technique whenever you want to edit adjustment settings, and collapse the **Properties** panel when you are done.

   b. In the **Adjustments** panel, click the **Brightness/Contrast** button.

      Instead of showing your former settings, it created a second adjustment layer. Each time you click an **Adjustment** button, it creates a new **Adjustment** layer.

      On rare occasions, you will use more than one of the same kind of **Adjustment** layer, but typically you will change the settings of the original adjustment rather than creating additional layers.

   c. Click the **Trash** button in the **Properties** panel because you do not want a second **Brightness/Contrast** adjustment. Instead, you want to modify the original adjustment layer.

7. When you are pleased with your adjustment, save the document as **maze_gr.psd** and leave it open for the next guided exercise.

LEVELS

The **Levels** adjustment, based on the **Histogram**, is used to identify an image's shadow and highlight points (blacks and whites) and set their target values.

The **Levels** adjustment comes with a number of preset adjustments to help you get started.

For a beginner, the most important item in the **Levels** adjustment is the **Auto** button.

The **Properties** panel for **Levels** opens to show the **Histogram** of the image with sliders and text boxes for changing image tonality.

Guided Exercise 10.4: Use Levels with the Auto Setting

In this guided exercise you will use the **Levels** adjustment to correct the tonality of **maze_gr.psd**.

1. Open **maze_gr.psd** if it is not already open.

2. Click the eye next to the **Brightness/Contrast** adjustment layer to hide that adjustment, and click the **Background** layer to activate it.

3. Click the **Levels button** in the **Adjustments** panel to add a **Levels** adjustment layer.

    The **Layers** panel now contains a **Levels** adjustment layer just above the **Background** layer and the **Properties** panel opens to show the **Levels** adjustment settings which are much more complicated and powerful than **Brightness/Contrast**.

4. Click the **Cache warning** button to update the **Properties** panel **Histogram**.

5. Click the **Auto** button.

    Auto has a dramatic effect on the image. On a grayscale image like this one, **Auto** stretches out the tones of the image so that they expand from shadows to highlights to fill the entire **Histogram**, thereby improving tonality and increasing contrast.

6. Now that the overall tones are balanced, you can fine tune the contrast in a variety of different ways. One way is to add a second **Levels** adjustment layer using one of the **Levels** presets:

    a. Click the **Levels button** in the **Adjustments** panel to make a second **Levels** adjustment layer.

    The **Properties** panel displays the **Levels** default settings for the second layer.

    b. In turn, try each of the **Increase Contrast** presets on your image. We liked **Increase Contrast 2**.

    Now you have two levels adjustment layers. **Auto** evens out the tones of the entire image, while **Increase Contrast 2** increased the contrast in the midtones of the previously adjusted image.

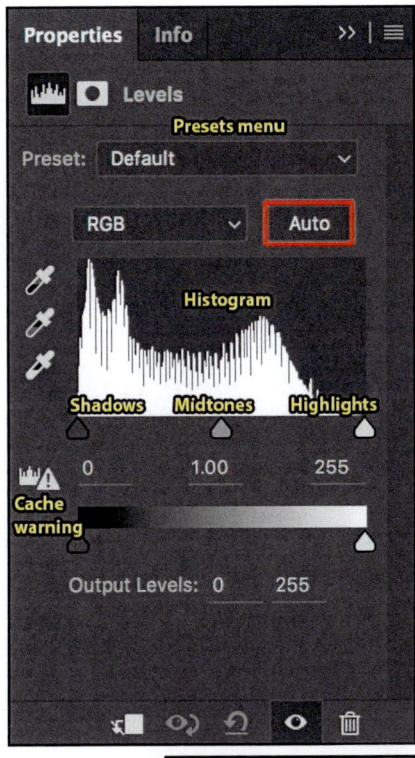

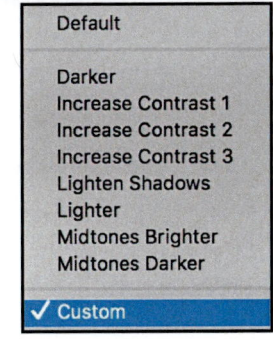

7. Refine the amount of contrast. Here are some suggestions:

   - Try some of the other presets for the **Levels 2** adjustment to see if you find any of them more pleasing. Be careful, as some of the presets will **CLIP** the highlights or shadows, losing detail by forcing the tones to pure white or pure black.

   - With the **Levels 2** adjustment layer active, lower its **Opacity** (using the slider at the top of the **Layers** panel) from **100%** to **50%** and observe how this affects the image. End up with the percentage of your choice.

8. When you are pleased with your adjustments, save the document as **maze_gr2.psd**.

9. Compare it with your original adjustment using **Brightness/Contrast**. Which version do you prefer and why?

NOTE: the adjustment method you used here is a beginners method. Photoshop professionals would fix the entire adjustment with a single adjustment layer, probably using the **Curves** adjustment. But, for now, this method definitely improves your image.

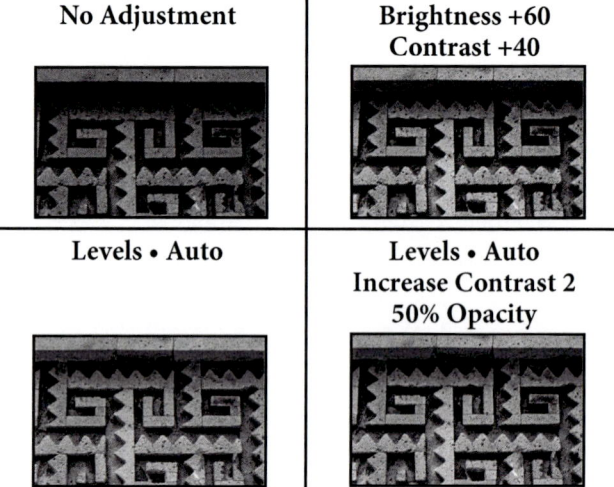

Adjusting the Tonality of Color Images

It is much simpler to adjust grayscale than color images because the human eye is very sensitive to color, and even small color shifts are quite noticeable to most people.

Here are the color versions of the maze image you worked on. On top is the original, in the middle the **Brightness/Contrast** version, and on the bottom the **Levels** version with two **Levels** adjustments just like you did in grayscale, but at **100% Opacity**.

It's better, but certainly not great. **Levels** is more versatile and yields better results. The bottom version is brighter, with more contrast than the other two.

Auto Color Correction Options

For grayscale images, the **Auto** button in the **Levels** adjustment is a one step fix. For color images, **Auto** hides the **Auto Color Correction Options** dialog box where you can try out different settings to get better results. One of the **Auto Color Correction Options** may be all you need to repair the color and tone, thereby saving you a lot of time. To view the **Auto Color Correction Options**, press **Alt** (Windows) or **Option** (Mac) as you click the **Auto** button in the **Levels Properties** panel:

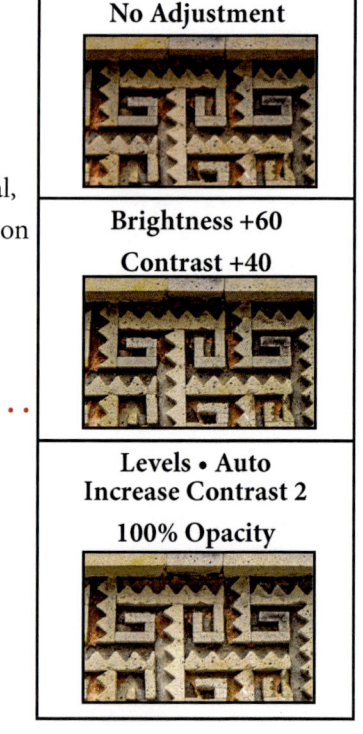

- **Enhance Monochromatic Contrast** increases contrast without adjusting color. This option changes the tonal range of the image by redistributing tones from pure white to pure black.

- **Enhance Per Channel Contrast** works individually on the red, green, and blue (**RGB**) components of the image to improve contrast and remove overall inappropriate colors known as **COLOR CASTS**.

- **Find Dark & Light Colors** analyzes an image to find the light and dark colors and then uses those colors as the new shadow and highlight colors to improve the contrast. It can also snap neutral midtones to help with color correcting.

- When **Snap Neutral Midtones** is checked for any of the first three options, it can further neutralize a color cast. Since this option sometimes removes too much color from an image, you can turn it on or off as desired.

   The default, **Enhance Brightness and Contrast**, analyzes the tonality of the image and then corrects it using Photoshop's special content-aware technology.

Guided Exercise 10.5: Use the Auto Color Correction Options

Each image is different, so the effectiveness of the **Auto Color Correction Options** can vary widely. Think of these options as a good place to start when correcting your image. In this guided exercise, you will open an image and compare the four **Auto Color Correction Options**.

1. Open the file called **10-seattle_compare.jpg**.

   This photograph was taken at the end of sunset, leaving the image dark and with dusky, muddy colors.

   There are five copies of the photo so that you can compare the original with the four **Auto Color Correction Options**.

2. Apply **Enhance Brightness and Contrast** to part of the document:

   a. Zoom in so that the image above **Enhance Brightness and Contrast** covers most of the document window.

   b. If you start with a selection, only that part of your document will be altered. Use the **Rectangular Marquee Tool** to select just that photo:

      1) Make sure the selection goes all the way out to the edges of the photo.

      2) If you didn't select quite right, choose **Select > Transform Selection** and drag the **Transform** handles to make your selection more precise.

   c. Click the **Levels** button in the **Adjustments** panel.

   d. Press the **alt** key (Win) or the **option** key (Mac) and click the **Auto** button in the **Levels Adjustments** panel to open the **Auto Color Correction Options** dialog box.

e. Click the **Enhance Brightness and Contrast** radio button and click **OK**.

f. Turn the visibility of **Levels 1** on and off to see how the adjustment changed the image's tones and colors.

Enhance Brightness and Contrast darkened the photo, compared with the original.

Notice the **Layer Mask** thumbnail in the **Layers** panel. The white part of the mask is your selected photo, and the black region is the deselected part. The **Levels** adjustment only changes the white or selected region, and the mask hides or protects the rest of the document from changing. You will learn much more about layer masks in Practical Photoshop Level 2.

3. Apply **Enhance Monochromatic Contrast** to part of the document:

   a. Select the photo above **Enhance Monochromatic Contrast**.

   b. Click the **Levels** icon in the **Adjustments** panel.

   c. Press the **alt** key (Win) or the **option** key (Mac) and click the **Auto** button in the **Levels Adjustments** panel to open the **Auto Color Correction Options** dialog box.

   d. Click the **Enhance Monochromatic Contrast** algorithm to see how it changes the photo, and click **OK**.

   Enhance Monochromatic Contrast lightened the image, increased its contrast, and made its overall colors a little pinker.

   You now have two **Levels** adjustment layers, each affecting a different part of the Background tones and colors.

4. Apply **Enhance Per Channel Contrast** to part of the document:

   a. Select the photo above **Enhance Per Channel Contrast**.

   b. Click the **Levels** icon in the **Adjustments** panel to make a third **Levels** adjustment layer.

   c. Press the **alt** key (Win) or the **option** key (Mac) and click the **Auto** button in the **Levels Adjustments** panel to open the **Auto Color Correction Options** dialog box.

   d. Click the **Enhance Per Channel Contrast** algorithm to see how it changes the photo. Experiment with **Snap Neutral Midtones** checked and unchecked, using the version you prefer and click **OK**.

   Notice the effects of **Enhance Per Channel Contrast** on the image. The image gets lighter, its contrast increases, and its overall color shifts toward blue.

5. Apply **Find Dark & Light Colors** to part of the document:

   a. Select the photo above **Find Dark & Light Colors**.

   b. Click the **Levels** icon in the **Adjustments** panel to make a fourth **Levels** adjustment layer.

c. Press the **alt** key (Win) or the **option** key (Mac) and click the **Auto** button in the **Levels Adjustments** panel to open the **Auto Color Correction Options** dialog box.

d. Click the **Find Dark & Light Colors** algorithm to see how it changes the photo.

e. Experiment with **Snap Neutral Midtones** checked and unchecked, using the version you prefer and click **OK**.

   Overall, **Find Dark & Light Colors** is the most subtle of the four. The image is lightened and its contrast is increased, but its color shift is minor compared with the original.

6. Save and print your document if desired.

On Your Own

- Improve the tonality of **10-loraine-gr_crop.psd**, experimenting with **Brightness/Contrast** and **Levels** adjustments. Be sure to use the **Adjustments** panel and not the **Image/Adjustments** menu, so that your adjustments are non-destructive. Our original is on the left, and the adjusted version on the right.

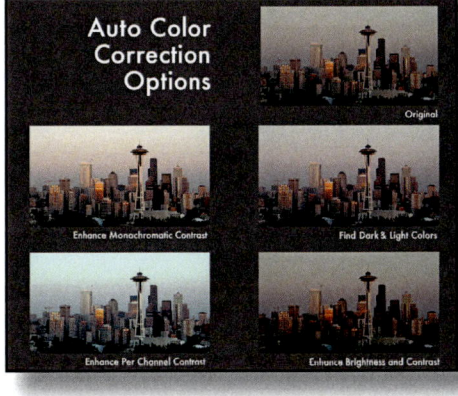

  Original   **Adjusted**

- Experiment with the **Auto Color Adjustment Options** for **10-maze.jpg**, the colored version of **10-maze-gr.jpg** that you worked with in this tutorial.

Resources and Videos

http://www.practical-photoshop.com/pages/CC2015-pp1-resources.html#10

Practical Photoshop CC 2015, Level 1
Tutorial 11: Adjusting Image Colors

Tutorial 10 focused on image tone. You assessed image tonality with the **Histogram** panel, and then used the **Image > Adjustments** commands and the **Adjustments** panel to improve the image tonality. Tutorial 11 continues the topic of image correction, concentrating on adjusting image colors.

Objectives

- Identify the additive (**RGB**) and subtractive (**CMY**) **PRIMARY COLORS** and memorize the opposite colors for each.

- Explain the purpose of **COLOR CHANNELS**.

- Use the **Info** panel to assess image tone and color.

- Identify and correct an image with a **COLOR CAST**.

- Make a **Color Balance** adjustment to improve an image.

- Use the **Color Range** command to select specific colors, and the **Replace Color** command to change specific colors.

- Differentiate among **HUE**, **SATURATION**, and **LIGHTNESS**.

- Use the **Hue/Saturation** adjustment to alter image colors and tones.

Color Science

The human eye perceives color according to the wavelength of the light that reaches it. The colors from these light sources can be divided into two categories: **TRANSMITTED COLOR** and **REFLECTED COLOR**.

PRIMARY COLORS are colors that cannot be made from other colors.

A **COLOR WHEEL** is a schematic way of showing relationships among colors. Digital software and printing relies heavily on this color wheel. The two triangles drawn on the wheel represent two sets of primary colors:

- The triangle for **red**, **green**, and **blue** (**RGB**) describes color that is **TRANSMITTED** to your eyes, such as from a computer monitor or television screen

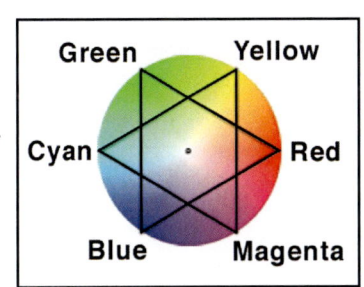

- The triangle for **cyan**, **magenta**, and **yellow** describes color that is **REFLECTED**, meaning when white light waves hit an object, some wave lengths are absorbed by its color, and others bounce back to our eyes to become the color we see.

The color information for Photoshop documents is stored in the **Channels** panel. In this book we are typically working with **RGB** images. Each of those images has three color channels—**Red**, **Green**, and **Blue**—in the **Channels** panel that store the image's color information.

The **Channels** panel also contains a composite **RGB** channel: the **RGB** channel is not a color channel because it does not hold the pixels of an individual color, either additive or subtractive.

Color Casts

Sometimes an image will have a **COLOR CAST** — an inappropriate color that affects the entire image. Technically, this happens because the pixels of one color channel are too strong or too weak for the other color channels.

The color wheel is very important for removing color casts in Photoshop. To remove a color cast, you add the color that is opposite on the color wheel:

- **RED** is opposite **CYAN**.
- **GREEN** is opposite **MAGENTA**.
- **BLUE** is opposite **YELLOW**.

But before we attempt to fix an image, we need to analyze its tones and colors to come up with an adjustment strategy.

Color Casts and the Info Panel

Most of the images you worked with in Tutorial 10 were **GRAYSCALE** images. That means that they were made up of shades of gray, but no colors. When you adjusted the tonality of these images, it was relatively simple. Most images you will work with, however, will be in color, and color introduces a whole new set of potential problems.

Sometimes a color cast is very obvious. Other times, you will look at an image and feel the colors are off, but you don't quite know what is wrong.

The Info Panel

The **Info** panel gives color and tonal information about individual pixels in an image to help you to recognize a color cast, so that you can correct it.

In the **Photography Workspace**, the **Info** panel is collapsed to a button with an **i** on it. If you are using a different workspace, like **Essentials**, you can choose the **Info** panel from the **Window** menu.

Tutorial 11: Adjusting Image Colors Page 218

In a color image, the top left section of the **Info** panel lists three values:

R, **G**, and **B**. These stand for **Red**, **Green**, and **Blue**, the primary colors of light that Photoshop uses to mix colors for most Photoshop images.

With any image open and any tool chosen, slowly move the cursor across the image without pressing the mouse button, and watch the numbers change as you move from pixels of one color to another. Here the values for the sampled color are **R = 0**, **G =24**, and **B = 46**. These values give a very dark turquoise color.

The **R**, **G**, or **B** values can range from **0** for complete absence of that color to **255** for complete presence of that color. **NEUTRAL TONES** are colors that have about the same value of **R**, **G**, and **B**. In other words:

- When **R**, **G**, and **B** are **0**, the color of that pixel is black, the complete absence of light.

- When **R**, **G**, and **B** are **255**, the color of that pixel is white, full light in the visible spectrum.

- When **R**, **G**, and **B** are **128**, the color of that pixel is medium gray.

If you check regions of an image with the **Info** panel that should be neutral — such as a white blouse or gray concrete — and the **R**, **G**, and **B** values are not close to the one another, the image probably has a color cast.

. . . .

GUIDED EXERCISE 11.1: IDENTIFY AND CORRECT A COLOR CAST

In this guided exercise you will open a photo of a child, use the **Info** panel to identify the color cast, and then apply a **Levels** adjustment with **Auto Color Correction** to fix the overall tonality of the image and improve its color somewhat.

1. Choose the **Photography** workspace.

2. Open the file named **11-blue-kid.jpg**. This photo was shot of a child in a shaded area on a sunny day, and the colors got a little off.

3. Look for areas in the image that should be neutral.

    The wall he's standing in front of is concrete, so it should be fairly neutral.

4. Use the **Info** panel to observe the color cast numbers:

    a. Click the **Info** panel button to expand the **Info** panel.

    b. Choose the **Eyedropper Tool**.

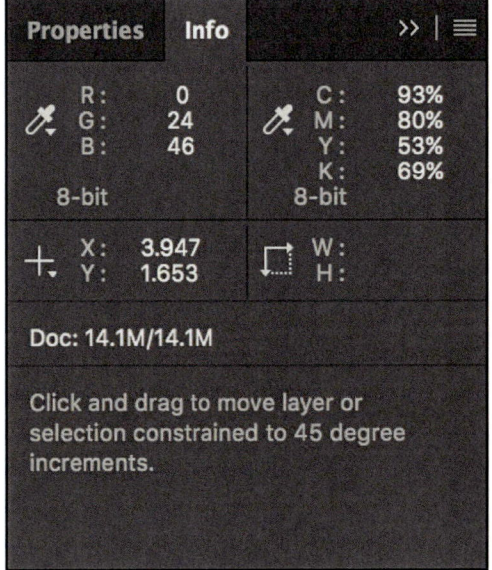

Although you can use any tool with the **Info** panel, we will use the **Eyedropper Tool** here to keep our instructions consistent.

c. Press the **Caps Lock** key to display the **precise cursor**.

Now the **Eyedropper Tool** pointer becomes a circle with a dot in its center. Whatever that dot covers is the pixel the **Info** panel is measuring.

d. Position the cursor over a dark area of concrete in the upper-right corner of the image and examine the **RGB** values in the **Info** panel. *Your numbers will probably be slightly different from ours, as it isn't likely that your cursor will be over the exact same pixel as ours.*

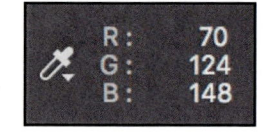

- In a neutral region, **R**, **G**, and **B** should have about the same values.
- Here, the **B** is much higher than either **R** or **G**, implying that the photo has a blue cast.

e. Position the cursor over one of the very lightest parts of the wall and check the **Info** panel numbers. Again **B** is significantly higher than the others.

When a color cast affects an entire image, the **Info** panel will show you color values that are "off" throughout the image, rather than just in one spot.

You should neutralize the cast for the entire image rather than to select and fix the individual areas of the image that look the most "off." Afterwards, you can spot-fix problems if still needed.

f. Press the **Caps Lock** key again to turn off the **precise cursor**.

5. Use a **Levels** adjustment layer to improve image contrast and hopefully remove the color cast:

    a. Click the **Levels** icon in the **Adjustments** panel.

    b. Press the **alt** key (Win) or the **option** key (Mac) and click the **Auto** button in the **Levels Adjustments** panel to open the **Auto Color Correction Options** dialog box to improve both image tonality and color. You used these options in the last tutorial, but here we will explain what they do in greater detail.

    ALGORITHMS are built-in formulas for correcting color and tone. You can click in each setting in turn to see how it affects the image.

    There are four choices because different images look better with different automatic corrections. All four of the algorithms will adjust your image by taking your darkest pixels and setting them to black and setting

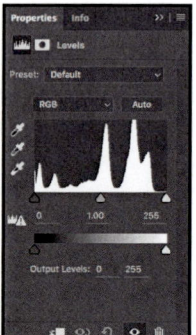

Tutorial 11: Adjusting Image Colors Page 220

the lightest pixels to white. Flat images that do not have darkest dark or brightest white pixels will look the most improved with increased contrast, but even photos with pixels throughout the tonal range often improve with a **Levels** adjustment.

Enhance Brightness and Contrast and **Enhance Monochromatic Contrast** do not fix color casts so we won't discuss them further. But you might want to look at them anyway just to see how they affect the photo.

Enhance Per Channel Contrast modifies color channels independently to improve contrast and remove color casts. In other words, **Enhance Per Channel Contrast** adjusts the input sliders by different amounts of **R**, **G**, and **B**.

Find Dark and Light Colors analyzes an image to find the light and dark colors and uses those colors as the shadow and highlight colors. The midtones are adjusted by selecting the colors closest to the neutral value and changing them to the target midtone color.

c. Experiment with the different algorithms in the **Auto Color Corrections Options** dialog box.

Based on the appearance on our monitor, **Enhance Per Channel Contrast** with **Snap Neutral Midtones** checked gave slightly better overall color, but there is still a definite color cast.

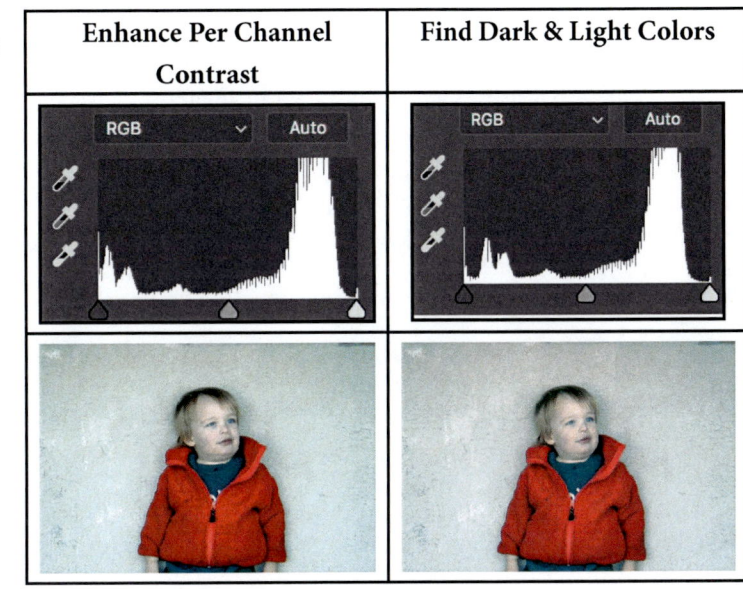

d. Choose **Enhance Per Channel Contrast** with **Snap Neutral Midtones** and click **OK** to accept these settings.

6. Save your image in the location of your choice as **kid.psd**. You may wish to print a before and an after image for comparison. You will use this image again to refine your adjustment.

Balancing Colors with their Opposites

You have already learned that the primary colors of red, green, and blue have opposite colors of cyan, magenta, and yellow. The **Color Balance** adjustment takes advantage of these opposites to fix either overall color casts, or specific problem colors in an image.

The Color Balance Adjustment

The **Color Balance** adjustment is typically used to make an image, layer, or selection **WARMER** (more red, magenta, or yellow) or **COOLER** (more green, blue, or cyan). **Color Balance** adjustments specifically adjust the highlights, midtones, or shadows of an image.

You use the **Color Balance** adjustment to correct an image with a color cast by moving the color sliders, increasing the color opposite to the cast.

For instance, you can correct for a red cast by moving the top color slider towards cyan. The sliders are colored to make it easier to visualize how the adjustment will affect your image.

Although **Color Balance** is not the most sophisticated way to correct a color cast, it is very easy to use, and provides a good starting point for beginners. Let's try it on the kid.

Guided Exercise 11.2: Use Color Balance to Further Correct a Color Cast

Take a good look at **kid.psd**. While the color cast is better, it is still there. In this guided exercise you will make a **Color Balance** adjustment layer above the **Levels 1** adjustment layer to correct the color non-destructively.

1. Open **kid.psd** if it is not already open.

2. Activate the **Levels 1** layer and then click the **Color Balance** button on the **Adjustments** panel to add a **Color Balance** adjustment layer above **Levels 1**.

   NOTE: The stacking order of adjustment layers is very important, as the adjustments take effect from the top down.

3. Add **red** (the opposite of **cyan**) to the shadows to neutralize the some of the overall cyan cast:

   a. At the top of the **Properties** panel, change the **Tone** from the default **Midtones** to **Shadows**.

   b. Highlight the number to the right of the **Cyan** to **Red** slider, and use the up arrow key on the keyboard to gradually move the slider to the right to increase the **Red** in the shadows.

   We use the keyboard instead of dragging the slider with the pointer because it is more precise. Often very small **Color Balance** adjustments can make a big difference in the overall appearance of the image.

4. Check with the **Info** panel again. We found that adding **Red** neutralized the **Cyan** cast, but there was still a slight **Green** cast so we countered it by adding some **Magenta** to the shadows as well.

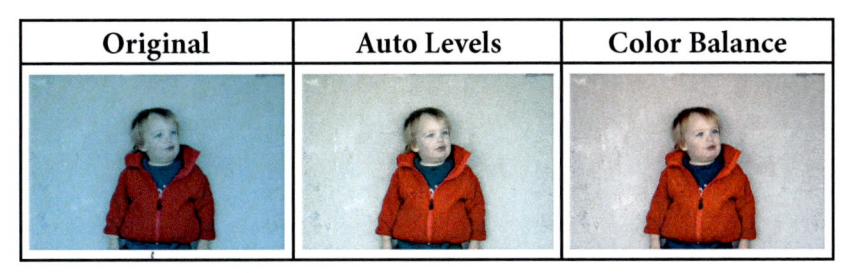

5. Save your image as **kid2.psd**. If you like, you may print it to compare with the printout you made in step 6 of Guided Exercise 11.1.

Guided Exercise 11.3: Apply a Color Balance Adjustment to a Multi-layered Document

In this exercise, you will use the **Adjustments** panel to apply a **Color Balance** adjustment to an image. As you work, you will see how layer order affects how the adjustments occur.

1. Begin in Bridge, because Bridge will let you easily combine three images into a single document.

2. Organize these three files into the same folder, and highlight all three in the Bridge **Content** panel: **11-cb_coastline.jpg**, **11-cb_giraffe.tif**, and **11-cb_goose.tif**.

   The **.tif** format is one you have not seen before. **TIFF** stands for **Tagged Image File Format**, and these files are a bit smaller than PSDs for faster download, but they have transparency so that the giraffe and the goose are on their own layers.

   If you have correctly highlighted all three images, then you will see the three images in the **Preview** panel of Bridge.

3. Choose **Tools > Photoshop > Load Files into Photoshop Layers**.

   This command takes the three images and combines them into a single document, with each original document becoming a layer of a new untitled document that opens in Photoshop.

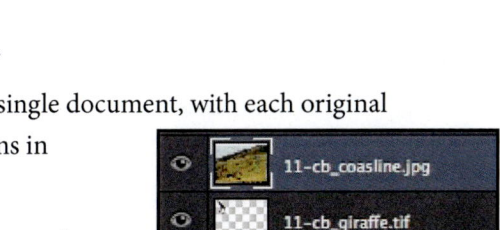

   Each layer has its old file name. If the order of your files in Bridge was the same as ours, then **11-cb_coastline.jpg** will be at the top of the stack, obscuring the other two layers. Notice that the new document does not have a **Background** layer.

4. Activate layer **11-cb_coastline.jpg**, and choose **Layer > New > Background from Layer** to simultaneously move the coastline layer to the bottom of the stack, and turn it into the **Background** layer.

5. Shorten the other two layer names to **goose** and **giraffe**.

6. With the **Move Tool**, rearrange the **goose** and **giraffe** layers until you like their positions in the image.

7. Save the document as **giraffe_goose.psd**.

8. Make a **Color Balance** adjustment layer:

    a. Activate the top layer (the giraffe here).

    b. Click the **Color Balance** icon in the **Adjustments** panel and examine its settings in more detail.

    The **Tone** section of the **Color Balance** adjustment allows you to alter the shadows, midtones, and highlights separately.

    Midtones is the default because most images have more midtones than either shadows or highlights.

    Preserve Luminosity is checked by default to prevent changing the luminosity or lightness values in the image while changing the color. If you uncheck it, you will change the overall tonal balance in the image. Keep **Preserve Luminosity** checked for this exercise.

    c. Make the hillside greener:

    1) In the **Color Balance** dialog box, move the top **Cyan to Red** slider to the left towards **Cyan**. As you move the slider it, examine its value box. Drag the slider so that its value is **-53**.

    2) Drag the middle **Magenta to Green** slider to the right towards **Green** and stop when its value box says **+53**.

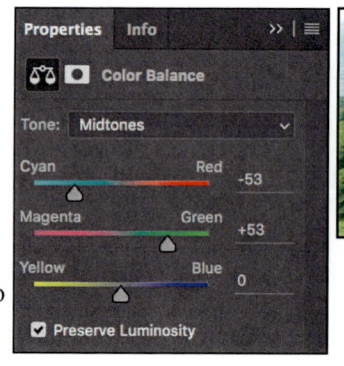

    Do not change the **Yellow to Blue** slider, as your initial adjustment is sufficient.

9. Look at the **Layers** panel. The **Color Balance** layer should be at the top of the stack. The **Color Balance** adjustment pumps up the cyan and green tones of the entire image.

The coastline looks much lusher, but both the giraffe and the goose have a green cast which is especially noticeable if you zoom in.

10. Drag the **Color Balance** adjustment layer just below the **giraffe** layer.

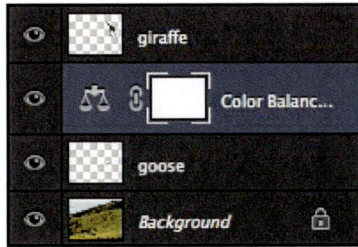

    The giraffe looks much better, but the goose has a green cast, most noticeably on its feet and beak that lose some of their orange color.

    NOTE: Every visible layer beneath an adjustment layer will be affected by that adjustment; the layers above the adjustment layer are not affected.

11. Finally, drag the **Color Balance** adjustment layer just above the **Background**.

    Now both the goose and giraffe have natural colors, and the hills and water are very blue-green.

12. Modify the adjustment because the green midtones are overwhelming:

    a. Activate the **Color Balance** adjustment layer if it is not currently active.

    b. Under **Tone**, choose **Shadows** to alter the darkest pixels in the image.

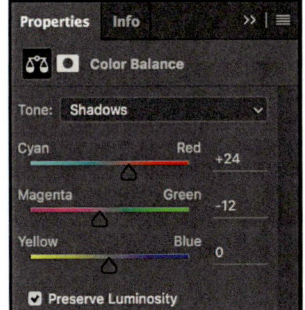

    c. Highlight the value box that controls **Cyan to Red**, and click the up arrow several times to pump up the red in the shadows.

    Using the arrow keys provides precise control, to help make a better adjustment.

    d. Highlight the value box that controls **Magenta to Green**, and press the down arrow several times to add magenta to the shadows.

    The image looks much better than when you started, but the new colors are quite intense.

13. Since your adjustment is on a layer, it is easy to tone down its strength by lowering the opacity of the adjustment layer. Lower the opacity of the **Color Balance** adjustment layer to **50%** and observe the change.

14. End up with the percentage of adjustment that you like.

15. Save and print if desired.

Creating an Adjustment Layer with a Selection

When you create an adjustment layer without a selection, the adjustment affects the whole document. If you create a selection before making an adjustment layer, the adjustment only affects the selected region.

A **MASK** is a visual representation of a selection, where the selected or active regions of the image are represented in white, and the deselected or protected areas represented in black.

This example shows a similar photo of the coast as **11-cb_coastline.jpg**, but taken as the sun is setting. It was made by first selecting the sky and then creating the adjustment layer.

When you create a selection before you create an adjustment layer, the mask created with the adjustment layer will be white in the selected area and black over the rest of the mask. The adjustment affects only the selected area. By selecting the sky *before* creating the **Color Balance** adjustment layer, the mask revealed only the sky area. Increasing the blue and cyan in the **Color Balance** dialog box improved the color of the sky and water without turning the hills blue.

WARNING: **Color Balance** is a good starting point for novices, but it is typically not recommended for professional level color adjustment because it can cause strange color shifts at the transitions between the highlights, midtones, and shadows.

Hue, Saturation, and Lightness

When Photoshop defines colors, one way of doing so is by assigning numbers to the red, green, and blue components of each color. Another way of defining colors is by their hue, saturation, and lightness or **HSL** values.

HUE is the pure color measured in degrees from **VISIBLE RED**, to **VISIBLE VIOLET**. Interestingly enough, 360 is the same as 0, which is visible red again… The hue graphic shown here is from Wikimedia Commons, http://commons.wikimedia.org/wiki/Main_Page.

SATURATION is the intensity or purity of the color, measured as a percentage of full color. When fully saturated, or **100%**, the color is the same as the hue. When fully desaturated, or **0%**, the color is completely neutral—black, white, or a shade of gray.

LIGHTNESS, also known as **BRIGHTNESS**, is how light or dark the color is, measured as a percentage of full light. **50%** lightness or brightness is neutral. Lowering lightness or brightness gradually increased the amount of black in the color with **0%** being pure black. Raising lightness or brightness gradually increases the amount of white in the color until it becomes pure white at **100%**.

The Hue/Saturation Adjustment

The **Hue/Saturation** adjustment allows you to increase or decrease saturation, to shift the hue of an image or selection, and to colorize images or selections.
Hue/Saturation has three sliders:

Hue adjusts the overall hue of the image or selection. Hue cycles through the color spectrum shown at the bottom of the dialog box from cyan, through blue, magenta, red, yellow, green, and back to cyan.

Saturation desaturates when moving to the left and adds saturation when moving to the right.

Lightness works poorly, like the **Legacy** brightness in the **Brightness/Contrast** adjustment. Avoid **Lightness** or use it sparingly. Instead use either **Brightness/Contrast**, or preferably **Levels**, to lighten or darken your overall image.

Colorize

The **Colorize** check box at the bottom-right of the **Hue/Saturation** dialog box, when checked, will limit the colors in an image or selection to black, shades of gray, or shades of whatever **Hue** and **Saturation** you have chosen.

- Click the **Colorize** check box and then use the **Hue** slider to cycle through the color spectrum.

- Control how strong the color appears by adjusting the **Saturation** slider. **Colorize** is typically used to add color to a grayscale image after first converting it from **grayscale** to **RGB**. You will do that later in this course.

Guided Exercise 11.4: Hue/Saturation Experimentation

In this guided exercise you will work with a brightly colored photo to observe the effects of the various **Hue/Saturation** settings

1. Open **11-yarn.jpg**.

2. Click the **Hue/Saturation** button in the **Adjustments** panel to add a **Hue/Saturation** adjustment layer to the document.

3. Adjust the **Hue** master slider to the right or left to change the colors of the yarn. This shows a **Master Hue** of **-59**.

4. Use the drop-down menu to target the colors of just one channel by choosing it from the drop-down menu and then adjusting its **Hue** slider.

5. Try changing some of the other colors with the **Hue** slider. As you do, look out for some strange color shifts. For example, when we upped the **Red Hue**, the bottom right purple skein of yarn became two-tone.

6. Use the **Saturation** slider. Dragging it to the left desaturates the colors; dragging it to the right brightens the colors.

7. Click the **Colorize** box and then drag the **Hue** slider from side to side.

   Colorize makes the entire image the same **Hue**.

8. Drag the **Saturation** slider from side to side.

   Using a very low **Saturation** with **Colorize** checked is a quick, non-destructive way to turn an image into a sepia-tone.

   WARNING: Be very cautions about using the **Lightness** slider. It works like clicking **Legacy** with the **Brightness/Contrast** adjustment and can really diminish the tonal quality of your image.

| Saturation +30 | Saturation -30 | Colorize | Lightness +30 |

Guided Exercise 11.5: Use the Hue/Saturation Adjustment to Change the Color of a Door

This red door is at Elsinore, otherwise known as Hamlet's Castle. In this guided exercise you will paint the door a different color, Photoshop style.

1. Open **11-door.jpg**.

2. Use the **Hue/Saturation Adjustment** to change the color of the door:

   a. Click the **Hue/Saturation** button in the **Adjustments** panel to add a **Hue/Saturation** adjustment layer to the document.

   b. Near the top of the **Properties** panel you will see **Master**, which changes all the colors in the image.

   c. Click on **Master** to display the **Presets** menu and choose **Reds** to target the red colors in the image.

   d. Drag the **Hue** slider to the left **-85** to paint the door purple.

   The bottom of the **Hue/Saturation Properties** panel visually shows the color change. The arrow we added shows the remapping of the colors as we drag left.

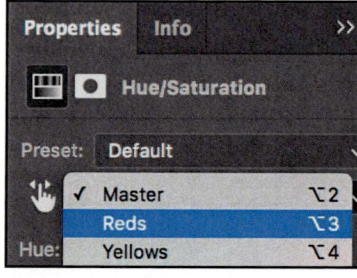

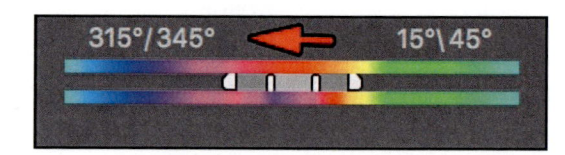

Tutorial 11: Adjusting Image Colors

3. Examine the right corner of the image to observe the color shifts. Apparently there were some yellow pixels that contained some red in them that also changed when you did the adjustment.

4. Change the door color by beginning with a selection to avoid the color shifts:

    a. Hide the **Hue/Saturation 1** adjustment layer and activate the Background layer.

    b. Select the red door. The **Quick Selection Tool** works well. Don't worry about including the metal nails and bolts; since they are not red, their color won't change.

    c. Make another **Hue/Saturation** adjustment layer (**Hue/Saturation 2**).

    Since you began with a selection, only the white portion will be affected — the door itself — and the black areas will not be affected.

    d. Drag the **Hue** slider to the left -85 to paint the door purple without changing the colors of the stone wall.

5. Compare changing the hue with extra saturation:

    a. Choose **Select > Reselect** to reload the door selection.

    b. Hide the **Hue/Saturation 2** adjustment layer.

    c. Make another **Hue/Saturation** adjustment layer (**Hue/Saturation 3**).

    d. Increase the **Saturation** to + 55 to make the color shifts very obvious.

    e. With **Master** chosen, change the **Hue** slider. Notice that the metal latch and the hobnails change color along with the door. You can see it now because the increased saturation makes small hue shifts more visible.

6. Save as **door.psd** and print if desired.

COLOR RANGE

You have already learned to select areas of an image with the **Quick Selection** and **Magic Wand** tools. The **Color Range** command works similarly with more control and finesse. You can work in the **Color Range** dialog box with a number of tools; when you click **OK**, it generates a selection. A selection created with **Color Range** will be more life-like than selections with the **Quick Selection** or **Magic Wand** tools. The **Color Range** command will read colors on all visible layers, but you will be editing only on the active layer.

Guided Exercise 11.6: Color Range + Color Balance

In this guided exercise, you will select portions of an image based on color and use an adjustment to change purple-pink flowers to salmon-orange.

1. Open **11-pinkflowers.jpg**.

2. Choose **Select > Color Range**.

3. Make sure you begin with the default settings:

   - **Select** should say **Sampled Colors**.
   - **Localized Color Clusters** should be unchecked in order to select the flowers throughout the image.
   - Below the image preview, **Selection** not **Image** should be chosen.
   - **Selection Preview** should be **None**.

4. Use the **Eyedroppers** to select the pink flowers:

   a. Click the left **Eyedropper** for the first click. This eyedropper begins a new selection

   b. In the document window, click anywhere on a pink flower to sample the color. The areas selected will show white in the **Color Range** preview.

   c. Select the **+Eyedropper** (add to selection) and continue to click in the pink areas of the document to add to the area selected.

   d. If a click adds too much to the selection, use the **-Eyedropper** to subtract from the selected area.

5. Experiment with adjusting the **Fuzziness** slider.

   FUZZINESS determines which pixels are included in the selection, and whether those pixels should be partly or fully selected (in contrast with the **Magic Wand Tool** where **Tolerance** is an all or nothing selection at 100% opacity). Increasing **Fuzziness** increases the range of colors to be selected.

   - Use more sample points at lower **Fuzziness** to avoid selecting stray pixels.
   - For fine details, use higher **Fuzziness** as fine areas are more "polluted" with colors from adjacent pixels.

6. When you are happy with the preview, click **OK**.

   You will see a selection in the document that can be modified or saved like any other selection.

7. Add a new **Color Balance** adjustment layer.

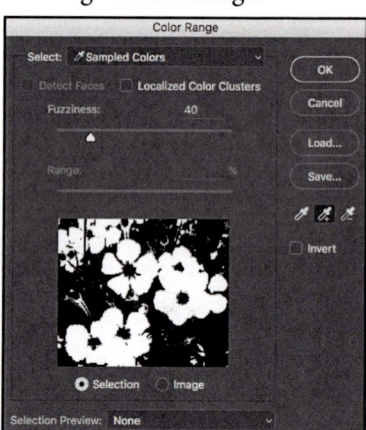

8. Adjust the colors to your liking in the **Color Balance** dialog box, and click **OK**. We used:

   - **Midtones**: **Color Levels** **+86** (red), **+19** (green), **-100** (yellow). You can type these numbers right into the **Color Level**s boxes.

   - **Highlights**: **Color Levels** were **0**, **0**, **-23** to add more yellow to the lighter areas.

   Your selection will only apply the adjustment to the selected area.

Replace Color

The **Replace Color** command combines **Color Range** with the ability to change the hue, saturation, and/or lightness of selected regions.

Replace Color directly changes the pixels of the active layer and cannot be used as an adjustment layer. Because of this, you should duplicate the layer you will be adjusting and activate the duplicate layer before using the **Replace Color** command.

Guided Exercise 11.7: Use Replace Color

In this guided exercise, you will change the colors of a girl's clothing.

1. Open **11-replacecolor.jpg**.

2. Duplicate the **Background** layer by dragging it to the **New Layer** button at the bottom of the **Layers** panel.

   The **Replace Color** command is destructive so you will work on a duplicate layer to preserve the original for safety.

3. Change the color of the girl's shirt:

   a. Choose **Image** > **Adjustments** > **Replace Color.**

   b. Select the **Eyedropper Tool** (for first click) in the **Replace Color** dialog box.

   c. Click to sample a lavender color in the document window. The areas that match that color will appear white in the dialog box preview.

   d. Select the **+ Eyedropper Tool** that appears to the right of the **Eyedropper Tool** and continue to click in the document to add to the area selected. Try dragging across a region for faster sampling. In case you select too much, the **– Eyedropper Tool** will subtract from the selected area.

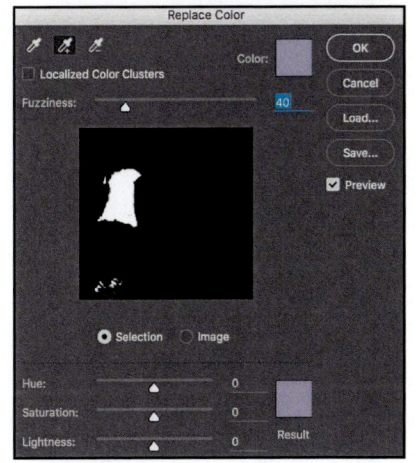

e. Experiment with adjusting the **Fuzziness** slider, dragging it to the right to increase the selection or to the left to decrease the selection.

f. Once you are satisfied with the preview, adjust the **Hue** all the way to the right (**+180**).

   There is a **Color swatch** to show the color selected in the upper part of the dialog box. In the bottom area, there is a **Result swatch** to represent the color you will be changing the selected area to. If you click on the **Result swatch**, you can change the color in the **Color Picker**.

   Pay careful attention to the color replacement edges. If you see shirt areas that are still lavender, use the **+ Eyedropper** to include them in the selection. If you zoom in on the actual document (the **Zoom** keyboard shortcuts work even though there is a dialog box open), it may be easier to see small areas that are still lavender. Click them in the document window to replace their color.

g. Click **OK**.

Compare the original, on the left, and the colorized on the right. Notice that the lavender areas in her shoes also changed color, as did the top of the cut log in the lower right corner.

4. Use one of these strategies to eliminate the color "leak:"

   - **Replace Color** only changes the pixels on the active layer. Because you worked on a duplicate layer, you can now erase areas that you want to restore.

     On the **Background copy** layer, use the **Eraser Tool** to erase the areas that have the unwanted color, and let the original show through from the **Background** layer underneath.

   - Start over. This time, after you duplicate the **Background** layer, make a rough selection around the shirt before choosing the **Replace Color** command. Now only the shirt will be affected.

5. Change the color of other parts of the photo and save as **replacecolor.psd**. Print if desired.

   Here is our version:

ON YOUR OWN

Use the adjustment, selection, and color-changing techniques you learned in this tutorial to improve the tonality of **11-howard.jpg**.

Here are our adjustments:

- **Levels Auto Color** adjustment
- **Color Balance** adjustment to slightly increase the red and yellow in the highlights to give Howard's skin a more healthy color.
- Made a composite or "stamped" layer and used **Replace Color** to change the color of some of the flowers. Here is how to make a **STAMPED** layer:
    a. Activate the top layer in the document.
    b. Press **Command + Option + Shift + E** (Mac) or **Ctrl + Alt + Shift + E** (Win).
    c. Rename the composite layer, **Replace Color Flowers** here.
- Selected Howard's sweatshirt and used **Hue/Saturation** with **Colorize** checked to change the color of his sweatshirt. After that, we did a rough selection with the **Lasso Tool** and then used **Color Balance** to warm up the color of the building in the background.

RESOURCES AND VIDEOS

http://www.practical-photoshop.com/pages/CC2015-pp1-resources.html#11

Practical Photoshop CC 2015, Level 1
Tutorial 12: Painting with Special Tools

This tutorial explores more of Photoshop's painting tools. You will work with three tools that are especially helpful for editing images: the **Clone Stamp Tool,** the **Spot Healing Brush Tool**, and the **Content-Aware Move Tool**. These tools help rid photographs of unwanted spots and elements and allow you to reposition elements. You will also compare their use with the **Fill > Content-Aware Fill** command. Finally, you will see how the **History Brush Tool** can be used to restore image portions to earlier states, and how the **Art History Brush Tool** can turn photographs into paintings.

Objectives

- Use the **Clone Stamp Tool** to remove unwanted artifacts in an image.
- Compare the **Clone Stamp Tool** with the **Spot Healing Brush Tool**.
- Improve some **Spot Healing Brush Tool** corrections by using the **Edit > Fill** command with the **Content-Aware** option.
- Reposition and fill "missing" image elements with the **Content-Aware Move Tool**.
- Use the **Red Eye Tool** to fix photographs with subjects with inappropriately red eyes.
- Paint with **History** states using the **History Brush Tool**.
- Compare the **History Brush Tool** with the **Art History Brush Tool**.

The Clone Stamp Tool

Think of the **Clone Stamp Tool** as a way to paint with photographic pixels. The **Clone Stamp Tool** is used to sample an area of an image and then paint the sampled area into another area on the same layer, a different layer, or even into another document. The **Clone Stamp Tool** has been widely used to clean up spots, dust, tears, or unwanted imagery by covering them up with sampled areas. The challenge for effective cloning is to make the sampled areas blend into the target areas seamlessly.

Cloning is a two step process:

1. Set your **SOURCE POINT**, the spot you wish to clone from:
    a. Press the **option** (Mac) or **alt** (Win) key.
    b. Click the spot you want to sample.
2. Paint with the brush of your choice to replace pixels on the active layer with those from your source.

Tutorial 12: Painting with Special Tools   Page 235

If you try to use the **Clone Stamp Tool** without first choosing a source point, you will be warned.

Cloning is **destructive** so it is best to either duplicate the layer you want to repair, or to create a new blank layer to paint on and use the **Sample All Layers** option.

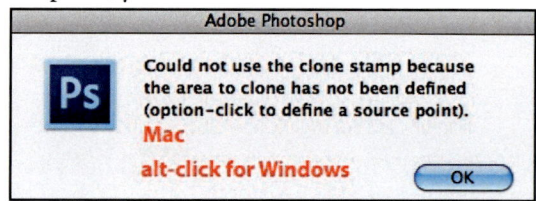

Guided Exercise 12.1: Use the Clone Stamp Tool

In this guided exercise, you will remove unsightly wires from a photo of grapevines. You will use the **Clone Stamp Tool** to sample pieces of the sky, and then paint to replace the wires with sky-colored pixels. This image works well because the sky is a fairly flat blue without much variation, so matching up the edited areas with the existing sky is fairly easy.

1. Reset all tools, and the default **Foreground** and **Background** colors.

2. Choose the **Painting** workspace from **Window > Workspace**.

   The **Painting** workspace displays the **Brush Preset Panel** on the right side of the workspace to more rapidly change your brush settings as you paint.

3. Open **12-leaves_wires.jpg** and save it as **leaves_wires.psd** in the location of your choice.

4. Zoom in to the wire on the left side of the image and choose the **Clone Stamp Tool**.

   Note two important default settings: **Aligned** checked and **Opacity 100%**.

5. In the **Brush Preset Picker**, choose a brush size that is quite a bit wider than the wire, about **45** pixels in diameter.

6. Set the **Hardness** to **50%**. The medium **Hardness** setting will soften the brush edge somewhat so that the **Clone Stamp Tool** replacement will blend better into the source image.

7. **Option + click** (Mac) or **alt + click** (Win) on the area you wish to sample.

   - Choose an area close by the area to repair, but far enough away so that the soft edge of the brush does not sample the wire.

   - Note that the brush tip cursor does not show the anti-aliasing brush edge so give the cursor a little more room when sampling.

8. Drag the cursor over the wire.

   - Make sure to paint thoroughly over the edge of the wire.

   - If you sampled too close to the wire, you will see the wire edge in your paint stroke. **Undo** and resample again, farther away from the wire.

9. You can paint with one stroke or many strokes.

    - Watch as the **CROSSHAIR CURSOR** follows the round brush tip cursor. The crosshair represents the area being sampled.

    - As you paint, the sampled area moves with the cursor.

    - Once you get close to the leaf on the right, you will need to resample again so that the wisp of the stem does not get painted in.

10. Use these same steps to remove the stretch of wire in the center of the photo, the metal post on the bottom right, and the curved metal at bottom-center. Sample each time from areas close to the target pixels. Although the blue sky looks like a single color, it contains slight variations of color.

Guided Exercise 12.2: Refine Clone Stamp Tool Usage

Here you will remove wires from an image with a lot of detail, not just a solid blue sky. Images like this one can also be repaired without too much difficulty using the **Clone Stamp Tool**.

1. Open **12-hairy_beast.jpg** and save it as **hairy_beast.psd** in the location of your choice.

2. Zoom in to the lower right corner.

3. Use the **Clone Stamp Tool**:

    a. In the **Options** bar, make sure **Align** is checked (the default setting) and **Opacity** is set to **100%**.

    b. Click the **Brush Preset Picker** and choose a brush size just wider than the wire, about **30 pixels** in diameter with **Hardness** of **30%**.

    TIP: To make your edits blend into the surrounding pixels invisibly, you may need to experiment with the **Hardness** setting of your brush in the **Brush Preset Panel**. Blending into textured pixels with a very soft brush (**0% Hardness**) can leave noticeable blurring at the edge of your edits. Try setting the **Hardness** between **30 - 60%**. For editing soft imagery such as clouds, a softer brush is called for (**0 - 30% Hardness**).

    c. Press the **option** (Mac) or **alt** (Win) key and click on the area you want to sample.

    d. Drag the cursor over the wire.

    Note that with detailed areas like dried grass, painting in small spurts and setting new samples very often will help keep the edits looking realistic. You may also find that using a non-round brush helps.

    If you find that a repeated pattern forms, sample more often and paint in smaller strokes. As you work across the bottom of the image, you will see the grass areas change tones due to shadows and light-filled areas. Be mindful that your samples match in tonal range to the areas that you are editing.

4. Next, remove the middle wire by sampling and editing from the hair of the beast.

   Editing the animal is like painting with tufts of hair.

   This requires a little more skill and patience. Pay close attention to the color, tone, and texture of your sampled areas, and paint your strokes in the direction of the animal's hair.

5. Removing the wire from the beast's eye is the biggest challenge:

   a. First, clone the surrounding pixels.

   b. Zoom in to **300%** and reduce the brush size small enough to just sample black pixels at the bottom of the eye.

   c. Paint in black pixels to form the top of the eye.

6. For the top wire, try a technique for editing pixels in a straight line to edit out the wire from the left side of the beast:

   a. Zoom into the top-left side of the wire.

   b. Set your brush size to a little larger than the wire.

      Remember the keyboard shortcuts of [to decrease brush size and] to increase brush size.

   c. Sample just above the wire at the far left of the image.

   d. Move the cursor so that it is centered over the wire at the far left and click with the mouse.

   e. Move the cursor to the right, centered over the wire, just to the left of where the beast starts. Hold down the **Shift** key and click. The **Shift** key constrains the edit to a straight line. The length of wire should now disappear, replaced by pixels of stone.

7. If you see obvious repeated markings, clean them up by sampling different areas without identifiable markings and by painting over them with the **Clone Stamp Tool**.

8. Try the same straight line method for removing the rest of the wire in two pieces—at the top of the animal and in the area to the right of the animal. Clean up as needed.

9. Save **hairy_beast.psd** to compare your first try with the repairs you will make in a later guided exercise.

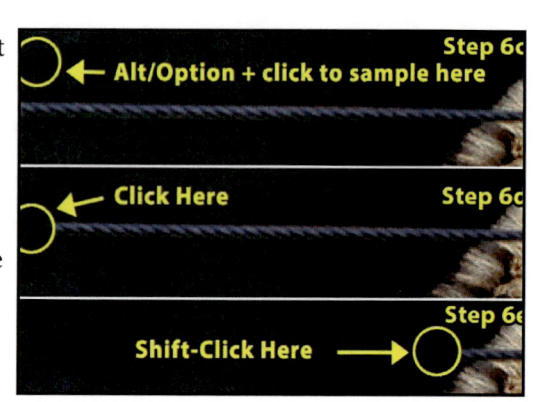

Content-Aware Technology

Content-Aware intelligently adds, removes, and changes image pixels based on what surrounds them. In turn, you will use the **Edit > Fill** with **Content-Aware** command, the **Content-Aware Move Tool**, and **Type: Content-Aware** for the **Spot Healing Brush Tool**. As a time-saver and sometimes magical image fixer, **Content-Aware** technology is very exciting. But, since **Content-Aware Fill** doesn't always work as planned, we taught you the "old" ways first because sometimes you need to use them. Now lets explore this relatively new approach.

The Edit > Fill Command

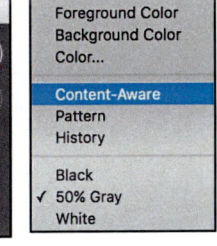

When a document has only a **Background** layer, and you erase pixels from that layer, those pixels are replaced by the **Background** color. If you erase pixels on a standard layer, those pixels erase to transparency. The **Edit > Fill** command allows you to replace selected regions of standard layers, or even entire layers, with **Contents** of your choice under the **Use** drop-down menu. The lower part of the dialog box lets you specify how the **Contents** will be blended with what it is filling (replacing).

Guided Exercise 12.3: Use Edit > Fill with Content-Aware

There can often be a frustrating discrepancy between the size of a photo captured with your digital camera and standard sizes for photographic printing. In this guided exercise you will use **Edit > Fill with Content-Aware** to extend out the edges of a photo to give it a standard print size.

1. Reset all tools, and the default **Foreground** and **Background** colors.

2. Open **12-cacti.jpg** and save as **cacti1.psd** in the location of your choice.

3. With **Doc** showing, press the **Status** bar to quickly see the **Width**, **Height**, and **Resolution** of this image.

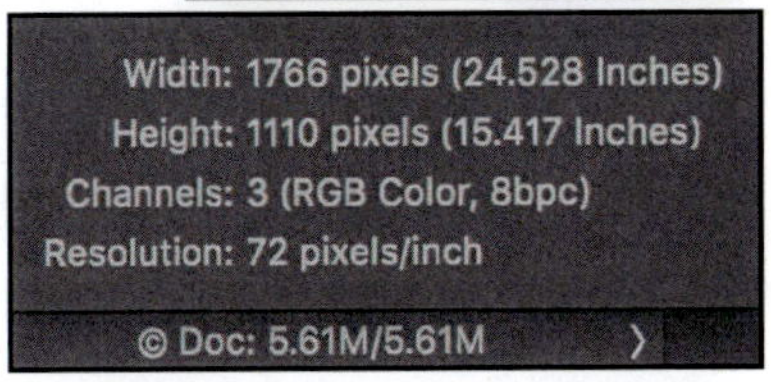

4. Use the **Image Size** command to change the print resolution to **300 pixels/inch**:

   a. Choose **Image > Image Size**.

   b. With **Resample** unchecked (to avoid resampling the image and diminishing its quality), change the **Resolution** to **300**, press the tab key to recalculate the image size, and click **OK**.

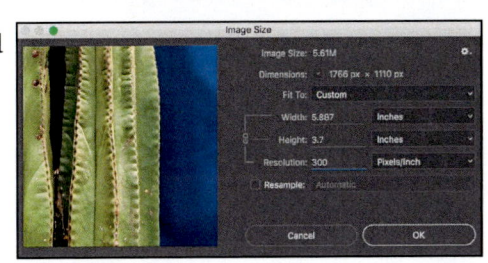

   The document is now **5.887 inches** in **Width** and **3.7 inches** in **Height**. It is *almost* 6 x 4 inches.

Tutorial 12: Painting with Special Tools   Page 239

5. Use the **Canvas Size** dialog box to place extra pixels around the edge of the current image:

   a. Choose **Image > Canvas Size**.

   b. Type in a **Width** of **6 inches**, a **Height** of **4 inches**. Be sure **Relative** is unchecked.

   c. Set the **Canvas extension color** to **White** to place a white edge around the photo, and click **OK**.

   For this image *do not* change the **Anchor**; it needs to stay in the center to extend the canvas all the way around the image. However, if you had an image that you didn't want to extend evenly, you could change the **Anchor** arrows to control where to add the pixels.

6. Fill in the edge pixels:

   a. Use the **Magic Wand Tool** with its default settings to click inside the white border to select just the white pixels.

   b. Choose **Edit > Fill**, choose the **Content-Aware** for **Use**, and click **OK**.

   c. Wait while **Content-Aware** generates new edges for the image from the current image pixels.

   It's better, but not perfect. There are some problems on the bottom right.

7. Save **cacti1.psd** and leave it open for the next guided exercise.

The Content-Aware Move Tool

The **Content-Aware Move Tool,** hiding under the **Spot Healing Brush Tool,** provides more control than **Edit > Fill** because you can drag the selected area to precisely where you want it, and the fill does not take place until you release the mouse button. In theory, you can you use **Content-Aware Move Tool** both to **extend** missing edges, and also to move **image** elements.

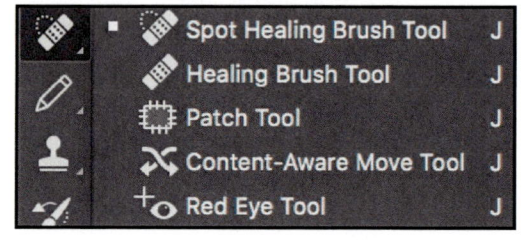

The **Content Aware Move Tool** works in two steps:

1. Select the area you want to move. You can use any selection tool to make the selection. If you use the **Content Aware Move Tool**, it behaves exactly like the regular **Lasso Tool**. Like other cursors in Photoshop CC 2015, the hot spot is the tip of the arrow.

2. Using the **Content Aware Move Tool**, click inside the selected area and drag to its new position. When you release the mouse, Photoshop will use **Content-Aware Fill** to fill the original selection.

∙∙

Guided Exercise 12.4: Use the Content-Aware Move Tool

In our experience, the **Content Aware Move Tool** is most effective on relatively simple images. Try it on the cacti in this short guided exercise:

1. Begin with **cacti1.psd** open.

2. Choose the **Content-Aware Move Tool**. By default it hides under the **Spot Healing Brush Tool**.

3. Examine the **Content-Aware Move Tool's Options** bar settings:

	Selection buttons like those found in many selection tools: **New selection**, **Add to selection**, **Subtract from selection**, and **Intersect with selection**
	Mode: Move repositions the selection and fills in the missing pixels. **Mode: Extend** fills out "blank" edges.
	Structure and **Color** controls the way in which the moved and filled pixels are generated.

We wasted a bunch of time trying to fill in the edges one at a time with **Mode: Extend** and did not get good results. There was lots of sloppiness and strange undesired fills.

4. Use **Mode: Move** to fix the bad spots. Here is what we did for one:

    a. Roughly selected a good area above the cactus blemish in the lower right corner of the image.

    b. Dragged down to the edge of the document and released to repair that strange leaf edge.

    c. Deselected (**Command/Ctrl +D**) to be ready to make the next repair.

5. Use **Mode: Move** to move the right cactus a bit closer to the others:

    a. Select the rightmost cactus. We used the **Quick Selection Tool**.

    b. Choose the **Content Aware Move Tool** set to **Mode: Move** and drag left to move the cactus near the others and fill in the old spot with the blue background.

6. Save **cacti1.psd** and close it for now.

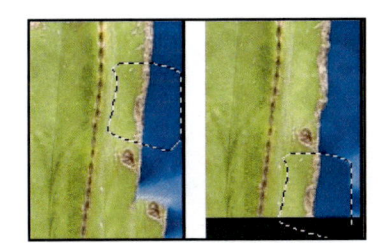

Don't worry if there are some rough areas; you can fix them on your own after you do the **Spot Healing Brush Tool** exercises.

- - -

The Spot Healing Brush Tool

As you work with the **Clone Stamp Tool**, you will find imagery that is difficult to edit because of gradual variations in tones. The flat sky in **12-leaves_wires.jpg** was easy to edit. If the photograph had been taken on a hazy day, with the sky gradually changing from blue to white, the wire removal would have been more difficult.

Skin tones are also a challenge because the gentle curves of a face capture light with varying highlights and shadows. The variation of skin texture adds to the complexity.

The **Spot Healing Brush Tool** works much better than the **Clone Stamp Tool** in these situations. With the **Spot Healing Brush Tool**, sampled pixels are first applied and then blended into the surrounding area with **Content-Aware** magic. When you use the **Clone Stamp Tool**, the sampled area needs to be close in color, texture, and tone to the target area. With the **Spot Healing Brush Tool**, texture is sampled as well as color, and **Content-Aware** matches the sampled area's texture to the target's surrounding color and brightness.

The **Spot Healing Brush Tool** is a simplified version of another tool that hides under it called **Healing Brush Tool.** *Be careful not to confuse them.*

The **Healing Brush Tool** offers more control in some ways, but the **Spot Healing Brush Tool** is easier to master and so we will use it here, leaving the **Healing Brush Tool** for more advanced students.

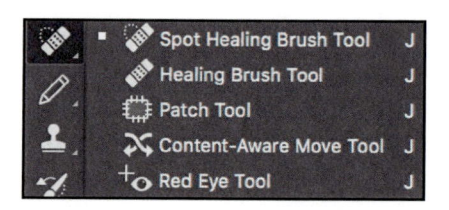

As its name implies, the **Spot Healing Brush Tool** works best on spots such as blemishes, dust specks, etc. This tool is designed to be a one-click spot remover. It will also work on large areas, but it requires more finesse to be successful. Instead of choosing a sample point as you do with the **Clone Stamp Tool**, the **Spot Healing Brush Tool** does the sampling automatically by analyzing surrounding pixels from the spot where you click with the tool.

An important limitation to the **Spot Healing Brush Tool** is that it is very sensitive to sudden changes of tones or areas of sharp contrast such as the edge of an object. The pixels of nearby contrasting areas easily bleed into the edits. If that is not successful, you should avoid healing areas close to contrasting tones and then refine your work with the **Clone Stamp Tool** in high-contrast areas. Changing the **Type** option as you work often lets you heal high contrast areas successfully.

Like the **Clone Stamp Tool**, the **Spot Healing Brush Tool** directly changes image pixels. For this reason, it is best to duplicate the layer you wish to repair, and spot heal the duplicate layer, preserving the original underneath in case you are unhappy with your repair.

Guided Exercise 12.5: Use the Spot Healing Brush Tool

In this guided exercise, you will correct spots on an image of a leaf, and experience the power of the **Spot Healing Brush** to heal with color, tone and texture.

1. Open **12-spot_leaf.jpg** and save it as **spot_leaf.psd** in the location of your choice.

2. Spot-heal the first leaf blemish:

   a. Choose the **Spot Healing Brush Tool**.

   b. In the **Brush Preset Panel**, choose a brush size slightly larger than the first spot you want to repair.

   c. Keep **Hardness** at the default setting of **100%**. Since the **Spot Healing Brush Tool** blends the edges of the edited area, you typically will not need a soft brush. As you work on this image, experiment with changing the **Hardness** percentage.

   d. **Type** sets a source sampling type. Begin with **Proximity Match**.

   Proximity Match samples the area surrounding the edited area.

   Create Texture analyzes all the pixels in the selection and creates a texture from it. This setting is sometimes used if there is not a clear enough area from which to sample, such as a face with many blemishes.

   Content-Aware matches the sampled area's texture to the target's surrounding color and brightness. Blemish removal is its forté.

   e. Position the cursor over a spot and click.

   The spot where you click initially turns dark gray. Upon release of the mouse, the area heals, sampling the texture and color.

3. Spot heal a second spot:

   a. Reposition the cursor over another spot, adjust the size of the brush as needed (use the bracket keys [and]) and click to edit.

   b. If the color change is great (such as the dark brown spots being replaced by yellow pixels), you may need to click again to remove the remnants of the original color. Touching up your edits with a smaller brush can help create the right texture lines.

4. Try painting a stroke instead of clicking. This will sometimes give you a better effect, especially if the color of pixels you want to sample are in proximity to one side but not all around the area to edit. In that case, paint with a stroke from the direction of the desired color.

5. Heal the big spot on the right side of the leaf:

    a. A third of the way up from the bottom is a dark area on the very edge of the leaf. The **Spot Healing Brush Tool** set to **Proximity Match** does not work here because the white background bleeds in.

    b. Undo, switch the **Type** to **Content-Aware** and try again. It works much better.

    c. Use the **Clone Stamp Tool** to touch up any problem spots where you still have a dark area or white bleed.

6. Use **Content-Aware Fill** with a selection instead of a brush:

    Beginning with a **Polygonal Marquee Tool** selection, notice what a good job it does to quickly clean up the spot on the edge of the leaf that was such a challenge without this new option. Great color and texture map, and a flawless leaf edge. Just select and fill and it will do the rest.

Select	Content-Aware Fill	Deselect

Guided Exercise 12.6: Use Content-Aware Heal and Fill to Remove Unwanted Image Elements

Content-Aware Fill intelligently adds, removes, and changes image selections based on what surrounds them. Let's try it on the hairy beast.

1. Open **12-hairy_beast.jpg** and save as **hairy_beast2.psd** in the location of your choice.

2. Use the **Spot Healing Brush Tool** to remove those distracting wires:

    a. Choose the **Spot Healing Brush Tool**, with a round brush somewhat bigger than the wire, like **70 pixels**, and set **Type** to **Content-Aware**.

    b. Paint a very straight stroke across the part of the upper wire that covers the beast, without touching its edges.

    c. Release the mouse and wait while Photoshop paints. Depending on the size and resolution of the image, it can sometimes take a while to make all its complex calculations to get the best match.

    While results differ, when the painted line was very straight, Photoshop tried to preserve the wire pattern, but used colors similar to the beast's fur. Interesting, but not quite right.

d. Undo and try again. This time, paint an uneven line. Much better!!

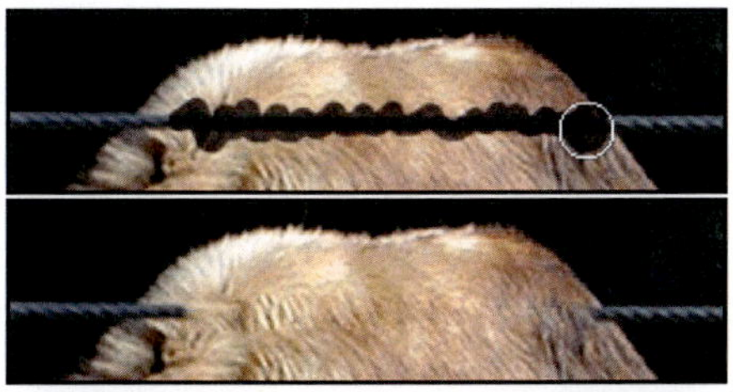

Remember how hard it was to use the **Spot Healing Brush Tool** when you got to sharp transitions?
The **Content-Aware** option does a much better job of recognizing and restoring edges.

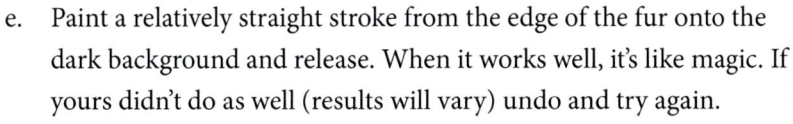

e. Paint a relatively straight stroke from the edge of the fur onto the dark background and release. When it works well, it's like magic. If yours didn't do as well (results will vary) undo and try again.

f. If desired, remove the remaining wires with the **Spot Healing Brush Tool**. Pay attention to which techniques work better than others.

3. Combine selections with the **Edit > Fill** command to remove those distracting wires. This technique works better on some images than others. It is really great on this one.

   a. Go back in history to the opening state of the hairy beast image.

   b. With the **Rectangular Marquee Tool**, quickly select the top wire and a bit above and below it.

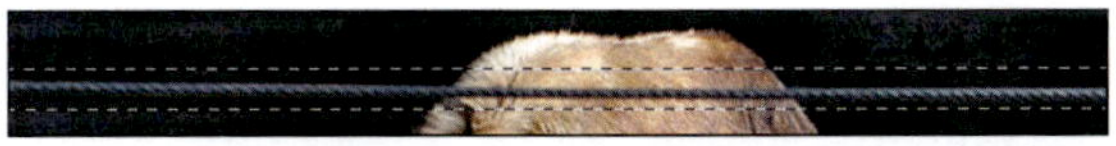

   c. Choose **Edit > Fill** — or to get there faster, press the **delete** key. Either way, you will open the **Fill** dialog box.

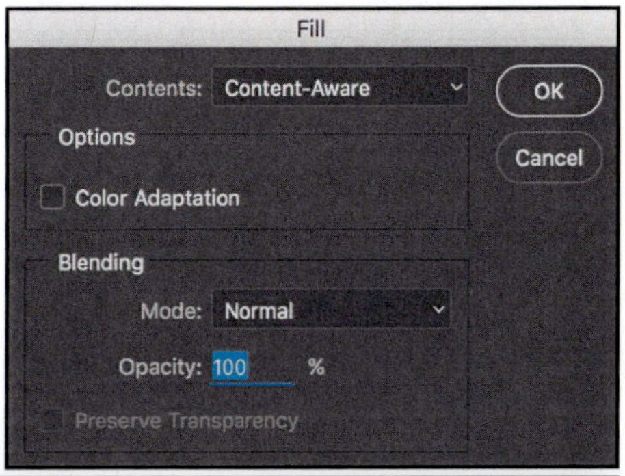

   d. By default, **Contents Use** should be set to **Content-Aware**. If you see a different choice, choose **Content-Aware** from the **Use** drop down menu.

   e. Make sure that the **Blending Mode** is **Normal** and the **Opacity** setting is **100%** and click **OK**.

   f. Wait while Photoshop magically removes the wire.

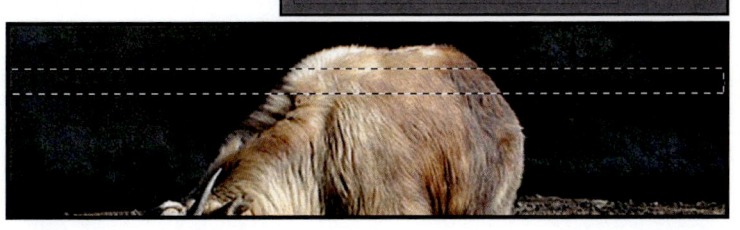

   g. Deselect and use the **Spot Healing Brush Tool** with small strokes to remove any wire residue. It seems to work best if you stroke as if you were painting hairs on the beast.

   h. Use the same technique to remove the other two wires. These are a bit trickier because there is more image detail, especially around the beast's eye and foot. Remember that beginning

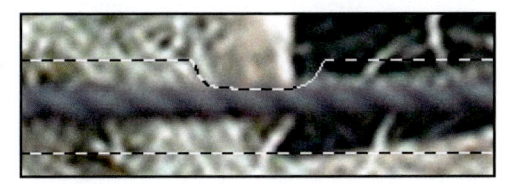

Tutorial 12: Painting with Special Tools

with the **Rectangular Marquee Tool** selection, you can modify that selection using your other selection tools for better precision.

4. Save **hairy_beast2.psd.**

The Red Eye Tool

RED EYES are caused by cameras with their flash too near to the lens of the camera, a common problem for many consumer-level cameras. There are many methods of removing red eyes in Photoshop, but the **Red Eye Tool** is quick and easy to use. When you click with the **Red Eye Tool**, it looks for red pixels that are inside an ellipse in close proximity to where you click. Because the tool is programmed to look for red, it does not work on animal photos, which typically show green or white eyes.

Guided Exercise 12.7: Use the Red Eye Tool

In this guided exercise, you will use the **Red Eye Tool** to remove the red from the pupils of a young woman. Then you will smooth out the dark lines under her right eye.

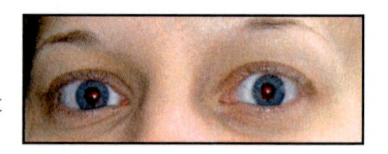

1. Open **12-redeyes.jpg** and save it as **redeyes.psd** in the location of your choice.

2. **Right-click** or **Ctrl + click** the **Background** layer just to the right of its name, and choose **Duplicate Layer** from the content menu that appears, and name the layer **Red Eye Repair**.

   Although we did not do so in the first few repairs to simplify the instructions, pixel editing restorations are typically done on duplicate layers, keeping the original underneath in case part of a repair does not work well.

3. Repair the red eyes:

   a. With the **Red Eye Repair** layer active, choose the **Red Eye Tool**, located under the **Spot Healing Brush Tool**.

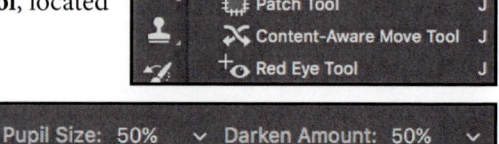

   b. Use the default settings in the **Options** bar of **50%** for **Pupil Size** and **50%** for **Darken Amount**.

   c. Drag diagonally from the top left to the bottom right of pupil of the eye, release the pointer, and wait a moment as Photoshop analyzes the surrounding pixels and removes the red color.

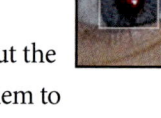

   The **Red Eye Tool** removes the red by removing color. The pupil should now turn black, but the eye color remains blue. If there are still small reddish areas at the edges of the pupils, click them to remove the red edge.

   In some photos, the pupils will turn gray.

   - If the pupils look too light, **Undo**, change the **Darken Amount** to a higher percentage, and try again.
   - If there is still red around the edges, **Undo**, increase the percentage for **Pupil Size**, and try again.

d. Repair the right pupil like you did the left one.

4. Gently soften the wrinkles under the right eye:

   a. Duplicate the **Red Eye Repair** layer, and name the new layer **Fewer Wrinkles**.

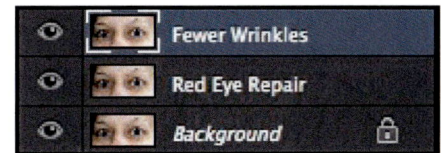

   b. Use the **Spot Healing Brush Tool** with **Content-Aware** to remove the wrinkles and bags under the left eye. The **Spot Healing Brush Tool** works best if you use short strokes in different directions to gradually smooth out the skin tones under her eye.

   c. Lower the opacity of the **Fewer Wrinkles** layer so that some of the definition of the eye remains, and her eye does not look totally airbrushed. Here we lowered the opacity to **50%**.

The History Brush Tool

As you learned in Tutorial 1, each time you use a tool or command to edit your image, the **History** panel automatically adds that particular version of the image to the bottom of the panel as a **HISTORY STATE**. The powerful **History Brush Tool** uses the **History** panel to paint backward and forward to different history states. With the **History Brush Tool**, you can make a change to an image, and then selectively paint it back to the way it was before the change was made. You can use either saved snapshots or automatically generated history states as the source for the **History Brush Tool**. Let's look at a few examples of how to make the **History Brush Tool** work for you.

Guided Exercise 12.8: Use the History Brush Tool

In this exercise, you will remove all the color from an image using the **Desaturate** command, and then use the **History Brush Tool** to selectively paint back color into the image.

By default the **History** panel saves only **50** automatic **History** states. Here you will make a **SNAPSHOT**, a named **History** state that will be preserved as long as the document is open. Remember, both automatic and named **History** states vanish when a document is closed, so this technique works only for a single Photoshop session.

1. Open **12-lilypads.jpg** and save it as **lilypads.jpg** in the location of your choice.

2. Open the **History** panel from the **Window** menu, if the **History** panel is not already visible.

   Upon opening the **History** panel, you will find a snapshot representing the beginning state of the image at the top of the panel with the **History Brush** icon next to it.

Tutorial 12: Painting with Special Tools   Page 247

This icon indicates the **SOURCE** that will be used when painting with the **History Brush Tool**.

3. Choose **Image > Adjustments > Desaturate**.

   The image loses all its color information, and now contains only shades of gray. Concurrently, the **History** panel automatically records a new state, called **Desaturate.**

4. Choose **Edit > Fade Desaturate**.

   Immediately after doing something to an image that changes it (not just zooming in or out), Photoshop gives you the opportunity to **FADE** or diminish the strength of that command or edit.

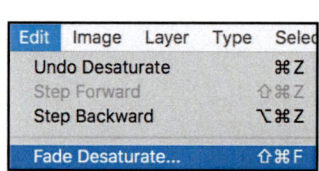

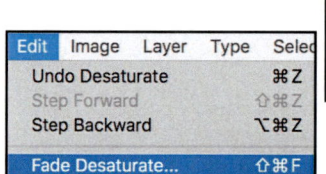

5. Lower the **Opacity** from **100%** to **75%**, so that just a little color returns to the image, and click **OK**.

6. Examine your **History** panel. Assuming that you followed these instructions precisely, you should have three automatically-generated **History** states:

   - **Open** for when you opened the image in Photoshop.
   - **Desaturate** for when you removed all color information from the image.
   - **Fade Desaturate** for when you restored about a quarter of the color information to the image.

7. Make a **Snapshot** — a named **History** state — of the desaturated version of the image:

   a. Click the **Desaturate** state to activate it.

   Notice that the state **Desaturate** is active, the document window displays the fully desaturated version of your image, and the **Fade Desaturate** state is grayed out. If you were to continue working on your image, **Fade Desaturate** would eventually be lost, replaced by whatever you did next to the image.

   b. **Alt + click** (Win) or **option + click** (Mac) the **Create new snapshot** button (**2**) at the bottom of the **History** panel to reveal the **New Snapshot** dialog box.

   c. Name the new snapshot **Desaturated 100%** and click **OK** to make the snapshot.

   The **Desaturated 100%** snapshot appears in the top section of the History panel, just below the automatic snapshot that Photoshop makes each time you open an image. We created this snapshot in order to keep a copy of the desaturated image that will not roll off of the list of history states in the panel.

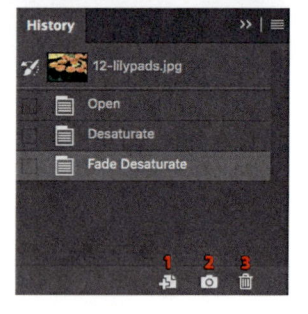

d. Click the **Fade Desaturate** state to restore just a bit of color.

8. Apply the steps used above to make a second user-defined snapshot, named **Fade Desaturate 75%**, and keep this snapshot active.

   You will use the **History Brush Tool** with these three snapshots to selectively paint or remove color on your image.

9. Choose the **History Brush Tool**, located between the **Clone Stamp Tool** and the **Eraser Tool**.

   Be careful not to choose the **Art History Brush Tool** that looks quite similar to the **History Brush Tool**, but paints very differently.

10. Change the **History Brush Tool** options:

    By default, the **History Brush Tool** paints with a small soft brush, only **21 pixels**.

    a. Click the **Brush Preset Picker** in the **Options** bar and change the brush size to **150 pixels**, a better size for painting on this high resolution image.

    b. Click outside the **Brush Preset Picker** to dismiss it.

11. Selectively add and remove color to parts of your image:

    a. With the **12-lilypads.jpg** snapshot chosen as the **History Brush Tool** source and the **Fade Desaturate 75%** History state active, paint on one of the big lily pads to restore its color. Do not worry about coloring outside the lines.

       Each time you release the mouse, Photoshop will record a new automatic **History** state.

    b. Change the **History Brush Tool** source to the **Fade Desaturate 75%** snapshot, and paint beyond the edge of the lily pad to clean up the edge. It may be easier to work with a smaller brush size to fine tune your edges.

       Be careful that you only click in the **History Brush** source and not on the actual **History** state, or you will revert your document to that state. If this happens, click on the very bottom automatic **History** state to restore the image to its most recent state.

    c. Lower the **History Brush Tool** opacity to **25%** in the **Options** bar, and continue painting with the **History Brush Tool**, changing your **History Brush Tool** source as desired to brush color onto or off of other lily pads.

Tutorial 12: Painting with Special Tools

12. Save **lilypads_desat.psd** and close the file.

13. Reopen **lilypads_desat.psd**. Notice that all the snapshots and **History** states are gone except for the default one that Photoshop generates.

History Brush Tool Uses and Limitations

Painting with the **History Brush Tool** permits a variety of ways to selectively change parts of an image that would be more complicated to accomplish using other techniques. Gradients, pattern fills, adjustments (like desaturate here), and filters can all be applied to an image, saved as a snapshot, and then selectively painted onto the original image state, as we did here.

NOTE: The major limitation to painting with the **History Brush Tool** is that all your painting must be done in a single editing session. All history states and snapshots are lost when a document is closed. Here are some other **History Brush Tool** limitations:

- The **History Brush Tool** will only work between image states that are the same size in pixels. If you resize your document by cropping, use the **Image Size** dialog box to change the number of pixels, or use the **Canvas Size** command, the **History Brush Tool** will not work on states before the resize. If you need to resize your image, make a snapshot after the resize, so you can reference it as your new "beginning" state.

- The **History Brush Tool** is limited to painting from and to layers made up of pixels. You cannot, for example, paint parts of a type layer onto another layer, or paint from one version of a type layer to another.

Guided Exercise 12.9: More History Brush Tool Experimentation

Here you will reopen to the original lily pad document, add a gradient to it, and then use the **History Brush Tool** to selectively paint gradient colors onto the lily pads.

1. Open **12-lilypads.jpg** and save it as **lilypads2.psd** in the location of your choice.

2. Choose the **Gradient** tool, and paint a colorful gradient over the **Background** layer. We used a radial rainbow gradient for our painting. This completely covered the image with the gradient.

3. Choose **Edit > Fade Gradient**, change the **Mode** from **Normal** to **Color**, and click **OK**. When **Mode: Color** mode is chosen, the details of the image are visible, but they are colorized by the gradient.

4. Make a snapshot of the image at this point, and name it **Fade Gradient: Color**.

    Notice that even though you saved the image with a different name, the opening **History** state is the original image.

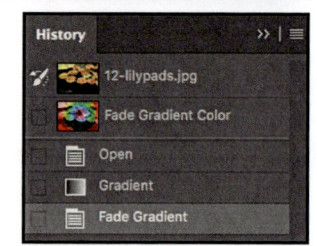

5. Activate the **12-lilypads.jpg** snapshot, set the **History Brush Tool** source to the **Fade Gradient: Color** state and selectively paint the rainbow colors onto your photograph.

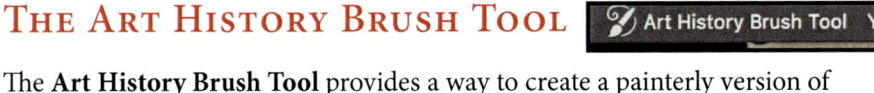

The Art History Brush Tool

The **Art History Brush Tool** provides a way to create a painterly version of a photograph. Using the **Art History Brush Tool** is similar to using the **History Brush Tool** in that you use the **History** panel to set a source for the history state you want to reference. The big difference between the two tools is that the **Art History Brush Tool** can paint in such a stylized way that image detail may not be very recognizable.

Once you choose the **Art History Brush Tool**, its **Options** let you pick from different brush stroke styles. The colors of the active history state are blended in a painterly way and brushed on the image in the shapes of the chosen style of brush stroke. You can simply open an image, choose the **Art History Brush Tool**, and begin painting. That is because by default, every document opened in Photoshop has a snapshot of the document in the **History** panel representing the image in the opening state.

The caution, of course, is that **Art History Brush Tool** replaces image pixels. Here are a few suggestions for effectively using the **Art History Brush Tool**:

1. Make a new blank layer above the **Background** layer and paint on the new layer to preserve the original pixels.

2. When using the **Art History Brush Tool**, choose a neutral color or one sampled from the source image for the blank layer. That way, where the brush strokes do not overlap, there will be a color instead of the underlying image to provide a more painterly effect.

Guided Exercise 12.10: Experiment with the Art History Brush Tool

In this guided exercise you will again work on the lily pads. You will add a new layer, fill with a solid color, and paint on it with the **Art History Brush Tool**.

1. Open **12-lilypads.jpg** and save as **lilypads_art.psd** in the location of your choice.

2. Create a new, blank layer by clicking the **New Layer** button at the bottom of the **Layers** panel and name it **Art History Brush Painting**.

3. Choose **Edit > Fill** and fill with **White** at **100% Opacity**.

4. Choose the **Art History Brush Tool**, located under the **History Brush Tool**. Remember that the **Art History Brush Tool** has that extra flourish to it.

5. In the **Brush Preset Picker**, use the panel menu to view the brushes by **Text** only and then scroll down the list of brush presets and choose the **Chalk 23 pixel** brush.

Tutorial 12: Painting with Special Tools

6. In the **Options** bar, set **Mode** to **Normal**, **Opacity** to **80%**, **Style** to **Dab**, **Area** to **30 px**, and **Tolerance** to **0%**.

7. Paint in the image. Try to get a painterly effect by leaving little spots untouched. Experiment with changing the brush **Size**, **Style**, and **Opacity**.

Take time to play with the different settings:

- Changing the brush preset will give you a wide variety of effects.

    Area changes the size of the area that the strokes can cover so that you can make fewer strokes to cover an area, but it can also increase the time it takes to generate each stroke. **Area** works in conjunction with the brush size. If your brush size is 10 pixels and the area is 50, each click will give you 10-pixel spots over a 50-pixel area. If you change the area to 200, you'll get 10-pixels spots over a 200-pixels area.

    Setting a high **Tolerance** limits the paint strokes to areas that differ from the colors in the snapshot or source state. Depending on the image, you may or may not notice a difference.

You will have more success with the **Art History Brush Tool** if you use an image with large, easily identifiable shapes. Images made up of many small details will not work as well. This example was created with the **Tight Medium** brush style and the brush preset chosen from the default presets in the **Brush Preset Picker** of **Hard Pastel on Canvas**.

The **History Brush Tool** was then used with a lowered opacity to softly paint back in hints of details.

NOTE: The **History Brush** and **Art History Brush Tools** can only paint between **History** states with identical pixel dimensions and image modes.

As you work on your own images, if you change an image's pixel dimensions by cropping or changing the **Image Size** or **Canvas Size**, **History Brush** and **Art History Brush Tools** will not work with the opening snapshot. To bypass this limitation, create a new snapshot just after changing image size or image mode.

ON YOUR OWN

Practice using the **Clone Stamp Tool** on different types of images. Dirt, stones, flat colored skies or other solid colored areas, puffy clouds, bushes, roads, wall textures, and water are some of the imagery that can be effectively edited with the **Clone Stamp Tool**.

Use the various tools and fills introduced in this tutorial to improve images of your own:

- Remove blemishes or wrinkles from someone's face with the **Spot Healing Brush Tool**. Compare the results when using the tool's various **Type** options: **Proximity Match**, **Texture Fill**, and **Content-Aware**. Which works best, and why?

- Remove wires or other distracting elements in an image.

- Remove "red eye" from an image that includes people.

- Practice with the **History Brush Tool** and the **Art History Brush Tool**. Remember to take **Snapshots** as you work for more effective editing.

- Reposition an element in an image using the **Content-Aware Move Tool**. After, use other repair tools to smooth out any residue from the element's original location.

Resources and Videos

http://www.practical-photoshop.com/pages/CC2015-pp1-resources.html#12

Practical Photoshop CC 2015, Level 1
Tutorial 13: Restoration Case Studies

Nearly everyone has old family snapshots that have not been properly cared for. Stuck in a box and placed in an attic or basement, these snapshots change color, fade or darken, and get scratched, torn, moldy, and/or spotted. Two of the photos used in this tutorial were found in just such a box—probably unopened for 20 years—and scanned for future restoration.

Photoshop provides many different ways to restore aged, damaged photographs. In this tutorial you will repair two damaged snapshots using just the skills you have already learned in this course. Then you will repair the old grayscale studio portrait of twins from 1921, and colorize the portrait to make it look hand tinted.

Finally, you will learn to sharpen photographs, a finishing touch for many images. When you complete this tutorial, you should be able to apply these techniques to images of your own.

Objectives

- Understand why it is important to avoid automatic scanning settings when scanning photographs for restoration.
- Repair an aged and damaged color photograph
- Fix an image with "pet eye."
- Restore a grayscale image.
- Colorize a grayscale image with **Hue/Saturation**, and by painting on a layer set to **Color** blend mode.
- Sharpen a photograph using the **High Pass Filter** technique.

Scanning Photographs for Restoration

Most flatbed scanners provide different levels of automation when they scan images. For example, the Epson scanner used to capture these images came from the factory set to scan images in **Fully Automatic Mode**. This setting determines the image resolution, makes color and other corrections as an image is scanned, and sharpens it as well. The problem with such automations is that they sometimes create as many, if not more, problems as they fix.

For this reason, you should disable any automatic corrections your scanner makes. By doing so, you can insure you are scanning at the correct resolution, and have more control to fix image problems in Photoshop. For the images used in this tutorial, we set Epson scanning software to operate in **Professional Mode**, and disabled continuous color correction and sharpening so that we could obtain a raw or unadjusted scan.

The first case study is a very tiny snapshot that was scanned at **300 ppi**. The original has since been lost. If the snapshot had been scanned at **600 ppi**, its document size could have been enlarged in Photoshop with **Resample Image** unchecked, to print twice as large, but still at **300 dpi**. Now, the only way to enlarge the photograph would be in the **Image Size** dialog box with **Resample** checked, which would diminish the image quality.

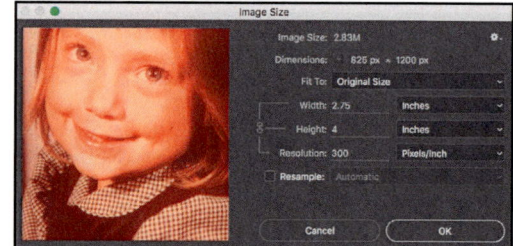

The take-home message: scan small images at a higher resolution if you ever plan to enlarge them.

Case Study 1: Repair an Aged & Damaged Color Photograph

This photo, taken in a studio more than fifty years ago, has muddied with age and acquired some small scratches. You will use **Levels** and **Hue/Saturation** adjustment layers to correct the tonality, and the **Spot Healing Brush Tool** and the **Clone Stamp Tool** to repair the scratches.

1. **Reset All Tools** and open **13-girl.jpg**.

2. Evaluate the image to determine what needs to be fixed:

   a. Visually, the image looks dark. Examine the **Histogram** panel to confirm the missing highlights. This image has darkened with age.

   b. Position the cursor over the dark part of one of the girl's eyes and note the **RGB** values in the **Info** panel.

   The **R** value is much larger than either **G** or **B**, indicating the image has a red cast.

   c. Confirm the cast in other parts of the image that you would not expect to be predominately red, such as the light checks in her blouse, or the whites of her eyes.

   Since the opposite of **Red** is **Cyan**, you will probably need to increase the **Cyan** in the photo to remove the cast and improve the color of the overall image.

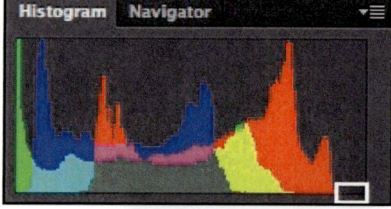

3. Add a **Levels** adjustment:

   a. Click the **Levels** button in the **Adjustments** panel to make a new **Levels** adjustment layer.

   b. **Alt + click** (Win) or **Option + click** (Mac) the **Auto** button in the **Properties** panel to open the **Auto Color Correction Options** dialog box.

c. Try each algorithm to determine which one looks best.

   We preferred **Find Dark & Light Colors** with **Snap Neutral Midtones** checked because these options neutralized much of the red cast without making the background too cyan.

d. Notice that the **Histogram** spreads out all the way across the tonal range and the red cast is gone.

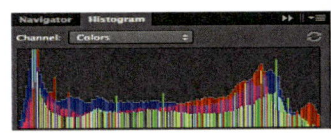

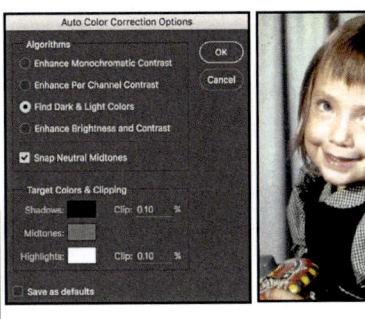

4. Add a **Hue/Saturation** adjustment layer:

   a. Click the **Hue/Saturation** button in the **Adjustments** panel to make a new **Hue/Saturation** adjustment layer.

   b. In the **Properties** panel, drag the **Saturation** slider slightly to the right to brighten up the colors in the child's face and the toy she is holding.

   We used **+12**, but it is a matter of taste. The image looks better, but her hair has some unnaturally red streaks, especially in the shadows near her left eye.

5. Use a **Color Balance** adjustment to fix the red streaks in her hair:

   a. Click the **Color Balance** button in the **Adjustments** panel to make a new **Color Balance** adjustment layer.

   b. In the **Properties** panel, change the **Tone** to **Shadows,** and then move the **Cyan-Red** slider to the left slightly to reduce the red in the girl's hair, and also to make her velvet jumper greener.

6. Restoring the image colors has accentuated image damage. Fix that next:

   a. Make a composite or "stamped" layer of the corrected image.

      1) Activate the top layer in the document.

      2) Press **Command + Option + Shift + E** (Mac) or **Ctrl + Alt + Shift + E** (Win).

      3) Rename the composite layer **repair**.

   b. Zoom in to **200%**, and use the **Spot Healing Brush Tool** and the **Clone Stamp tool** to repair the damage to the image. For best results, set your brush size just a tiny bit larger than the damaged area, and keep your brush strokes short.

   c. Select just the toy top and increase its saturation (**Hue/Saturation** adjustment).

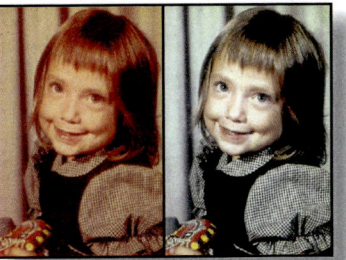

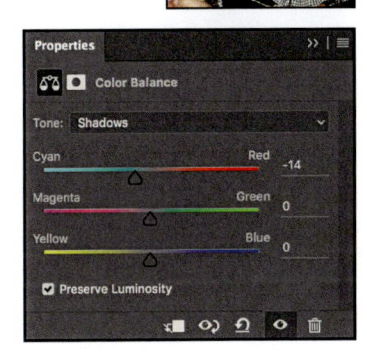

Tutorial 13: Restoration Case Studies

Case Study 2: Repair An Aged Color Snapshot

Here is a snapshot of the same girl with her dog that was taken a few years later. It has a red color cast, is crooked, and has a distracting background. Improve it in this guided exercise:

1. **Reset All Tools,** open **13-girl_dog.jpg** and save as **13-girl_dog.psd** in the location of your choice.

2. Use the **Histogram** and **Info** panels to confirm your visual inspection of the image:

    a. In the **Histogram** panel, use the panel menu in the upper right corner to change the view to **Expanded View**.

    b. Change the **Channel** from **Colors** to **Luminosity** to better assess the image's tonality and notice the lacking **Highlights** and **Shadows**.

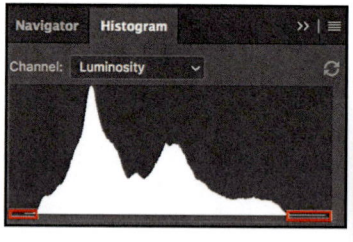

    c. In the **Info** panel, inspect areas that should be neutral like the gray dog to confirm the red cast.

3. Use the **Crop Tool** with the **Straighten** button to minimize the distracting background and focus on the girl and her dog:

    a. With so many angles in this small kitchen, it is hard to know which angle to make vertical. We chose the edge of the dishwasher.

    b. Additionally crop the image as desired. We decided to remove as much of the busy kitchen as possible without overly crowding the subjects.

4. Apply a **Levels** adjustment layer to neutralize the color cast. For this image, we preferred **Find Light and Dark Colors** with **Snap Neutral Midtones** checked.

5. Zoom in to **100%** and notice that the dog's eyes look very strange. This light cyan is the dog (or cat) equivalent of red eye, and sometimes occurs when the flash goes off in an animal's eyes. This problem is sometimes called **PET EYE**.

6. Fix the dog's eyes by making a new layer and carefully painting the cyan areas black. Then lower the opacity of the layer until the eyes look more natural.

    Alternately, try fixing the eyes with the **Spot Healing Brush Tool** and **Content-Aware Fill**. It's not quite as good as above, but very fast for a start (done here on non-adjusted version of the image).

Tutorial 13: Restoration Case Studies

7. At **100%**, you can see that the girl's eyes have a slight red eye. The default settings for the **Red Eye Tool** are too strong, and make the entire eye regions too vividly green. Even using very low tool settings (**Pupil Size 11 %** and **Darken 21%**) the correction was too strong. Careful use of the **History Brush Tool** at low opacity will let you lessen the correction so that her eyes look more natural.

8. Repair any other damage you may find.

9. Save and print, if desired.

Case Study 3: Restore and Colorize An Aged Black and White Photo

You already looked at the **Histogram** of this image in an earlier tutorial. Now that you have more skills, you can restore and colorize the photo.

1. Open **10-twins.jpg** and save it as **twins.psd** in the location of your choice.

2. Get information about the photo to help to restore it:

    a. Examine the image's **Title** bar or **Tab**.

    Gray means it is a **GRAYSCALE** image, containing pixels of only black, white, or shades of gray.

    b. With the **Status** bar menu set to **Document Sizes**, press the menu to quickly view **Document Information**:

    When opened in Photoshop, the image is approximately 1.88 M. (Your size may be slightly different; it's an imprecise measurement.)

    This document will print at *approximately* **4 x 5.6 inches** at **300 ppi**. It has one color channel, **Grayscale**.

3. Choose **Image > Mode > RGB Color** to convert the **Grayscale** into an **RGB Color** image, so that you can add color to it.

4. Again view **Document Information**:

    The document size enlarges to approximately **5.63 M** and it now has three color channels, **R**, **G**, and **B**. Although you have not yet edited the image, it needs to be three times as large as it was in grayscale to accommodate the color information.

5. Add a **Levels** adjustment layer:

    a. Click the **Levels** icon in the **Adjustments** panel to make a new **Levels** adjustment layer.

    b. **Alt/Option + click** the **Auto** button in the **Properties** panel to open the **Auto Color Correction Options** dialog box. The default, **Enhance Brightness and Contrast**, works poorly. Its **Histogram** lacks the brightest **Highlights** and most of the **Shadows**.

6. Since this image started out in **Grayscale** mode, the other three **Auto Color** options will be identical. Choose one of them and click **OK**.

7. Make a composite layer and use it to repair the damage to the image:

    a. With the top layer active, press **Command + Option + Shift + E** (Mac) or **Ctrl + Alt + Shift + E** (Win) to place a composite layer at the top of the **Layers** panel.

    b. Name the composite layer **Repair**; and repair the damage to the image as best you can.
    Here is a quick trick for fixing the faded bottom of the chair:

    1) Select the chair bottom; the **Quick Selection Tool** with **Sample all layers** checked worked well.

    2) Make a new layer named **Chair** bottom above the **Repair** layer.

    3) Sample a gray Foreground color just above the selection and choose **Edit > Fill** to fill the selection with the Foreground color.

    4) Lower the **Opacity** of the **Chair** layer until the colors blend in.
    We liked **35%**, but it will depend on what color you sampled.

    5) Deselect and then use the **Spot Healing Brush Tool** or **Clone Stamp Tool** to blend in the line at the edge of the chair repair. Remember to work with **Sample All Layers** checked to grab the underlying colors as you work.

Original	Levels Adjustment	Repaired

Tutorial 13: Restoration Case Studies

8. Colorize the image. Here is how to do a single region:

    a. Carefully select the region you want to make a single color. We selected the standing boy's romper, his socks, and his eyes.

    b. Make a **Hue/Saturation** adjustment layer, check **Colorize**, and then set the color you want by adjusting the **Hue**, **Saturation**, and maybe the **Brightness** sliders in the **Adjustments** panel. (Remember that **Brightness** can be dangerous.)

    c. The colorized region will look very harsh. In the **Layers** panel, change the blend mode from **Normal** to **Color**, and observe how much more natural the colored regions look.

    d. Adjust the layer opacity until you get a pleasing tint.

9. Repeat step 8 for each distinct region you want to colorize.

10. Tweak any of the colored regions by activating the **Hue/Saturation** adjustment layer in question, and adjusting its **Properties**.

11. Save your completed document, and print if desired.

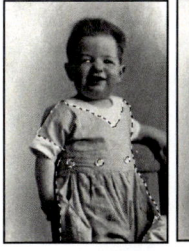

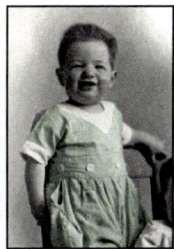

Sharpening Images

Input and output devices tend to reduce sharpness even with the best scanners and digital cameras. Printing also reduces image sharpness, especially half-toned (printing press) and dithered (ink jet) printing. Photoshop tools and filters can often restore the sharpness that is lost when the image is digitized or printed.

Because image editing can slightly soften an image, sharpening is usually done at the end of the image correction work cycle, after virtually all the other changes have been made.

DIGITAL SHARPENING means enhancing edges or transitions between tones or colors. The correct amount of sharpening for each image is highly subjective. The more abrupt or distinct the transition between one region of an image and another, the sharper that image appears.

Proper sharpening enhances the edges in the image. Sharpening is tricky because over-sharpening a photo can make areas that should be smooth, like the petals of a rose, rough or pixilated.

Before Sharpening	Sharpened	Over Sharpened

Tutorial 13: Restoration Case Studies

Photoshop provides so many ways to sharpen images that whole books have been written on the topic. We are only going to use one technique here, using the **High Pass** filter, because we find it is the easiest for beginners to master, and it provides good results in many cases.

One final warning before we get started. Photoshop sharpening works best on images that are in focus, and just need a little help.

Remember, no amount of Photoshop magic can fix a really blurry photograph.

The High Pass Filter

Let's repeat this important concept: **DIGITAL SHARPENING** means enhancing *edges* or *transitions* between tones or colors. The sharpening challenge is to find a way to strengthen the transitions between the meaningful parts of an image, such as between the subject and its background—without harming those parts of the image that should have gradual changes in color and tone.

The **High Pass** filter's job is to look for areas in the image where sharp color transitions occur, and to suppress the rest of the image to neutral gray. It has one slider, **Radius**. The higher the **Radius**, the more color transitions **High Pass** will identify.

To sharpen with the **High Pass** filter, you apply it to a copy of the **Background**, or to a composite layer for a multiple layered document. After you use the **High Pass** filter to identify the transitions, you change the blend mode of the filtered layer to accentuate those edges in the underlying document.

Case Study 4: Sharpen an Image with the High Pass Filter

In this case study you will sharpen an image to improve its focus. As you work, you will explore many strategies to enhance detail where desired, and to avoid introducing unwanted detail or **ARTIFACTS** whenever possible.

1. Begin with **13-rose.jpg** open in Photoshop.

2. Duplicate the **Background** layer and name the new layer **high pass sharpening**.

3. Zoom in to **50%**, and be sure the rose shows in the center of the document window.

    As you sharpen, your zoom should be between **50%** and **100%** to best observe the sharpening effects on the image.

4. Apply the **High Pass** filter to the **high pass sharpening** layer:

    a. Choose **Filter > Other > High Pass** to open the **High Pass** dialog box.

    The **High Pass** filter retains edge details in the specified **Radius** where sharp color transitions occur and suppresses the transition in the rest of the image.

b. Slowly drag the **High Pass** dialog box as far to the right of the document window as you can, previewing the effects within the document as the **Radius** setting increases.

c. Drag the **Radius** all the way to the left, to **0.1 pixels**, and notice that the image is virtually solid gray.

d. Highlight the **Radius** value, and press the up arrow on the keyboard repeatedly. As you do, the outlines of the image start to appear, resembling a line drawing of the image.

e. Stop when you can just see nice edge detail and click **OK**. We used a **Radius** setting of **3 Pixels**.

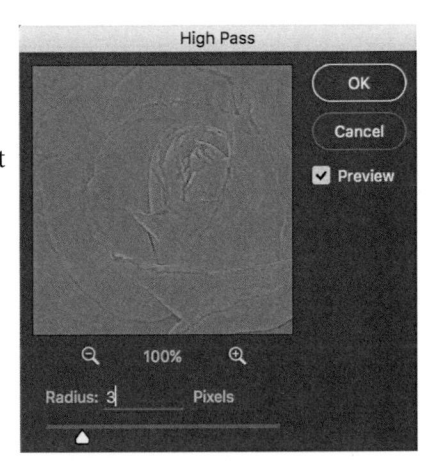

5. Experiment with blending modes other than **Normal** on the **high pass sharpening** layer to enhance detail:

    a. Change the blending mode of the **high pass sharpening** layer from **Normal** to **Overlay**. **Overlay** does not change the color of underlying pixels covered by neutral gray, but it lightens pixels that are lighter on the **high pass sharpening** layer and darkens pixels that are darker.

    b. Change the blend mode from **Overlay** to **Soft Light**. **Soft Light** works like **Overlay**, but more subtly. Try using the **Soft Light** blend mode when **Overlay** seems too extreme.

    c. Change the blend mode from **Soft Light** to **Hard Light**. **Hard Light** gives a sharper edge transition

    d. Finally, you can lower the **Opacity** of the **high pass sharpening** layer to less than **100%** to further diminish the sharpening effects if they still seem too strong.

6. Spot adjust areas where the sharpening generated artifacts:

    A common problem with sharpening damaged photos is that sharpening accentuates debris along with desired detail. When you sharpen portraits, it is easy to accentuate unflattering details such as skin blemishes or wrinkles.

    a. Begin with the blending mode of the **high pass sharpening** layer at **Normal**, **100% Opacity**.

    b. Use the **Eyedropper Tool** to sample a solid gray area.

    c. Return the blending mode back to the sharpening blending mode and opacity you preferred and choose the **Brush Tool**.

    d. Paint on the **high pass sharpening** layer wherever you find unwanted detail to spot-remove the overly sharpened areas.

    e. As you work, switch back to **Normal** to paint out more of the unwanted detail. We painted out all the foliage to accentuate the shallow depth of field. We increased the contrast of our screenshot so it will show up better here. Yours will probably be more subtle.

7. End up with the blending mode of your choice.

Original	Radius 3 pixels, Overlay mode	Cleaned up with gray brush	Finished

8. Save the image, and print it if desired, to compare the sharpened and unsharpened versions.

On Your Own

Sharpen other images using the **High Pass** technique. Here are two you might find challenging:

- **Casa de Estudillo** in Old Town San Diego, **13-casa.jpg**. Your goal is to sharpen the adobe without making the sky grainy. Donald Laird, who took the photo, tells us this is California Landmark #53. You can find out more about California landmarks on his Web site: http://www.calandmarks.com.

- One of the buildings from the ghost town in Garlock, California, **13-garlock.jpg**, California Landmark #671. For this image, you will need to adjust it before you sharpen it. Begin with the **Levels Auto Color Adjustment Options**. Then, figure out how the sharpen the building without over sharpening the hillside.

For a real challenge, try sharpening the twins. Begin with a composite layer at the top of the layers panel. Its very tricky to give more detail to their faces without adding a lot of debris.

Resources and Videos

http://www.practical-photoshop.com/pages/CC2015-pp1-resources.html#13

Practical Photoshop CC 2015, Level 1
Tutorial 14: Fun with Filters

As you already know, **FILTERS** are 'mini programs' that add functionality to Photoshop. Over a hundred filters come pre-installed within Photoshop with thousands more available from commercial and free sources. Each filter can be used to make modifications to your images. Some filters make image improvements and others add special effects. In this tutorial, we will discuss just a handful of filters.

Objectives

- List guidelines for achieving optimal results from Photoshop filters.
- Identify the various sections of the **Filter** menu.
- Apply the **Clouds** and **Difference Clouds** filters.
- Compare the use of the **Motion Blur** filter on an entire layer with its use on selected regions of that layer.
- Use the **Lens Flare** filter.
- Use the **Liquify** filter to stretch, twist, and distort images.

Filter Guidelines

In order to get the best results when working with filters, here are a few things to know and do:

- A filter can only be applied to an active, visible layer that contains pixels, not to a **Type** or **Shape** layer unless you either **RASTERIZE** the layer (turn it into a pixel layer), or convert the layer into a special layer called a **Smart Object** (discussed in Practical Photoshop Level 2).
    - Without a selection, the filter will affect the entire layer.
    - When you start with a selection, only the selected area will be filtered.
    - Linking or grouping layers will not cause the filter to apply to more than the active layer.
    - If the active layer is not visible (its eye clicked off in the **Layers** panel), a filter cannot be applied.
- Filters are destructive. Take precautions before applying them:
    - As you work, take a **History Snapshot** before performing a filter so that you can go back to the snapshot if you don't like the filter results, or you can use the **History Brush Tool** to selectively paint back some of the layer to its pre-filtered state.

- Duplicate the target layer and perform the filter on the duplicate layer. That way you have both the filtered and pre-filtered versions saved with the image for future editing. You can then erase (or mask) on the duplicate layer to selectively let the original show through.
- Save before you apply a filter, especially when using third party filters.
- Filter results are typically resolution-dependent. Applying an effect to a low resolution image can be quite different than applying the identical effect to a higher resolution version of the same image.
- Filters can be memory intensive and take a long time to apply, especially on large images. If you are working on a large image, test out the filter on a small portion of the layer first. You can also test out filters on a lower resolution file, remembering that you may need to change your filter settings to achieve the same results on the high resolution version.
- To undo or cancel a filter:
  - As the filter is being applied, press the **Escape** (**esc**) key to simultaneously cancel a filter and close its dialog box.
  - After applying the filter, *immediately* type **Command + Z** (Mac) or **Ctrl + Z** (Win) to undo the filter.
  - Back up in the **History** panel to reverse the effects of a filter.
- To diminish the effects of a filter or to provide a special effect with a blend mode, choose **Edit > Fade**.

  Immediately after applying a filter, the **Edit** menu will permit you to fade that filter. For example, if you had just applied the **Clouds** filter, you would see **Fade Clouds** listed in the **Edit** menu.

  Command + Shift + F (Mac) or **Ctrl + Shift + F** (Win) is the **Fade** keyboard shortcut. *Make sure to include Shift to avoid reapplying the last filter.*

The Filter Menu

Photoshop's filters are organized in the **Filter** menu.

- The top menu command, **Last Filter**, lets you reapply the last filter used since Photoshop was opened. It is grayed out until you use a filter.

  Choosing **Last Filter** or using the shortcut, **Command / Ctrl + F** applies the last filter used with its last settings.

  To open the filter's dialog box to view or change the settings, use **Command + Option + F** (Mac) or **Ctrl + Alt + F** (Windows).

- The second menu command is **Convert for Smart Filters**. We cover **Smart Objects** and **Smart Filters** in the Practical Photoshop Level 2 book.

- Below **Convert for Smart Filters** is a collection of **Specialty Filters**. You will use the **Liquify** filter shortly.

- Next are eleven **Filter Groupings** beginning with **3D** and ending with **Other**. These groupings hold the majority of Photoshop's filters.

- Near the bottom of the **Filter** menu, you may see one or more **THIRD PARTY FILTERS**, filters produced by software companies other than Adobe. If you installed the **Digimarc** filters when reading Tutorial 7, they will appear here.

- Finally, **Browse Filters Online** at the bottom of the list links to the **Adobe Marketplace**, https://creative.adobe.com/addons?pp=PHSP, where you can purchase additional third party filters and other goodies.

  Before making a filter or other purchase at the marketplace, make sure the item works with Photoshop CC 2015. Sometimes the older items have not been updated.

With so many filters, it is hard to know where to start and what to include in an introductory Photoshop course. Let's begin with the **Clouds** filter because it is so simple to use.

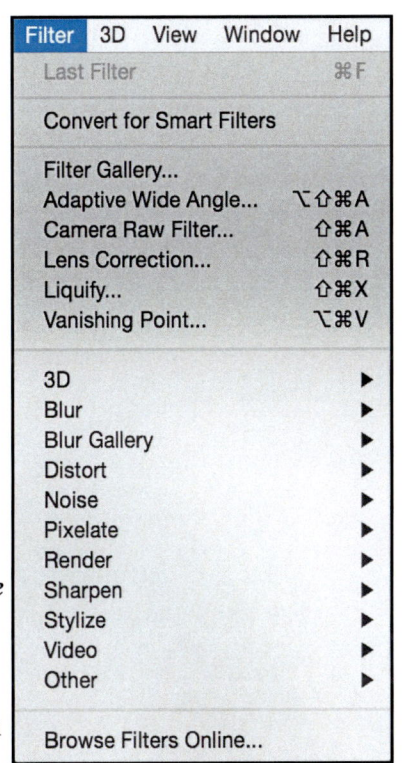

The Clouds Filter

A beautiful blue sky adds a lot to an outdoor photograph. What about pictures taken on gray, overcast days?

Thanks to the **Clouds** filter, you can create a replacement sky with just the right amount of fluffy white clouds. The **Clouds** filter uses the **Foreground** and **Background** colors to make abstract clouds. You can also use the **Clouds** filter to simulate a sky near sunset.

Guided Exercise 14.1: Use the Clouds Filter to Make a Replacement Sky

In this guided exercise you will use the **Clouds** filter to replace the existing sky in an otherwise colorful photo of Sedona, Arizona.

1. Open **14-newsky.jpg** and save it as **newsky.psd** in the location of your choice.

2. Make a new layer above the **Background**, and name the layer **sky**.

3. Choose your sky colors: sample from the **Swatches** panel to set the **Foreground** color to a nice soft blue, and the **Background** color to white.

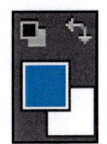

The greater the difference between the **Foreground** (sky) color and the **Background** (cloud) color, the more distinct the clouds will be. Set the **Background** color to white for bright clouds or a color close to your **Foreground** color for barely visible clouds.

4. Use the **Quick Selection Tool** with **Sample All Layers** checked to select the sky; modify your selection in **Refine Edge** or **Select and Mask** with gentle feathering to smooth the transition between the rock formation and the sky.

5. Make four versions of clouds to choose from:

   a. With the sky layer active, choose **Filter > Render > Clouds** to fill the selected region with a randomly-generated cloudy sky.

   b. Choose **Clouds** from the top of the **Filter** menu to generate another random clouds pattern.

   c. Repeat two more times.

      Each time you choose **Filter > Clouds**, a new sky is generated.

   d. Once you have made several skies, you can use the **History** panel to look at each rendering and pick the one you prefer. Display the **History** panel, view each of the cloud patterns in turn, and click the **History** state you like the best.

   e. All the skies are quite bright. Lower the layer **Opacity** to tone down the intensity of the new sky.

      Here we lowered the opacity to **50%**.

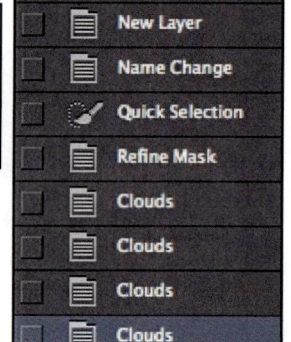

6. Add a touch of sunset colors to your clouds:

   a. Be sure your clouds layer has **100%** opacity.

   b. From the **Swatches** panel, sample a bright red **Foreground** color and a light yellow **Background** color.

   c. Duplicate the **clouds** layer and name the duplicate layer **sunset**.

   d. Activate the **sunset** layer and **Command + click** (Mac) or **Ctrl + click** (Win) its layer thumbnail to reload the sky selection you made earlier.

   e. Choose **Filter > Clouds** to create some reddish clouds.

   f. Change the blend mode of the **sunset** layer to **Soft Light** to tone down these clouds because they are way too bright to be realistic.

   g. If desired, you can duplicate the **sunset** layer, leaving it at **Soft Light** blend mode, to intensify the sunset colors.

Guided Exercise 14.2:
Use the Clouds Filter to Change the Color and Tone of an Image

The problem with using the **Clouds** filter is that while it helps in a pinch, the new sky still looks pretty fake. Used gently, however, the **Clouds** filter can have some pretty impressive results. In this guided exercise, you will apply the **Clouds** filter to another photo of Sedona, taken at noon, and make that image look like it was shot closer to sunset.

1. Open **14-sedona2.jpg** and notice its "real" clouds. Save it as **sedona2.psd** in the location of your choice.

2. Make a new layer above the **Background**, and name the layer **sunset**.

3. Change the **Background** color to a soft orange.

4. Apply the **Clouds** filter to the entire **sunset** layer. All you will see is the clouds pattern.

5. Change the blend mode of the **sunset** layer to **Color** to colorize the entire image with the colors the **Clouds** filter generated.

    The results are quite intense.

6. Reduce the opacity of the **sunset** layer to **30%**.

    The unevenness of the **Clouds** filter works nicely to change the colors of both the sky and the rocks less uniformly, as would be seen in a "real" sunset.

    For comparison, we colorized the second version by placing a solid red **Color Fill** layer above the **Background** layer, set to **Color** blend mode, with the same **30%** opacity. Notice that its colors are much more uniform, and the image looks artificially colored compared to the one to the left of it.

Difference Clouds

The **Difference Clouds filter** resembles the **Clouds** filter, except that:

- The **Clouds** filter uses only the **Foreground** and **Background** colors to create the clouds, completely replacing the pixels on the current layer.
- The **Difference Clouds** filter takes the existing pixels into consideration when creating the clouds.

Guided Exercise 14.3: Use the Difference Clouds Filter

In this guided exercise you will use the **Difference Clouds** filter to modify a photo of fish in an aquarium.

1. Open **14-aquarium.jpg** and save it as **14-aquarium.psd** in the location of your choice.

2. Duplicate the **Background** layer and activate **Background copy**.

3. Reset the **Foreground** and **Background** colors to their default black and white, and choose **Filter > Render > Difference Clouds** to apply the filter.

   The photo now has vivid colors to go along with the clouds running through it.

4. Make the colors even more interesting:

   a. Choose **Edit > Fade Difference Clouds** to display the **Fade** dialog box.

   b. Experiment with the various blending modes to see which one gives you the results you like the best. Here we used **Fade 100%** with the **Pin Light** blending mode.

Motion Blur

The **Motion Blur** filter can be used to blur an image, making it look like the camera or the subject was in motion when the picture was taken. Use it in the next guided exercise:

Guided Exercise 14.4: Use the Motion Blur Filter

Let's start with a nice, sharply-focused image, like this one of a bee on a thistle, and use the **Motion Blur** filter to selectively change its focus. It is a small file, just for on-screen experimentation.

1. Open **14-bee.jpg** and save it as **bee.psd** in the location of your choice.

2. Choose **Filter > Blur > Motion Blur** to bring up the **Motion Blur** dialog box. The **Motion Blur** filter is quite simple with only two controls: **Angle** and **Distance**:

   - **Angle** determines the direction of the blur—the direction the movement takes place.
   - **Distance** determines how strong the blur will be—the speed of the movement.

3. Experiment with different settings to produce different results.
   You can get quite a variety of results from the same filter.

Angle: **0˚**, **Distance**: **10 pixels**.

Angle: **62˚**, **Distance**: **81 pixels**. Makes a diagonal blur

Angle: **0˚**, **Distance**: **999 pixels**. Makes an abstract background using colors from the source image.

Filter a selected area. Here, the bee was selected and then filtered with **Angle: 25˚, Distance: 6 pixels** to add just a little movement to the bee.

Blur everything but the bee to get this image, with **Angle: -39˚, Distance: 13 pixels**.

Tutorial 14: Fun with Filters

Guided Exercise 14.5: Use the Motion Blur Filter to Soften a Distracting Background

In one of the above examples, the **Motion Blur** filter was used to change the image into an abstract version of itself. In this guided exercise you will expand upon that procedure to blur a distracting background to focus on the subject: the proud owner of the shiny new red Corvette.

1. Close any open Photoshop documents, and open **14-new_corvette.jpg**. This is a low-quality image that you will work with on screen, but not print.

2. Duplicate the **Background** layer and name the duplicate layer **blurred**.

3. Use the **Motion Blur** filter on the **blurred** layer, so that the blur works in the direction of the car. We used an **Angle** of **52°** and a **Distance** of **118 pixels**.

4. Choose the **Eraser Tool** and set a big hard brush, around **90 pixels**.

5. In the **History** panel, make a new snapshot called **blurred**.

6. On the **blurred** layer, erase the subject of the image—the guy and the car—going a little around him so that the entire subject is included.

7. In the **History** panel, set the source for the **History Brush Tool** to the **blurred** snapshot.

8. Choose the **History Brush Tool** with a smaller soft brush and carefully paint back in the blur, just to the edges of the guy and his car.

9. If you go too far, switch back to the **Eraser Tool**, with a small soft brush, and erase the edges as needed.

The Lens Flare Filter

For years, photographers have struggled when photographing extremely bright objects, like metal objects in full sunlight, to avoid the glare that results. The **Lens Flare** filter simulates these glares. Why would you want to add this type of glare to an image? To make it look more realistic. A lens flare can make an image have a certain believable, imperfect quality. Try it out in this guided exercise.

Guided Exercise 14.6: Use the Lens Flare Filter

In this guided exercise you will start with an image of a lady bug on a spherical fence post top and add a lens flare to the shiny spot on the sphere.

1. Open **14-ladybug.jpg** and save it as **ladybug.psd** in the location of your choice. This is another low-quality image that you will not print.

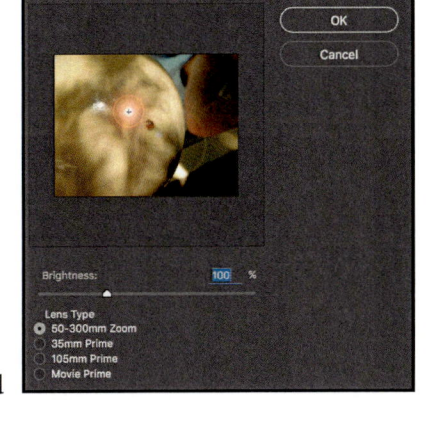

2. Duplicate the **Background** layer and name the duplicate **lens flare** and be sure **lens flare** is the active layer.

3. Choose **Filter > Render > Lens Flare** to bring up the **Lens Flare** dialog box.

    Lens Flare has only two controls: **Brightness** and **Lens Type**. We kept the **Brightness** at **100%** and used the **50-300mm Zoom Lens Type**, but you may use whatever settings you like.

4. Once you've changed the settings to give you the flare you want, you need to position the flare.

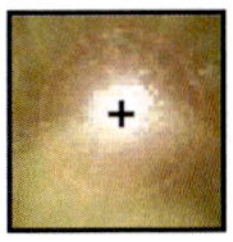

    Look for the small cross hair in the image preview portion of the dialog box. The cross hair determines the focal point of the flare. Click in the image preview to position the cross hair exactly where you want the flare centered—on the shiny spot in this example.

5. Click **OK** to get the final result.

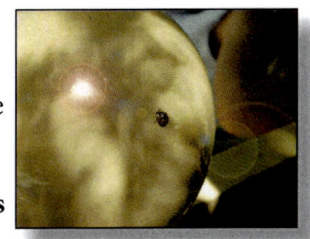

    Notice the complex lens flare, simulating the reflections that take place within the elements of the camera lens.

6. If you think the lens flare effect is too strong, simply lower the opacity of the **Lens Flare** layer to soften it.

The Liquify Filter

The **Liquify** filter is a very fun feature in Photoshop that allows you to stretch, twist, and distort images. Like all other filters, the **Liquify** filter will only affect the active layer which must be visible. **Liquify** is available to images only in **RGB**, **CMYK**, **Duotone**, **Lab** or **Grayscale** mode. If you have an active selection, the filter will be applied to just the selected area(s). You can limit how much area the **Liquify** filter will affect by using a selection, and you can fade the effect of the filter by choosing **Edit > Fade > Liquify** immediately after you have applied the filter.

It is best to duplicate the layer to receive the **Liquify** filter to because you will be altering the pixels of that layer.

WARNING: the **Liquify** filter requires more from your computer's graphics card and its video memory, called VRAM, than most other filters. If you have trouble getting **Liquify** to work, it may be because of your computer's video card.

The Liquify Filter Dialog Box

The Liquify filter was changed a lot in the update to Photoshop CC 2015.5 (June 2016). Here is the earlier version of the dialog box:

When you first open the **Liquify** filter dialog box, there will be fewer tools and controls than shown here. Click the **Advanced Mode** check box (toggle) on the right side of the image preview to see the additional tools and settings.

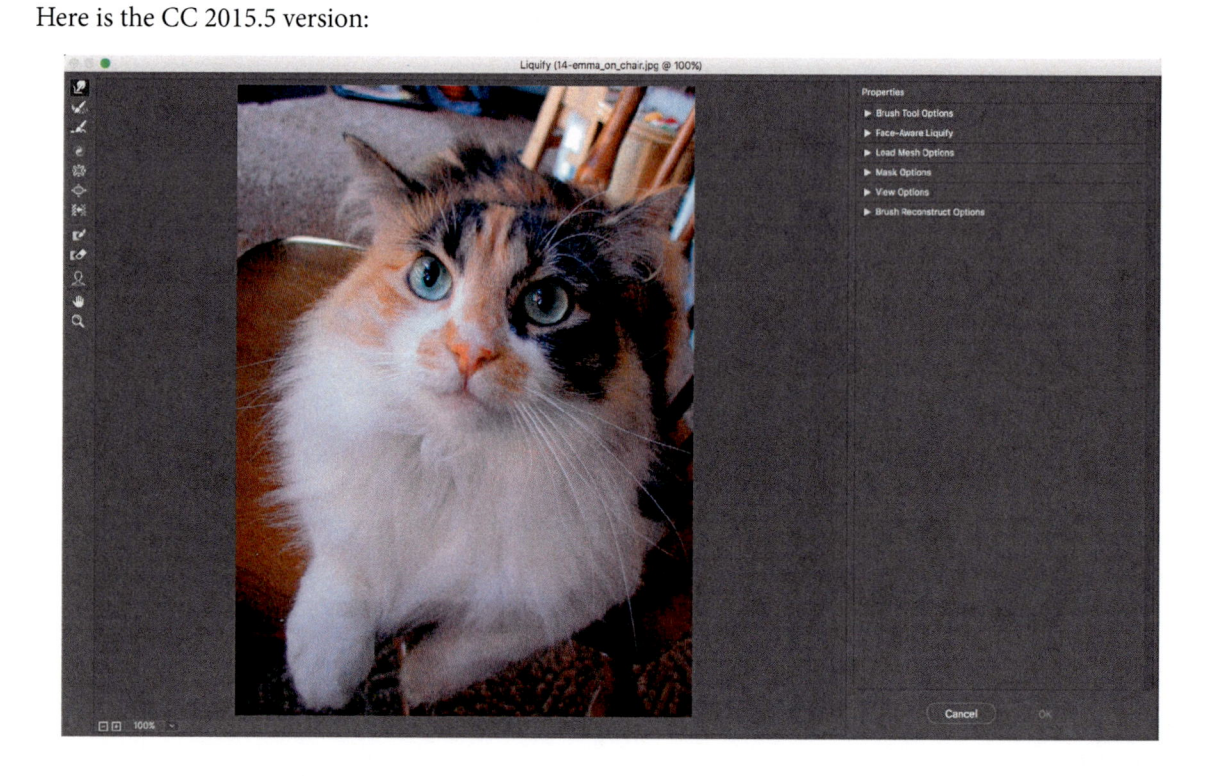

Here is the CC 2015.5 version:

Tutorial 14: Fun with Filters

THE LIQUIFY TOOLS

The tools for using the **Liquify** filter are on the left side of the dialog box. If you want to play with some of these tools as you read on, open **14-emma_on_chair.jpg**.

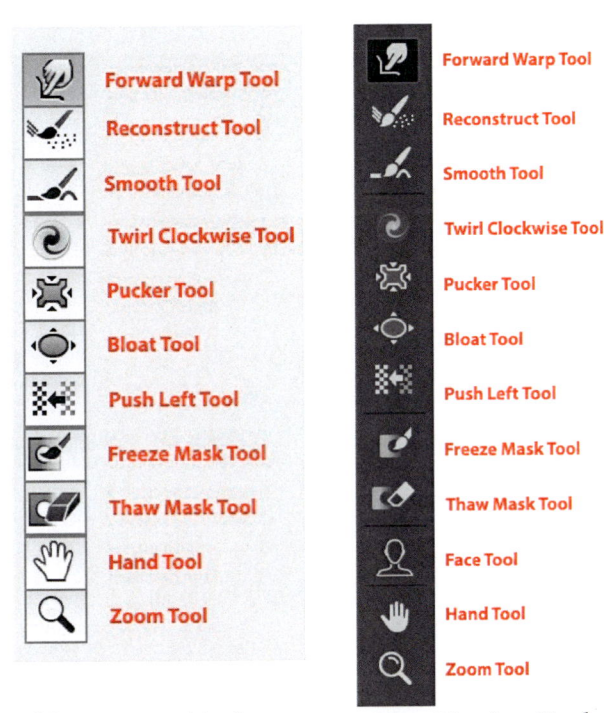

Older Version Tools	New Version Tools
Forward Warp Tool	Forward Warp Tool
Reconstruct Tool	Reconstruct Tool
Smooth Tool	Smooth Tool
Twirl Clockwise Tool	Twirl Clockwise Tool
Pucker Tool	Pucker Tool
Bloat Tool	Bloat Tool
Push Left Tool	Push Left Tool
Freeze Mask Tool	Freeze Mask Tool
Thaw Mask Tool	Thaw Mask Tool
Hand Tool	Face Tool
Zoom Tool	Hand Tool
	Zoom Tool

The default **Forward Warp Tool** pushes pixels in the direction you drag the cursor.

The **Reconstruct Tool** restores areas back to their original states. The **Reconstruct Tool** lets you paint the areas to their pre-liquified state, like using the **History Brush Tool**.

The **Smooth Tool** acts like the **Reconstruct Tool**, eventually restoring the image to its original state, by smoothing out any areas that have been modified.

The **Twirl Clockwise Tool** will continue to rotate pixels as long as you hold down the mouse or drag the cursor. Press **alt** or **option** as you drag to twirl the affected pixels counter clockwise.

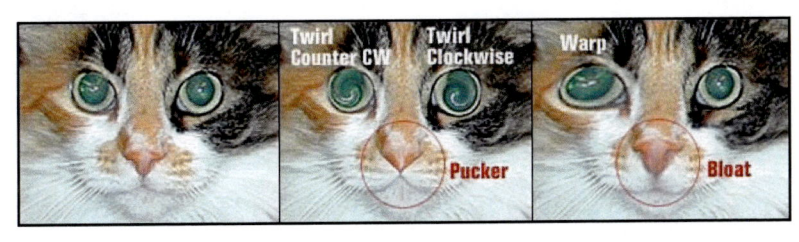

Tutorial 14: Fun with Filters — Page 275

The **Pucker** and **Bloat** tools do the opposite of each other; the **Pucker Tool** pulls in pixels towards the center of the brush and the **Bloat Tool** pushes pixels away from the center.

The **Push Left Tool** moves pixels at right angles from the direction the brush is moved. In other words, the direction of your stroke determines which direction the tool moves the pixels.

- To widen Emma's nose using the **Push Left Tool**, paint a stroke from the bottom to the top on the left side of her nose and then paint a stroke from the top to the bottom on the right side of her nose.

- To narrow her nose, paint a stroke from the top to the bottom on the left side of her nose and then from the bottom to the top on the right side of her nose.

The **Zoom** and **Hand Tools** work like those on the main **Tools** panel.

The **Freeze Tool** lets you mask out areas that you don't want to affect with the filter. The **Thaw Tool** unfreezes masked areas so that they can be edited. If you had an irregular selection active when choosing the filter, your unselected areas will be frozen. You can thaw these areas with the **Thaw Tool**.

The new **Face Tool** attempts to recognize facial features and allows you to easily manipulate their qualities.

If you have a rectangular selection active when you choose the filter, only the selected area is previewed in the dialog box. An irregularly shaped selection will show as a squared off area cropped in around the selected area with the non-selected areas masked (by default in red) so as not to be affected by the filter.

Here, the cat's nose is selected in the document window on the left, and within the **Liquify** dialog box on the right.

When **Liquify** is chosen, the **Liquify** dialog box represents that selection with the non-selected areas masked in red so that it cannot be affected by the **Liquify** filter, and the selected area revealed for editing.

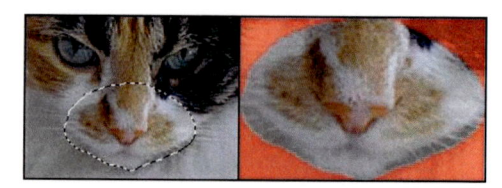

OTHER LIQUIFY SETTINGS

In the **Mask Options** area on the right side of the dialog box:

- **None** thaws all frozen areas.
- **Mask All** freezes everything.
- **Invert All** thaws frozen areas and freezes unfrozen areas.

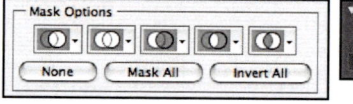

Once you start using any of the **Liquify** tools, the **Reconstruct Options** area become available:

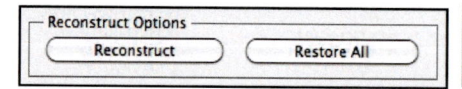

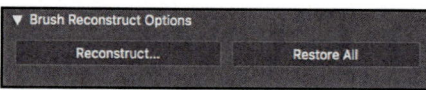

Tutorial 14: Fun with Filters

- The **Restore All** button will instantly revert your image back to the way it was when you opened the **Liquify** dialog box.
- The **Reconstruct** button opens the **Revert Reconstruction** dialog box with its **Amount** slider. The default **100 (%)** is the same as clicking **Revert**.
- Slowly drag the **Amount** to the left to gradually apply your **Liquify** changes to the image. Watch the preview to see the effects, and click **OK** when there is a **Liquify Amount** you like.

On the right side of the **Liquify** dialog box you have a number of other settings. The **Tool Options** area lets you set a **Brush Size** from **1-600** pixels that applies to all of the tools. You can choose a **Brush Pressure** from 1-100% to control the rate at which the distortion will be applied. Check **Stylus Pressure** if you are using a tablet and stylus to use pressure to further control how your brush paints.

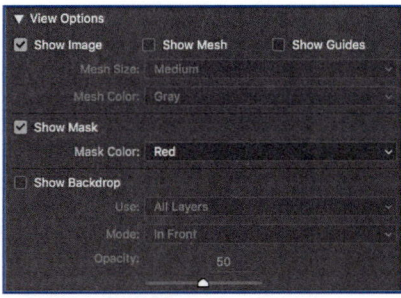

No matter which layers are displayed, the **Liquify** filter will only affect the active layer.

- In a multi-layered document, uncheck **Show Backdrop** setting in **View Options** section to view only the active layer within the dialog box.
- When **Show Backdrop** is checked, you can choose a layer to display and set an opacity for the display.

The Liquify Mesh

Behind the scenes, the **Liquify** filter creates a **MESH**, a grid pattern that visually shows how the distortion affects the image.

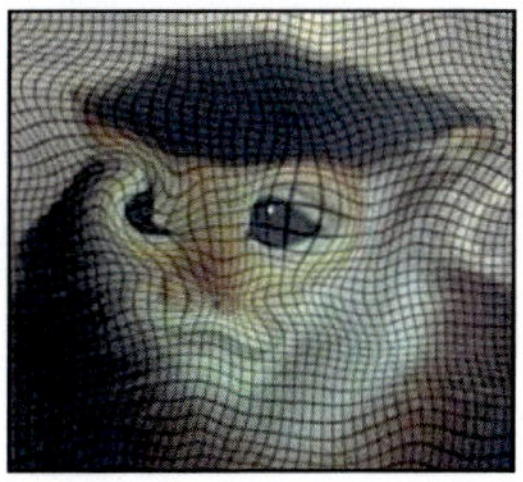

- Toggle the mesh visibility with the **Show Mesh** check box. Viewing the mesh can help you see what areas you have affected. This can be helpful when working with the **Reconstruct Tool**.

If you are unsure about your **Liquify** settings and might want to tweak them later, save the mesh for that specific **Liquify** filter session. That way, if you decide after the **Liquify** dialog box is closed you want to tweak your settings, you can open **Liquify** again and load the mesh.

To save a mesh:

- Click the **Save Mesh** button in the top right of the **Liquify** dialog box. You will save the mesh to a file with a **.msh** file extension.

To load a mesh:

- Select the layer that originally had **Liquify** applied to it.
- Choose **Filter > Liquify**.
- Click the **Load Mesh** button.

You can also load the **.msh** file to give other layers or images the same **Liquify** distortion.

Guided Exercise 14.7A: Use the Liquify Filter to Modify a Boy's Portrait (for Photoshop CC 2015.2 and Earlier)

The **Liquify** filter can be used to greatly distort an image, as you have already seen from the preceding examples. In this guided exercise you will use the **Liquify** filter to subtly change the subject's expression, while keeping the image as realistic as possible. Be sure to also read the next Guided Exercise to see how much the **Liquify** filter has improved in Photoshop CC 2015.5.

1. Open **14-face.jpg** and save it as **face.psd** in the location of your choice.

2. Duplicate the **Background** layer and name the duplicate **frown**.

3. With the **frown** layer active, choose **Filter > Liquify** to open the **Liquify** dialog box.

4. Check the **Advanced Mode** box near the upper-right corner of the **Liquify** dialog box to display all of the **Liquify** filter's tools and settings.

5. Change the boy's mouth to a frown:

    a. Choose the **Forward Warp** tool.

    b. Be sure the **Brush Size** is set to the default setting of **100**.

    c. Using short strokes gently push the corners of his mouth downward and slightly to the center.

    d. Gently push the upper lip downward and the lower lip upward.

6. Before closing the **Liquify** dialog box, check and tweak your results:

    a. Check **Show Backdrop** and set the **Opacity** to **100** to see your original starting image.

    b. Toggle **Show Backdrop** off and on to compare your before and after versions.

    c. Continue to adjust the mouth as desired. Try to keep your image as realistic as possible.

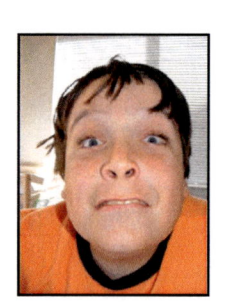

7. Use the **Push Left Tool** to modify his eyebrows:

   a. Change the **Brush Size** to **50**.

   b. Click on the inside edge of his right eyebrow and drag slowly to the left to push his eyebrow downward and flatten it out somewhat.

   c. Starting on his left eyebrow, right next to the curl of hair that covers it, drag slowly to the left to flatten the arch.

8. Shrink his eyes:

   a. Choose the **Pucker Tool** and set the **Brush Size** to **150**.

   b. Click exactly on the center of the pupil of each eye to shrink it a little. Make very quick clicks; the longer the mouse button is held down, the more the **Pucker Tool** will shrink the eyes.

   c. Use **Edit > Undo** or **Step Backward** if you go too far.

9. Toggle the **Show Backdrop** check box to see your before and after image.

   If any of your adjustments look too unrealistic, choose the **Reconstruct** tool and paint over the area as desired.

   If you have used **Liquify** properly, you should end up with a very realistic change of mood.

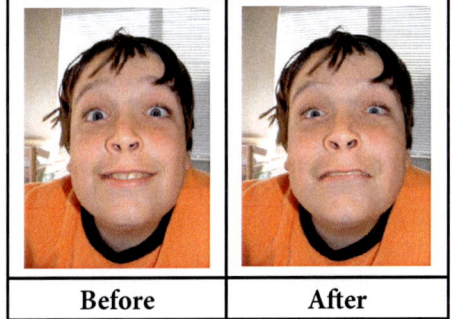

   Before   **After**

Guided Exercise 14.7B: Use the Liquify Filter to Modify a Boy's Portrait (for Photoshop CC 2015.5)

In this guided exercise you will use the **Liquify** filter to change the subject's expression from happy to sad, while taking advantage of the new face-detection features in the Photoshop CC 2015.5 version.

1. Open **14-face.jpg** and save it as **face.psd** in the location of your choice.

2. Duplicate the **Background** layer and name the duplicate **frown**.

3. With the **frown** layer active, choose **Filter > Liquify** to open the **Liquify** dialog box.

4. Choose the Face Tool. Notice that Photoshop has detected a face in the image, and put two curved lines around the general area. As you move the cursor over the face itself, you will see controls appear on the eyes, nose, and mouth. You can change these features from the controls, but we will use the settings in the **Face-Aware Liquify** section of the dialog box, for more precise adjustments.

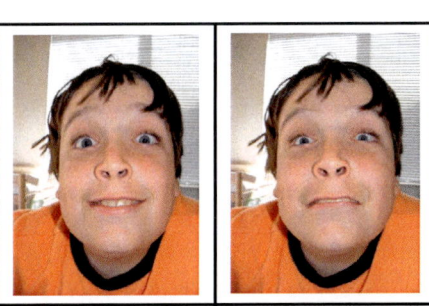

Tutorial 14: Fun with Filters

5. Click the triangle next to **Face-Aware Liquify** to expand the section.

6. Let's change the boy's expression, by starting with the overall shape of his face:

    a. Expand the **Face Shape** area.

    b. Correct for some distortion caused by the use of a wide-angle lens with a close-up image:

    1) Bring the top of the head a bit lower by setting the **Forehead** to -70.

    2) Bring the chin up by setting the **Chin Height** to 29.

    3) Narrow the jaw slightly by setting **Jawline** to -4.

    4) Finally, set the **Face Width** to -4. Now the overall shape looks much more natural.

7. He looks too happy. Next, expand the **Mouth** section to make changes there:

    a. Move the **Smile** slider all the way to the left.

    b. Narrow the mouth by setting the **Mouth Width** to -70.

    c. Flatten the mouth by setting the **Mouth Height** to -100. That's better.

8. Now it's time for the nose:

    a. Expand the **Nose** section.

    b. Lower the **Nose Height** to -37.

    c. Narrow the nose a little by setting the **Nose Width** to -68.

9. Time to turn up the sadness by modifying his eyes:

    a. Expand the **Eyes** section.

    b. Set all the sections to -100 to make his eyes smaller and closer together.

    c. Click OK to confirm your changes.

    d. If you want to go for a little extra sadness, choose **Filter** > **Liquify** again and lower the smile setting in the **Mouth** section again.

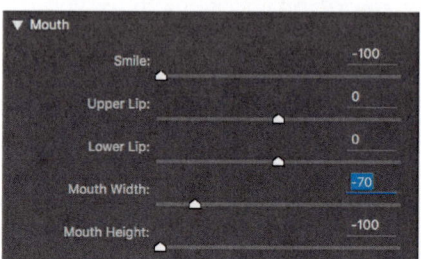

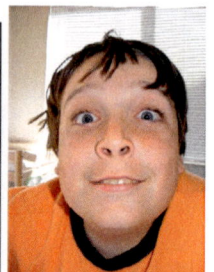

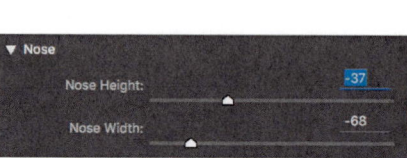

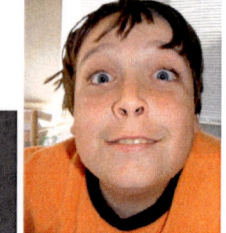

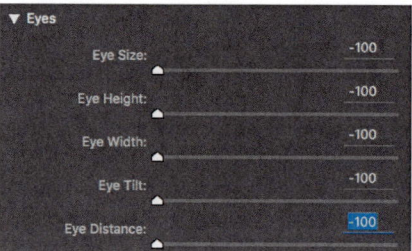

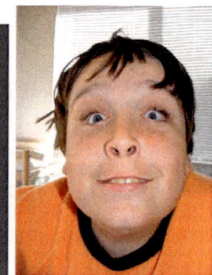

Tutorial 14: Fun with Filters   Page 280

10. As you can see from the original image on the left, to the modified one on the right, the changes are visible, but still believable.

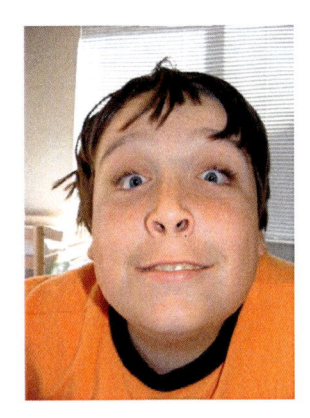

11. To make additional chages, review the tools in Guided Exercise 14.7A — all of the tools mentioned there are still available in the latest version of the Liquify filter. They also allow you to make more drastic changes to your images.

12. Save your image, if desired.

On Your Own

Use the tools and settings in the **Liquify** dialog box to change the boy's expression in a different way. Make him angry, scared, or any other expression you want.

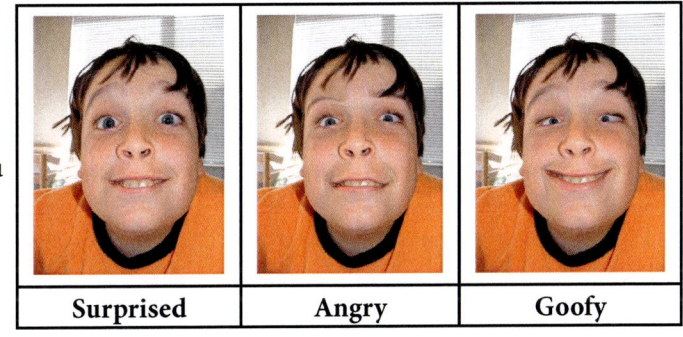

| Surprised | Angry | Goofy |

Resources and Videos

http://www.practical-photoshop.com/pages/CC2015-pp1-resources.html#14

Practical Photoshop CC 2015, Level 1
Tutorial 15: Putting It All Together

This final tutorial combines many of the skills you have acquired to complete a practical project—making your own postcards. As you work through the project, you will learn some tricks about using the **Eraser Tools**, and you will make, load, and use **PRESETS**—saved sets of tool or panel options—to streamline your workflow. As you work, you will use brush, gradient, and color swatch presets, define some of your own, and build some preset libraries.

You will also use the **Define Pattern** command to create your own patterns, use them to make new backgrounds for images, and paint with them using the **Pattern Stamp Tool**.

Objectives

- Compare the (standard) **Eraser Tool** with the **Magic Eraser Tool** and the **Background Eraser Tool**.
- Define custom patterns.
- Use the **Pattern Stamp Tool**.
- Define **Presets**.
- Save and load **Preset Libraries** from the **Preset Manager**.
- Make at least two custom postcards.

The Eraser Tools Revisited

You have already used the **Eraser Tool** to remove unnecessary pixels. Let's take a further look at the (standard) **Eraser Tool**, see how its options increase its functionality and compare it to both the **Magic Eraser Tool** and the **Background Eraser Tool**.

The Eraser Tool

Remember that the **Eraser Tool** erases to the background color on the **Background** layer, and erases to transparent on other layers. **Mode** determines the **Eraser Tool's** brush shape and properties. As you change from one **Mode** to another, the **Options** bar settings will change to reflect that mode's available options.

- **Brush** and **Pencil Modes** use brushes to erase to either the background color or to transparency.
- **Brush Mode** erases using anti-aliasing; **Pencil Mode** does not.
- **Block Mode** changes the eraser to a square, hard-edged, fixed-size eraser.

Tutorial 15: Putting it all Together

Use **Block Mode** either to completely erase areas or to fine-tune a highly-magnified image. As you zoom in, **Block** covers fewer pixels because it is zoom level dependent.

The Magic Eraser Tool

The **Magic Eraser Tool** does not use a brush. Instead, it is like first clicking, not dragging, with the **Magic Wand Tool** and then pressing the **delete** key to erase the selected area to transparent pixels. Notice that its options resemble those of the **Magic Wand Tool**.

Tolerance controls the range of tonality to be removed, based on the clicked pixel.

Anti-aliased gives a softer edge to the selected area.

Contiguous erases only neighboring pixels.

Sample All Layers bases the selection on the composite image tonality rather than that of the active layer—but will only remove pixels from the active layer.

Opacity below 100% lets you partially erase parts of a layer.

When you use the **Magic Eraser Tool** on the **Background** layer, it automatically becomes a standard pixel layer to support transparency. The **Magic Eraser Tool** works best when the area you want to remove is quite uniform in color. If the **Magic Eraser Tool** does not perform as you had hoped, **Undo**, adjust your **Tolerance**, and try again.

The Background Eraser Tool

The **Background Eraser Tool** lets you erase pixels on a layer as you drag. By specifying different sampling and tolerance options, you can control the range of background removal and the sharpness of the removal boundary. Think of it as the **Magic Eraser Tool** on a brush.

The **Background Eraser Tool** works best to clean up the selection edges after you remove an object from its surrounding pixels. The greater the contrast between the image and its background, the better the **Background Eraser Tool** will work.

Eraser Cautions

- All the **Eraser Tools** permanently remove pixels from the active layer. If you are unsure exactly what you want to erase, copy the layer or even duplicate the entire document before you start erasing.

- Although you can select pixels from individual layers or the composite image (**Sample All Layers**), you can only erase pixels or remove backgrounds from individual layers.

- The **Magic Eraser Tool** and the **Background Eraser Tool** change the **Background** layer into a standard pixel layer, and erase to transparent — not always in the way that you hoped. Before using an eraser tool, you should preserve an intact copy of the original layer or image for safekeeping.

Guided Exercise 15.1: Use the Eraser Tools to Clean Up a Selection

In this guided exercise, you will use the **Eraser** tools to remove the background from a photo of a red fire hydrant.

1. **Reset All Tools** before you begin so that your tool settings will match the ones described here.

2. Open **15-hydrant.jpg** and save it as **hydrant.psd** in the location of your choice.

3. Duplicate the **Background** layer, and name the duplicate layer **hydrant**.

4. Activate the **Background** layer, make a new **Color Fill** layer filled with a bright green color, and rename that layer **green**.

   Making an intermediate layer filled with a contrasting color helps to differentiate the edges of an item from the transparent parts of a layer. Using a **Color Fill** layer does not add much to the file size. Once the layer is cleaned up, you can discard the intermediate layer.

5. On the **hydrant** layer, select the background as carefully as you can. The **Quick Selection Tool** works pretty well. As you select, be careful that you do not select any of the chain. Don't worry about the insides of the chain—you will erase them shortly.

6. Press the delete key to remove the selected area, leaving just the hydrant with a green layer underneath it.

7. Zoom in to **200%** and carefully inspect the hydrant to be sure it is entirely there.

8. If you have missing regions, like part of the chain here on the left, paint the missing regions back using the **History Brush Tool**. Your source will be the state just before the **delete** state. Don't worry if you leave a bit of extra edge.

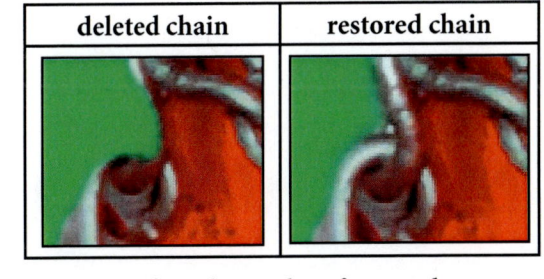

9. Choose the **Eraser Tool** and zoom to **400%** to more carefully identify any problems with the hydrant edges.

10. Attempt to erase the extra pixels using the default Eraser settings. You can remove much of the edge, but the brush is too big to erase in tight areas, and it can sometimes leave a small dark edge of anti-aliased pixels.

11. Change to **Pencil** mode, and continue to erase the dark area. Now you can erase more without leaving an anti-aliased edge. In some cases, this is good; in others, the edge is too harsh and stair-stepped. Here we have zoomed in to **400%** to see the rough edge.

Tutorial 15: Putting it all Together

12. The best use of **Pencil** mode is to clean up individual pixels and the tiniest, a one pixel brush, gives you the most control.

    Save a **TOOL PRESET** for this special use:

    a. Change the **Eraser Tool** brush size to **1 pixel**.

    b. Click the **Tool Preset picker** button in the upper left corner of the **Options** bar to open the **Tool Preset picker**.

    c. Click the **Create new tool preset** button, give the tool a meaningful name like **Eraser one pixel cleanup**, and click **OK** to save the tool as a preset.

    d. Choose your new tool preset from the **Tool Preset Picker** whenever you want to use it.

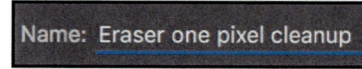

13. Change the **Eraser Tool** to **Block** mode and continue to erase the stray pixels.

    The pointer changes to become a white block, and you cannot change its size from the **Options** bar. If you zoom in, the block eraser gets proportionately smaller. If you zoom out, the block size increases. Erasing in **Block** mode can be very effective at high magnification, because you can erase pixel by pixel.

14. Using the **Eraser** options of your choice, remove as much of the unwanted edges as possible. Also, use a small brush to carefully clean up the insides of the chain. Do not worry about the very thin anti-aliased edge; you will fix that soon.

15. Make sure the hydrant layer is active and choose **Layer > Matting > Defringe** (at the very bottom of the **Layer** menu) to remove the outer layer of contrasting pixels.

    When the **Defringe** dialog box appears, leave the **Width** at the default of **1 pixel**, and click **OK**.

    If the dark edge is still prominent, choose the **Defringe** command a second time. It seems to work better this way than to set a larger pixel width.

16. Save the document one more time.

17. **Alt /option + click** the eye in the **hydrant** layer to hide all layers but the hydrant to view the cleaned up hydrant on its own layer.

18. Delete the hidden layers, and save the document as **hydrant_only.psd**.

    This document will not have a **Background** layer.

Semi-Guided Exercise 15.2: Make a Custom Postcard

In this guided exercise you will create a new **document preset**, perfectly sized for postcards that meet the US Postal Service's size requirements, and use that preset to make a custom postcard.

1. Choose **File > New** to display the **New** dialog box.

2. Enter these values for your postcard:

    Name: postcard 6 in x 4.25 in
    Width: 6 inches
    Height: 4.25 inches
    Resolution: 300 ppi (for commercial printing)
    Color Mode: RGB

3. Click the **Save Preset** button to make a new **Document Preset** using these settings.

4. Be sure the **Preset Name** is "postcard 6 in x 4.25 in" and click **OK** to return to the **New** dialog box.

    When you click the **Preset** drop-down menu arrow, you will see your postcard document preset near the top of the list.

5. Choose **postcard 6 in x 4.25 in** from the **Preset** menu and click **OK**.

6. Open the **hydrant_only.psd** file if necessary.

7. With the **Move Tool**, drag the **hydrant** layer onto the new (untitled) document.

8. Save the document as **postcard1.psd** in the location of your choice.

9. Activate the **Background** layer.

10. Sample a light blue color for your foreground color and white for your background color; then choose **Render > Clouds** to fill the **Background** layer with clouds. If you want, you can use other filters to make your background more interesting.

11. Copy the **hydrant** layer a few times; you decide how many hydrants to use in your postcard.

12. Drag the **hydrant** layers around the image until they look pleasing.

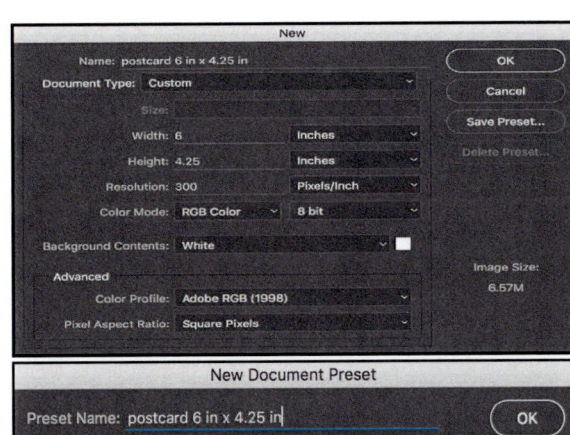

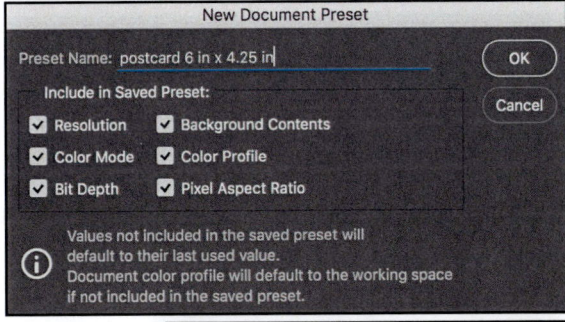

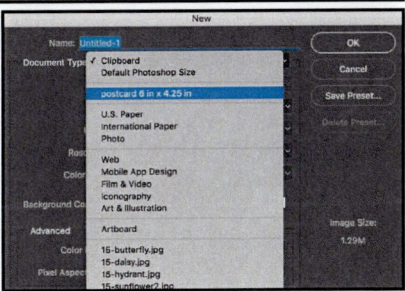

Tutorial 15: Putting it all Together

13. Colorize the hydrants individually. Here is an easy way to colorize a layer:

    a. Activate the layer.

    b. Choose **Image** > **Adjustments** > **Hue/Saturation**.

    c. Drag the **Hue** slider until you find a color you like.

    d. Adjust **Saturation** and **Lightness** as desired, and click **OK**.

    Notice that you did not use an adjustment layer. That's because in this beginning class you won't have time to learn how to make an adjustment layer that only affects a single layer.

14. Finish the document as you choose. Experiment with many of the skills you have learned in this course. Be playful. For example, you could:

    - Transform hydrants.
    - Liquify or otherwise filter hydrants.
    - Paint on hydrants or other layers of your own making.
    - Clone hydrants or elements from other images.

15. As you work, you may want to save snapshots of different versions, or even choose **Image** > **Duplicate** and make more than one hydrant postcard. Don't forget to save those documents, too.

Here are a couple of simple examples. You can certainly do better!

Guided Exercise 15.3: Use the Magic Eraser Tool

If an image has a fairly consistent background, the **Magic Eraser Tool** can quickly remove it for you. In this guided exercise you will use the **Magic Eraser Tool** to remove the blue sky background from a photo of a sunflower.

1. **Reset All Tools** and open **15-sunflower2.jpg**.

2. Choose the **Magic Eraser Tool** and click *once* in the blue sky of the image.

Tutorial 15: Putting it all Together   Page 288

The **Magic Eraser Tool** only removes some of the blue sky because the default **Tolerance** setting of **32** is too low. **Undo**!

3. Change the **Tolerance** setting to **70** and click *once* in the blue sky.

   Much better, except that there are still patches of blue enclosed within the flower. **Undo** again.

4. Uncheck the **Contiguous** option and click once in the blue sky of the image.

   That does it. Notice that the **Background** has become **Layer 0**.

5. Change the name of **Layer 0** to **sunflower**

6. Crop the image as there is no reason to work with a bigger file than you need.

7. Save the image as **15-sunflower.psd** in the location of your choice.

How good a job does the **Magic Eraser Tool** do? On this image, it removed the blue sky from the sunflower both quickly and cleanly. However, if you put a solid white layer under the sunflower layer and you zoom in on the stem, you can see a blue halo that may cause problems in some situations. Sometimes, you can remove such a halo with **Refine Edge** or **Select and Mask**. Here is another technique that provides more control.

Guided Exercise 15.4: Use the Background Eraser Tool

The **Background Eraser Tool** will help you to clean up the remaining blue halos. As appropriate, you will save and use a tool preset for the **Background Eraser Tool**.

1. Begin with **15-sunflower.psd** open.

2. Make a new layer, name it **white**, fill it with **100% white**, and place it below the **sunflower** layer.

3. Zoom in to **300%** and inspect an edge of the flower stem.

4. Activate the sunflower layer.

5. Choose the **Background Eraser Tool**, and move it across the document without pressing the mouse key to view the tool's distinctive pointer.

   The **Background Eraser Tool** uses a **cross hair circular pointer**. As you erase, Photoshop samples the pixel at the center of the cross hair. The sampled color controls what is removed, and erases by brush size everything within its **Tolerance** setting. Here we clicked once and removed stray pixels based on the **Background** color.

6. Examine the default **Background Eraser Tool** options and the results of changing these settings.

   The **Background Eraser Tool** is set to use a **13 pixel hard-edged** brush. Changing that setting to a soft-edged brush will erase more completely at the center of the brush than towards its edges.

Tutorial 15: Putting it all Together

Sampling controls how the color to be erased is chosen.

- **Continuous**, the default, adjusts erasure as you drag across different image pixels. The **Background Eraser Tool** removes all the pixels in its swath that are within the tolerance of the pixels the cross hair passes over.

- **Once** only erases pixels that match the first pixel you drag across. With **Sampling** set to **Once**, the **Background Eraser Tool** only removes pixels within the tolerance of the color under the cross hair when you first press the mouse. Each time you release the mouse button, move its location, and press again, you redefine the color to be removed.

- **Background swatch** erases only those pixels that match the current background color. This setting works best with fairly uniform backgrounds and low tolerance settings. We won't use it here.

Limits control where erasure occurs.

- **Contiguous**, the default, erases areas of the sampled color which are connected to each other.

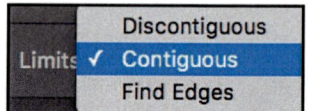

- **Discontiguous** erases the sampled color wherever it occurs in the layer, within the limits of the brush shape.

- **Find Edges** erases connected areas containing the sampled color while better preserving the sharpness of the object's edges. This setting works best with high contrast borders.

Tolerance is similar to the **Magic Wand Tool**, but measured in percentage (**0** to **100%**) rather than **256 levels**. The default **Tolerance** of **50%** is the same as **128** for the **Magic Wand Tool**.

By default, **Protect Foreground Color** is not checked. When **Protect Foreground Color** is checked, pixels of the foreground color will not be erased. This option works best when **Sampling** is set to **Once**.

7. Drag across an unwanted edge on the stem to remove it.

    Dragging here does not work very well. With continuous sampling, a high tolerance, and the small default brush, you either leave pixels behind or remove partial round circles from the flower itself.

8. **Undo** and change the **Background Eraser Tool** options. Try these settings:

    Sampling: Once
    Limits: Find Edges
    Tolerance: 25%

    You may need to drag more than once to get most of the blue area removed. Be careful not to drag the cross hair across the petal or stem, or you will remove their color as well.

9. Use a combination of the **Background Eraser Tool** with its default settings and the (standard) **Eraser Tool** to delete any stray pixels.

10. These settings worked better than the default. Save them as a tool preset to use in the future:

    a. Open the **Tool Preset Picker** and click the **Create new tool preset** button.

    b. Give the tool a more meaningful name, like **Background Eraser edge remover** and click **OK**.

    Now you can choose your new tool preset from the **Tool Preset Picker** whenever you want to use it.

11. Use any techniques you like to clean up the rest of the edges, and save the document when you finish.

On Your Own: Make a Sunflower Postcard

Start with a new document using the **postcard new document preset**, drag the sunflower layer onto the new document, resize it as desired, and make your own postcard.

Patterns

A **PATTERN** is a square or rectangular swatch that **TILES** or repeats throughout a layer or selection. Patterns are used by the **Pattern Stamp Tool**, the **Paint Bucket Tool** with the **Pattern** option chosen, the **Pattern Overlay** layer effect, **Pattern Fill** layers, or when choosing **Edit > Fill** and filling with a pattern. Patterns are organized in the **Pattern Picker**.

Here is one way to view the **Pattern Picker**:

1. Choose the **Pattern Stamp Tool** hiding under the **Clone Stamp Tool**.

2. Click the triangle next to the **Pattern** preview near the center of the **Options** bar to view the **Pattern Picker**.

By default the **Pattern Picker** shows only a few pattern thumbnails. However, like gradients, you can load and use additional patterns from the **Pattern Picker** menu. You can also define your own pattern.

To Define a Pattern by Selection:

If you want to try it, there is a tiny image called **15-butterfly.jpg** that you can work with.

1. With the **Rectangular Marquee Tool**, select the area to become your tile, like this section of a butterfly wing.

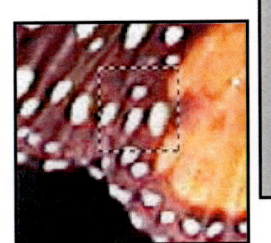

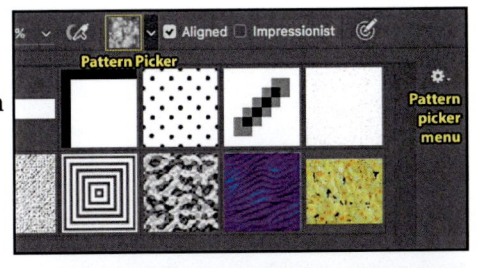

2. Choose **Edit > Define Pattern**.

3. Name the pattern in the **Pattern Name** dialog box that appears, and click **OK**.

   The pattern will appear at the end of the **Pattern Picker**.

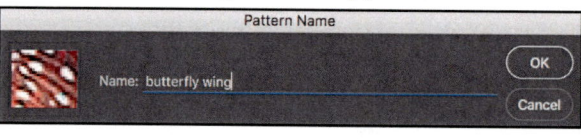

4. Use your pattern. Here, the left sample was painted with the **Pattern Stamp Tool**, and the right sample was filled using the **Paint Bucket Tool** set to fill with the pattern.

Guided Exercise 15.5: Making Patterns

In this guided exercise you will make some patterns to use later in the tutorial.

1. **Reset All Tools** before you begin so that your tool settings will match the ones described here.

2. Open **15-daisy.jpg**.

3. Zoom in to **100%** and make a small rectangular selection in the central part of the flower.

4. With the flower layer active, choose **Edit > Define Pattern**.

5. Name the pattern **daisy-patch** in the **Pattern Name** dialog box that appears, and click **OK**.

6. Duplicate the **Background** layer, and apply a fairly strong **Motion Blur** filter to the duplicate layer.

7. Make a similar selection to your last one, in the center of the flower, and choose **Edit > Define Pattern**.

8. Name the pattern **daisy-blur** in the **Pattern Name** dialog box and click **OK**.

   Now you have two saved patterns.

9. Close **15-daisy.jpg** as you won't need it for a while.

10. Compare your patterns:

    a. Make a new document, choosing **Default Photoshop Size** from the **Presets** drop down list. This will make a small document (504 x 360 pixels) that is too small for quality printing, but good for experimentation.

    b. With the **Rectangular Marquee Tool**, select approximately the left half of the document.

    c. Choose the **Paint Bucket Tool**, set to **Pattern** and click the arrow to the right of the pattern swatch to view the **Pattern Picker**.

    d. Click the thumbnail of the first pattern you made to select it and then click inside the selection in your document window to fill the selection with your first pattern.

e. Choose **Select > Inverse** to select the other half of the image.

f. In the **Pattern Picker**, choose your second custom pattern, and then click inside the selection to fill the other half of the document with the second pattern.

The two patterns look quite different. Notice that both of them contain quite visible squares of pattern. That is to be expected when you define patterns. There are all kinds of tips on the Internet for making the seams less visible.

Presets, Libraries, & the Preset Manager

Nearly every Photoshop tool has a variety of settings and options that expand the tool's functionality. Reconfiguring each tool for special uses can be time consuming. Fortunately, Photoshop has ways to save and reuse some of these settings in what are called **PRESETS**.

Each **PRESET** is a saved set of options such as the shape of a brush or the distribution of colors in a gradient.

PRESET PICKERS display thumbnails of specific categories of presets.

A saved collection of presets is called a **LIBRARY**.

Different tools have different techniques for making presets. For example, you can make a preset by:

- Setting options for a tool, and then clicking the **New Tool Preset** button in the **Tool Preset Picker.**
- Defining a pattern from the **Edit** menu.
- Adding a color to the **Swatches** panel.

Each of these techniques only stores the preset temporarily. The new preset appears at the bottom of the picker (or panel). These presets will be permanently lost if you reinstall Photoshop or use the **Replace** command to load another library of presets or choose **Reset** (Brushes, Gradients, etc.) and then click **Replace** rather than **Append**.

Guided Exercise 15.6: Making and Loading Libraries

The **Preset Manager** is like a central command center for organizing all your presets rather than going to each one at a time. You cannot create presets with the **Preset Manager**, but you can organize, append, replace and reset, rename and delete items from within the **Preset Manager**.

If you have one or more presets that you want to preserve, you should save them as a **LIBRARY** file on your hard drive. By placing presets into libraries, you can organize them for your own work, back them up, and easily share them with others.

In this guided exercise you will first make a pattern library and then you will load gradient and pattern libraries.

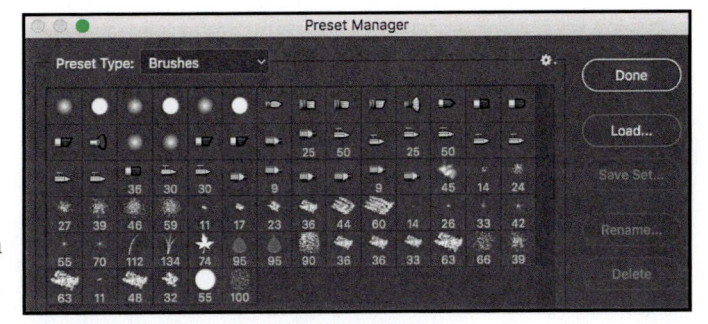

1. Choose **Edit > Presets > Preset Manager** to open the **Preset Manager**.

    By default, it opens to show thumbnails of the **Brushes** presets.

2. Click the arrow to the right of **Brushes** to display the **Preset Type menu**, and choose **Patterns**. Now you can see your pattern presets.

3. Click on one of the daisy pattern thumbnails to select it.

    The thumbnail will be outlined and if you hover over the thumbnail the **Pattern** tool tip will appear with its name, pixel dimensions, and image mode.

4. **Command + click** (Mac) or **control + click** (Win) to select additional thumbnails to add to your library.

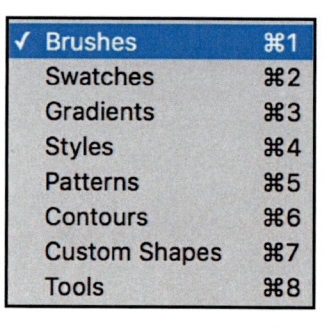

5. Click the **Save Set** button, and name and save the library where you choose.

    Each preset library type has its own file extension such as **.grd** for gradients, **.abr** for brushes, or **.pat** for patterns. If you store a library inside the appropriate folder within the **Presets** folder nested inside the **Adobe Photoshop folder**, the preset will appear in the **Preset Manager** menu once you quit and restart Photoshop.

6. Click the tiny gear symbol to the left of the **Done** button to reveal the **Preset Manager** panel menu.

7. Pick one of the **Preset Pattern** libraries from the bottom of the menu to load that library.

8. Choose **Append** from the dialog box that appears to add the chosen library to the bottom of the thumbnails.

    If you had clicked **OK** you would have deleted all the patterns except for the library you chose to load. Any user-defined patterns you had not already saved would have been lost.

NOTE: If you save a library to a different place on your hard drive than the appropriate **Presets** folder, the library will not appear in the picker (or panel) pop-out list. You will need to click the **Load** button from the pop-out panel menu and browse to the library's location. Using the **Load** button will append the chosen library to the current preset list. Scroll down the picker or pop-out list to the bottom to find your new library.

. . . .

Semi-Guided Exercise 15.7: Use Presets to Make a Postcard

This long, detailed, semi-guided exercise has several parts. You will begin with a photograph of a Shasta daisy (hybridized by Luther Burbank in Sonoma County, CA where this book is being written). First you will place the daisy on its own layer, resize it, and clean up its imperfections. Next, you will create a black background for the daisy to show it off better. Finally, you will use your postcard document preset and pattern presets you made to create another original postcard.

1. Open **15-daisy.jpg** and save the file in the location of your choice as **15-daisy.psd**.

2. Place the daisy on its own layer with very clean edges. You have learned at least two ways to do this:

    - Select the daisy and use the **Layer > New > Layer via Copy** command to put the daisy onto its own layer.

    - Use the **Eraser Tools** to erase the background, beginning with the **Magic Eraser Tool** to change the **Background** into a standard pixel layer.

3. Delete any layers except the one that contains the isolated daisy on a transparent background, and name this layer **daisy**.

4. **Crop** the image to remove most of the transparent areas around the daisy itself, and save the document.

5. Open the **Image Size** dialog box to check and change the document size if necessary. Remember that the final **300 ppi** postcard will be 6 inches wide and 4.25 high.

    a. Examine the document size. Your document might have slightly different values, depending on how the image is cropped.

    The digital camera that took this image assigned a resolution of **72 ppi**—too low for our purposes.

    b. With **Resample** unchecked, change the resolution to **300 pixels/inch**.

    Remember, with **Resample** unchecked, no image pixels change; but the to be printed **Document Size** changes—in this case it gets quite a bit smaller.

    c. The image is still taller than the postcard will be, so you will need to reduce the pixel dimensions with **Resample** checked.

    We changed the **Height** to **4 inches**, and kept the resolution at **300 pixels/inch** with **Bicubic Sharper** chosen for the interpolation method. That gave the image the correct height, but it is still not wide enough.

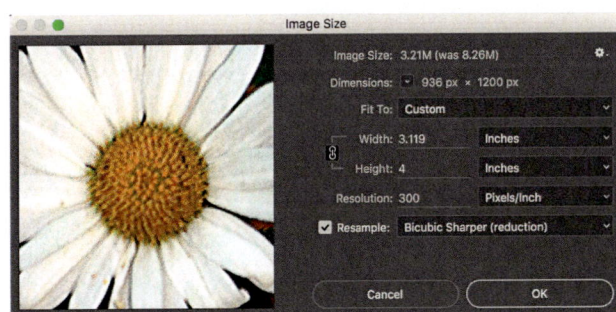

6. Add extra space to the sides of the canvas to make it the correct size:

    a. Choose **Image > Canvas Size** and change the canvas size from its current size to **5.5 x 4 inches**.

    The **Canvas Size** command is used to expand the size of a document by adding pixels around the perimeter of the original document.

The dark square in the center of the **Anchor** area is called the **proxy**. When the **proxy** is in its central position, the original image stays centered when canvas pixels are added. If you click on one of the side squares, pixels will add based on that new location, and the original image will not be centered.

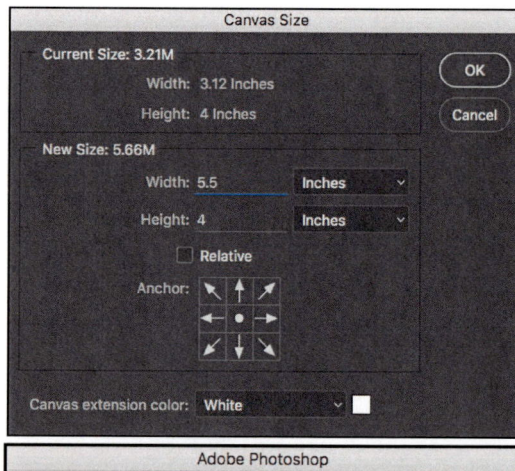

When a document has a **Background** layer, the **Canvas Size** command adds a border of new background-colored pixels on the **Background** layer. In this case, since the document does not have a **Background** layer, transparent pixels are added to the perimeter.

If you type smaller dimensions than the original document size into the **Width** or **Height** boxes, Photoshop will warn you that the document will be **CLIPPED**. In other words, some of the original pixels will be removed from the perimeter.

Notice that instead of clipping off the unwanted pixels, you first cropped the image, and then added back some of the pixels with the **Canvas Size** command. The advantage to using the **Crop Tool** instead of the **Canvas Size** command is to reduce document dimensions so that you can precisely control which pixels will be removed from the current document.

    b.   Click **OK**.

7. Zoom in to **100%** and use the **Spot Healing Brush** to clean up the debris on the daisy.

   Experiment with the various healing **Types**. On this image we had good results with **Content-Aware**.

8. White daisies don't show up well on white backgrounds. Place the daisy onto a black background:

   a. Reset your **Foreground** and **Background** colors to the default black and white, and then click the **Swap Foreground and Background** button to make **black** the background color.

   b. Make a new layer, and keep it active. Its stacking position doesn't matter.

   c. Choose **Layer > New > Background from Layer** to make the new layer a solid black **Background** layer.

9. Save your document; you have worked hard to get it to this point. Keep the document open.

10. Make a new document using your **postcard 6 in x 4.25 in** document preset and save the file in the location of your choice as **daisy_postcard.psd**. (If you are working in a computer lab, you may need to recreate the preset that you made earlier in this tutorial.)

11. Zoom out so that your document magnification is about **33%**.

12. Choose **Window > Arrange >2-up Vertical** so that the two documents will appear side by side. This arrangement tiles the images vertically.

13. On the **15-daisy.psd** document, highlight both the **daisy** and the **background** layers, and choose the **Move Tool**.

14. Press the **Shift** key, drag the layers from the right side of the **Layers** panel on top of the **daisy_postcard.psd** window, and release the mouse button first, then the **Shift** key.

    The new layers will be copied into the center of the **daisy_postcard.psd** document.

15. Use the **Paint Bucket Tool** to fill the background with one of your custom daisy patterns.

16. Experiment with different layer locations and settings (blend modes, opacity, fill, and layer styles) to make your postcard more interesting. Feel free to resize the daisy, or make more daisies as you see fit.
    Consider using the **Style** presets in the **Styles** panel, and remember you can load more presets from either the **Styles** panel menu or from the **Preset Manager**.

Resources and Videos

http://www.practical-photoshop.com/pages/CC2015-pp1-resources.html#15

Where Do You Go From Here?

The best way to develop your Photoshop skills is to practice, experiment, and then practice some more. Have fun as you explore on your own! For more in-depth training, we have a second course to follow: **Practical Photoshop Level 2**. Find it at http://www.practical-photoshop.com/

Practical Photoshop CC 2015, Level 1
Index

Symbols

3D Material Drop Tool 128

A

Active Layer. *See* Layer Types: Active layer
Adjusting Image Colors 217
Adjustment layers. *See* Layer Types: Adjustment Layers
Adjustments panel 207, 208, 209, 210, 211, 213, 214, 215
   Adjustment button 210
Adobe Acrobat 174, 194, 195
Adobe Bridge 173, 174, 177, 185
   Collections panel 189
   Content panel 174, 179, 181
      Preview thumbnail
      Loupe Tool 184, 185
      Thumbnail order 185
      Thumbnails 174, 179
   Favorites panel 175, 182, 183, 189
      Add to Favorites 183
      Remove from Favorites 183
   File > Browse in Bridge 174, 181
   Filter panel 173, 180, 187, 188, 199
   Folders panel 182
   Keywords panel 186
      Add a Keyword 188
      Delete a Keyword or Set 187
      Make a New Keyword Set 187
      Make a Sub Keyword 187
      Remove a Keyword 188
   Menu bar 174, 179
   Metadata panel 188, 189
      Camera Data 189
      File Properties 188
      IPTC Core (International Press Telecommunications Council) 188

   Output panel 173, 180, 187, 188, 199
      PDF Slideshow 173, 180, 187, 188, 198, 199
   Path bar 174, 177, 179, 180, 182, 185, 195
      Organization buttons 180
      Delete 180
      New folder 180
      Open recent 180
      Preview quality 174, 177, 180, 182, 185, 195
      High Quality 178
      Prefer Embedded (Faster) 178
      Rating Images 178
      Filter Items by Rating Menu 179
      To Change the Rating of an Individual Image 179
      To Change the Rating of Multiple Images 179
      To Rate a Group of Images with the Label menu 178
      To Rate an Image from its Thumbnail 178
      To Rate Selected Images with Keystrokes 179
      Sort by menu 180
   Rename images 184
      Batch Rename 176, 185, 186
   Standard Workspace 174
   Status bar
      Thumbnail Size Slider 183
   Tools bar 175
      Camera Raw 175, 176. *See also* Camera Raw
      Open in Camera Raw 176
      Get Photos from Camera 175, 176
      Photo Downloader 175, 176
      Navigation buttons 175
      Back and Forward buttons 175
      Back (to opening application) button 175
      Favorites button 175
      Recent button 175
      Quick Search 177
      Refine 175, 176

Batch Rename 175, 176

File Info 175, 176

Review Mode 175, 176

  Thumbnail Rotation 183

  View Modes 177

Compact 177

Full Screen 177

  Workspace Switcher 177

Workspaces and the Workspace Switcher 174, 175, 177, 181

  Essentials workspace 174, 175, 177, 181, 189

  Filmstrip workspace 174, 175, 177, 181, 189

  Keywords workspace 189

  Light Table workspace 174, 175, 177, 181, 190

  Metadata workspace 174, 175, 177, 181, 189

  Output workspace 174, 175, 177, 181

Adobe Certified Associate (ACA) exam 161

Adobe Creative Suites

Requirements 4

Adobe ID 6

Adobe Marketplace 267

Adobe Photoshop 1

Activation & Deactivation 5

Adobe Photoshop Help 9, 30

Hardware and Software Requirements 3

Installation 5

Settings File 6

  Restore Default Settings 7

Uninstall Photoshop 6

Updates 6

Uses 1

Adobe Photoshop Elements® 3

Adobe Reader 174, 193, 194, 195

Algorithms 220

Alignment 101. *See also* **Design Principles (PARC): Alignment**

Centered 101

Left aligned 101

Right aligned 101

Alt/Option drag 70

Anti-aliasing 51

Application Frame 10, 12

Archival paper 36

Archival Version of an Image 201

Arrange documents 106, 113

  Window > Arrange> 2-up Vertical 106, 297

Art History Brush Tool 235, 249, 250, 251, 252, 253

Artifacts 201, 235, 262, 263

Aspect Ratio 168

Auto Color Correction Options 212, 213, 214, 215, 220, 221, 256

  Enhance Brightness and Contrast 213, 214, 221

  Enhance Monochromatic Contrast 213, 214, 221

  Enhance Per Channel Contrast 212, 213, 214, 221

  Find Light & Dark Colors 213, 214, 215, 221, 257

  Snap Neutral Midtones 213, 214, 215, 221, 257, 258

Auto Enhance. *See* **Quick Selection Tool**

Automations 173, 190

  Contact Sheet II 173, 191, 192, 193, 199

Auto-Select Layer or Group 111, 114

B

Background color. *See* **Colors: Background color**

Background Eraser Tool 13, 283, 284, 285, 289, 290, 291

Limits

  Contiguous 290

  Discontiguous 290

  Find Edges 290

Protect Foreground Color 290

Sampling

  Background Swatch 290

  Continuous 290

  Once 290

Tolerance 290

Background layer 14, 22, 27, 29, 75, 76, 79, 83, 86, 88, 89, 90, 93, 103, 104, 106, 110, 111, 112, 113, 117, 121, 127, 133, 134, 211, 223, 224, 231, 232, 239, 246, 250, 251, 262, 269, 270, 272, 273, 278, 283, 284, 285, 286, 287, 292, 296, 279.
See **Layer Types: Background layer**

Bicubic. *See* **Image Interpolation: Bicubic**

Bicubic Automatic. *See* **Image Interpolation: Bicubic**

Automatic

Bicubic Sharper. *See* Image Interpolation: Bicubic Sharper

Bicubic Smoother. *See* Image Interpolation: Bicubic Smoother

Bilinear. *See* Image Interpolation: Bilinear

Bit 44

Blend Modes. *See* Layers panel: Blend Modes:

Bridge. *See* Adobe Bridge

Brightness/Contrast 202, 205, 206, 207, 208, 209, 210, 211, 212, 215

   Brightness slider 206

   Contrast slider 206, 207

   Image > Adjustments > Brightness/Contrast 206

   Use Legacy check box 207

Browse Filters Online. *See* Filters: Filter menu sections: Browse Filters Online

Browsing Software 174. *See also* Adobe Bridge

Brushes panel 123, 124, 125, 126

Brush Preset Picker 23, 117, 123, 124, 125, 126, 143, 144, 236, 237, 243, 249, 251, 252

   Built-In Brush Presets 124

      Calligraphic Brushes 124

      Faux Finish Brushes 124

      Natural Brushes 124

      Wet Media Brushes 124

   Hardness 123, 144, 236, 237, 243

      0% 123

      100% 123, 144

   Load Brushes 124

   Replace Brushes 124

   Size 123, 144

   Thumbnail 123, 144

Brush thumbnail 23

Brush Tool 23, 117, 118, 123, 124, 125, 126, 127, 128, 139, 143, 144

   Airbrush 75, 76, 86, 87, 93, 105, 106, 107, 108, 113, 117, 125, 126, 127, 128, 132, 133, 136, 139, 144

   Flow 75, 76, 86, 87, 93, 105, 106, 107, 108, 113, 117, 125, 126, 127, 128, 132, 133, 136, 139, 144

   Hardness 75, 76, 86, 87, 93, 105, 106, 107, 108, 113, 117, 125, 126, 127, 128, 132, 133, 136, 139, 144

   Opacity 75, 76, 86, 87, 93, 105, 106, 107, 108, 113, 117, 125, 126, 127, 128, 132, 133, 136, 139, 144

   Painting modes

      Normal 86, 103, 107, 108, 125, 128, 130, 131

   Painting Modes 125

      Color 59, 105, 87, 91, 93, 104, 108, 109, 117, 125, 130, 63, 135, 136, 137, 141

      Difference 59, 105, 87, 91, 93, 104, 108, 109, 117, 125, 130, 63, 135, 136, 137, 141

      Overlay 59, 105, 87, 91, 93, 104, 108, 109, 117, 125, 130, 63, 135, 136, 137, 141

   Size 75, 76, 86, 87, 93, 105, 106, 107, 108, 113, 117, 125, 126, 127, 128, 132, 133, 136, 139, 144

Byte 44

C

Camera Data (Exif). *See* Adobe Bridge: Metadata panel: Camera Data

Camera Raw 173, 176, 189

Cancel button 99

Canvas Size. *See* Image > Canvas Size dialog box

Centered. *See* Alignment: Centered

Channels panel 58, 218

   RGB channel 218

Clipboard 105

   Edit > Purge > Clipboard 105

Clipping 207

   Clipped Image 296

Clone Stamp Tool 235, 236, 237, 238, 242, 244, 249, 252

   Aligned 236

   Constrain with the Shift Key 238

   Crosshair cursor 237

   Hardness 236, 237, 243

   Opacity 236

   Sample All Layers 236. *See* Clone Stamp Tool: Source Point

   Source Point 235, 236

      Option + click (Mac) or alt + click (Win) on the area you wish to sample 236

Close Box 13

Close button 12

Clouds filter 265, 266, 267, 268, 269, 270, 287

Filter > Clouds 268

Color Balance adjustment 217, 221, 222, 223, 224, 225, 226, 230, 233, 257

Color Cast 213, 217, 218, 219, 220, 221, 222, 258

   Neutral 213, 219, 220, 221, 226

   To remove a color cast 218

Color channels 203, 204, 213, 214, 217, 218, 221

Color Depth 4

Color Models 119

   CMYK 119. *See* Specific tools, by name

   RGB 119

Color panel 14, 16, 23, 117, 118, 120, 121, 122, 142, 143

   Change Foreground and Background colors 121

   Color Ramp 121

Color Picker 101, 117, 118, 119, 120, 121, 125, 126, 131, 134, 137, 138, 139, 141

   Color Field 118, 119, 138, 139

   Gamut indicator 119

   Only Web Colors 119

   Web Warning Indicator 119

Color Range command 217, 229

   Default settings 211, 230

   Eyedroppers 230

   Fuzziness 230, 232

   Localized Color Clusters 211, 230

   Sampled Colors 211, 230

   Selection Preview 211, 230

Colors

   Background color 22, 23, 24, 28, 48, 89, 118, 120, 121, 122, 129, 132, 133, 134, 137, 140, 142, 143, 203, 236, 239, 267, 268, 269

   Color Controls 23, 118

   Cooler colors 222

   Foreground color 22, 23, 28, 89, 118, 120, 121, 122, 129, 132, 133, 134, 137, 140, 142, 143, 203, 236, 239, 267, 268

   Opposite colors 217, 221

   Primary colors 217, 219, 221

      Additive 217, 219, 221

      Subtractive 217, 219, 221

   Reflected color 217

   Restore default Foreground and Background colors 11

   Transmitted color 217

   Warmer colors 222

Color Science 217

Color Table 40. *See also* **File Formats: GIF**

Color Wheel 217, 218

Commit button 53, 99

Composite Images 97, 103, 161

Composite (stamped) layer 233, 257, 260, 262, 264

Constraining (a selection) 47

Contact Sheet II 173, 191, 192, 193, 199. *See* **File > Automate: Contact Sheet II**

Content-Aware Fill 133, 235, 238, 239, 240, 241, 242, 243, 244, 245, 247, 252, 253, 258, 296

Content-Aware Move Tool 235, 239, 240, 241, 253

   Adaptation 241

   Mode: Extend 241

   Mode: Move 241

Context Menu. *See* **Menus: Context Menu**

Contiguous 51

Contrast. *See also* **Design Principles (PARC): Contrast**

Copyright 13, 147, 148, 150

Creative Suites. *See* **Adobe Creative Suites**

Crop and Straighten Photos. *See* **File > Automate: Crop and Straighten Photos**

Cropping and the Crop Tool 168, 169, 170, 171, 190, 201, 205, 258

   Aspect Ratio Presets Menu 168, 169, 170, 171

   Commit button 169, 170

   Shielded 169, 170

   Straighten button 171, 205, 258

Cursors

   Crosshair Cursor 67

   Precise Cursor 67

D

Default Photoshop Size 98

Defaults 6

Defringe 286

   Layer > Matting > Defringe 286

Desaturate. *See* **Image > Adjustments > Desaturate**

Deselect 48

Deselect menu commands and keyboard shortcuts 46

Design Principles (PARC) 161

    Alignment 161, 162, 163

        Center Alignment 162

        Left Alignment 162

        Right Alignment 162

    Contrast 161, 162, 163

    Proximity 161, 162, 163

    Repetition 161, 162, 163

Destructive Editing 201, 207, 215, 228, 231, 236, 265

Difference Clouds filter 269, 270

    Filter > Render > Difference Clouds 270

Digimarc filter 148

Digital Cameras 153

    Digital Camera Resolution 154

Digital Sharpening. *See* Sharpening Images: Digital Sharpening

Digital Watermark 147, 149, 150

Dithering 119

Docks 10

    Dock Manipulation 15

Document Resolution. *See* Resolution: Document Resolution

Document Window 11, 13

Dots per Inch (dpi) 34

Download Photos From Camera. *See* Adobe Bridge: Download Photos from Camera

Downsampling. *See* Resampling: Downsampling

Drop Shadow 93. *See also* Layers panel: Settings: Layer Styles: Drop Shadow

Dynamic Range. *See* Tonal Range

E

Edit > Copy 104

Edit > Fade 248, 250, 266, 270, 273

Edit > Fill 235, 239, 240, 245, 251

Editing Type Layers. *See* Layer Types: Type layer: Editing Type layers

Edit > Paste 104

Edit > Transform > Flip Horizontal 71

Edit > Transform menu 51

Edit > Transform > Rotate 55, 69

Edit > Transform > Scale 52

Elliptical Marquee Tool 45, 47, 49, 108

Enhance Brightness and Contrast. *See* Auto Color Correction Options: Enhance Brightness and Contrast

Enhance Monochromatic Contrast. *See* Auto Color Correction Options: Enhance Monochromatic Contrast

Enhance Per Channel Contrast. *See* Auto Color Correction Options: Enhance Per Channel Contrast

Eraser Tool 13, 22, 23, 24, 29, 117, 121, 127, 128, 139, 143, 144, 232, 249, 272, 283, 284, 285, 286, 288, 289, 290, 291, 295

    Block Mode 128

    Brush Mode 128

    Mode 283

    Pencil Mode 128

Eraser Tools 283. *See also* Background Eraser Tool; *See also* Eraser Tool; *See also* Magic Eraser Tool

Essentials workspace. *See* Panels: History panel

Eyedropper Tool 117, 121, 122, 219, 220, 231

    Sample a color 118, 121

    Sample Size 122

        Point Sample 122

    Sampling Ring 121

F

Fade. *See* Edit > Fade

File > Automate 179, 180, 187, 188, 190, 193, 198, 199

    Contact Sheet II 173, 180, 187, 188, 190, 198, 199

    Crop and Straighten Photos 173, 180, 187, 188, 190, 198, 199

File > Automate > Crop and Straighten Photos 205

File > Browse in Bridge. *See* Adobe Bridge: File > Browse in Bridge

File Formats

    GIF 40

    JPEG 26, 40, 176, 180, 181, 188

        JPEG artifacting 43

        JPEG Quality 42

        Maximum Quality 43

    PSD 26, 176, 180, 181, 188

    TIFF (.tif)

Tagged Image File Format 159, 176, 223
File > New command 97, 98
   New Document templates 109
      Photo preset 109
   Preset menu 287
File > Print One Copy 36
File > Save for Web. *See* **Resolution: Print Resolution**
File Size 44
   Dimension Size 44
Fill 128
   Content-Aware fill. *See* Content-Aware Fill
   Fill Command (Edit > Fill) 133
   Fill shortcuts 134
Fill > Content-Aware Fill 235
Fill Tools 128
Filters 265, 266, 267. *See also* **Specific filters by name**
   Filter Guidelines 265
   Filter menu sections 265, 266, 267, 268
      Convert for Smart Filters 266, 267
      Filter Groupings 267
      Last Filter 266
      Specialty Filters 267
      Third Party Filters 267
Find Dark & Light Colors. *See* **Auto Color Correction Options: Find Light & Dark Colors**
Fit in Window. *See* **View: Fit in Window**
Flatten Image. *See* **Layers: Flattened**
Focal Point. *See* **Photographic Design Principles: Framing**
Font family 101
Font size 101
font style 101
Foreground color. *See* **Colors: Foreground color**
Formatting Type Layers. *See* **Layer Types: Type layer: Formatting Type layers**

G

GIF (.gif). *See* **File Formats: GIF**
Gradient Tool 117, 121, 128, 129, 131, 142
   Angle Gradient 94, 129
   Diamond Gradient 94, 129
   Gradient Picker 94, 129, 136
   Linear Gradient 128, 130, 142
   Radial Gradient 128, 130, 142
   Reflected Gradient 94, 129
Grayscale images 203, 204, 211, 212, 218, 227, 255, 259
Guides 106
   View > Clear Guides 106

H

Hand Tool 9, 19, 48, 49, 60, 65. *See* **Tools: Hand Tool**
   Hand Tool. *See* Hand Tool
Hardware and Software Requirements. *See* **Adobe Photoshop: Hardware and Software Requirements**
Healing Brush Tool 235, 239, 240, 241, 242, 243, 244, 245, 246, 247, 252
Highlights 203, 204, 205, 206, 208, 209, 211, 212
High Pass filter 262
   Radius setting 262, 263
Histogram panel 202, 203, 204, 205, 206, 207, 210, 211, 217, 256, 257, 258, 259, 260
   Cached Data Warning triangle 204
   Compact View 204
   Expanded View 204
History Brush Tool 235, 247, 248, 249, 250, 251, 252, 253, 265, 272, 275, 285
   Uses and Limitations 250
History panel 9, 24, 25, 26, 27, 29, 89, 97, 107, 108, 266, 268, 272. *See* **Workspace: Painting Workspace**
   History state 24, 25, 97, 107, 235, 247, 248, 249, 250
      Create new snapshot 107
      Delete current state 107
      Snapshot 25, 247, 248, 249, 250, 251, 252, 265
   Keyboard Shortcuts 27
Horizontal Type Tool. *See* **Type Tools: Horizontal Type Tool**
Hue 217, 226, 231
Hue/Saturation adjustment 205, 217, 226, 227, 228, 229, 256, 257, 261
   Colorize 227, 228, 233, 288

I

Image > Adjustments > Brightness/Contrast.

See **Brightness/Contrast: Image > Adjustments > Brightness/Contrast**

Image > Adjustments > Desaturate 248

Image > Adjustments menu 205, 208, 209. *See* **Specific Adjustments**

Image > Adjustments > Replace Color. *See* **Replace Color command**

Image > Canvas Size dialog box 240, 295
    Anchor area 296
        Proxy 296

Image Correction 201. *See also* **specific image adjustment commands and layers**
    Image Correction Steps 201
        Global Adjustments 201
        Local Adjustments 201

Image > Duplicate 149, 157, 288

Image Interpolation 147, 149, 150, 153
    Bicubic. *See* **File Formats: PNG**
    Bicubic Automatic 153, 157
    Bicubic Sharper 153. *See* **File Formats: PNG**
    Bicubic Smoother 153. *See* **File Formats: PNG**
    Bilinear. *See* **File Formats: PNG**
    Nearest Neighbor. *See* **File Formats: PNG**

Image Key 202, 203, 213, 214, 215
    Average Key 202, 203, 213, 214, 215
    High Key 202, 203, 213, 214, 215
    Low Key 202, 203, 213, 214, 215

Image Longevity 36

Image Processor 181
    Tools > Photoshop > Image Processor 181

Image Size 147, 149, 150, 151
    Image Size dialog box 147, 151, 153, 156, 157, 239, 250, 256, 295
        Constrain Proportions 152
        Document Size 151, 154
        Pixel Dimensions 151, 154
        Pixels to Percent 151, 154
        Resample Image 152
        Scale Styles 152

Image Size dialog box. *See* **Image Size: Image Size dialog box**

Image Sources 147, 149, 150
    FreeFoto 150
    Free Stock Photos 150
    Google Image Source 150
    Library of Congress 147, 149, 150
    NASA 147, 149, 150
    Online 147, 149, 150
    Public Domain Photos 150

Image Use Ethics 147

Info panel 217, 218, 219, 220, 222, 223, 256, 258
    RGB values 220, 256

Ink Jet Paper Quality 36

IPTC Core (International Press Telecommunications Council). *See* **Adobe Bridge: Metadata panel**

J

JPEG (.jpg) 41. *See* **File Formats: JPEG**

K

Key. *See* **Image Key**

Keyboard Shortcuts 13, 21

Keywords 186. *See also* **Adobe Bridge: Keywords panel**

Kilobyte 44

L

Landscape printing. *See* **Printing Photoshop Documents: Print Dialog Box: Landscape orientation button**

Lasso Tool 45, 46, 53, 54, 233, 240

Lasso Tools. *See* **Lasso Tool**; *See* **Magnetic Lasso Tool**; *See* **Polygonal Lasso Tool**

Layer Blend Modes. *See* **Layers panel: Blend Modes**

Layer Groups 77, 81, 97
    Delete Group 83
    Layer > New > Group from Layers 82, 111
    New Group button 81
    New Group command 81, 84
    Remove layers from a group 82

Layer > New > Layer Via Copy. *See* **Layers: Creating New Layers: Layer > New > Layer Via Copy**

Layers 27, 83
    Active layer 28

Background layer 27
Creating New Layers 80, 113
    Copy part of a layer into a new layer 80
    Copy/Paste 110
    Creating a Layer from a Selection 80
    Duplicate a layer 80, 105
    Layer > New > Layer Via Copy 103, 110, 295
Delete Layer 82
Fill setting 29
Flattened 79, 83, 104
Hidden layer 28
Layer mask 135
Layer Options 85
Merging Layers 83
    Merge Down 83
    Merge Linked 83
    Merge Visible 83
Naming Layers 80
New Layer button 27
Organizing Layers 78
    Linking layers 80

Layers panel 27, 75, 76, 100. *See* **Layers panel: Settings: Layer Locking**

Blend Modes 75, 76, 85
    Base color 85
    Blend color 85
    Color 86, 87, 91, 269
    Difference 86, 89
    Dissolve 87, 107
    Multiply 87
    Overlay 86, 109
    Pass Through 88
    Result color 85
    Screen 86
    Shortcuts 87
    Soft Light 268
Components 77
    Layer Filter Controls 78
    Layer mask 78, 214
    Layers Panel Menu 78

    Name 77
    Show/Hide Box 77, 79
    Thumbnail 77
Organization 112
Panel buttons 76, 78
    Add a layer style 78
    Add layer mask 78
    Delete layer 78
    Layer group 78
    Link layers 78
    New fill or adjustment layer 78, 137
    New layer 78
Settings
    Fill 75, 93
    Layer Group 76
    Layer Locking 88
    Lock All 88, 89
    Lock Image Pixels 88, 89
    Lock Position 88, 89
    Lock Transparency 88, 139
    Layer Styles 75, 90, 134
    Bevel and Emboss 29, 91, 93, 106
    Color Overlay 90, 136
    Contour settings 95
    Drop Shadow 90, 94
    Effects 29, 94
    Expanding and Contracting the Effects List 92
    Gradient Overlay 90
    Inner Glow 90, 94
    Inner Shadow 90
    Normal 107
    Outer Glow 90
    Pattern Overlay 90
    Satin 90
    Stroke 91, 117, 140, 141
    Turning Styles and Effects On and Off 92
    Opacity 75, 86, 93
Stacking order 76, 108

Layer Styles. *See* **Layers panel: Settings: Layer Styles**

Layer Types 75
    Active layer 77
    Adjustment Layers 208
        Adjustment Layer with a Selection 225
    Background layer 75, 79, 92, 117, 211, 223, 224, 231, 232
    Fill Layers 134
        Gradient Fill 134
        Modifying Fill Layers 135
        Pattern Fill 134
        Solid Color Fill 134, 285, 142
    Pixel layers 75, 76, 117
    Standard layer 75
    Target Layer 77. *See* Layers panel: Blend Modes:
    Type layer 97, 99, 105
        Editing Type layers 100, 101
        Formatting Type layers 100, 101
        Type Layer Options and Use 101

Left aligned. *See* **Alignment: Left aligned**

Lens Flare filter 265, 272
    Brightness 273
    Filter > Render > Lens Flare 273
    Lens Type 273

Levels 202, 205, 210, 211, 212, 213, 214, 215, 219, 220, 221, 222, 223, 226, 227, 230, 231, 232, 233, 256, 258, 260, 264
    Auto Color Correction Options. *See* Auto Color Correction Options

Lightness 217, 224, 226, 231

Liquify filter 265, 267, 273, 275, 276, 277, 278, 279
    Advanced Mode 274, 278
    Bloat Tool 274, 278
    Forward Warp Tool 274, 278
    Freeze Mask Tool 274, 278
    Hand Tool 274, 278
    Liquify Mesh 277
        Load a mesh 277
        Save a mesh 277
        Show Mesh 277
    Mask Options 276
        Invert All 276
        Mask All 276
        None 276
    Pucker Tool 274, 278
    Push Left Tool 274, 278
    Reconstruct Options 276
        Reconstruct 276
        Reconstruct dialog box with Amount slider 276
        Restore All 276
    Reconstruct Tool 274, 278
    Thaw Mask Tool 274, 278
    Tool Options 277
        Brush Pressure 277
        Brush Size 277
        Stylus Pressure 277
    Twirl Clockwise Tool 274, 278
    View Options 277
        Show Backdrop 277
    Zoom Tool 274, 278

Load Files into Photoshop Layers. *See* **Tools > Photoshop > Load Files into Photoshop Layers**

Load Selection. *See* **Selections: Select > Load Selection**

Loupe Tool. *See* **Adobe Bridge: Content panel: Preview thumbnail: Loupe Tool**

M

Macro photography 166

Magic Eraser Tool 13, 283, 284, 285, 288, 289, 295
    Anti-aliased 284
    Contiguous 284
    Opacity 284
    Sample All Layers 284
    Tolerance 284, 289

Magic Wand Tool 45, 46, 50, 51, 52, 71, 132

Magnetic Lasso Tool 45, 46, 54, 70

Maintain aspect ratio button 52

Marquee Tools 46, 47. *See also* **Elliptical Marquee Tool**; *See also* **Rectangular Marquee Tool**

Maximize/Restore button 12

Megabyte 44

Megapixels 147, 154

Menu bar 12

Menus 9
    Context Menu 9, 21
    Menu bar 9, 10
    Window menu 10. *See* Panels: History panel

Mesh 277, 278

Metadata 173, 176, 188, 189. *See also* Adobe Bridge: Metadata panel

Midtones 202, 204, 211, 213

Mini Bridge 174. *See also* Adobe Bridge

Minimize button 12

Modifier Keys 3

Modifying a Selection. *See* Selections: Modifying a Selection

Monitor 4

Monitor Resolution 4

Motion Blur filter 265, 270, 272
    Angle 94, 270, 271, 272
    Distance 94, 270, 271, 272
    Filter > Blur > Motion Blur 270

Move Tool 11, 46, 47, 48, 49, 52, 53, 55, 69, 70, 71, 72, 76, 81, 88, 89, 100, 102, 106, 107, 109, 111, 114, 115, 224, 235, 239, 240, 241, 253, 287, 297

N

Navigation
    Document Navigation 17. *See* Panels: History panel
    Navigation Shortcuts 21, 31
    Navigator panel 9
    Navigator Panel 19
    View Menu Commands 17

Nearest Neighbor. *See* Image Interpolation: Nearest Neighbor

New Photoshop document. *See* File > New command

O

Open Recent command 14

Optimized for Web 39

Options bar 9, 11, 12, 14, 15, 16, 18, 20, 21, 22, 23, 24, 47, 49, 52, 53, 54, 55, 56, 57, 61, 62, 67, 68, 71, 72, 84, 99, 100, 102, 65, 65, 66

output printer 34

Output to PDF. *See* Adobe Bridge: Output panel: Output to PDF

P

Paint Bucket Tool 117, 118, 128, 132, 133, 134, 291, 292, 297

Painting Workspace. *See* Workspace: Painting Workspace

Panels 9, 11, 14
    Free-float a Panel 16
    Grouped or Clustered 14
    History panel 9. *See* Brush Tool
    Panel Menus 16
    Relocate an Individual Panel 17
    Relocate a Panel Group 17
    Swatches panel. *See* Swatches panel

Paragraph Type 99

Password. *See also* Adobe Bridge: Output panel: Output to PDF: Passwording a PDF

Patterns 4, 33, 117, 133, 137, 138, 268, 283, 291, 292, 293, 294, 297
    Define Pattern 4, 33, 117, 133, 137, 138, 268, 283, 291, 292, 293, 294, 297
        Edit > Define Pattern 4, 33, 117, 133, 137, 138, 268, 283, 291, 292, 293, 294, 297
        Pattern Name dialog box 292
    Pattern Picker 291, 292, 293

Pattern Stamp Tool 283, 291, 292. *See also* Patterns

PDF Slideshow. *See* Adobe Bridge: Output panel: PDF Slideshow

Pencil Tool 22, 117, 118, 123, 127, 128
    Block Mode 283
    Brush Mode 283
    Pencil Mode 283

Pet Eye 255, 258

Photographic Design Principles 165. *See also* Design Principles (PARC)
    Angle of View 165
    Arrangement 168
    Balance 167
    Close Ups 166
    Contrast 167
    Emphasis 165

    Focal Point 165

    Framing 165

    Line and Shape 168

    Rule of Thirds 165

    Tone and Sharpness 168

Photography Workspace. *See* **Workspace: Photography Workspace**

Photoshop Help. *See* **Adobe Photoshop: Adobe Photoshop Help**

Pixel layers. *See* **Layer Types: Pixel layers**

Pixels 4

Pixels per inch (ppi) 33

Pixilated 38

Point Type 99

Polygonal Lasso Tool 45, 46, 54, 68, 70, 111

Polygonal Marquee Tool 244

Precise Cursor 220. *See* **Cursors: Precise Cursor**

Preferences 6

Preset Manager. *See* **Presets: Preset Manager**

Presets 129, 141, 143, 144, 145, 211, 212, 251, 252, 283, 293, 294, 297

    Preset Libraries 283

    Preset Manager 283

    Tool Preset 286, 289, 291

        Tool Preset Picker

        Create new tool preset button 286, 291

Presets folder 124

Print dialog box. *See* **Printing Photoshop Documents: Print Dialog Box**

Printer Driver 35

Printer Margins 154

Printer Resolution. *See* **Resolution: Print Resolution**

Printer Setup 37

Printing Photoshop Documents 33, 36, 155

    Print Dialog Box 36

        Landscape orientation button 37, 155, 156

        Position and Size 38, 155

        Scale to Fit Media 38, 155, 156

Print resolution. *See* **Resolution: Print Resolution**

Process color. *See* **Color Models: CMYK**

Properties panel 202, 208, 209, 210, 211, 212, 222, 228, 256, 257, 260

    Clip to layer button 209

    Reset to adjustment defaults button 209

    Trash button 209

    View previous state button 209

    Visibility button 209

Proximity. *See* **Design Principles (PARC): Proximity**

PSD (.psd). *See* **: PSD**

Q

Quick Selection Tool 46, 49, 50, 56, 57, 110, 68, 70, 229, 111, 228, 229, 241, 260, 46

    Auto Enhance option 57

    Sample all layers 260

R

Rasterize 265

Rectangular Marquee Tool 45, 47, 48, 49, 60, 71, 103, 131, 130, 131, 213, 245, 246, 291, 64

Red Eye 235, 246, 247, 253, 258, 259

Red Eye Tool 235, 245, 246, 259

    Darken Amount 246

    Pupil Size 246

Refine Edge dialog box 45, 62, 111

    Adjust Edge 60

        Contract/Expand 67

        Contrast 61, 65, 67

        Shift Edge 61, 65, 67

        Smooth 60

    Edge Detection 59, 64

        Smart Radius 59, 64

    Output 61, 65

        Remember Settings 61, 65

    View Mode 59, 63

        Black & White 59, 62, 63, 66

        Marching Ants 59, 63

        On Black 59, 62, 63, 66

        On Layers 59, 63

        On White 59, 62, 63, 66

        Overlay 59, 63

Reveal Layers 59, 63

Repetition. *See also* Design Principles (PARC): Repetition

Replace Color command 217, 230, 231, 232

Resampling 147, 149, 150, 152, 153, 154, 155, 157. *See also* Image Size: Image Size dialog box: Resample Image

   Downsampling 152, 154

   Resample Image off (unchecked) 153, 154, 155

   Resample Image on (checked) 156, 157

   Upsampling 152, 154

Resolution 33, 147, 149, 150

   Document Resolution 34

   High-resolution 154

   Monitor Resolution 33

   Print Resolution 34, 147, 149, 150

      Print Resolution Chart 35

Restoration Case Studies 255

Restore a photograph 202

RGB channel. *See* Channels panel: RGB channel

Right aligned. *See* Alignment: Right aligned

Robin Williams 161, 162, 163, 164

Rotate a selection. *See* Selections: Transform a Selection

Rule of Thirds 170. *See also* Photographic Design Principles: Rule of Thirds

S

Sample All Layers 51

Saturation 217, 226, 227, 231

Save for Web and Devices

   Avoid the Most Common Save for Web Mistake 44

   Image Size tab 41, 42

   Save for Web dialog box 40, 42

Saving a File for Fast Online Transmission 38

Scale to Fit Media. *See* Printing Photoshop Documents: Print Dialog Box: Scale to Fit Media

Scan 147

   Scanners 147, 149, 150, 158

      To Scan Directly into Photoshop 158

   Scanning Photographs for Restoration 255

      Disable or avoid Automatic Mode 255

Screen resolution. *See* Resolution: Monitor Resolution

Scrubbing Cursor 60, 64

Scrubby Zoom. *See* Zoom Tool; *See* Zoom Tool: Scrubby Zoom

Selections 45

   Combining Selection Tools 71

   Copying and Pasting Selections 72

   Creating a Selection from a Layer 80

   Hide Selection Edges 66

   Modifying a Selection 49

   Options 49

      Add to selection button 49, 52, 56, 241

      Auto-Select Layer vs. Group 111

      Intersect with selection button 50, 241

      Make new selection button 49, 56

      Subtract from selection button 50, 56, 68, 241

      Tolerance. *See* Tolerance

   Select > All 67

   Select > Deselect 48, 67

   Selection Border 46, 48. *See* Hand Tool

   Selection Principles 45

   Select > Load Selection 55

   Select menu 66

   Select > Save Selection 55

   Show Selection Edges 66

   Shrink Selections 67

   Stored Selections (alpha channels) 58. *See* Quick Selection Tool

   Transform a Selection 52

      Edit > Free Transform 105, 114

      Edit > Transform > Flip Vertical or Horizontal 56

      Edit > Transform > Rotate 56

Shadows 203, 205, 206, 207, 211, 212

Sharpening Images 261

   Digital Sharpening 261, 262

Size slider 23

Slideshow. *See* Adobe Bridge: Output panel: PDF Slideshow

Smart Object (Layer) 265

Snap Neutral Midtones. *See* Auto Color Correction Options: Snap Neutral Midtones

Snapshot 25. *See also* History panel: History state:

Snapshot

Source point. *See* Clone Stamp Tool: Source Point

Spot Healing Brush Tool 235, 239, 240, 241, 242, 243, 244, 245, 246, 247, 252

   Hardness 236, 237, 243

   Type

      Content-Aware 236, 237, 243

      Create Texture 236, 237, 243

      Proximity Match 236, 237, 243

Status bar 14, 79, 102, 156

   Document Sizes 259

      Document Information 259

Stroke 128, 138

   Stroke Command (Edit > Stroke) 138

      Drawbacks 140

Stroke Layer Style. *See* Layers panel: Settings: Layer Styles: Stroke

Styles panel 92, 95. *See also* Layers panel: Settings: Layer Styles

   No Style button 92, 95

Swatch 23, 89, 92, 95, 120, 121, 138, 140, 143, 144

Swatches panel 12, 14, 15, 23, 117, 118, 120, 121, 143, 267, 268

   Add a Swatch 120

   Delete a Swatch 120

   Reset swatches 120

   Sample a swatch color 120

T

Target Layer. *See* Layer Types: Target Layer

Template 97, 112, 113

The Non-Designer's Design Book 161, 162, 163, 164

Thumbnails 173, 174, 176, 177, 178, 180, 182, 183, 184, 185, 188, 189, 191, 192, 193

TIFF. *See* File Formats: TIFF (.tif)

Title bar 259

Tolerance 50

Tonal Range 202

Tool Preset picker 123, 286

Tools 9. *See also* Specific tools, by name

   Active tool 11. *See* Panels: History panel

Reset Tool (restore defaults) 11, 21, 22

Tools panel 9, 13

Tools > Photoshop > Load Files into Photoshop Layers 223

Tool tip 13

Transform a Selection. *See* Selections: Transform a Selection

Tutorial Files 7

Tutorial Guidelines 2

Type layers. *See* Layer Types: Type layer

Type Tools 98

   Horizontal Type Tool 98, 99, 101, 102, 105

U

Undo 23

Undo commands 9

Upgrades 3

Upsampling. *See* Resampling: Upsampling

Use Legacy check box. *See* Brightness/Contrast: Use Legacy check box

V

View > Actual Pixels 18

View Menu Commands. *See* Panels: History panel

View > Zoom In 18

W

Watermark. *See* Digital Watermark; *See also* Adobe Bridge: Output panel: Output to PDF: Watermark tab; *See also* Digimarc filter

Web-safe colors 119

White space 161, 163, 164

Workspace 9

   Essentials workspace 14

      Landmarks 10

         Windows 10

   Painting Workspace 236

   Photography Workspace 203, 204, 218

   Reset the Essentials workspace 11

Workspace Switcher 9, 11, 12

Z

Zoom level 14
Zoom Tool 9, 11, 18, 48, 60, 65
   Scrubby Zoom 19, 48, 57
   Zoom in or Zoom out 18

Made in the USA
Middletown, DE
24 January 2017